Maid War Chronicle

1

Translated and adapted by Gemma Collinge
Lettered by North Market Street Graphics

DEL
REY

Ballantine Books • New York

A Del Rey Manga/Kodansha Trade Paperback Original

Maid War Chronicle volume 1 copyright © 2007 by RAN.
English translation copyright © 2009 by RAN.

Published in the United States by Del Rey Books, an imprint of The Random House Publishing Group, a division of Random House, Inc., New York.

DEL REY is a registered trademark and the Del Rey colophon is a trademark of Random House, Inc.

Publication rights arranged through Kodansha Ltd.

First published in Japan in 2007 by Kodansha Ltd., Tokyo as Maid Senki

ISBN 978-0-345-51246-8

Printed in the United States of America

www.delreymanga.com

9 8 7 6 5 4 3 2 1

Translator/Adapter—Gemma Collinge
Lettering—North Market Street Graphics

CONTENTS

Honorifics Explained

Throughout the Del Rey Manga books, you will find Japanese honorifics left intact in the translations. For those not familiar with how the Japanese use honorifics and, more important, how they differ from American honorifics, we present this brief overview.

Politeness has always been a critical facet of Japanese culture. Ever since the feudal era, when Japan was a highly stratified society, use of honorifics—which can be defined as polite speech that indicates relationship or status—has played an essential role in the Japanese language. When addressing someone in Japanese, an honorific usually takes the form of a suffix attached to one's name (example: "Asuna-san"), is used as a title at the end of one's name, or appears in place of the name itself (example: "Negi-sensei," or simply "Sensei!").

Honorifics can be expressions of respect or endearment. In the context of manga and anime, honorifics give insight into the nature of the relationship between characters. Many English translations leave out these important honorifics and therefore distort the feel of the original Japanese. Because Japanese honorifics contain nuances that English honorifics lack, it is our policy at Del Rey not to translate them. Here, instead, is a guide to some of the honorifics you may encounter in Del Rey Manga.

-san: This is the most common honorific and is equivalent to Mr., Miss, Ms., or Mrs. It is the all-purpose honorific and can be used in any situation where politeness is required.

-sama: This is one level higher than "-san" and is used to confer great respect.

-dono: This comes from the word "tono," which means "lord." It is an even higher level than "-sama" and confers utmost respect.

-kun: This suffix is used at the end of boys' names to express familiarity or endearment. It is also sometimes used by men among friends, or when addressing someone younger or of a lower station.

-chan: This is used to express endearment, mostly toward girls. It is also used for little boys, pets, and even among lovers. It gives a sense of childish cuteness.

Bozu: This is an informal way to refer to a boy, similar to the English terms "kid" and "squirt."

Sempai/
Senpai: This title suggests that the addressee is one's senior in a group or organization. It is most often used in a school setting, where underclassmen refer to their upperclassmen as "sempai." It can also be used in the workplace, such as when a newer employee addresses an employee who has seniority in the company.

Kohai: This is the opposite of "sempai" and is used toward underclassmen in school or newcomers in the workplace. It connotes that the addressee is of a lower station.

Sensei: Literally meaning "one who has come before," this title is used for teachers, doctors, or masters of any profession or art.

-[blank]: This is usually forgotten in these lists, but it is perhaps the most significant difference between Japanese and English. The lack of honorific means that the speaker has permission to address the person in a very intimate way. Usually, only family, spouses, or very close friends have this kind of permission. Known as *yobisute*, it can be gratifying when someone who has earned the intimacy starts to call one by one's name without an honorific. But when that intimacy hasn't been earned, it can be very insulting.

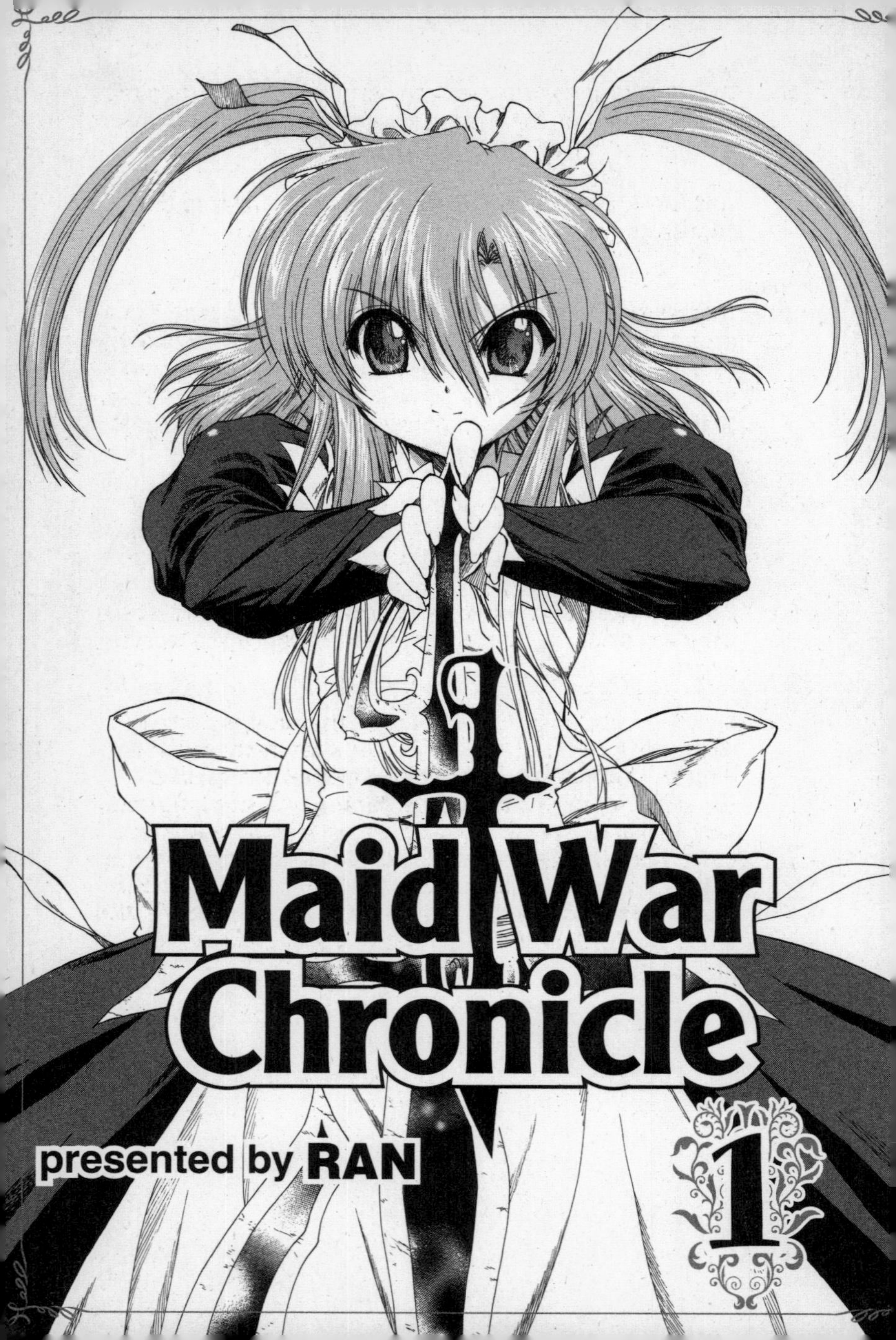
Maid War Chronicle
1
presented by RAN

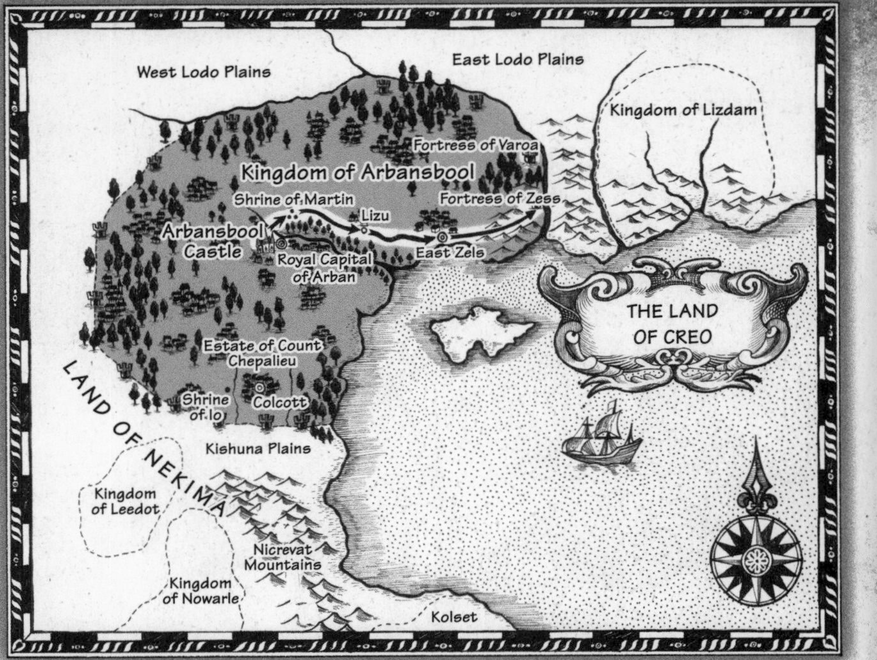
West Lodo Plains
East Lodo Plains
Kingdom of Lizdam
Fortress of Varoa
Kingdom of Arbansbool
Shrine of Martin
Fortress of Zess
Lizu
Arbansbool Castle
Royal Capital of Arban
East Zels
THE LAND OF CREO
Estate of Count Chepalieu
LAND OF NEKIMA
Shrine of Io
Colcott
Kishuna Plains
Kingdom of Leedot
Nicrevat Mountains
Kingdom of Nowarle
Kolset

CONTENTS

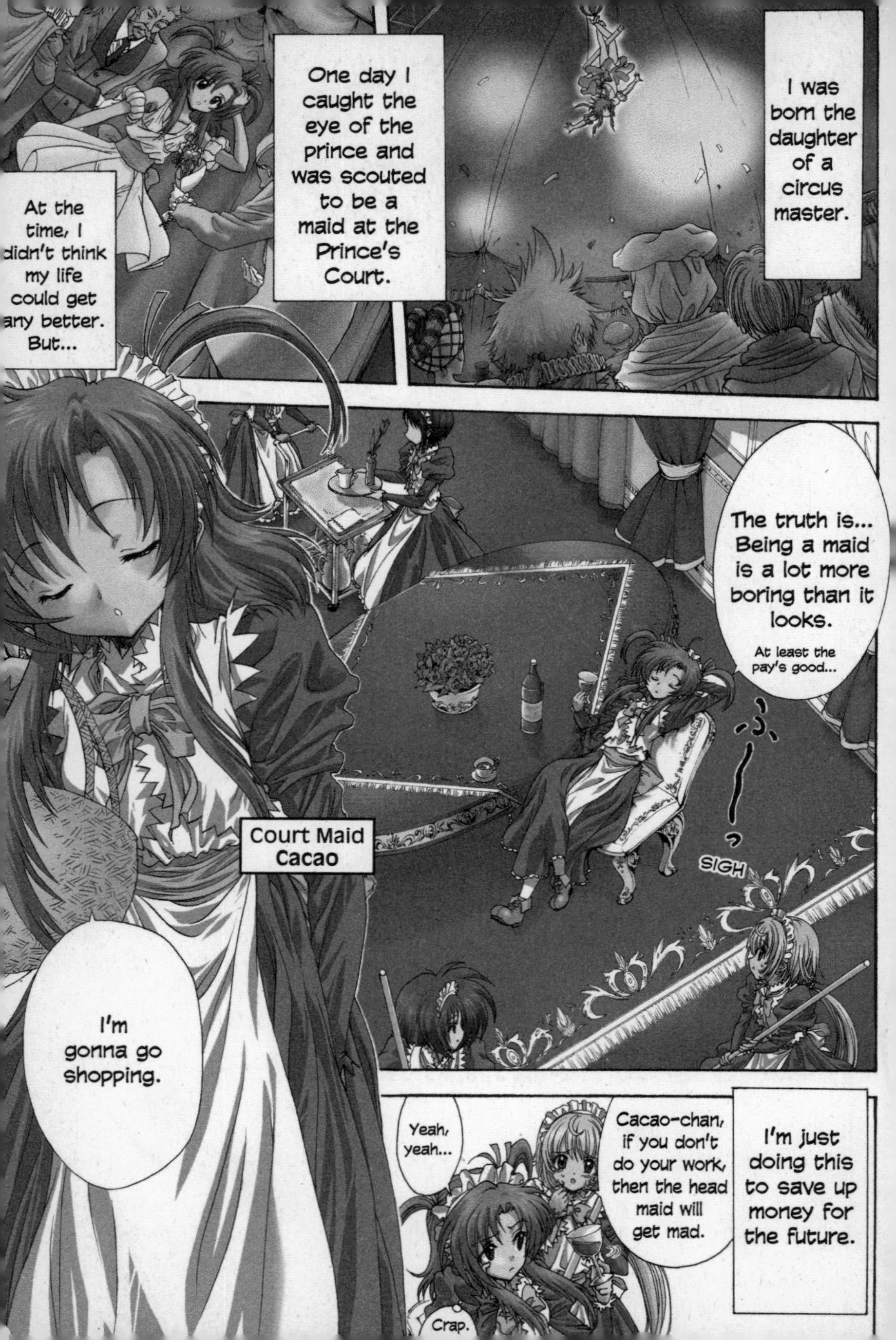
I was born the daughter of a circus master.
One day I caught the eye of the prince and was scouted to be a maid at the Prince's Court.
At the time, I didn't think my life could get any better. But...
The truth is... Being a maid is a lot more boring than it looks.
At least the pay's good...
ふー
SIGH
I'm just doing this to save up money for the future.
Cacao-chan, if you don't do your work, then the head maid will get mad.
Yeah, yeah...
Crap.
Court Maid Cacao
I'm gonna go shopping.

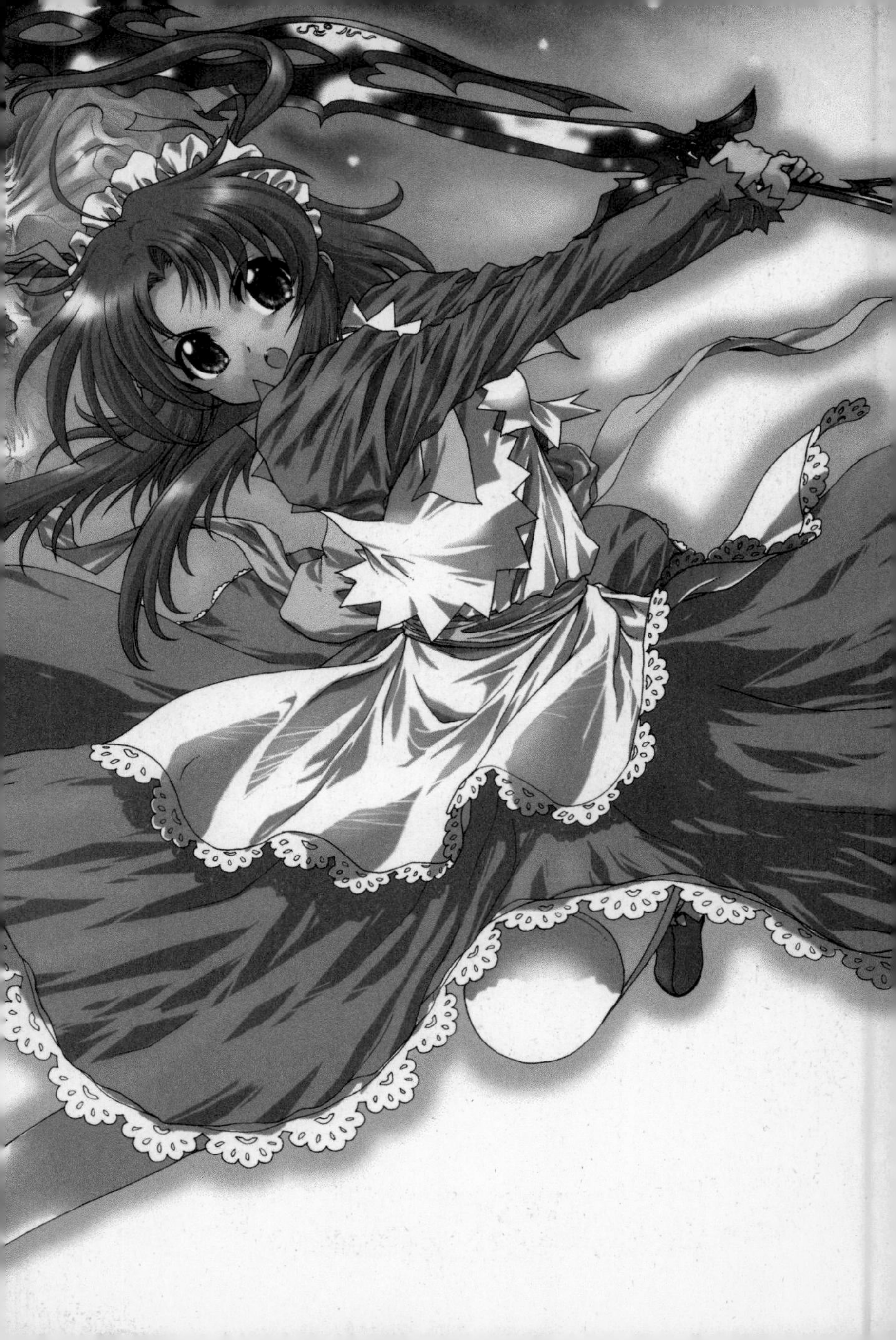

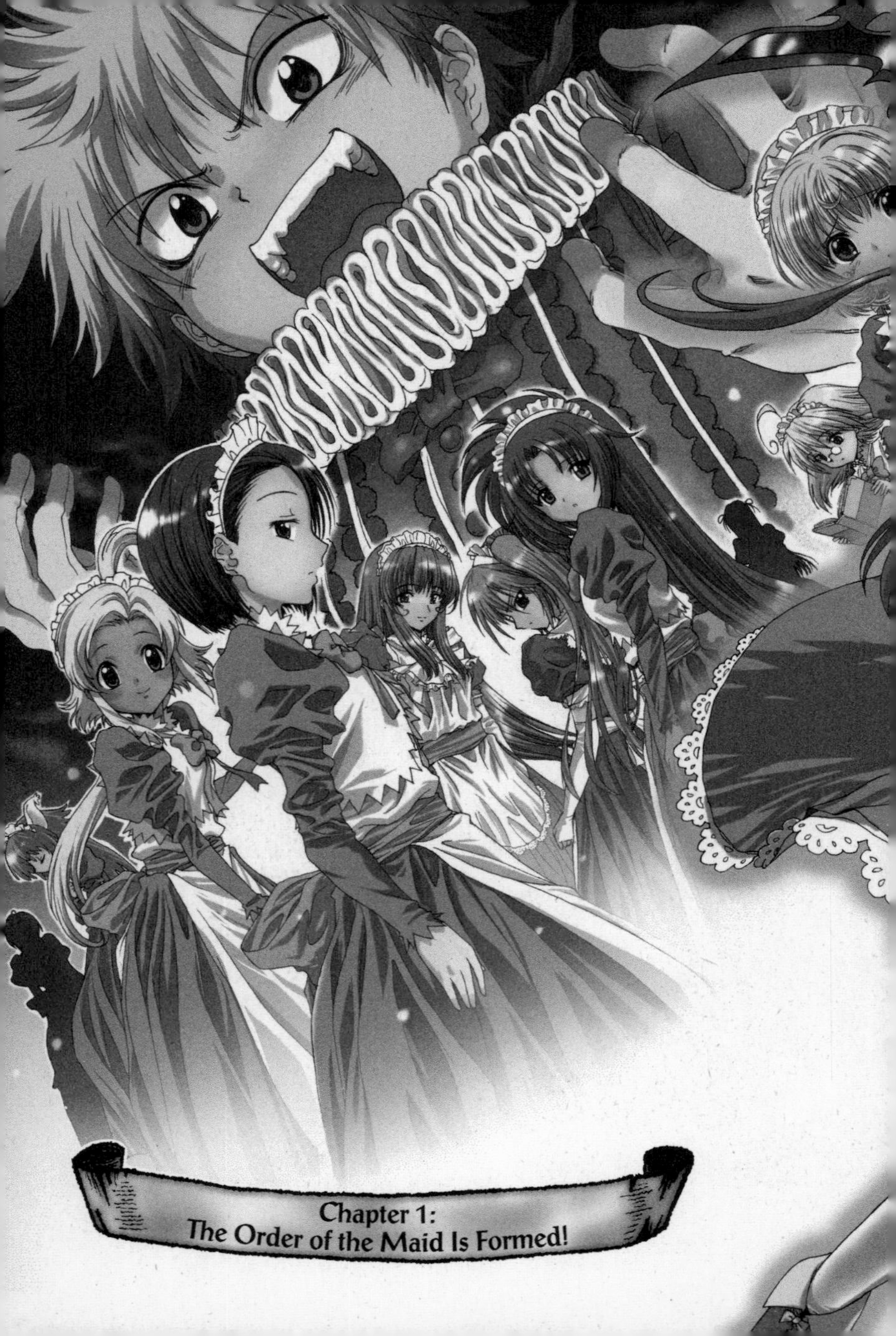
Chapter 1:
The Order of the Maid Is Formed!

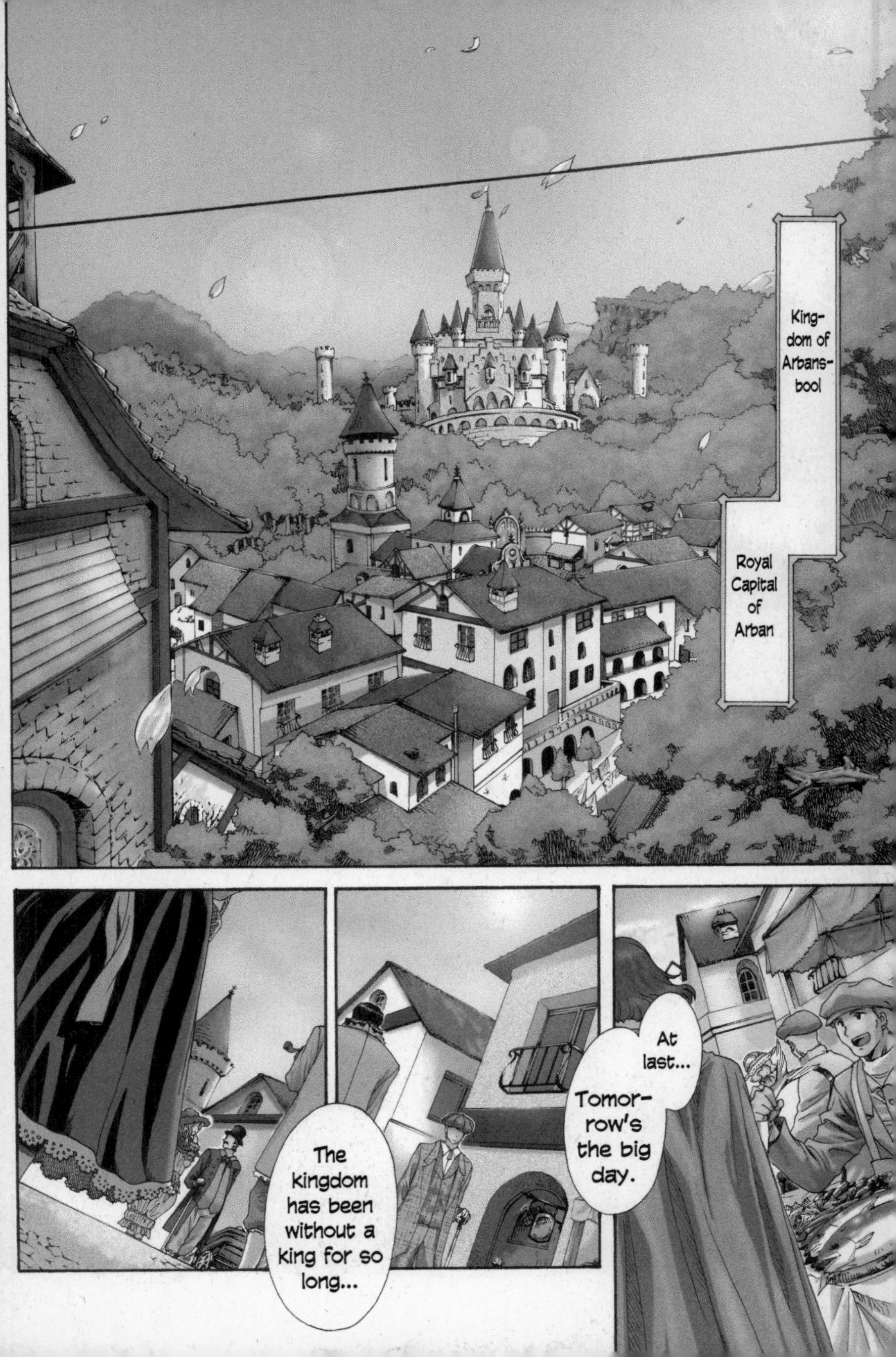
King-dom of Arbans-bool
Royal Capital of Arban
At last...
Tomor-row's the big day.
The kingdom has been without a king for so long...

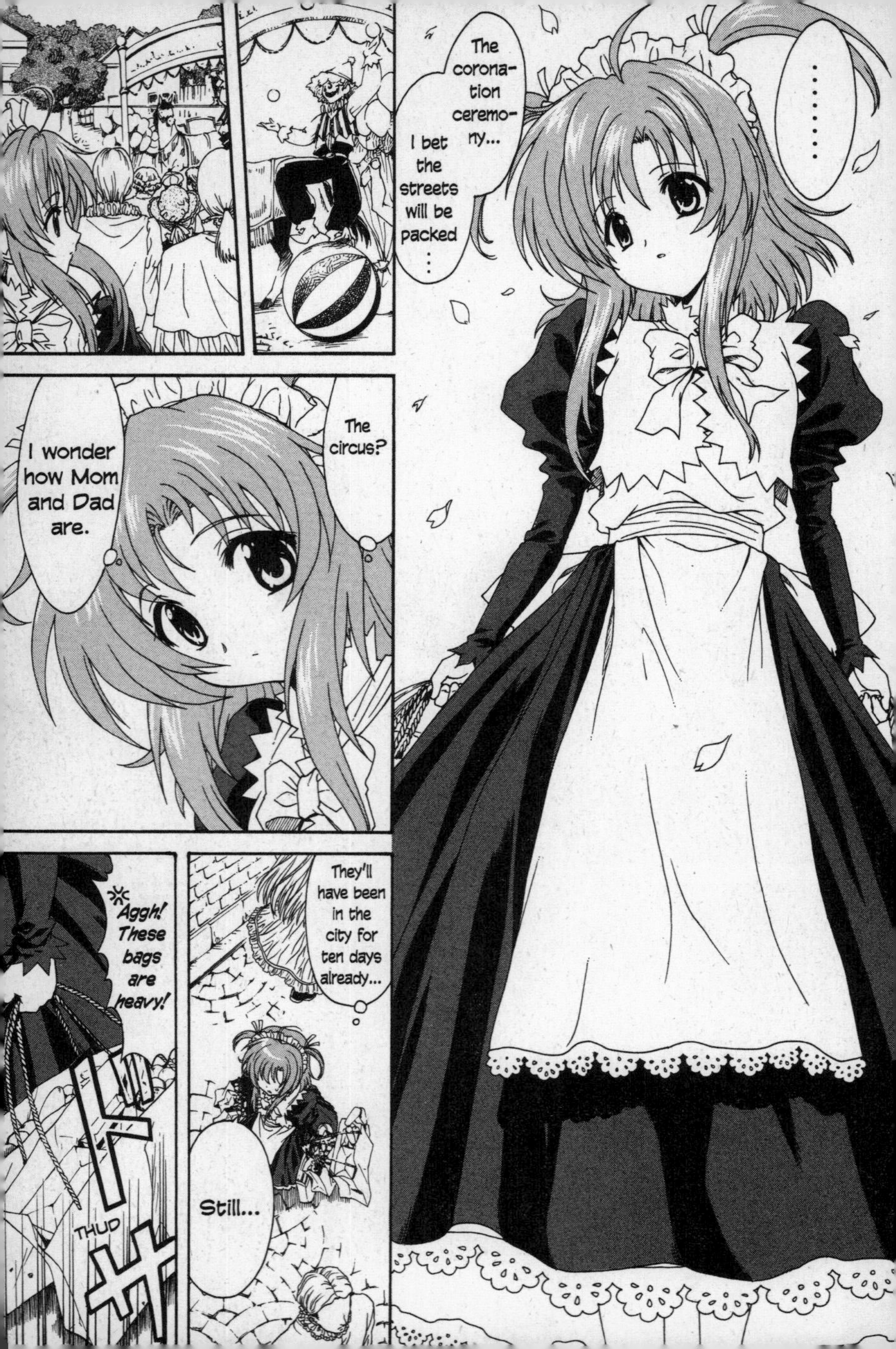
......
The coronation ceremony... I bet the streets will be packed...
The circus?
I wonder how Mom and Dad are.
They'll have been in the city for ten days already...
Still...
Aggh! These bags are heavy!
THUD

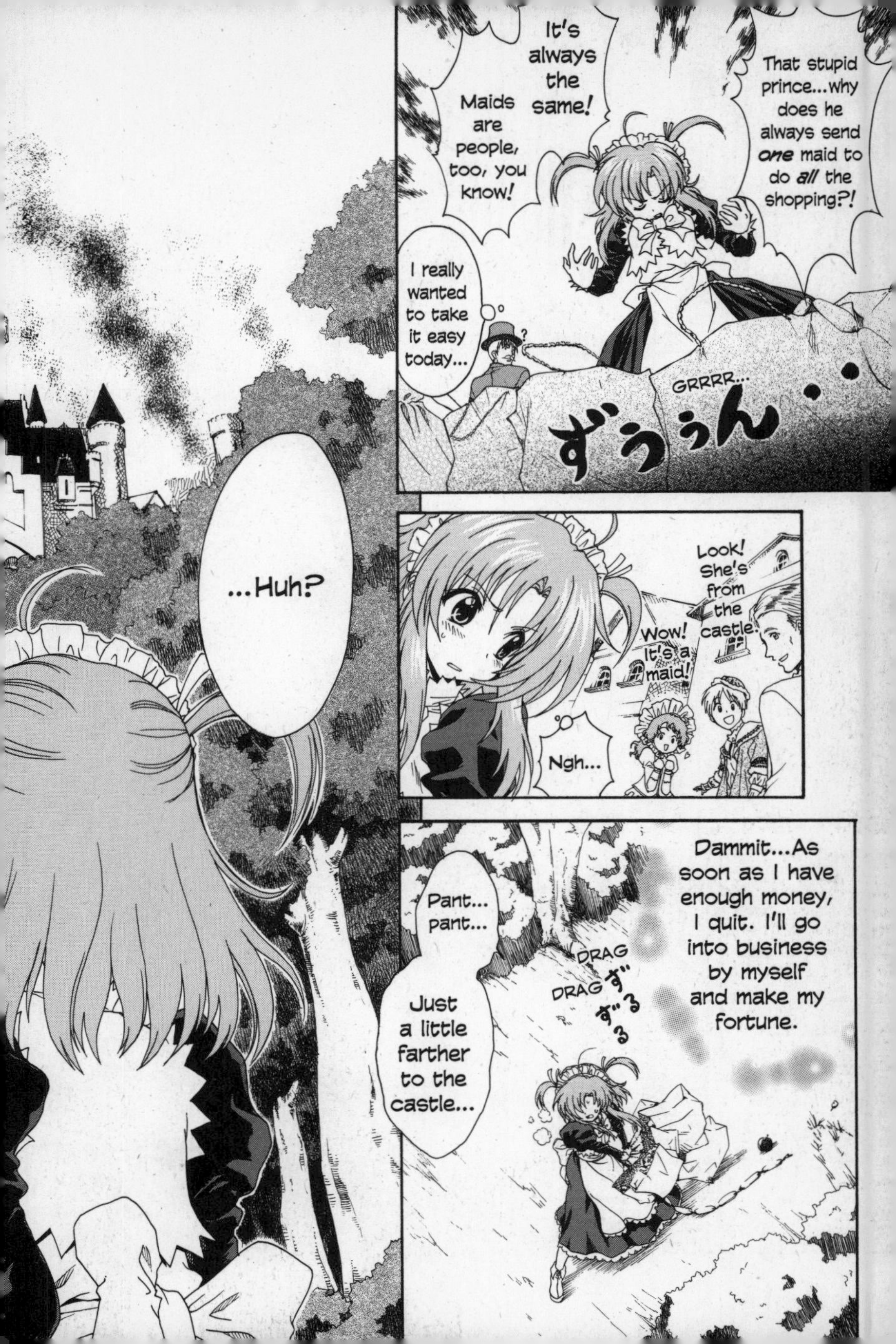
That stupid prince...why does he always send *one* maid to do *all* the shopping?!
It's always the same!
Maids are people, too, you know!
GRRRR...
ずううん
I really wanted to take it easy today...
Look! She's from the castle.
Wow! It's a maid!
Ngh...
Dammit...As soon as I have enough money, I quit. I'll go into business by myself and make my fortune.
Pant... pant...
DRAG DRAG
ずるずる
Just a little farther to the castle...
...Huh?

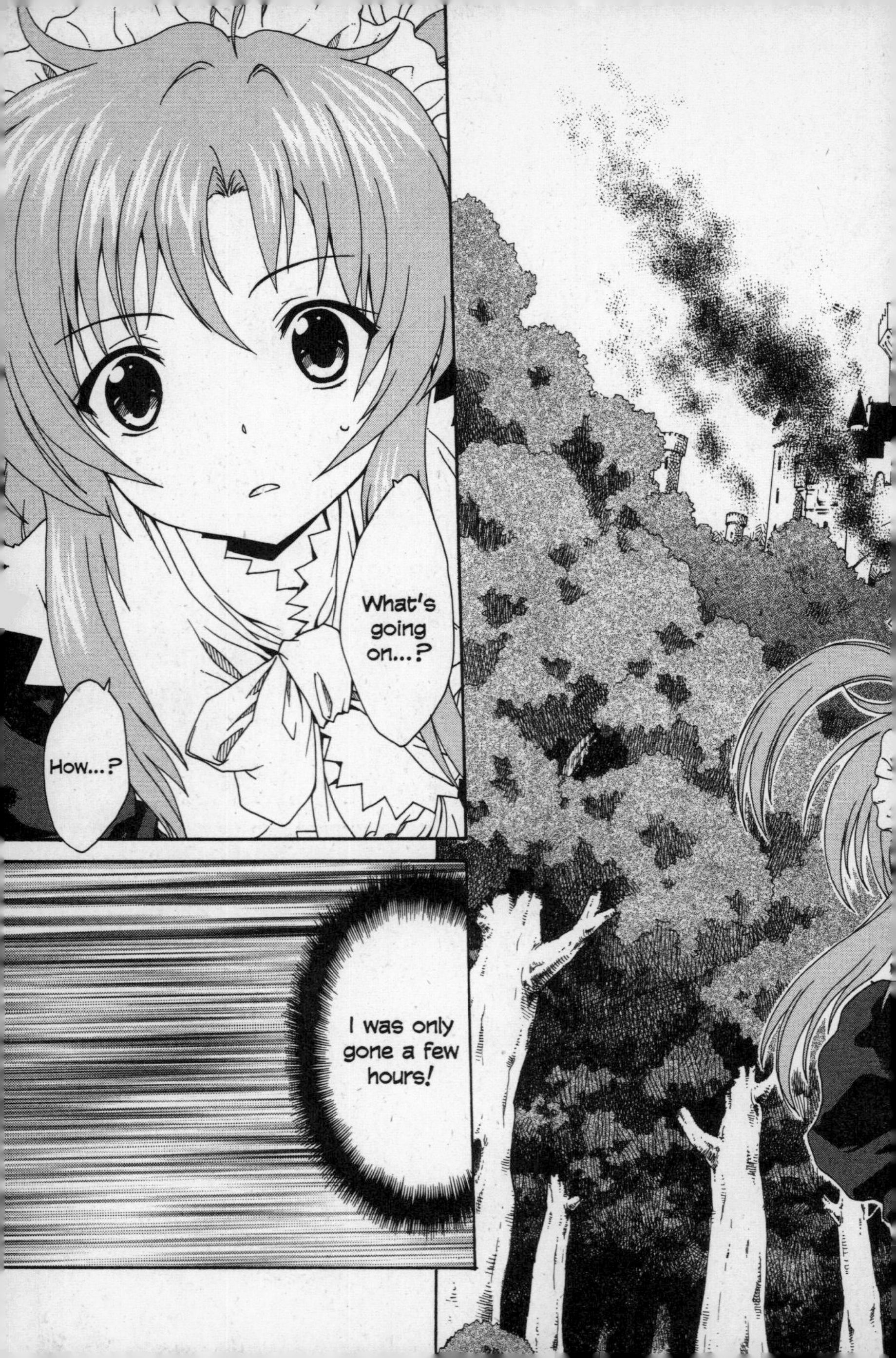
What's going on...?
How...?
I was only gone a few hours!

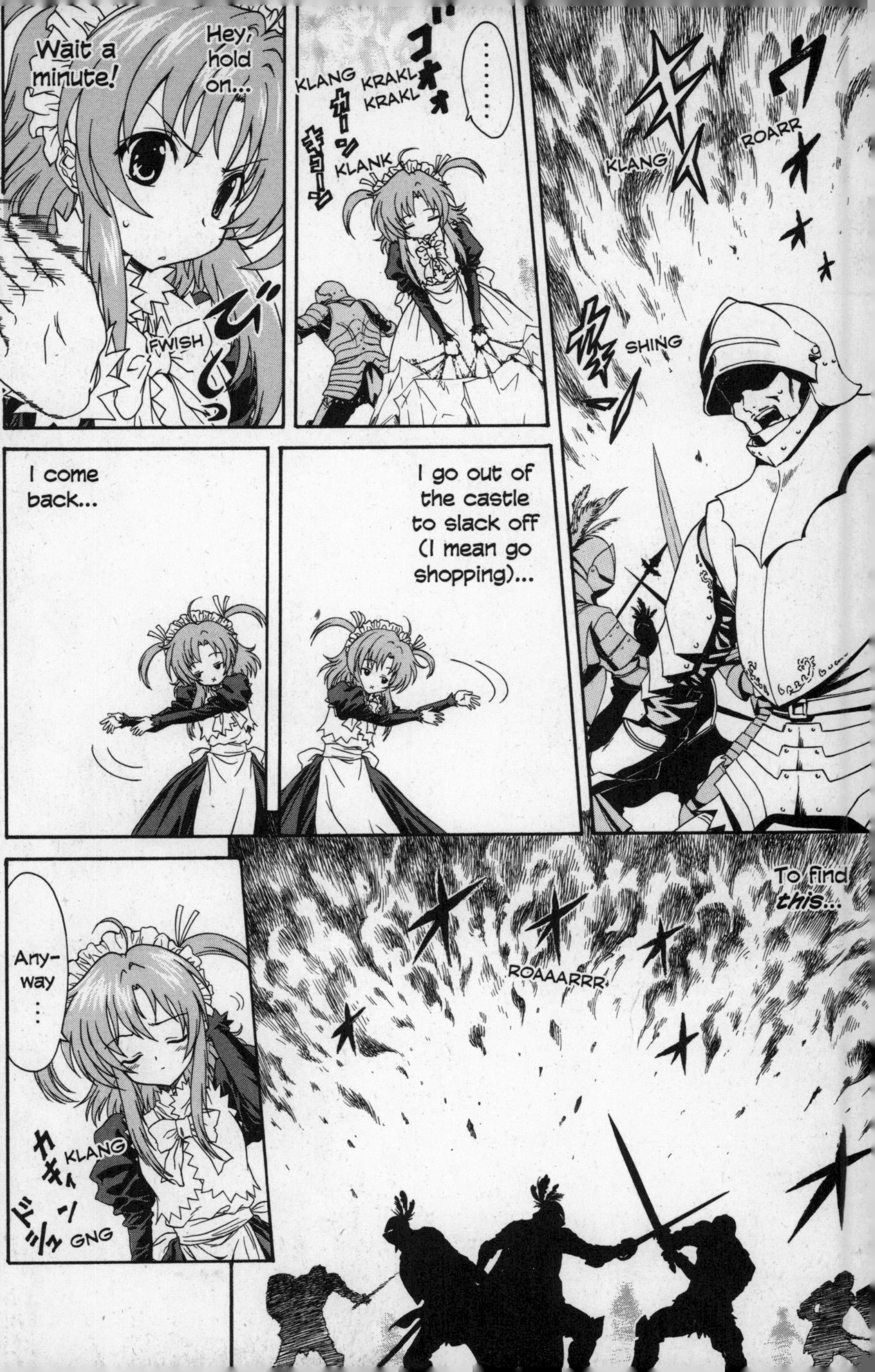

ROARR
KLANG
SHING
......
KRAKL KRAKL
KLANG
KLANK
Hey, hold on...
Wait a minute!
FWISH
I go out of the castle to slack off (I mean go shopping)...
I come back...
To find *this*...
ROAAARRR
Any-way...
KLANG
GNG

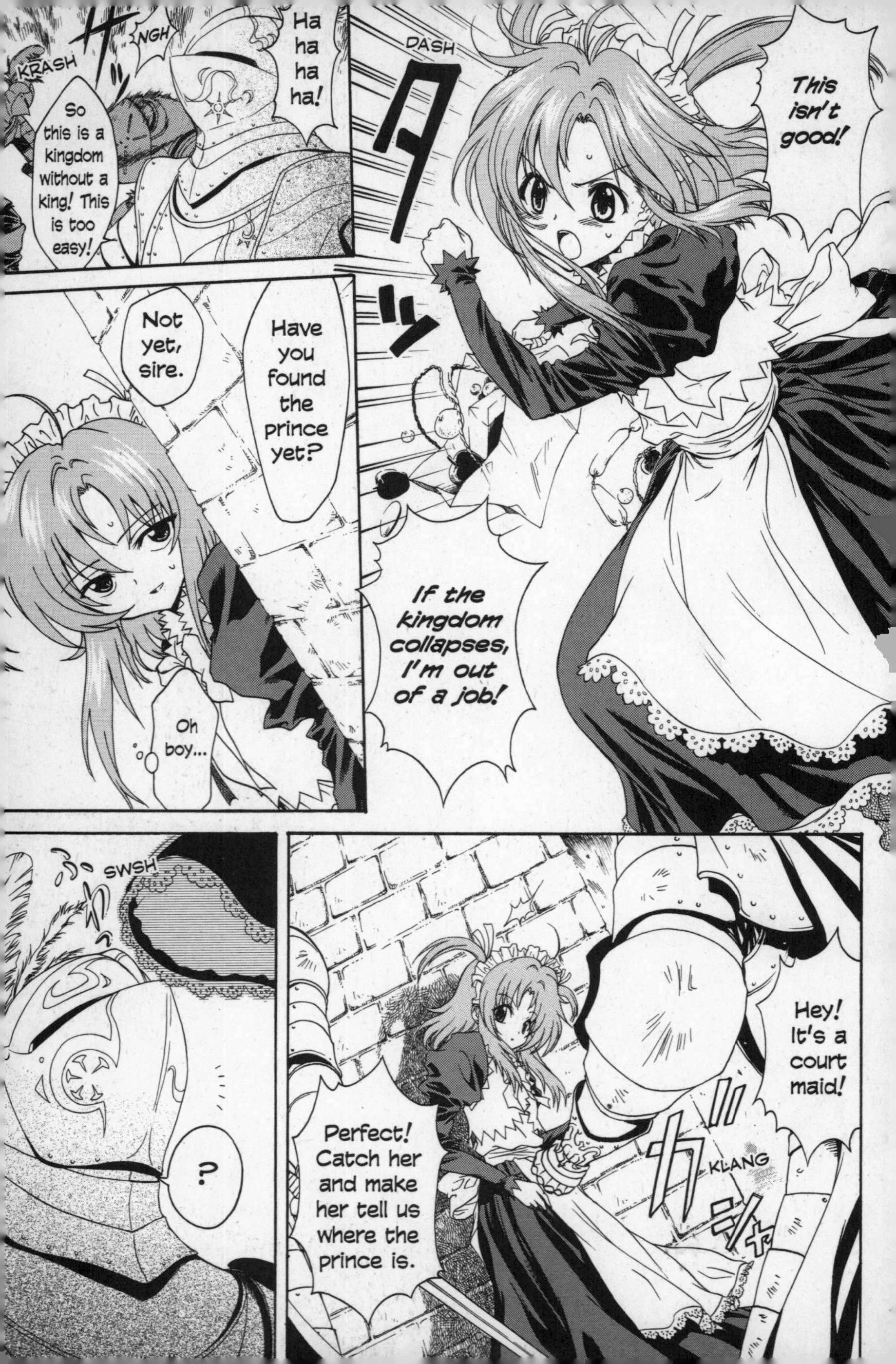

DASH
This isn't good!
If the kingdom collapses, I'm out of a job!
Ha ha ha ha!
NGH
KRASH
So this is a kingdom without a king! This is too easy!
Have you found the prince yet?
Not yet, sire.
Oh boy...
Hey! It's a court maid!
KLANG
Perfect! Catch her and make her tell us where the prince is.
SWSH
?

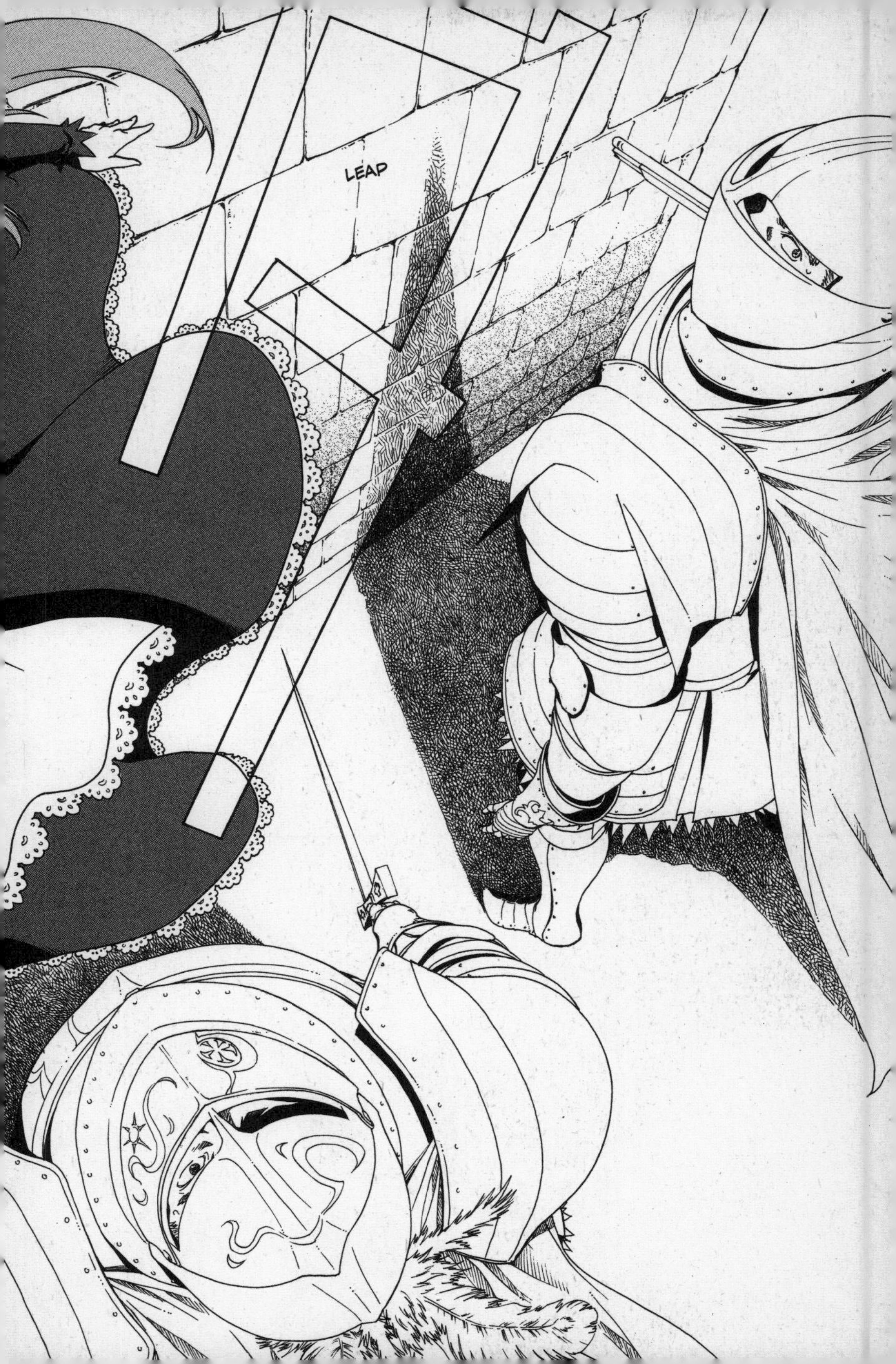
LEAP

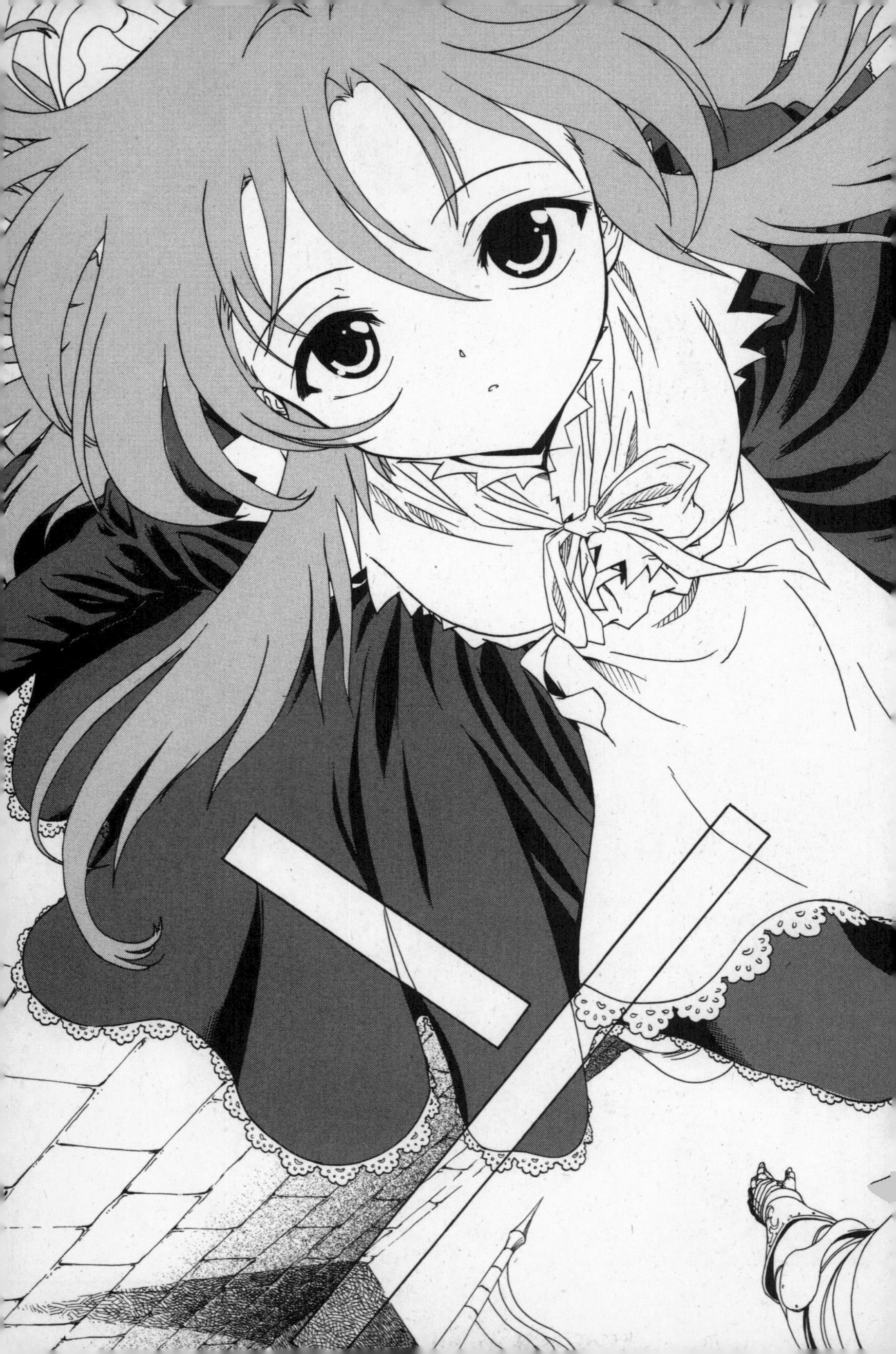

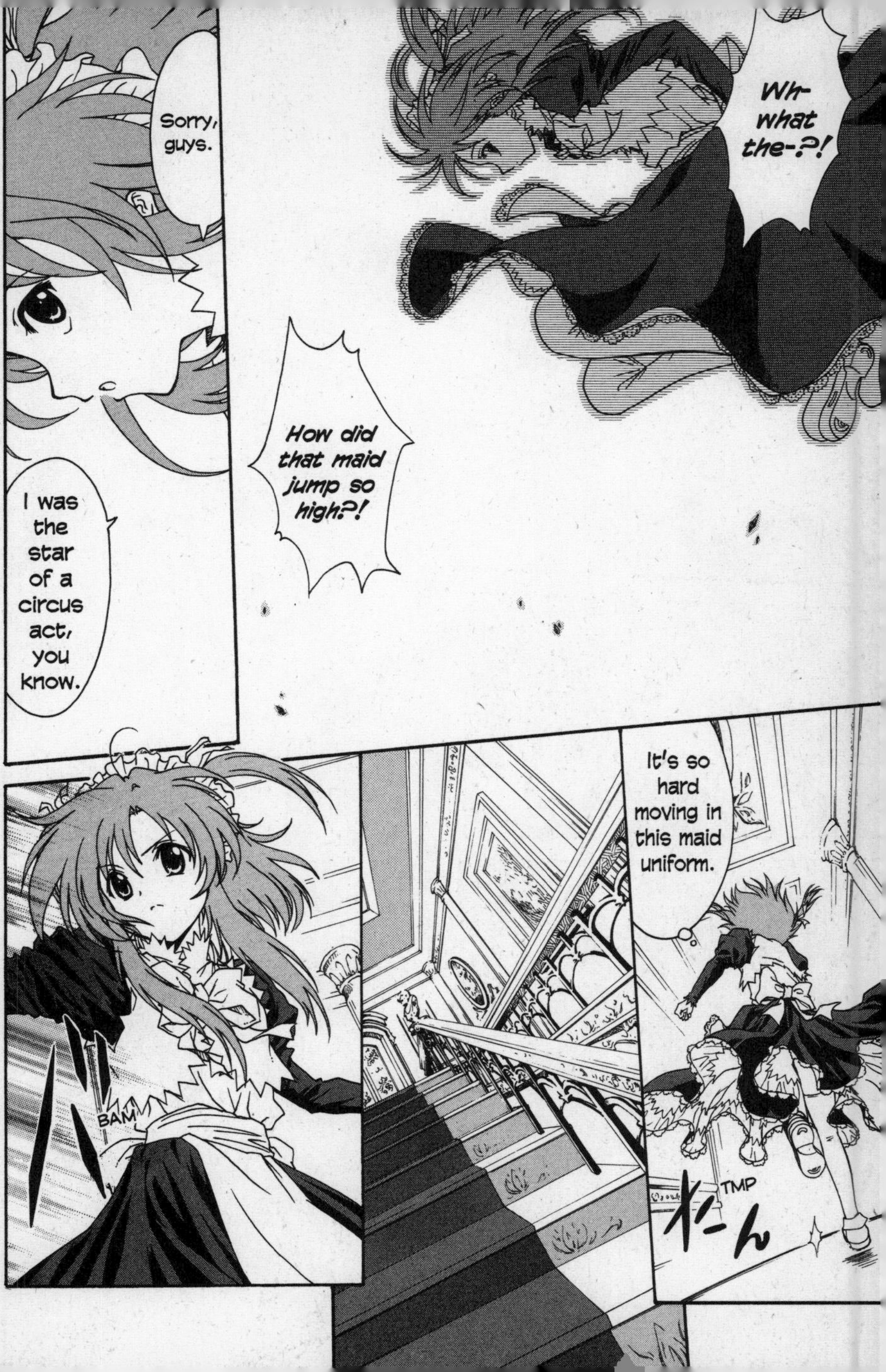
Wh- what the-?!
How did that maid jump so high?!
Sorry, guys.
I was the star of a circus act, you know.
It's so hard moving in this maid uniform.
TMP
BAM

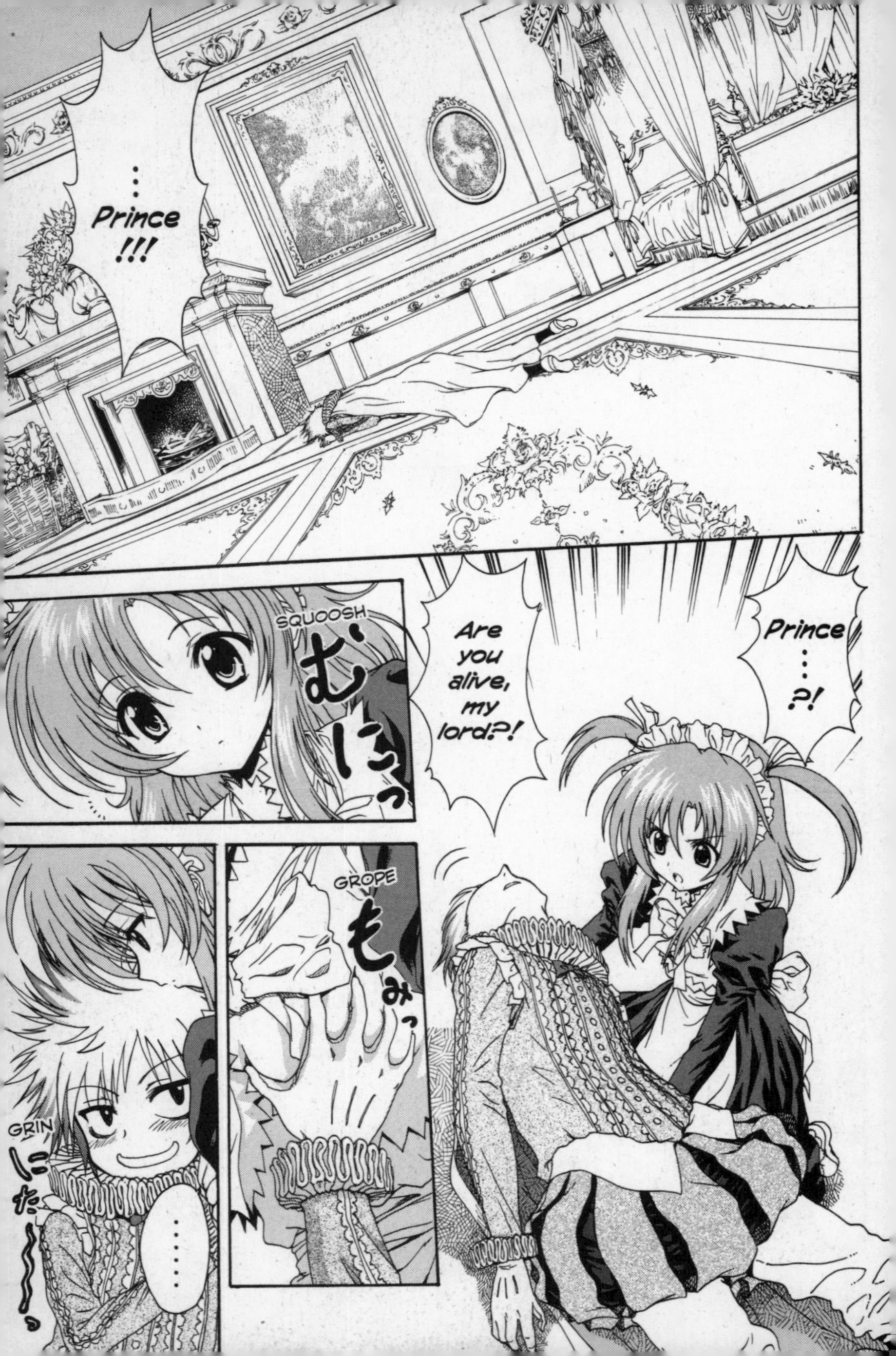

...Prince!!!
Prince...?!
Are you alive, my lord?!
SQUOOSH
むにっ
GROPE
もみっ
GRIN
にた～～～
.....

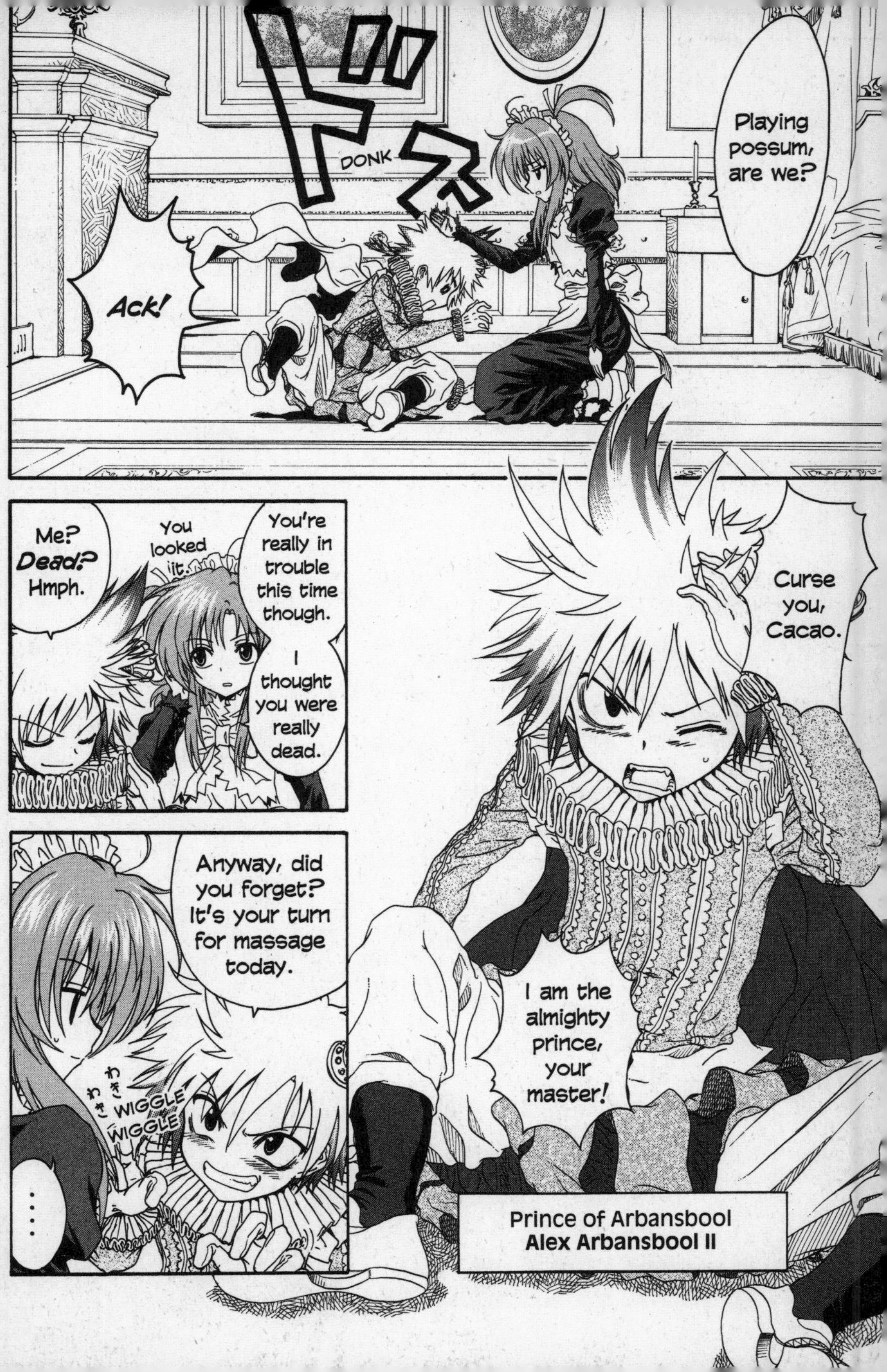

Playing possum, are we?
DONK
Ack!
Curse you, Cacao.
I am the almighty prince, your master!
Prince of Arbansbool
Alex Arbansbool II
You're really in trouble this time though.
I thought you were really dead.
You looked it.
Me? *Dead?* Hmph.
Anyway, did you forget? It's your turn for massage today.
わき わき
WIGGLE WIGGLE
....

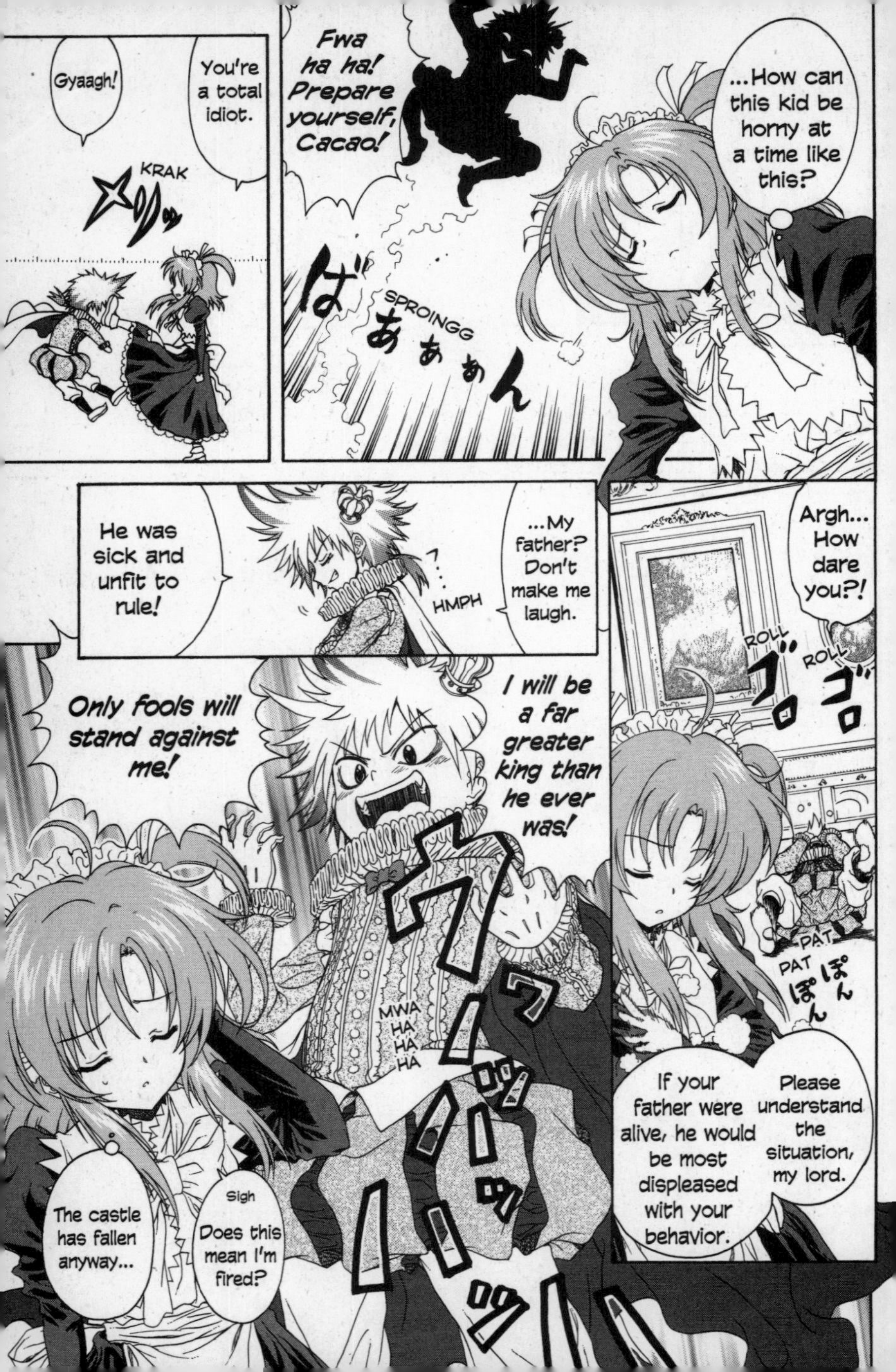

...How can this kid be horny at a time like this?
Fwa ha ha! Prepare yourself, Cacao!
SPROINGG
ばあぁぁん
You're a total idiot.
Gyaagh!
KRAK
Argh... How dare you?!
ROLL
ROLL
ゴロゴロ
PAT
PAT
ぽんぽん
Please understand the situation, my lord.
If your father were alive, he would be most displeased with your behavior.
...My father? Don't make me laugh.
HMPH
He was sick and unfit to rule!
I will be a far greater king than he ever was!
Only fools will stand against me!
MWA HA HA HA
Sigh
Does this mean I'm fired?
The castle has fallen anyway...

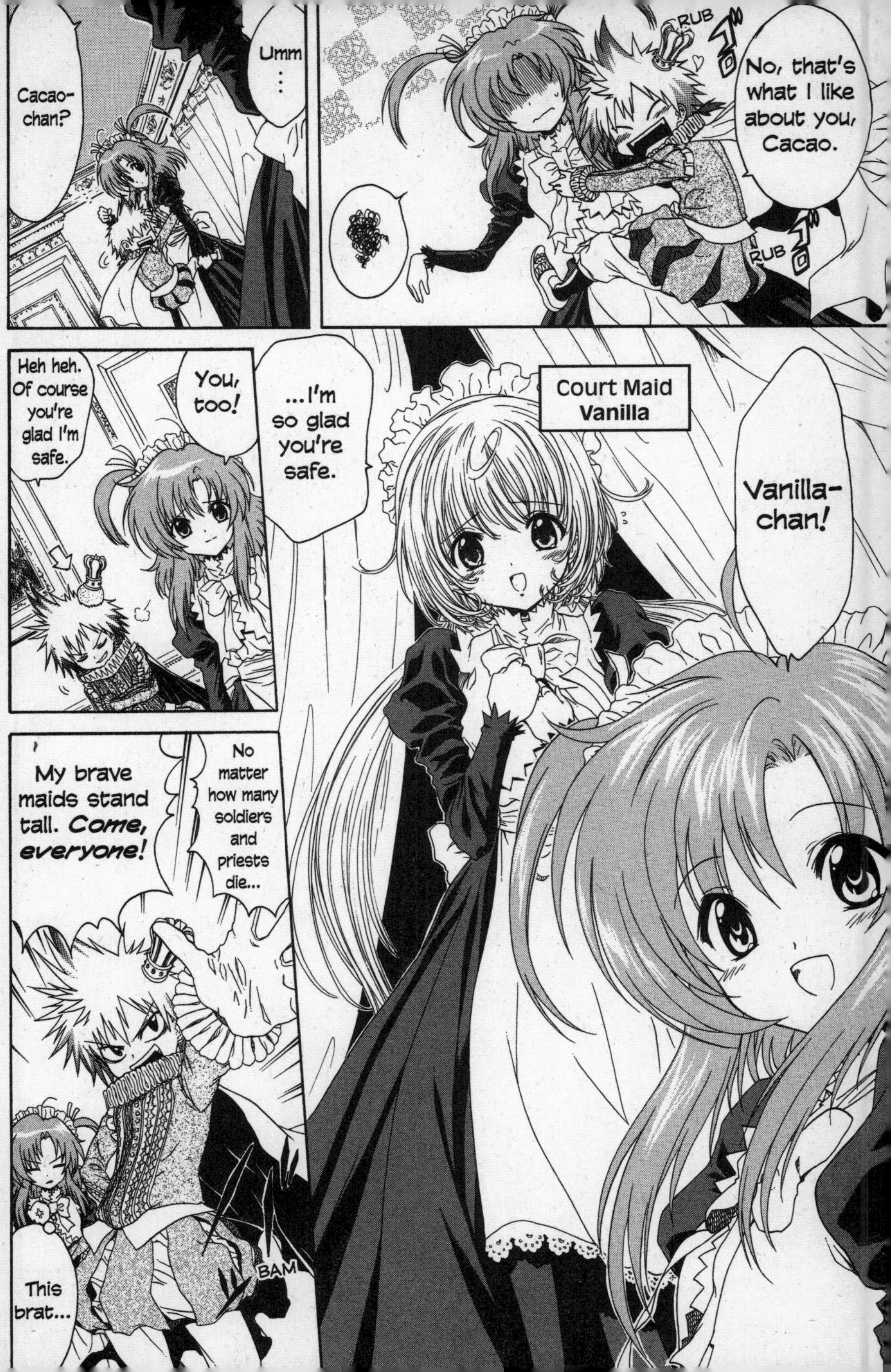
RUB
No, that's what I like about you, Cacao.
RUB
Umm ...
Cacao-chan?
Vanilla-chan!
Court Maid Vanilla
...I'm so glad you're safe.
You, too!
Heh heh. Of course you're glad I'm safe.
No matter how many soldiers and priests die...
My brave maids stand tall. *Come, everyone!*
BAM
This brat...

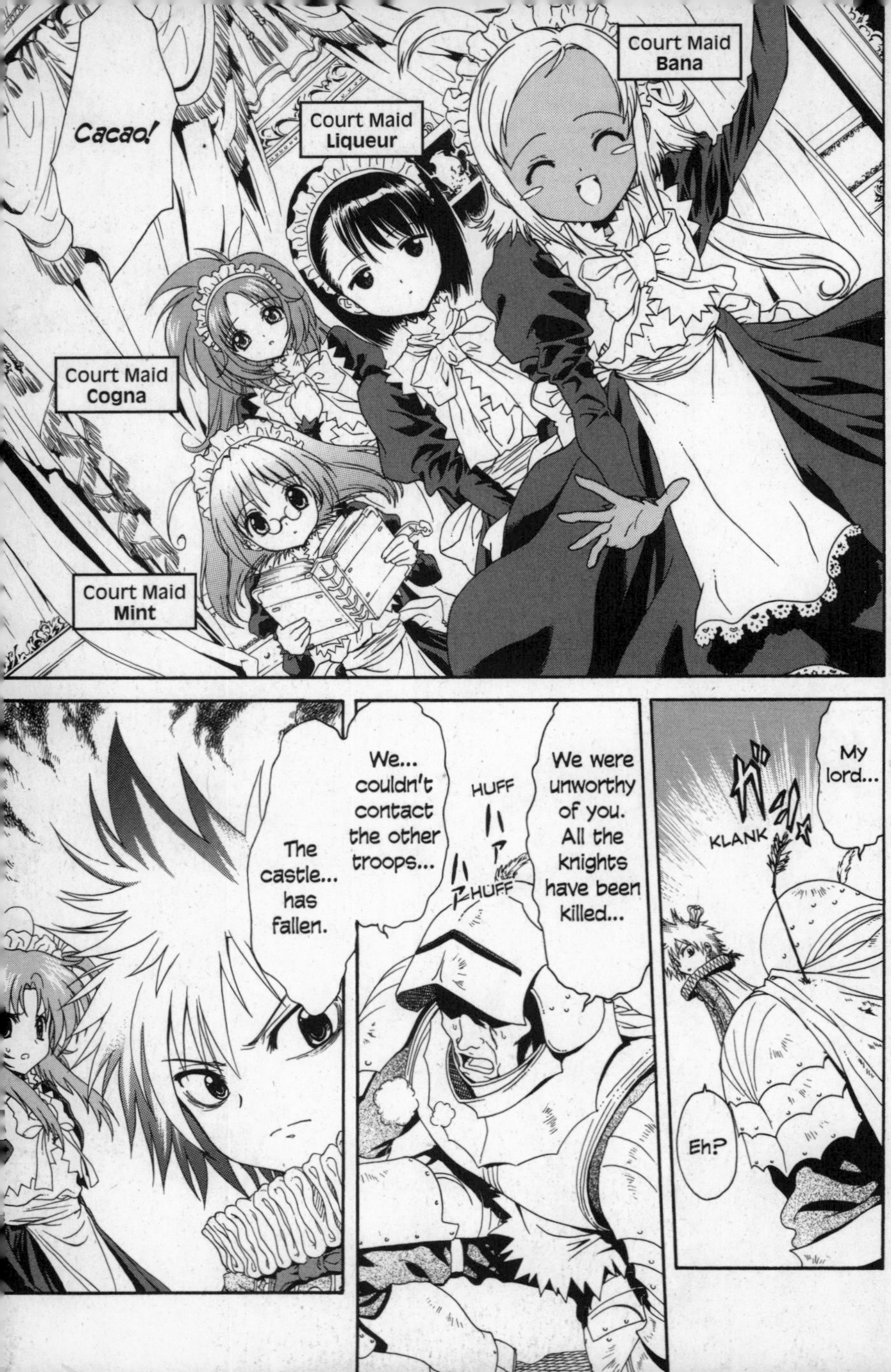
Court Maid Bana
Court Maid Liqueur
Cacao!
Court Maid Cogna
Court Maid Mint
My lord...
KLANK
Eh?
We were unworthy of you. All the knights have been killed...
HUFF
HUFF
We... couldn't contact the other troops...
The castle... has fallen.

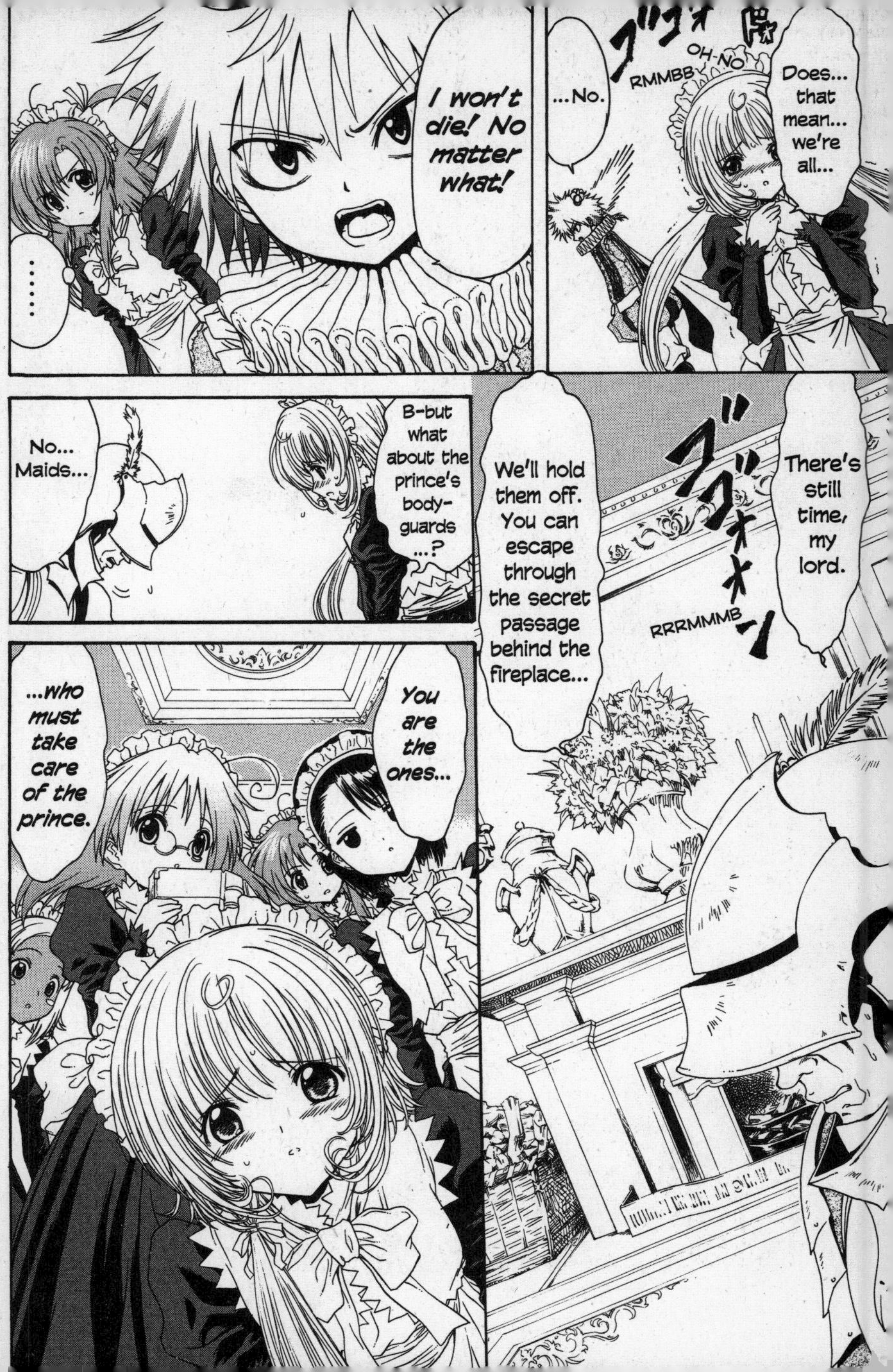
RMMBB
OH-NO
Does... that mean... we're all...
...No.
I won't die! No matter what!
......
There's still time, my lord.
RRRMMMB
We'll hold them off. You can escape through the secret passage behind the fireplace...
B-but what about the prince's body-guards ...?
No... Maids...
You are the ones...
...who must take care of the prince.

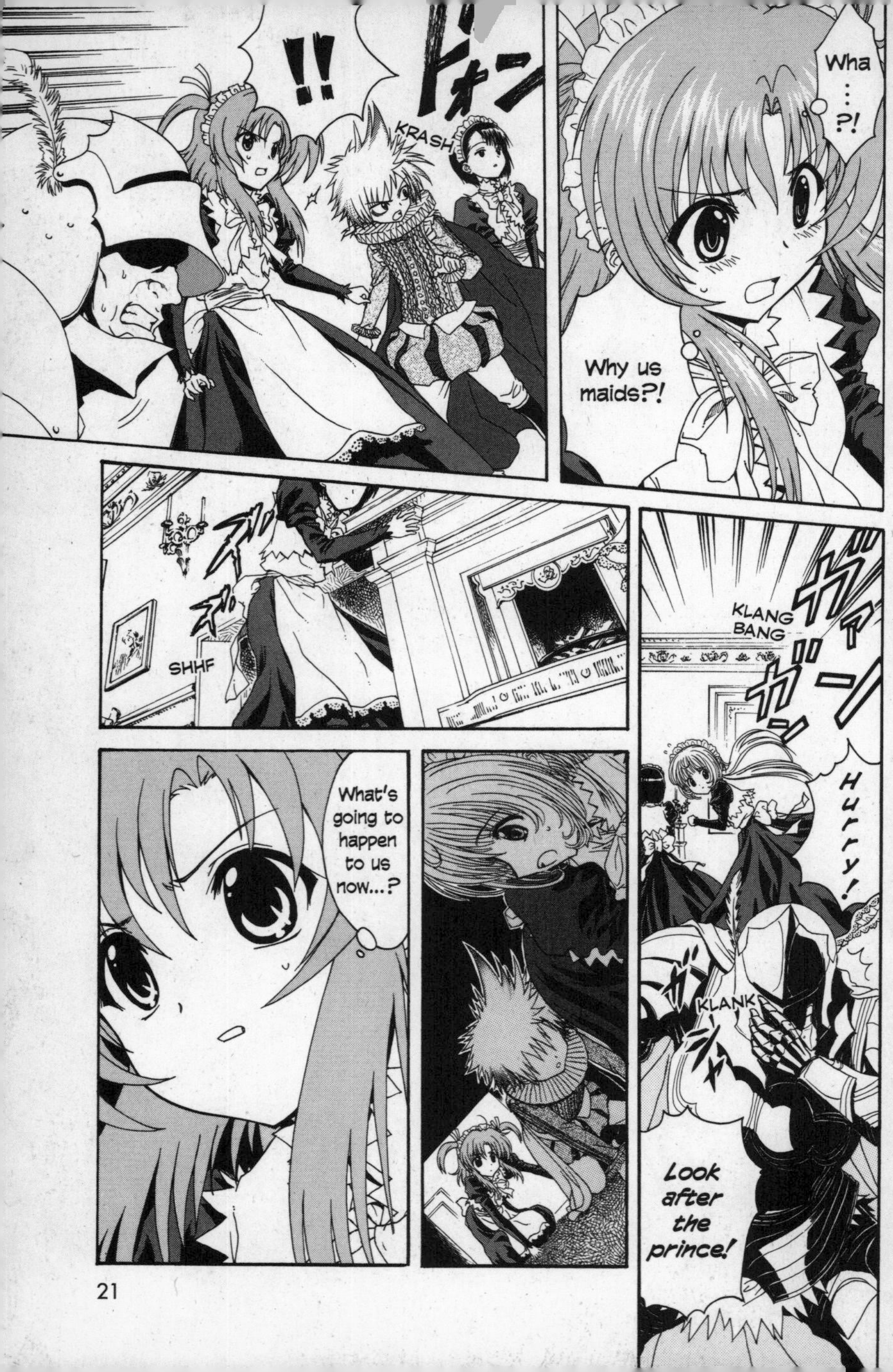
Wha...?!
Why us maids?!
!!
KRASH
KLANG
BANG
Hurry!
KLANK
Look after the prince!
SHHF
What's going to happen to us now...?

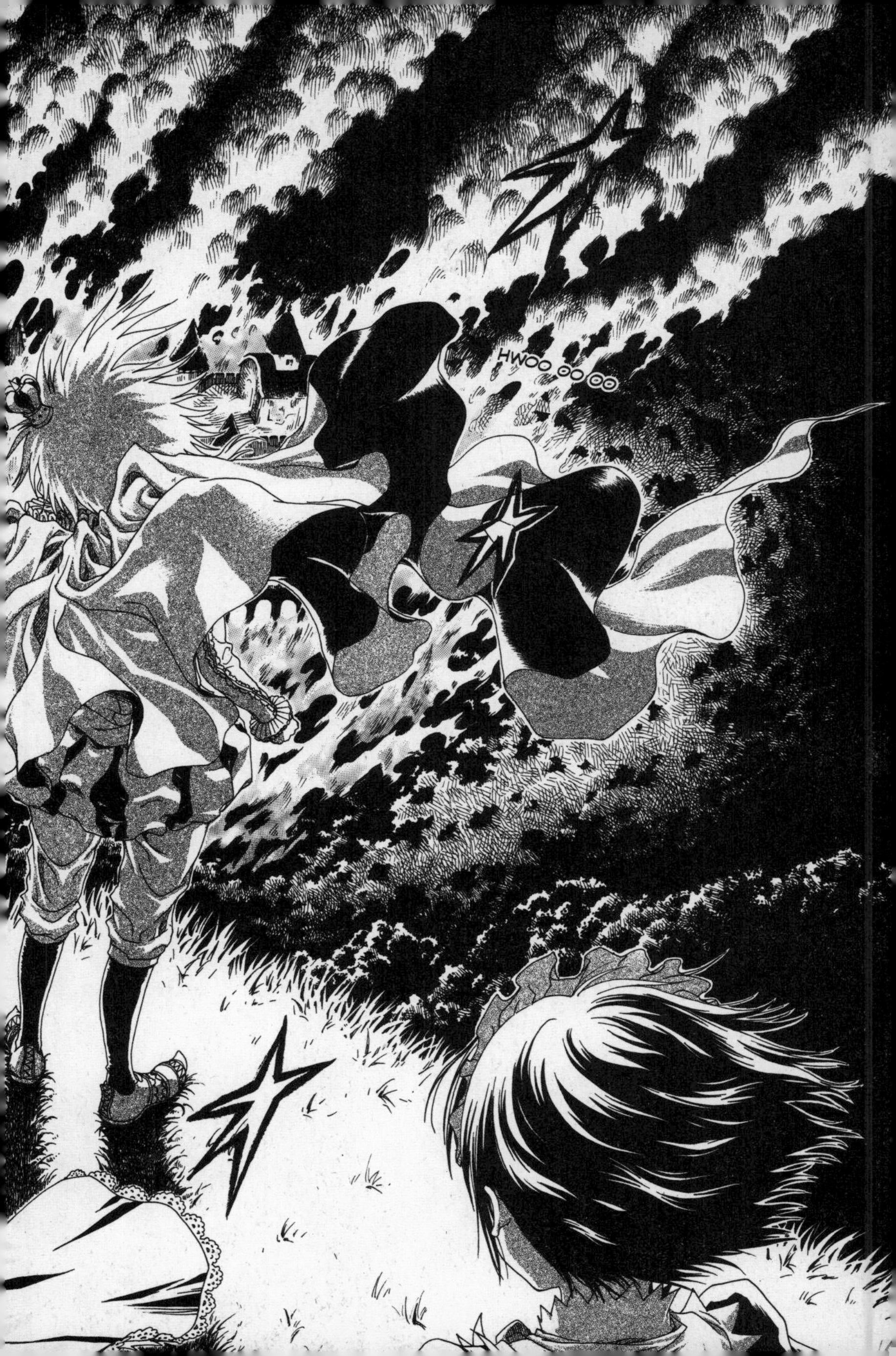
HWOO OO OO

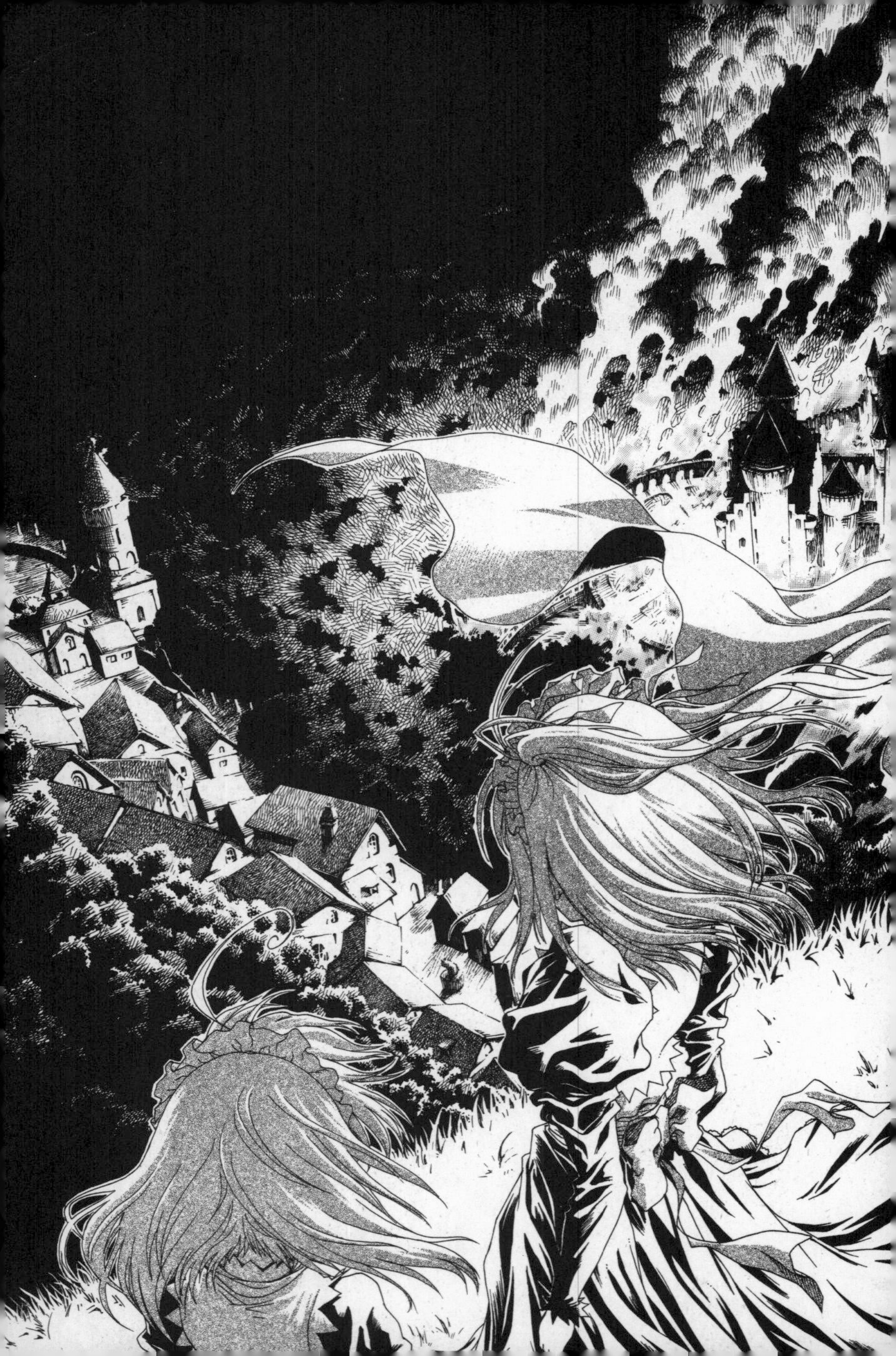

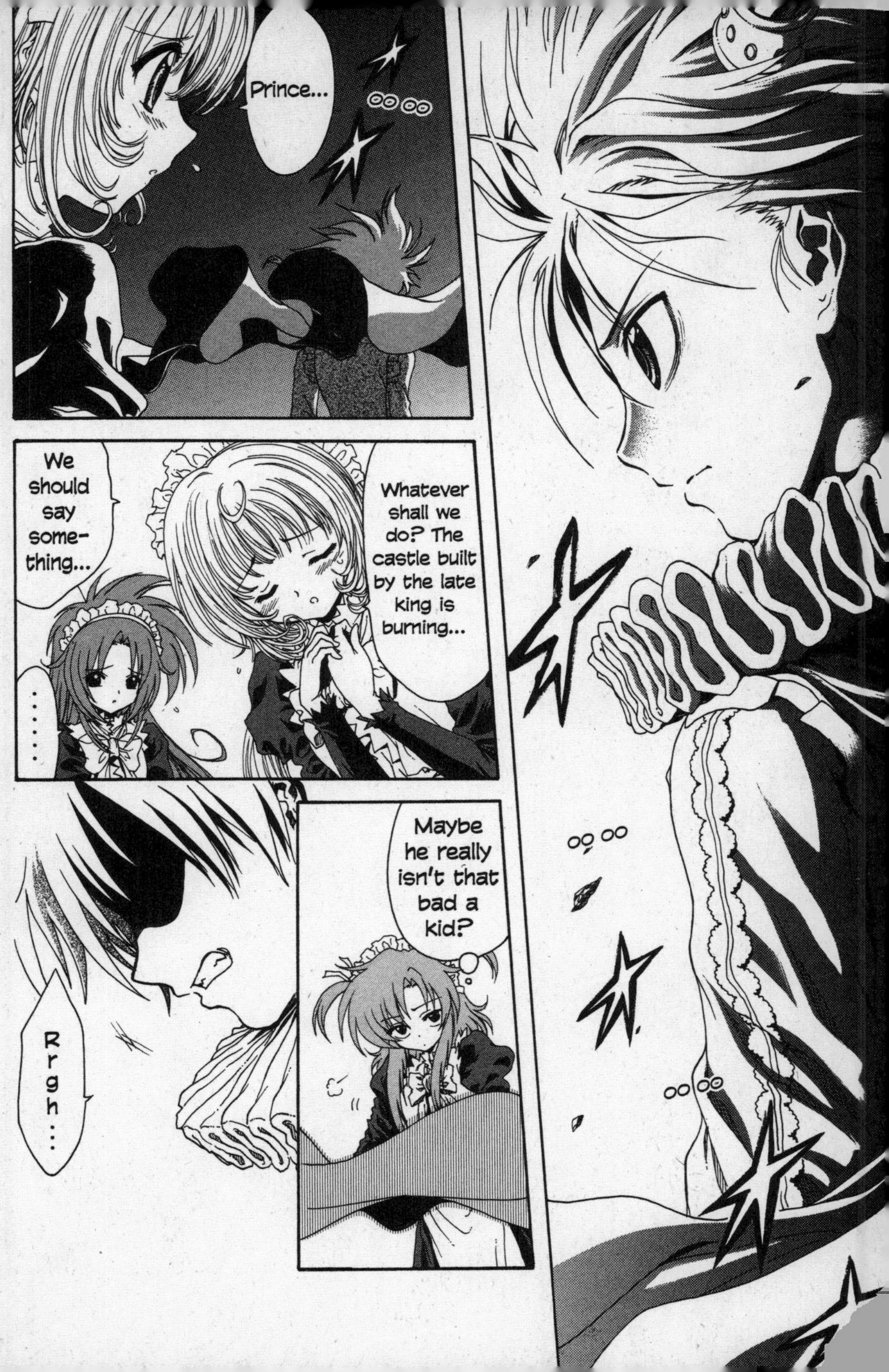
Prince...
Whatever shall we do? The castle built by the late king is burning...
We should say some-thing...
......
Maybe he really isn't that bad a kid?
Rrgh...

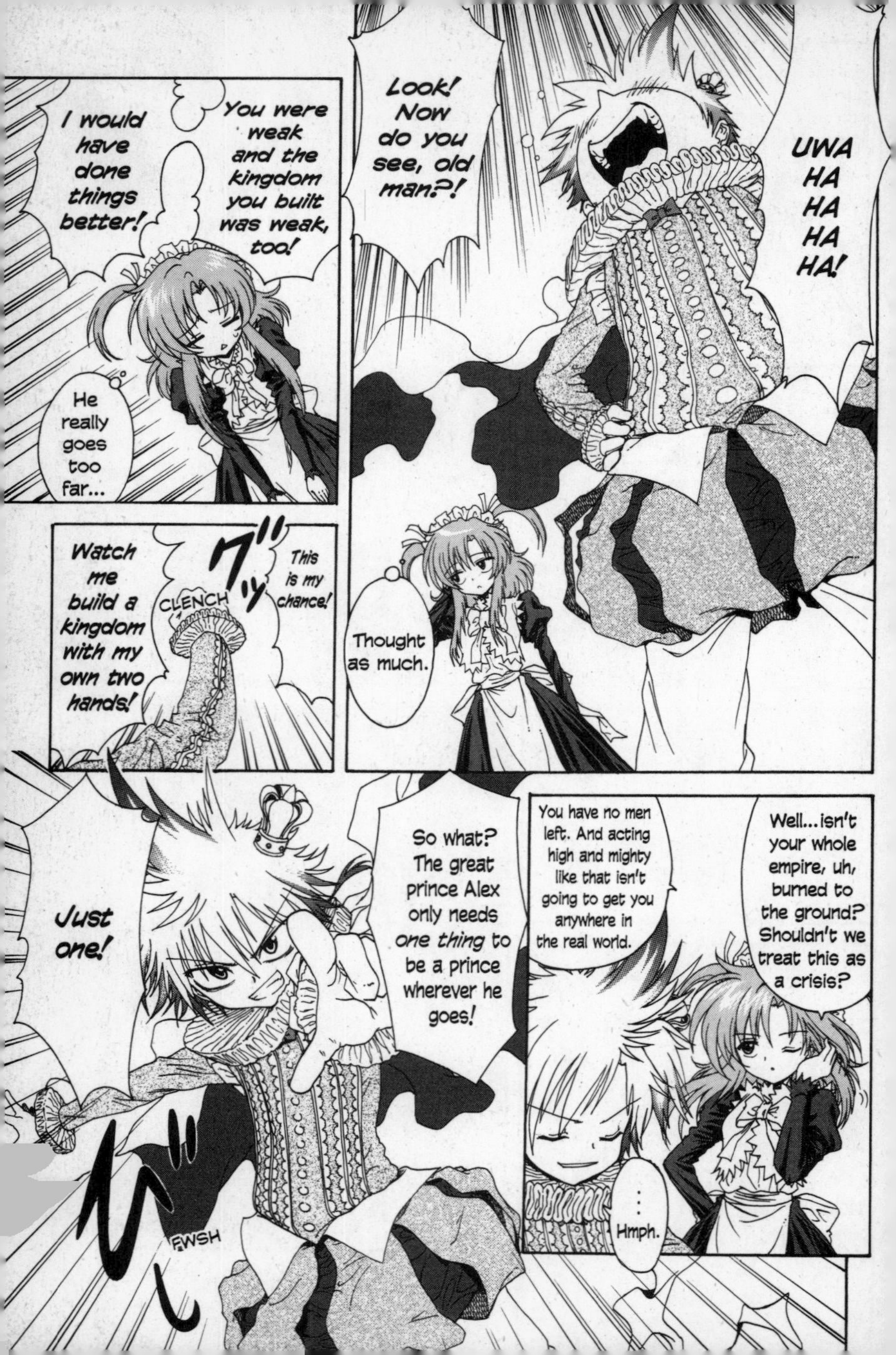
UWA HA HA HA HA!
Look! Now do you see, old man?!
Thought as much.
You were weak and the kingdom you built was weak, too!
I would have done things better!
He really goes too far...
This is my chance!
CLENCH
Watch me build a kingdom with my own two hands!
Well...isn't your whole empire, uh, burned to the ground? Shouldn't we treat this as a crisis?
You have no men left. And acting high and mighty like that isn't going to get you anywhere in the real world.
... Hmph.
So what? The great prince Alex only needs *one thing* to be a prince wherever he goes!
Just one!
FWSH

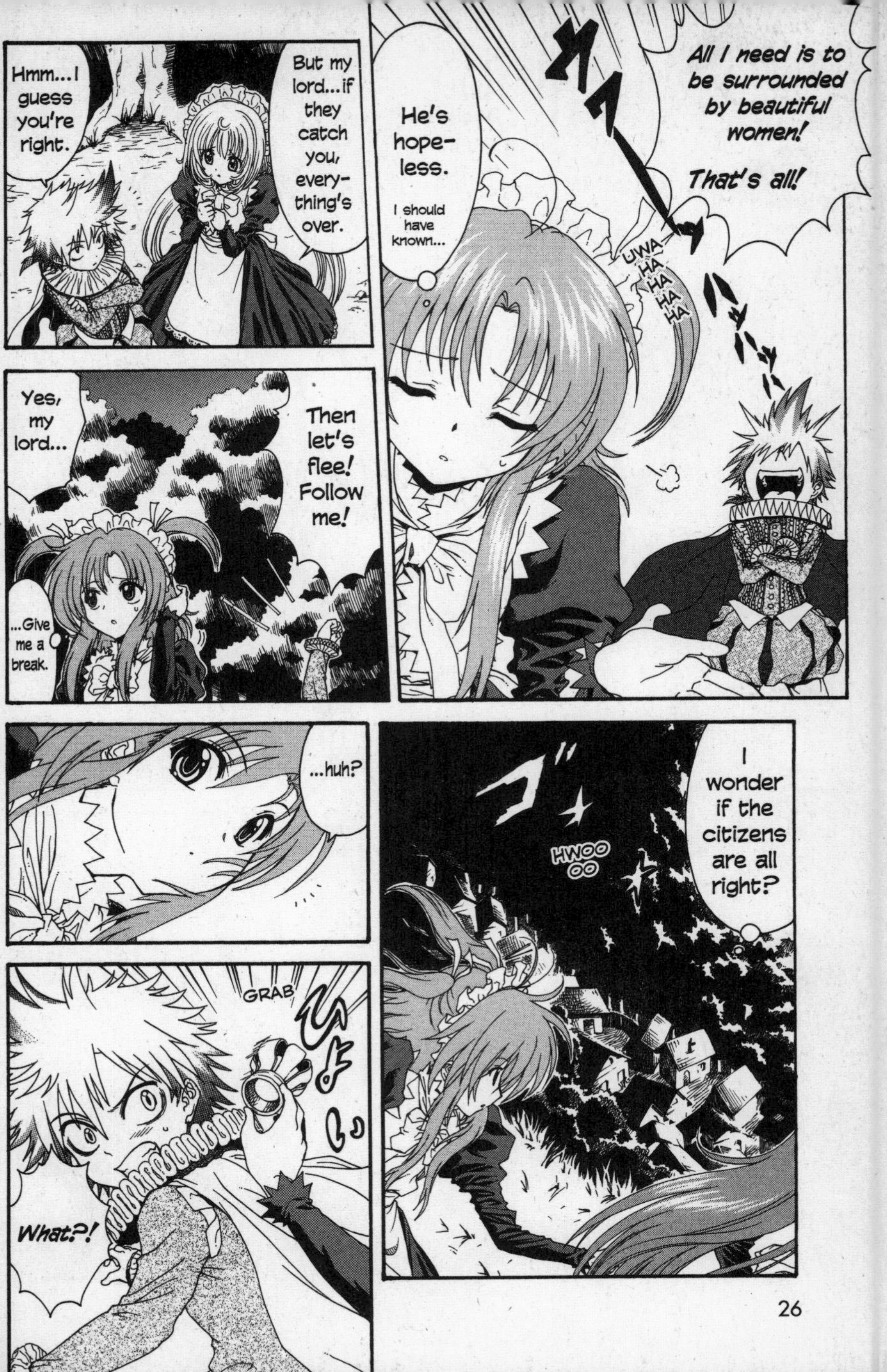

All I need is to be surrounded by beautiful women!
That's all!
UWA HA HA HA HA
He's hopeless.
I should have known...
But my lord...if they catch you, everything's over.
Hmm...I guess you're right.
Then let's flee! Follow me!
Yes, my lord...
...Give me a break.
I wonder if the citizens are all right?
HWOOOO
...huh?
GRAB
What?!

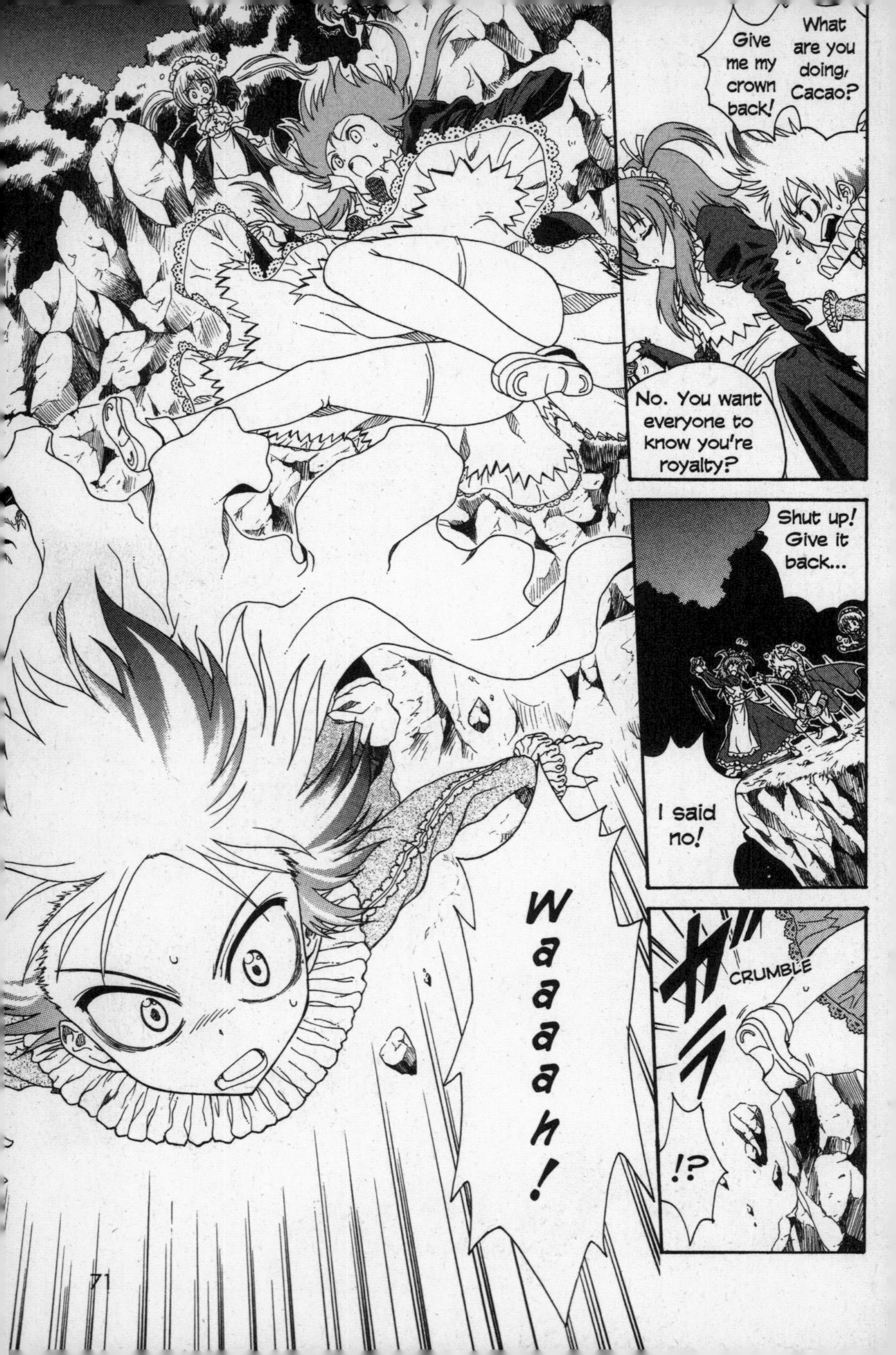
What are you doing, Cacao?
Give me my crown back!
No. You want everyone to know you're royalty?
Shut up! Give it back...
I said no!
CRUMBLE
!?
Waaaaah!

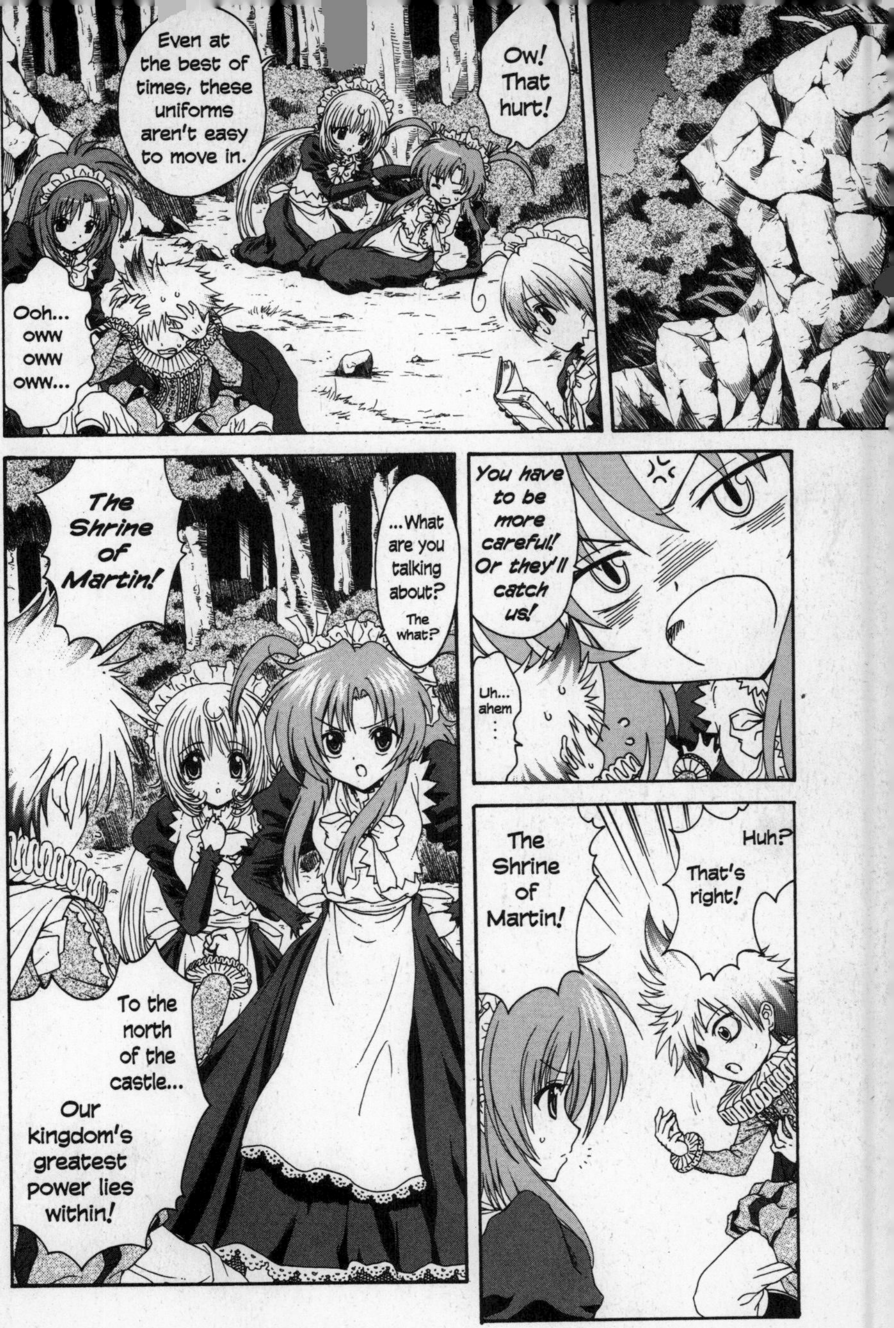

Ow! That hurt!
Even at the best of times, these uniforms aren't easy to move in.
Ooh... oww oww oww...
You have to be more careful! Or they'll catch us!
Uh... ahem...
Huh?
That's right!
The Shrine of Martin!
...What are you talking about?
The what?
The Shrine of Martin!
To the north of the castle...
Our kingdom's greatest power lies within!

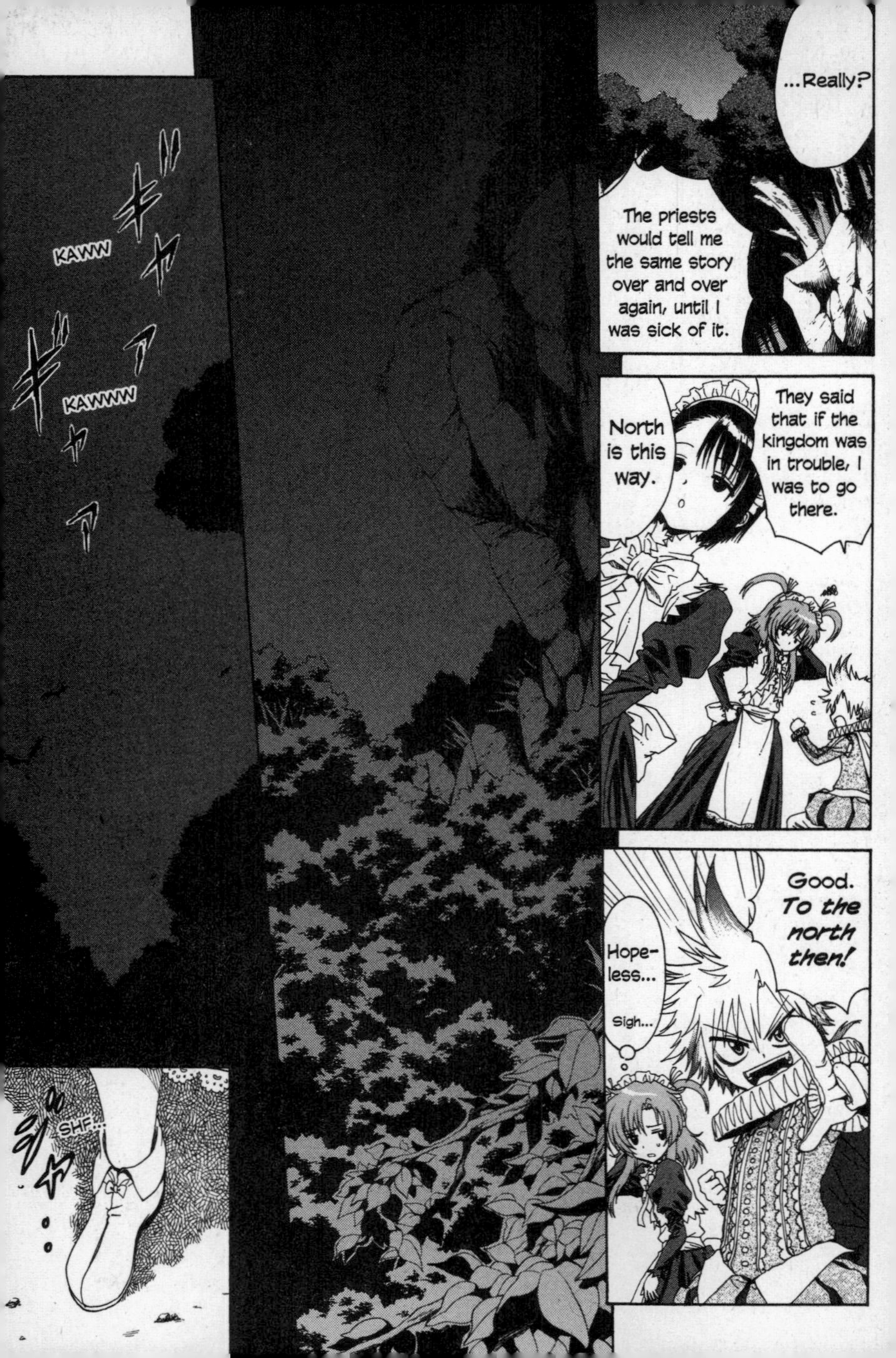
...Really?
The priests would tell me the same story over and over again, until I was sick of it.
They said that if the kingdom was in trouble, I was to go there.
North is this way.
Good. To the north then!
Hope-less...
Sigh...
KAWW
KAWWW
SHF...

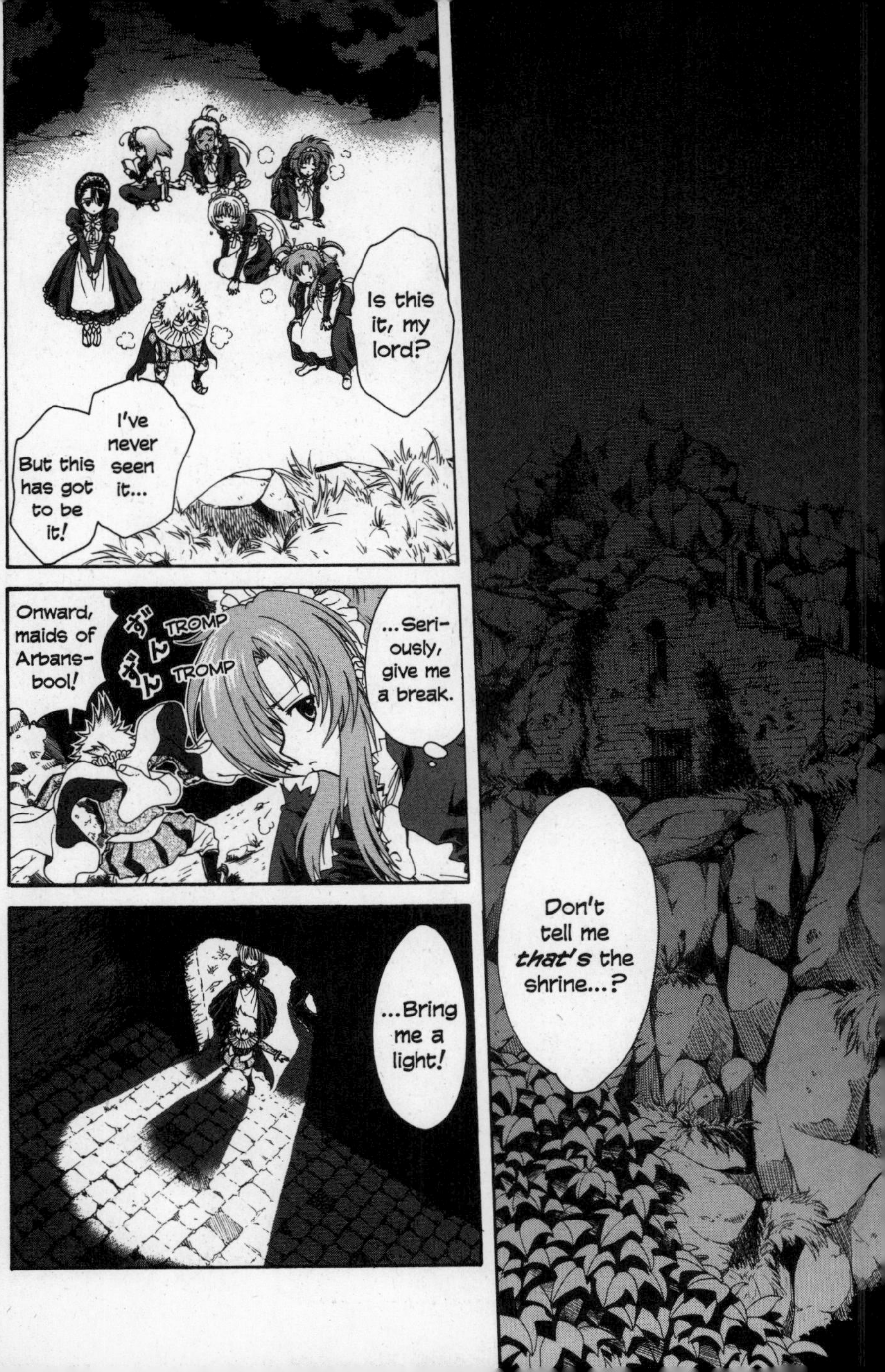
Don't tell me *that's* the shrine...?
Is this it, my lord?
I've never seen it...
But this has got to be it!
...Seriously, give me a break.
TROMP
TROMP
Onward, maids of Arbans-bool!
...Bring me a light!

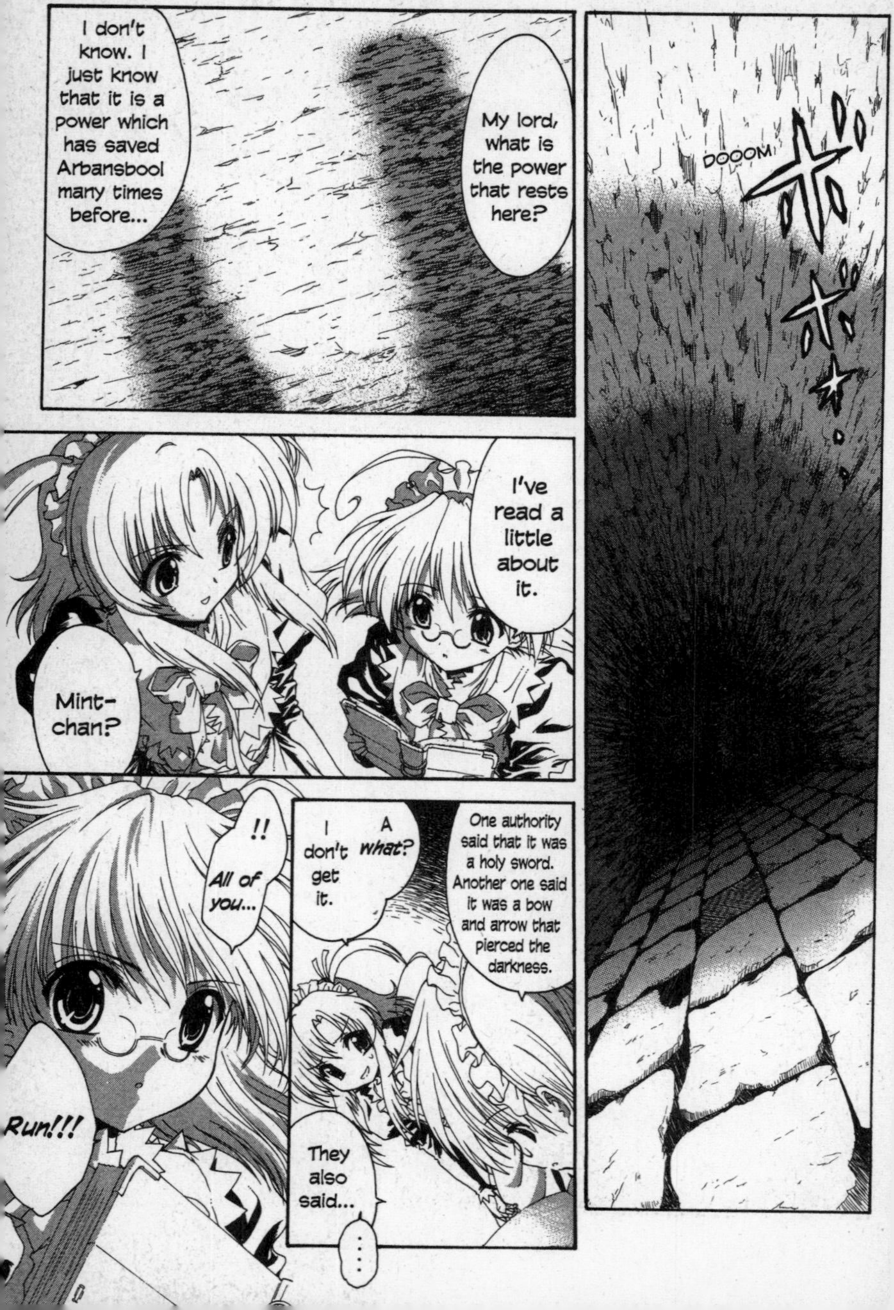
DOOOM
My lord, what is the power that rests here?
I don't know. I just know that it is a power which has saved Arbansbool many times before...
I've read a little about it.
Mint-chan?
One authority said that it was a holy sword. Another one said it was a bow and arrow that pierced the darkness.
A what?
I don't get it.
They also said...
....
!!
All of you...
Run!!!

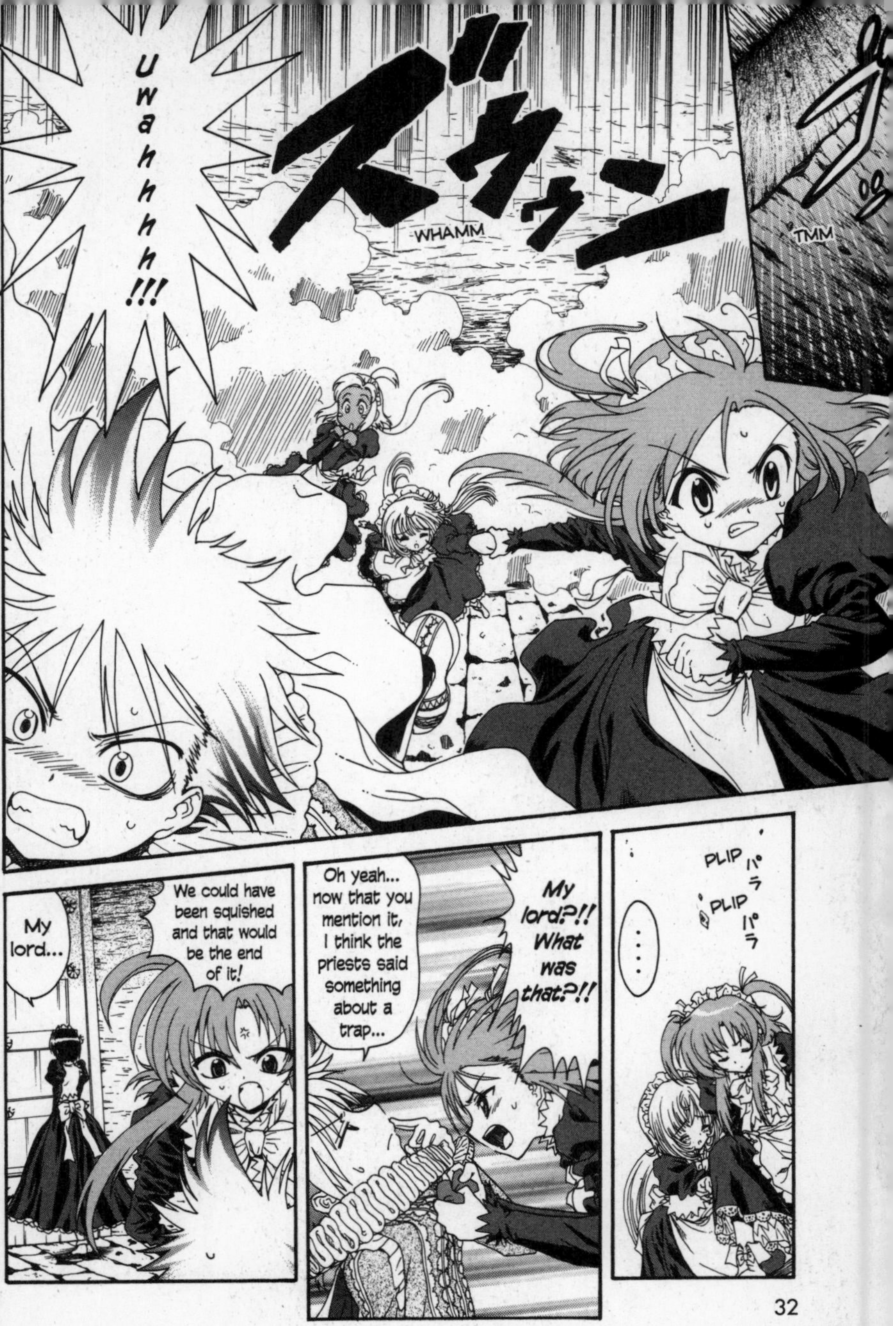
TMM
WHAMM
Uwahhhhh!!!
PLIP パラ
PLIP パラ
....
My lord?!! What was that?!!
Oh yeah... now that you mention it, I think the priests said something about a trap...
We could have been squished and that would be the end of it!
My lord...

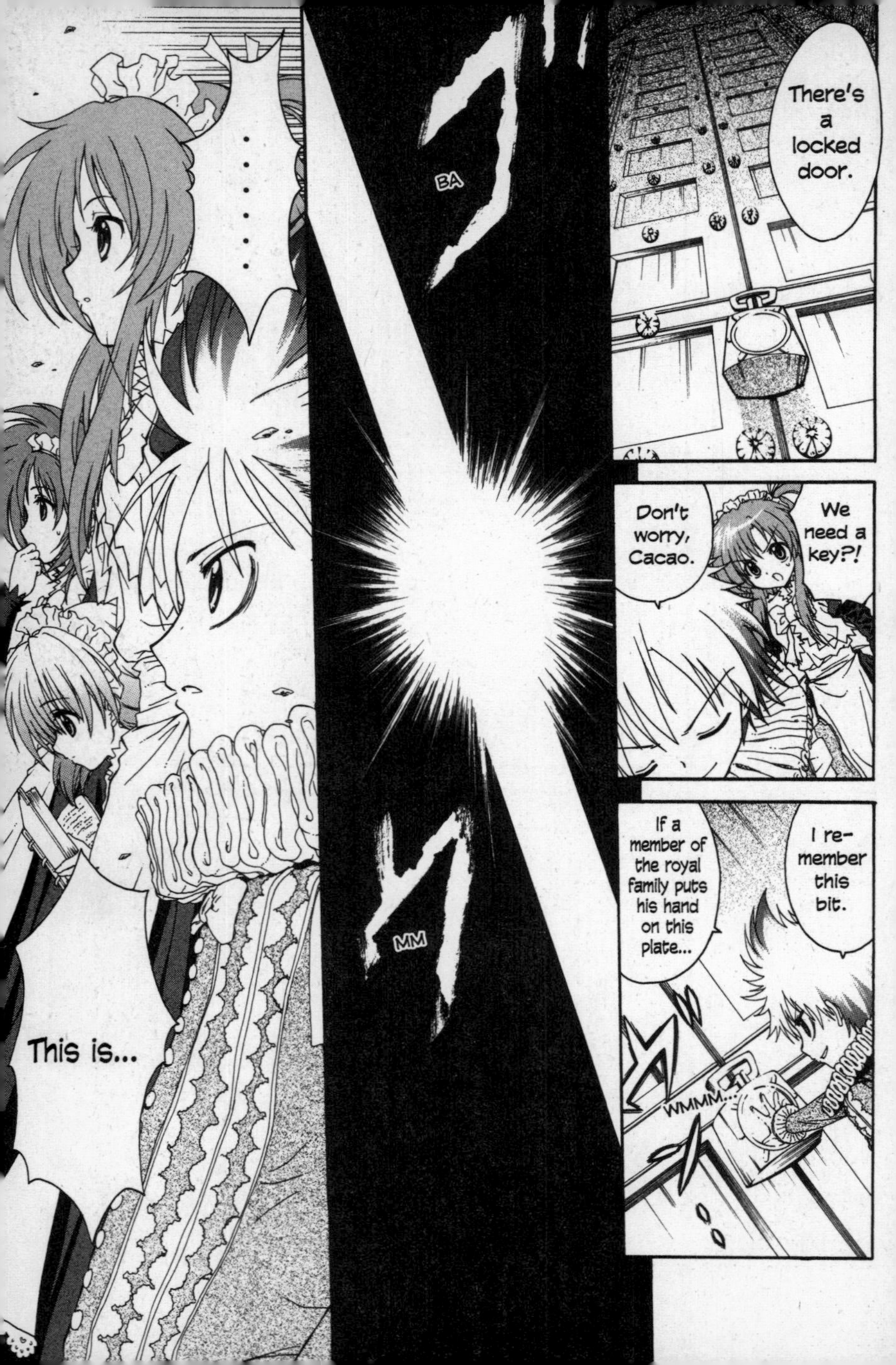
There's a locked door.
We need a key?!
Don't worry, Cacao.
I re-member this bit.
If a member of the royal family puts his hand on this plate...
WMMM...
BA
MM
This is...

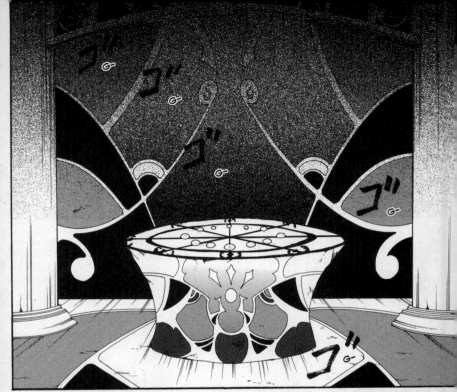

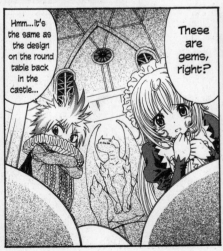

These are gems, right?

Hmm...it's the same as the design on the round table back in the castle...

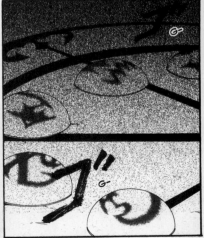

34

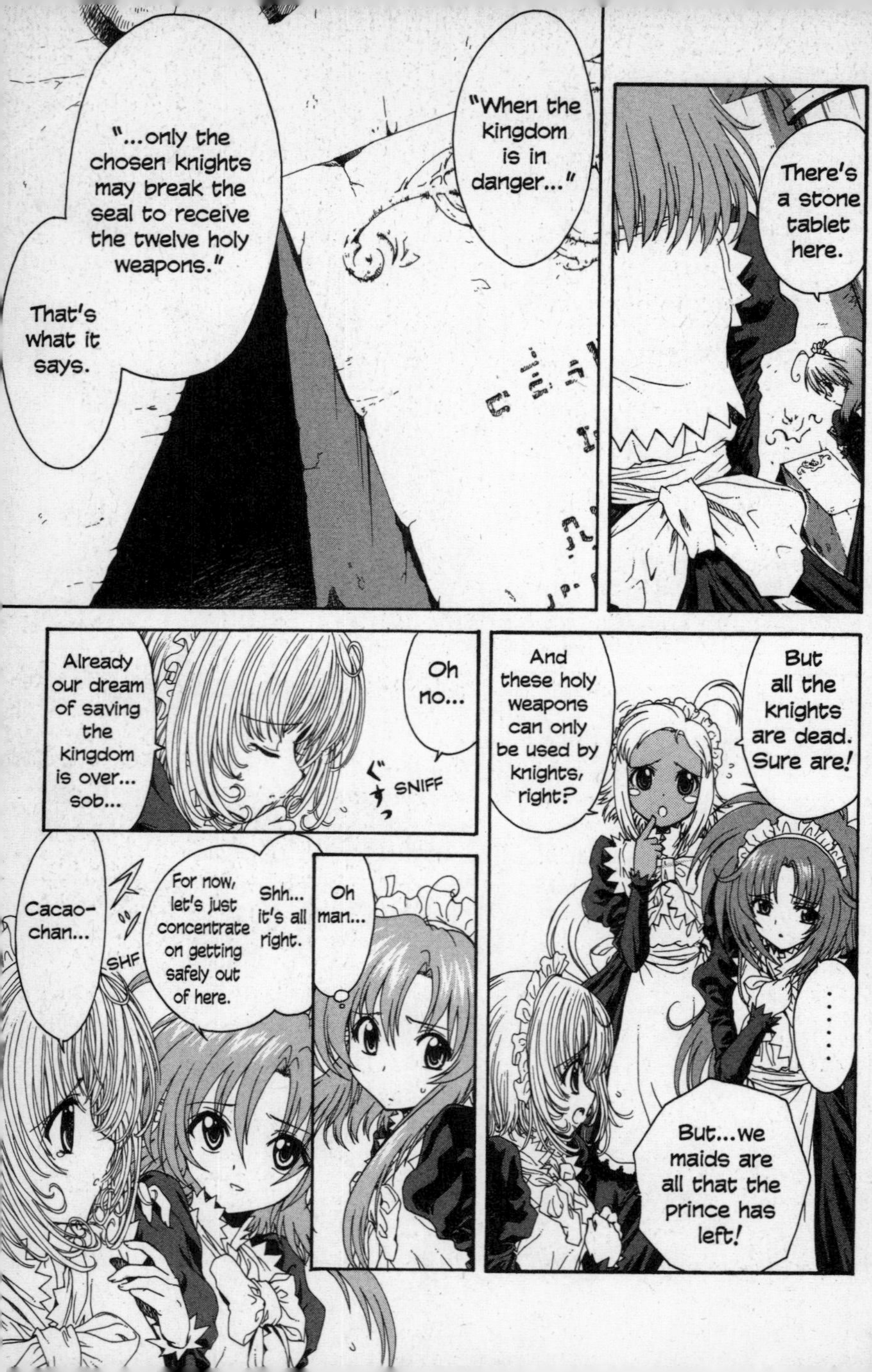
There's a stone tablet here.
"When the kingdom is in danger..."
"...only the chosen knights may break the seal to receive the twelve holy weapons."
That's what it says.
But all the knights are dead. Sure are!
And these holy weapons can only be used by knights, right?
......
But...we maids are all that the prince has left!
Oh no...
ぐすっ SNIFF
Already our dream of saving the kingdom is over... sob...
Oh man...
Shh... it's all right.
For now, let's just concentrate on getting safely out of here.
Cacao-chan...
SHF

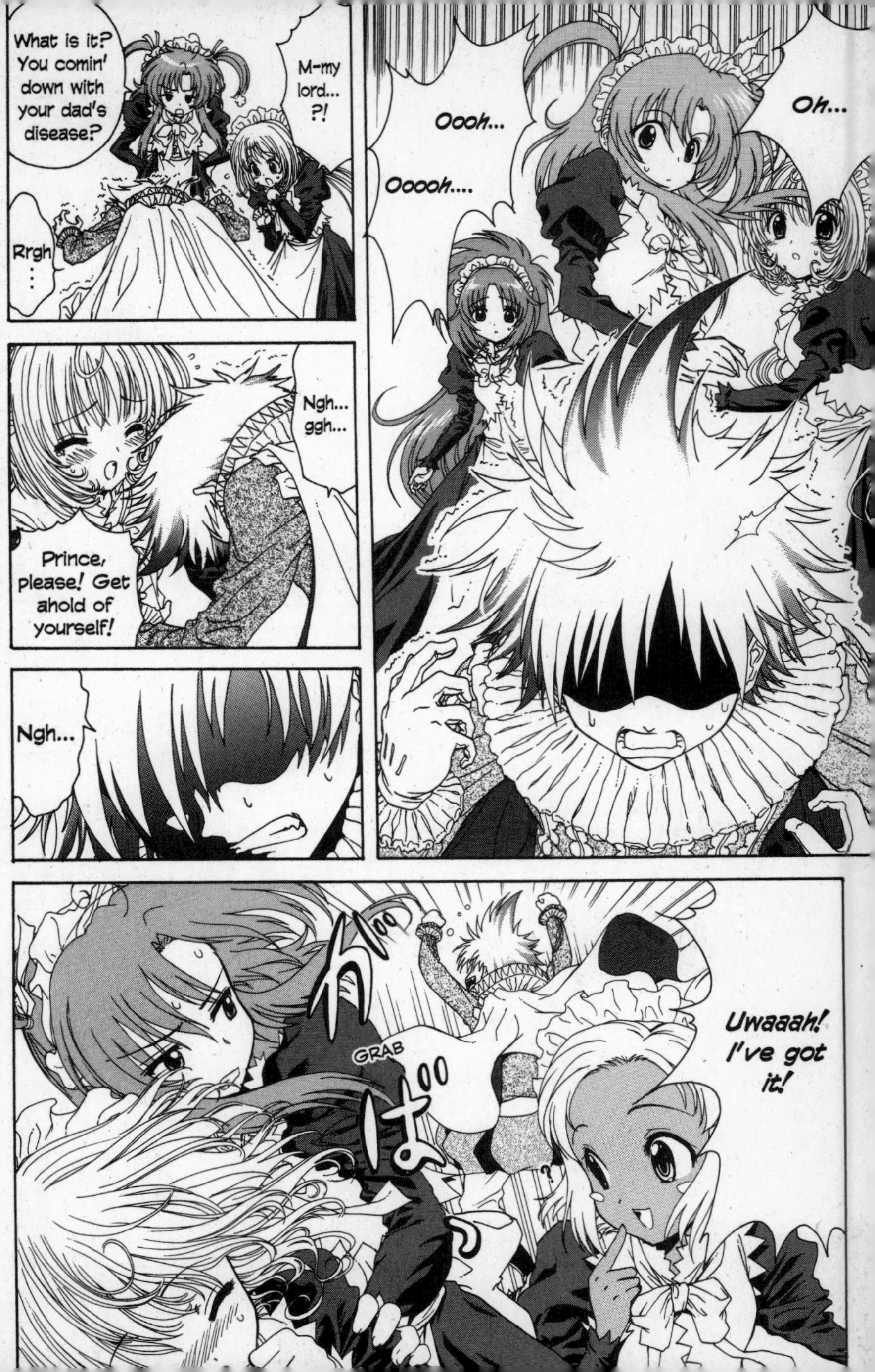
Oh...
Oooh...
Ooooh....
M-my lord...?!
What is it? You comin' down with your dad's disease?
Rrgh...
Ngh... ggh...
Prince, please! Get ahold of yourself!
Ngh...
Uwaaah! I've got it!
GRAB

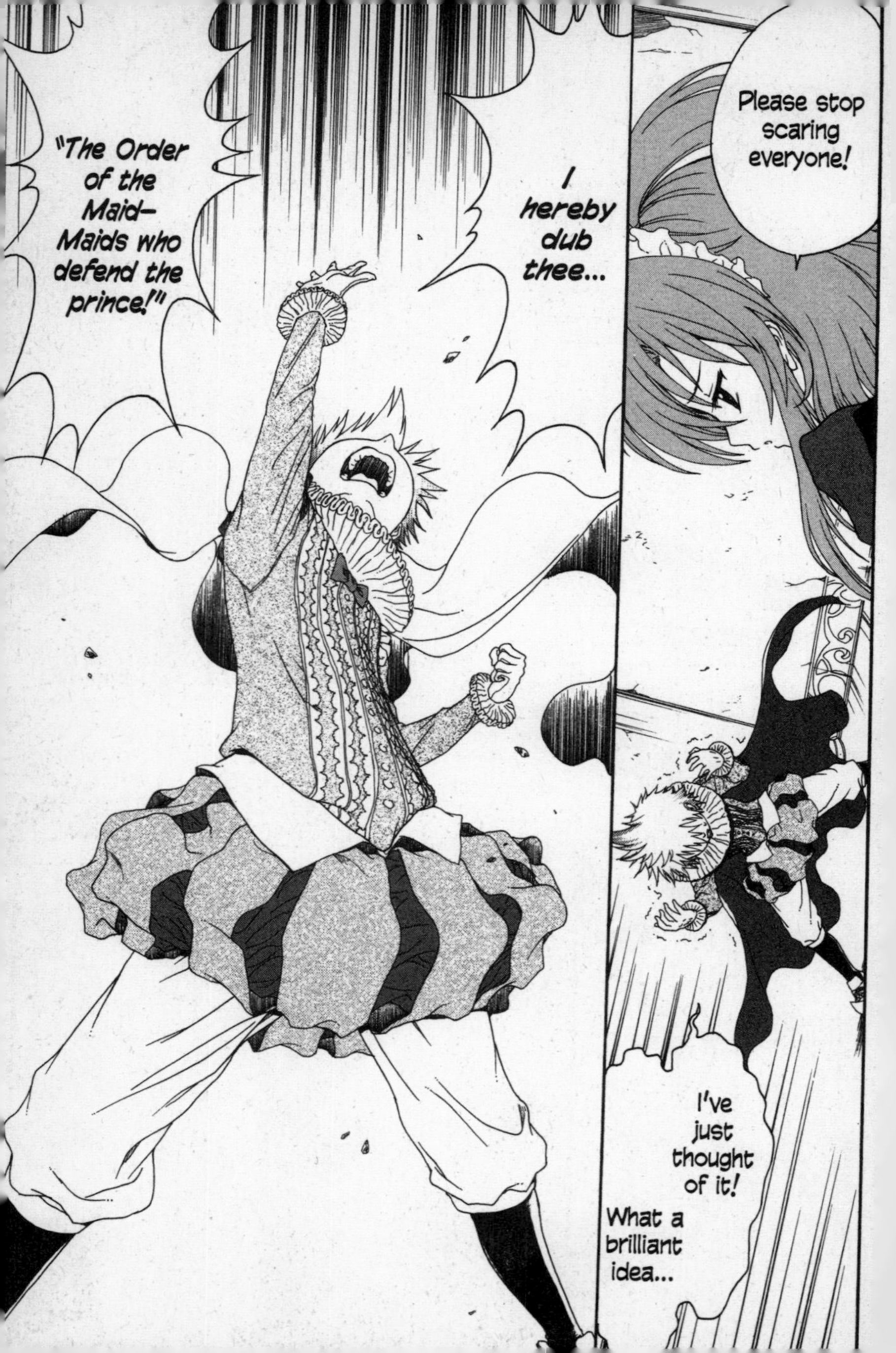
Please stop scaring everyone!
I've just thought of it!
What a brilliant idea...
I hereby dub thee...
"The Order of the Maid-Maids who defend the prince!"

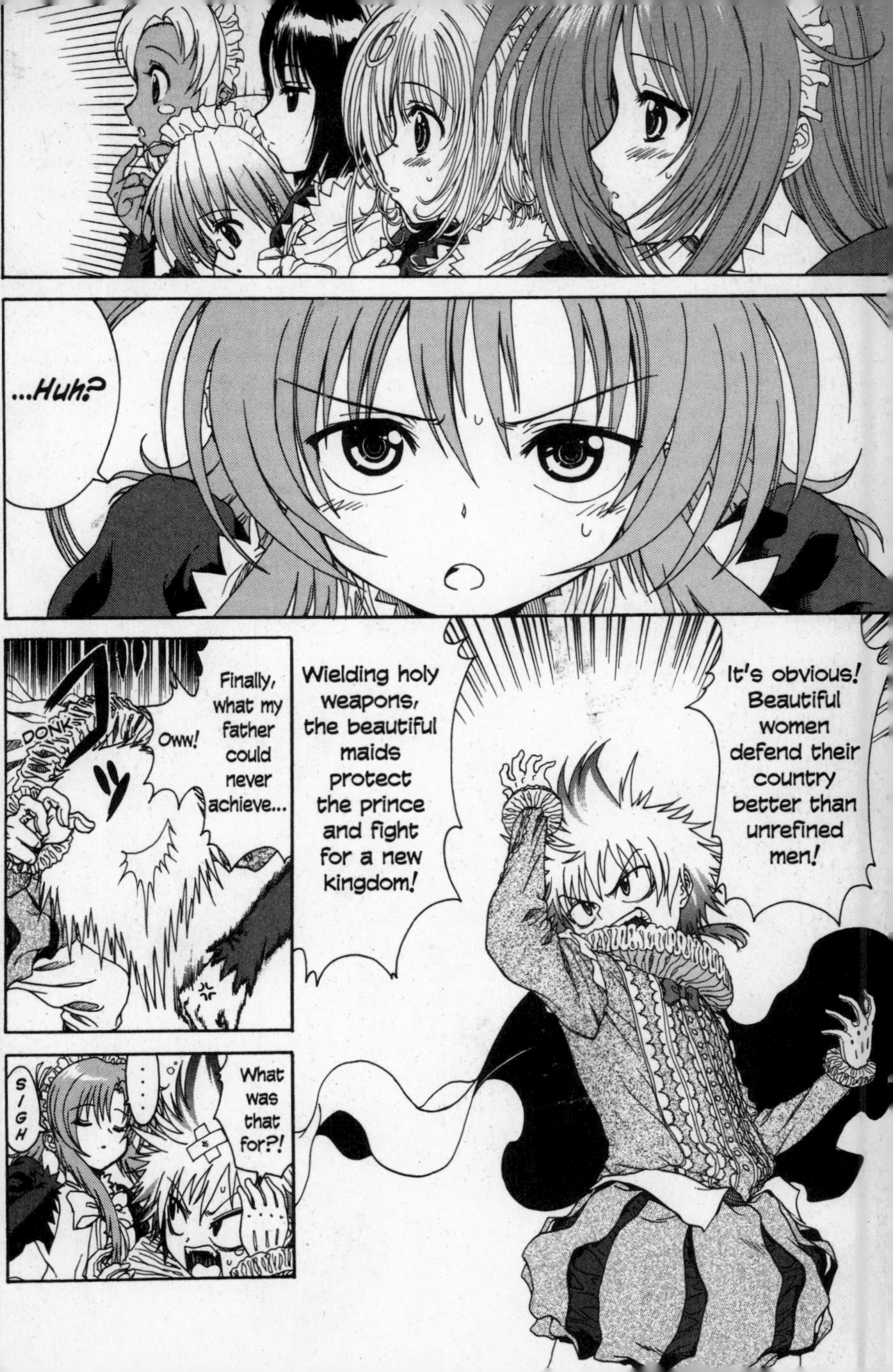
...Huh?
It's obvious! Beautiful women defend their country better than unrefined men!
Wielding holy weapons, the beautiful maids protect the prince and fight for a new kingdom!
Finally, what my father could never achieve...
Oww!
DONK
What was that for?!
...
SIGH

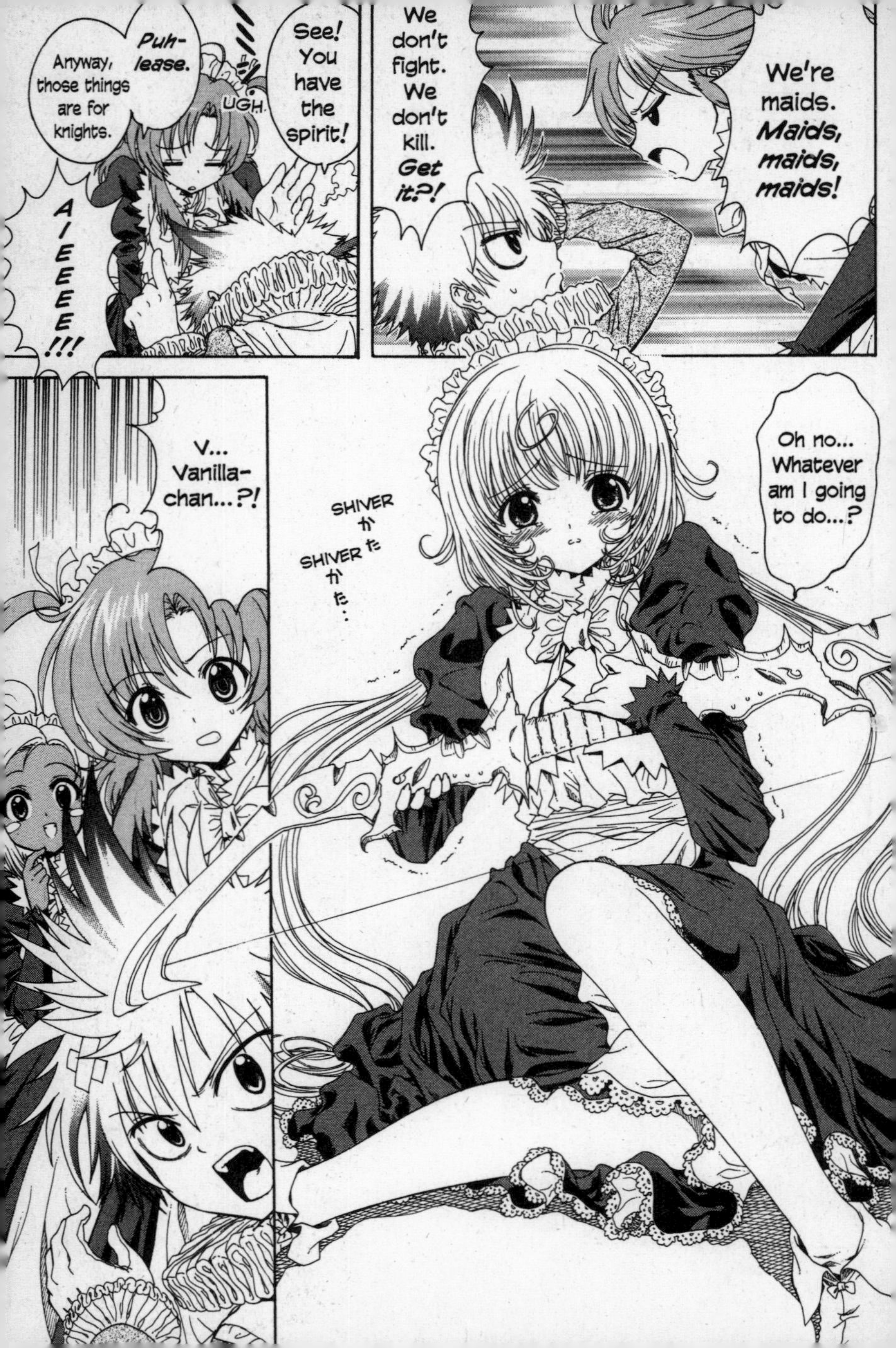
We're maids. Maids, maids, maids!
We don't fight. We don't kill. Get it?!
See! You have the spirit!
UGH.
Puh-lease.
Anyway, those things are for knights.
AIEEEEE!!!
Oh no... Whatever am I going to do...?
SHIVER かた
SHIVER かた...
V... Vanilla-chan...?!

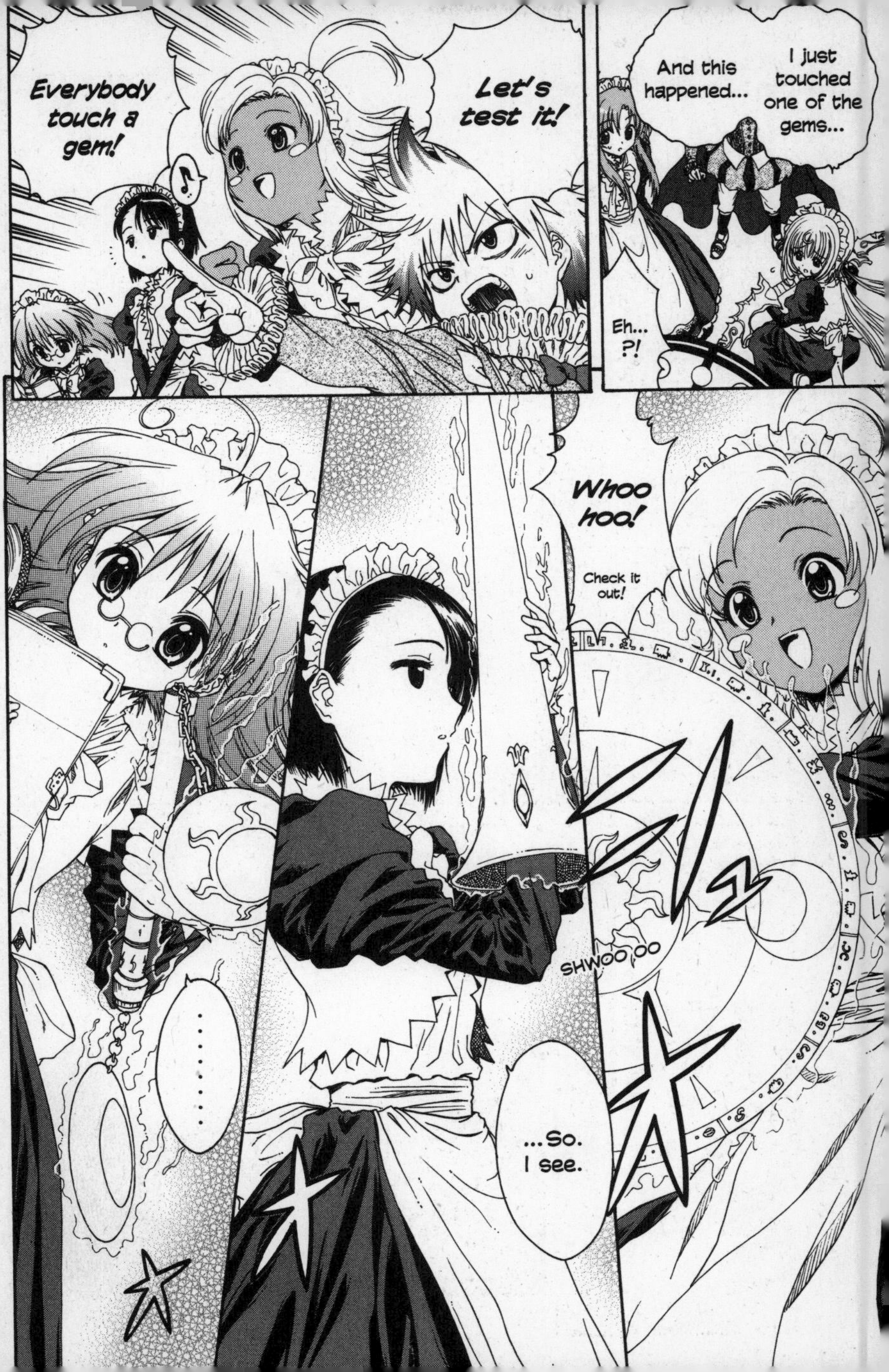
I just touched one of the gems...
And this happened...
Eh... ?!
Let's test it!
Everybody touch a gem!
Whoo hoo!
Check it out!
SHWOO OO
...So. I see.
......

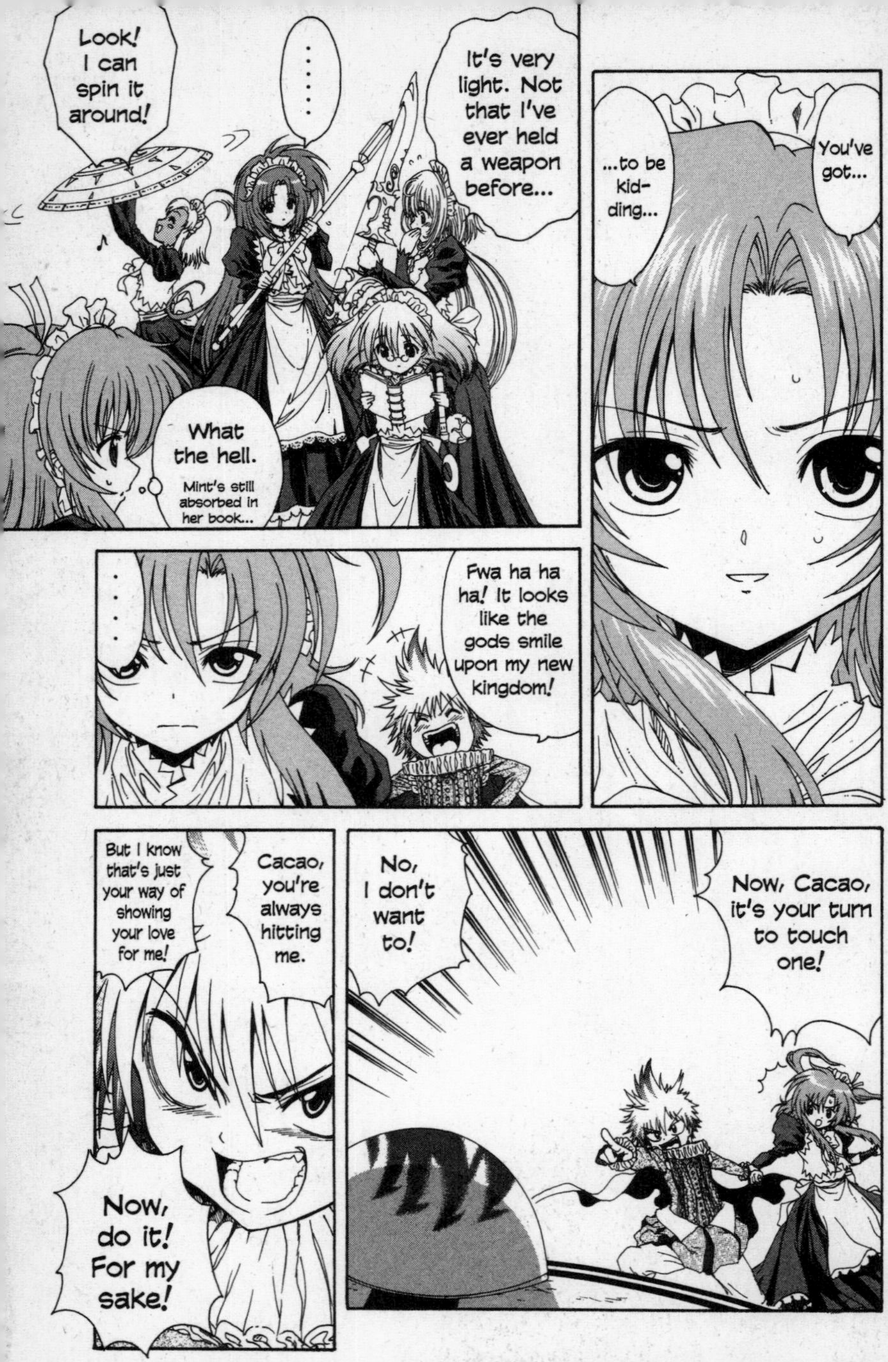
You've got...
...to be kid-ding...
It's very light. Not that I've ever held a weapon before...
......
Look! I can spin it around!
What the hell.
Mint's still absorbed in her book...
Fwa ha ha ha! It looks like the gods smile upon my new kingdom!
.....
Now, Cacao, it's your turn to touch one!
No, I don't want to!
Cacao, you're always hitting me.
But I know that's just your way of showing your love for me!
Now, do it! For my sake!

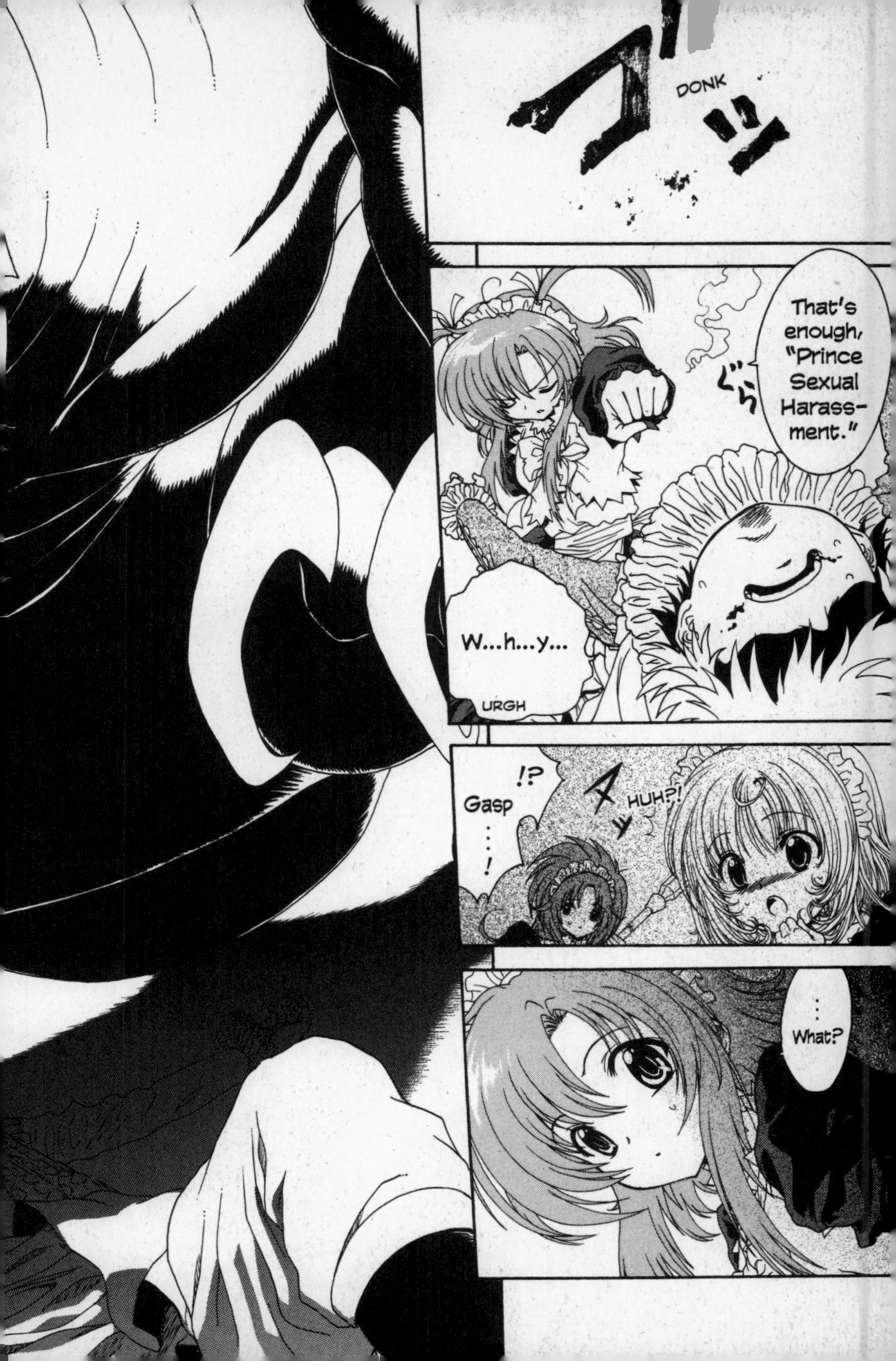

ゴッ
DONK
That's enough, "Prince Sexual Harass-ment."
ぐら
W...h...y...
URGH
HUH?!
!?
Gasp
...!
... What?

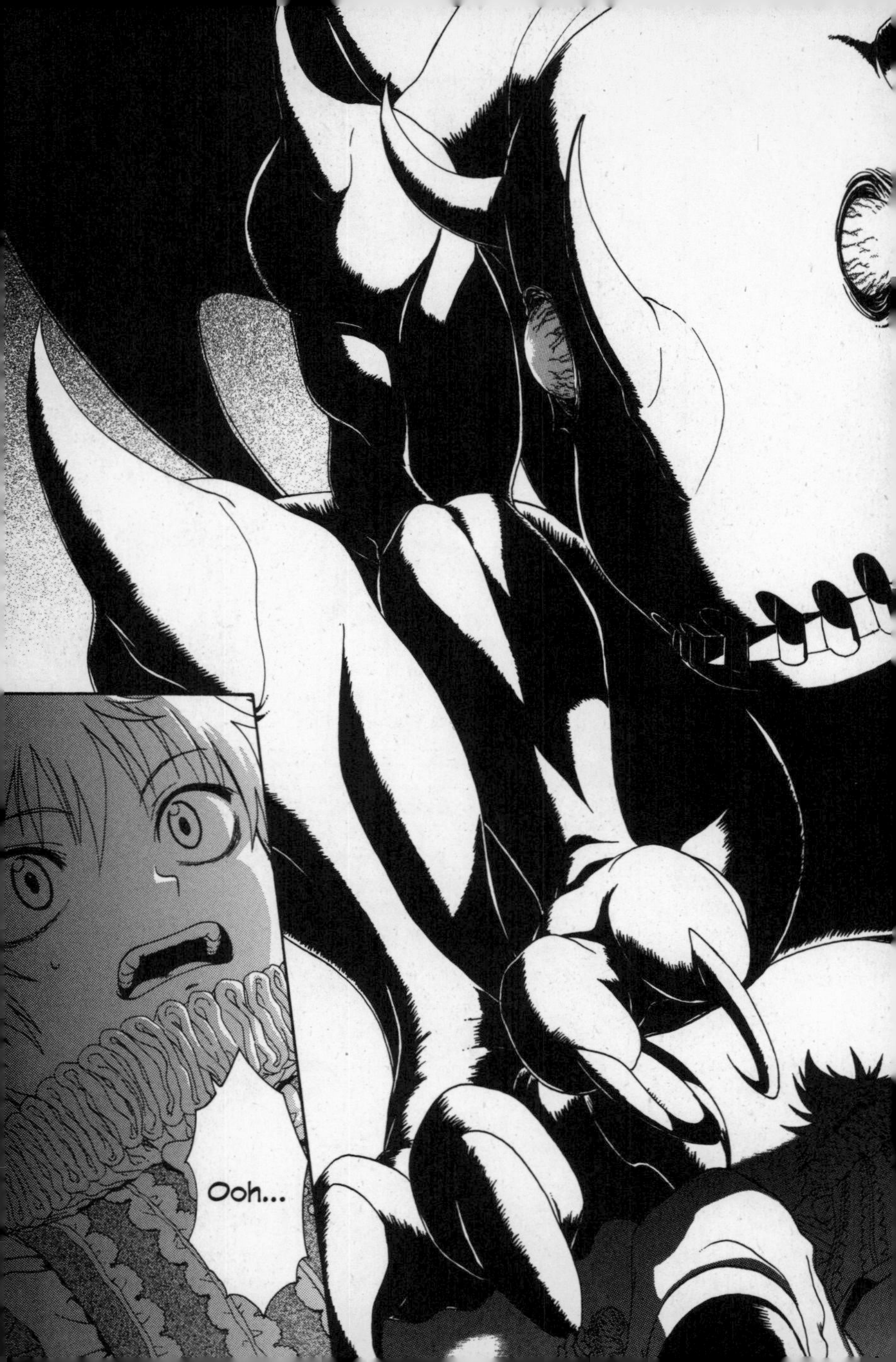
Ooh...

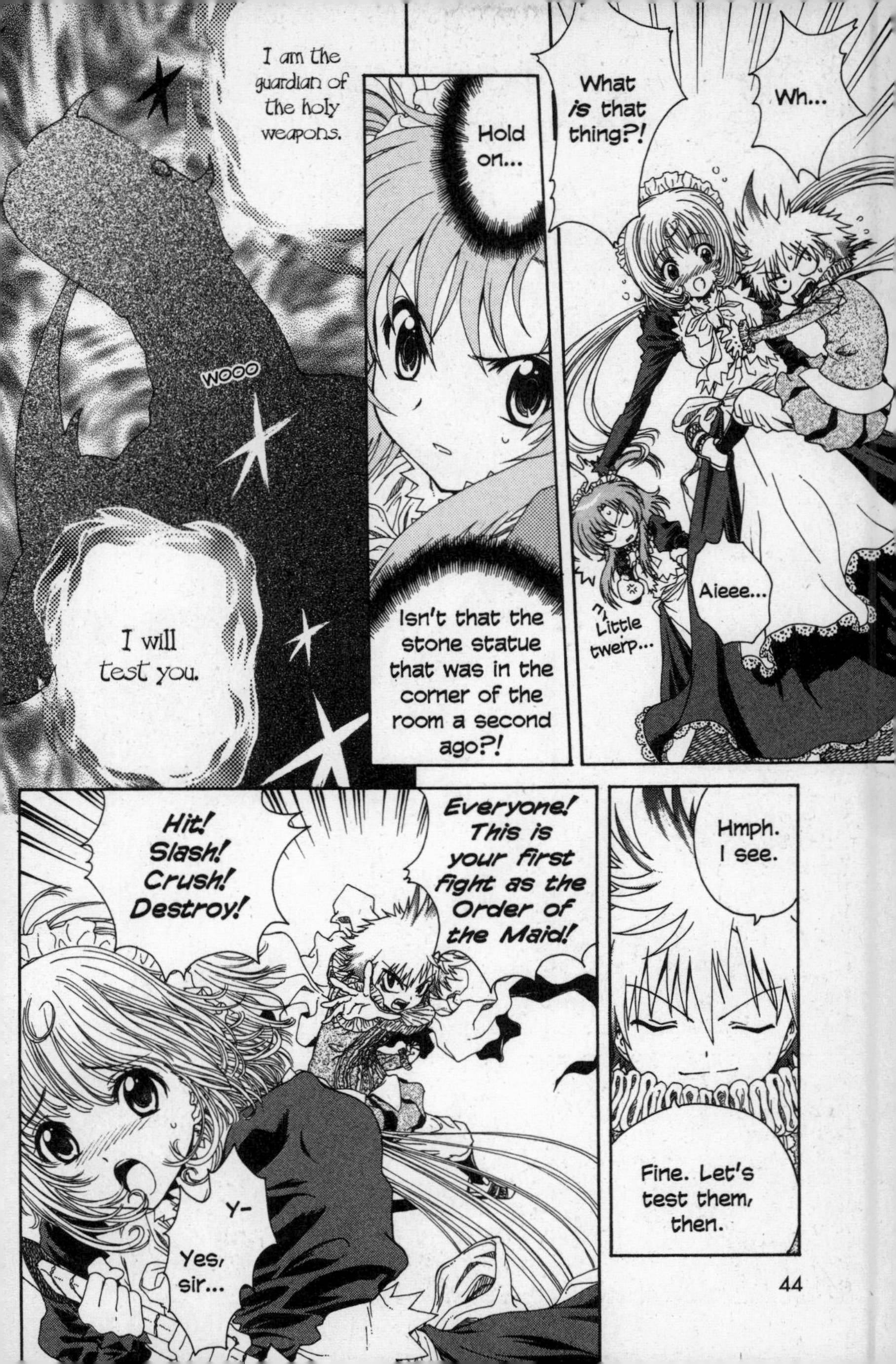
Wh...
What *is* that thing?!
Aieee...
Little twerp...
Hold on...
Isn't that the stone statue that was in the corner of the room a second ago?!
I am the guardian of the holy weapons.
WOOO
I will test you.
Hmph. I see.
Fine. Let's test them, then.
Everyone! This is your first fight as the Order of the Maid!
Hit! Slash! Crush! Destroy!
Y-
Yes, sir...

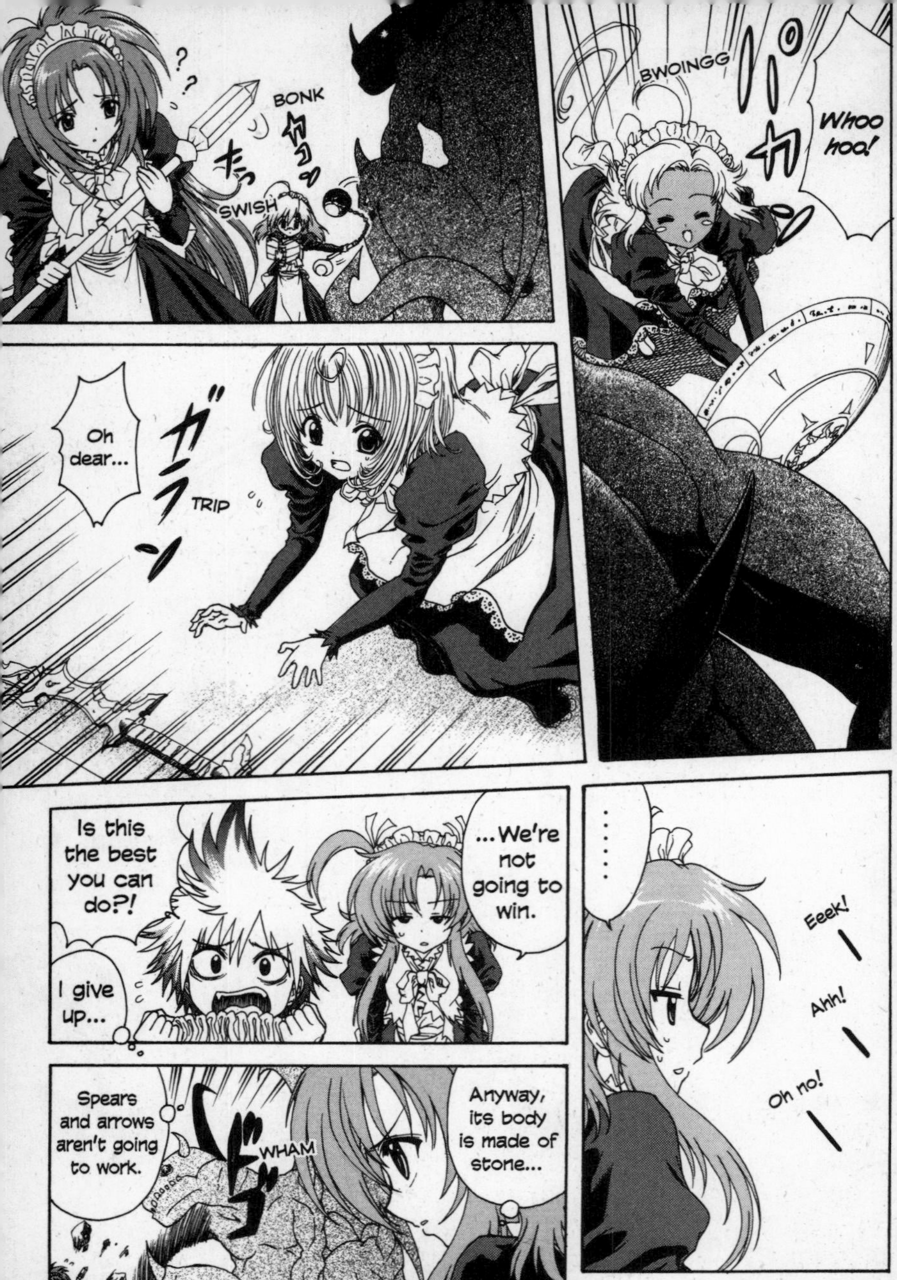

BWOINGG
Whoo hoo!
??
BONK
SWISH
Oh dear...
TRIP
....
Eeek!
Ahh!
Oh no!
...We're not going to win.
Is this the best you can do?!
I give up...
Anyway, its body is made of stone...
WHAM
Spears and arrows aren't going to work.

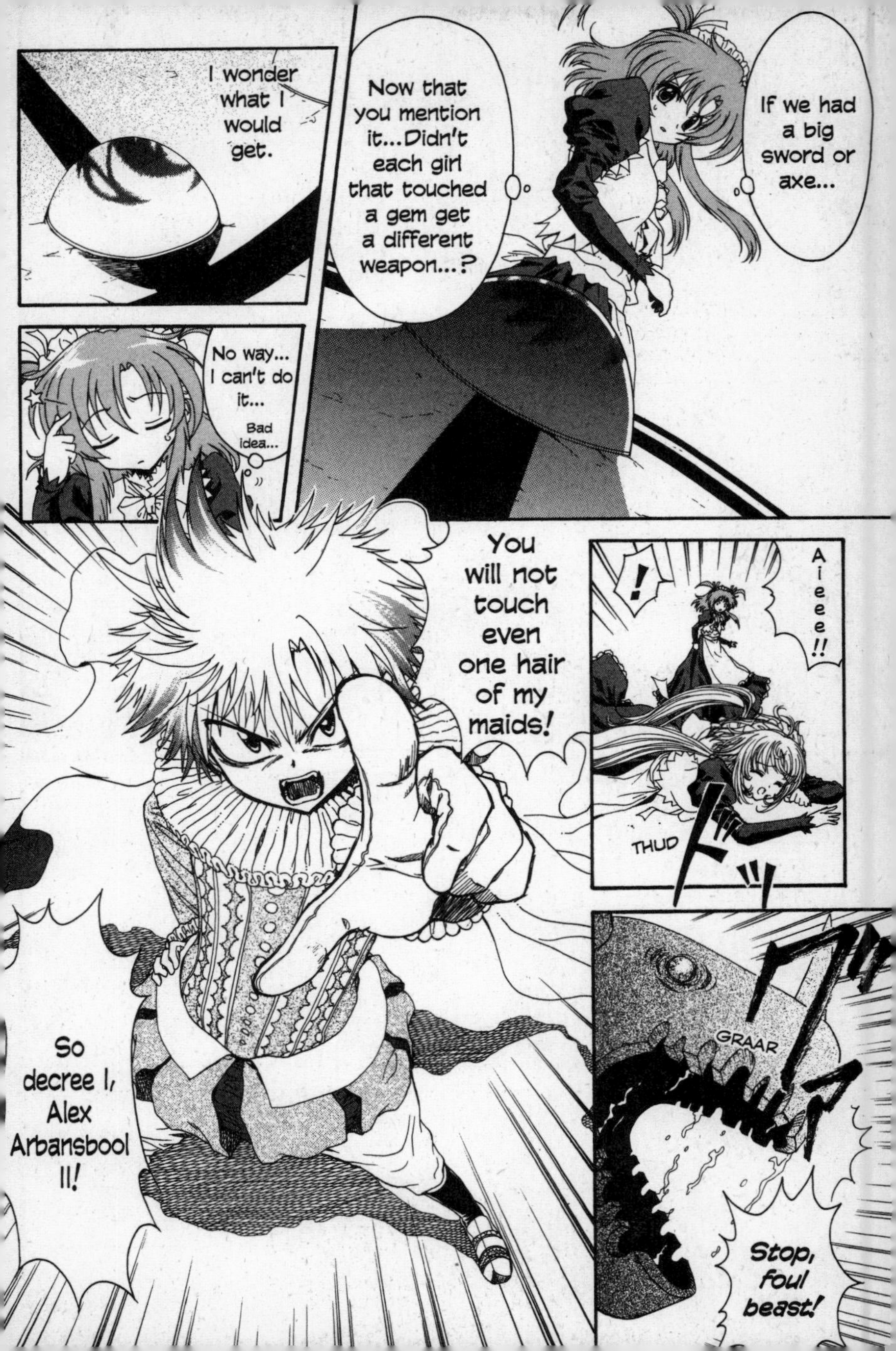
If we had a big sword or axe...
Now that you mention it...Didn't each girl that touched a gem get a different weapon...?
I wonder what I would get.
No way... I can't do it...
Bad idea...
!
Aieee!!
THUD
GRAAR
Stop, foul beast!
You will not touch even one hair of my maids!
So decree I, Alex Arbansbool II!

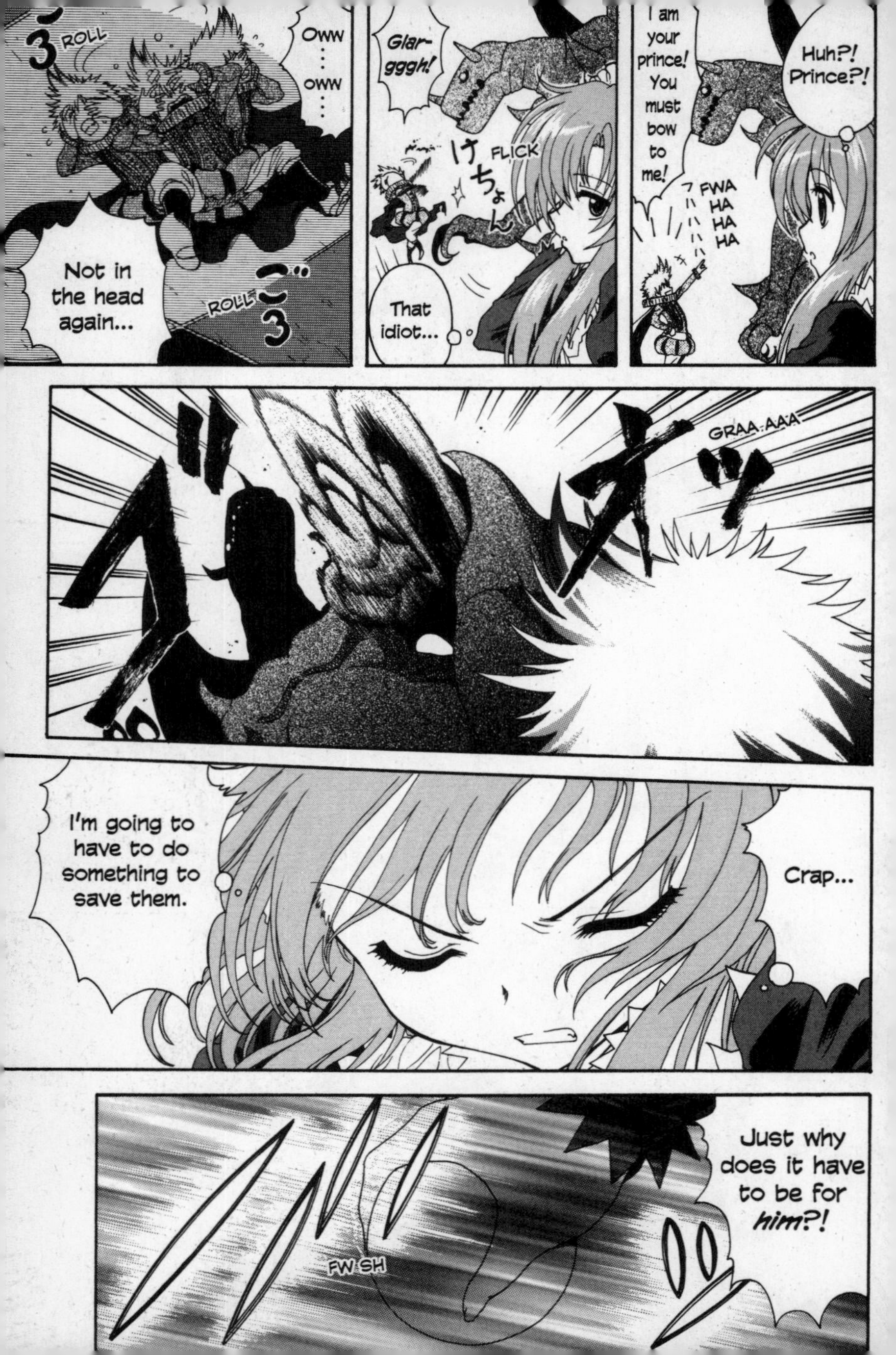
Huh?! Prince?!
I am your prince! You must bow to me!
FWA HA HA HA
Glar-gggh!
けちょん
FLICK
That idiot...
Oww... oww...
ROLL
Not in the head again...
ROLL
GRAA AAA
Crap...
I'm going to have to do something to save them.
Just why does it have to be for *him*?!
FW SH

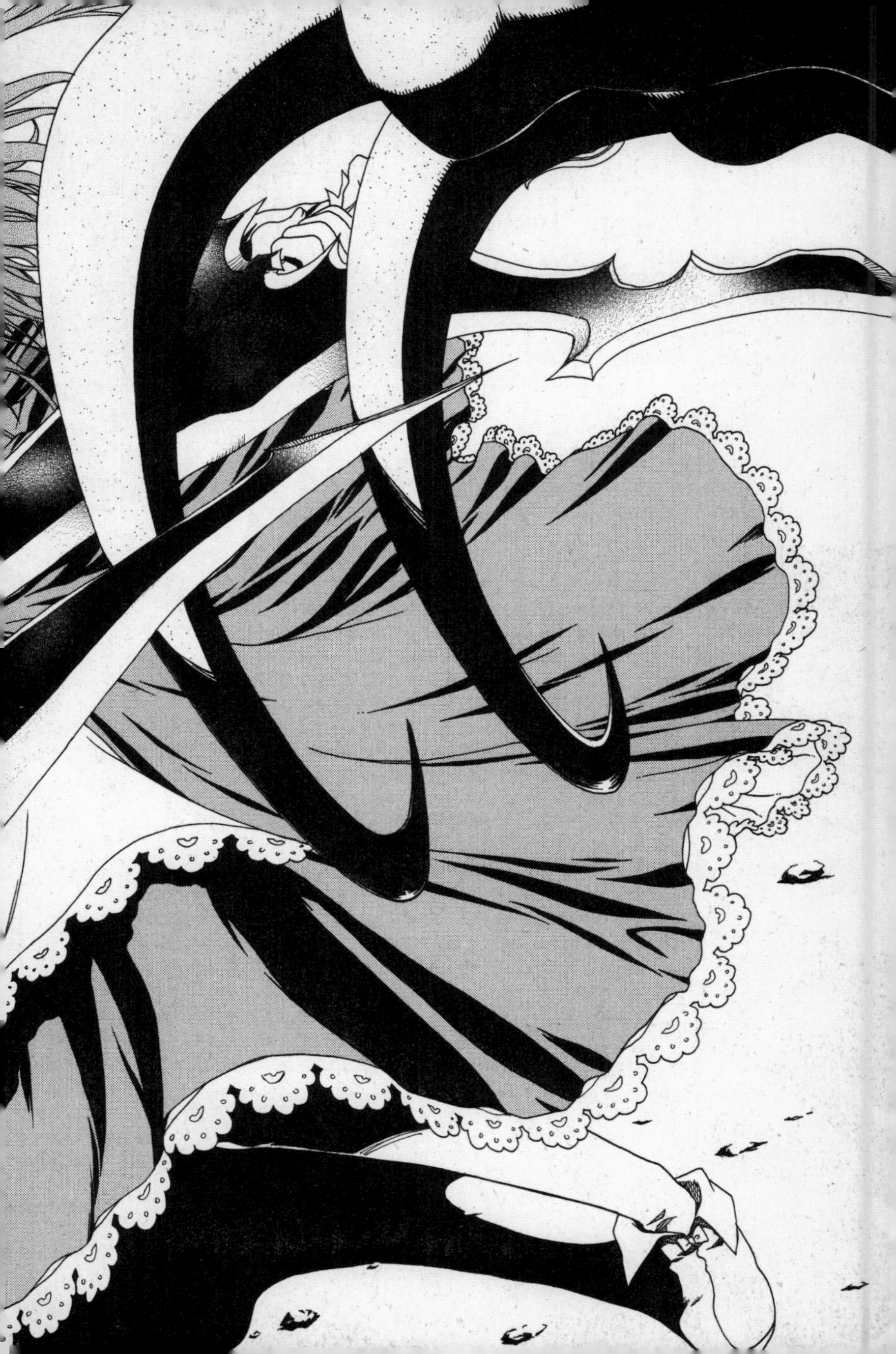

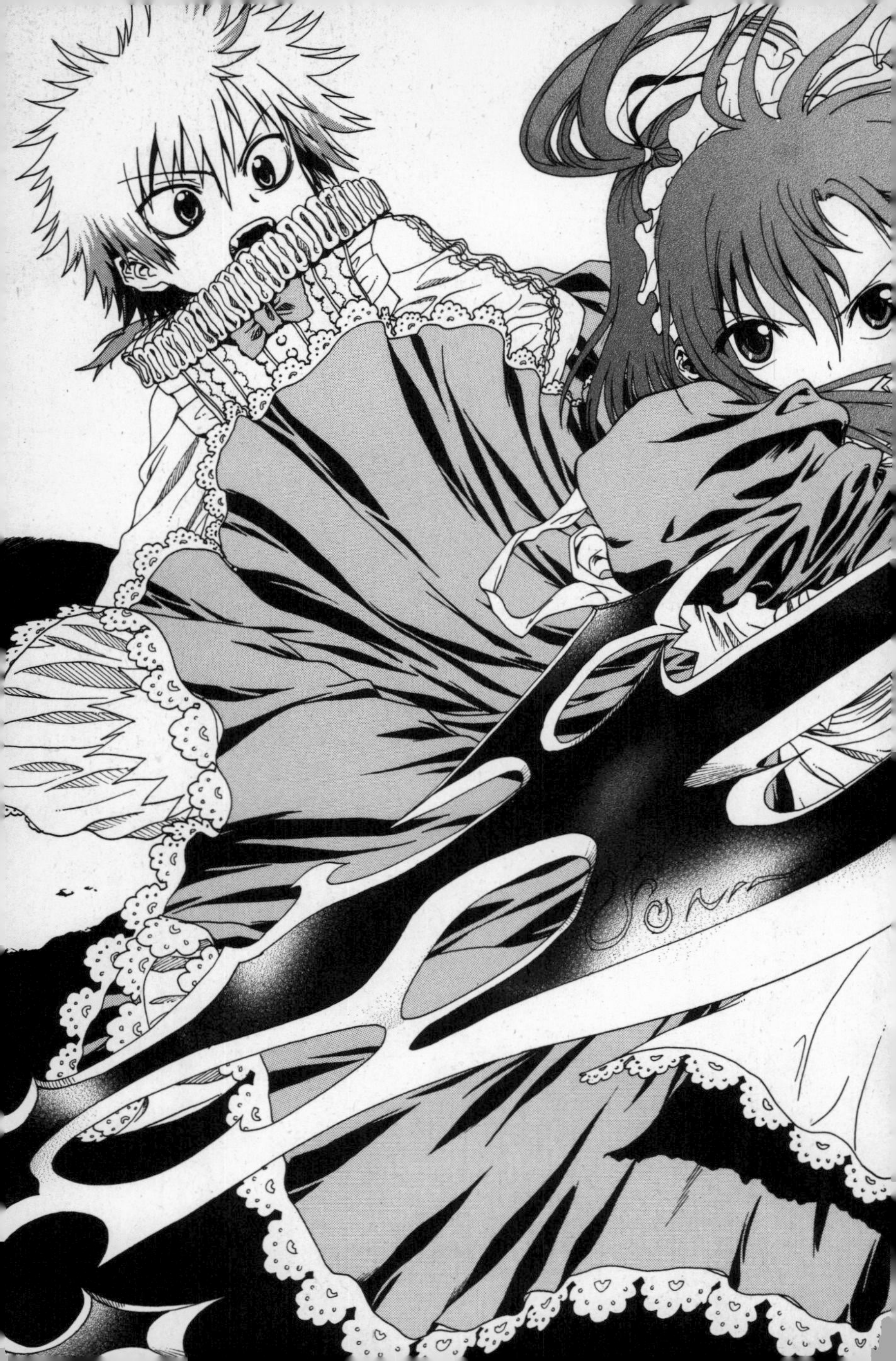

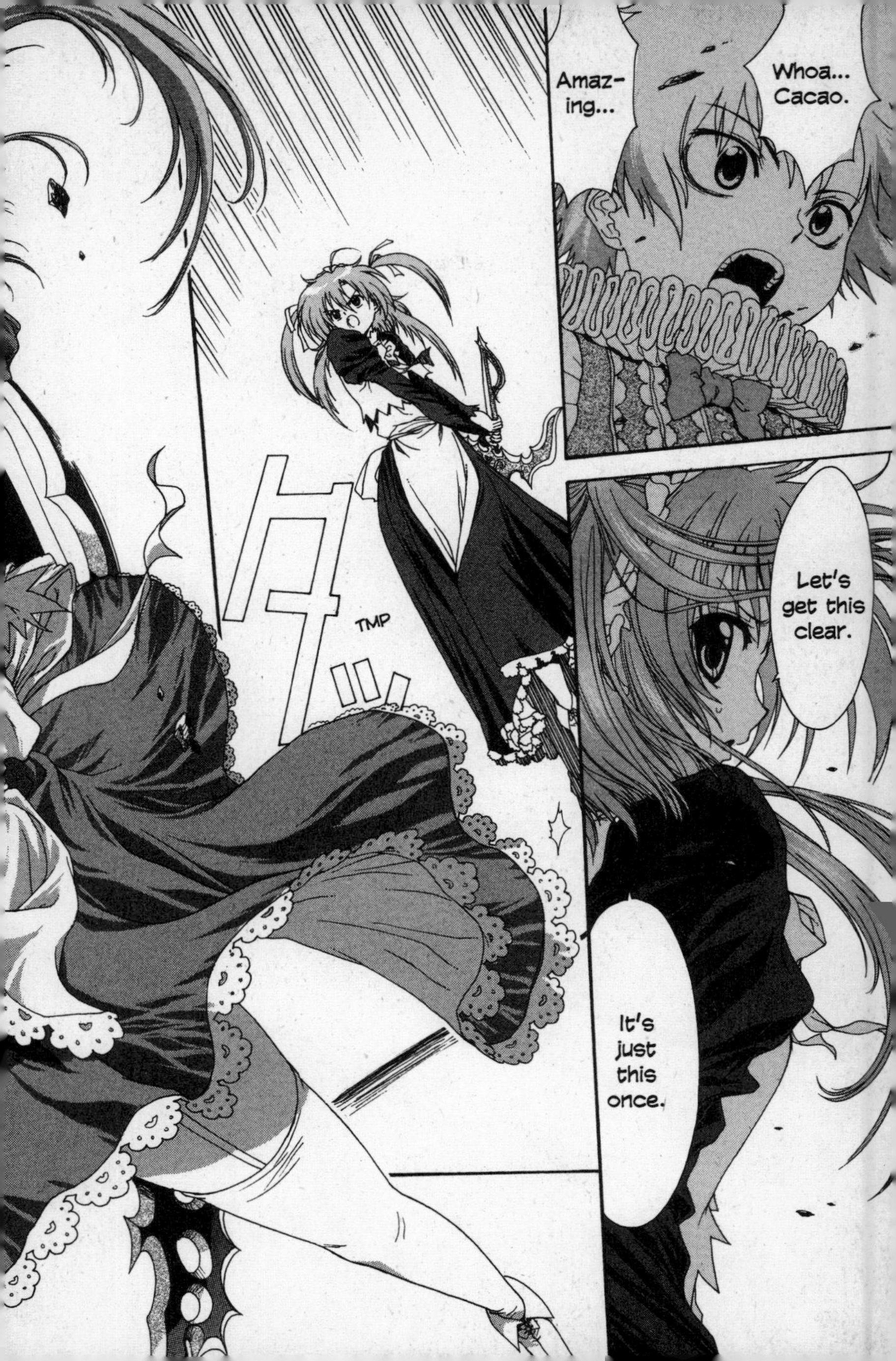
Whoa... Cacao.
Amaz-ing...
Let's get this clear.
It's just this once.
TMP

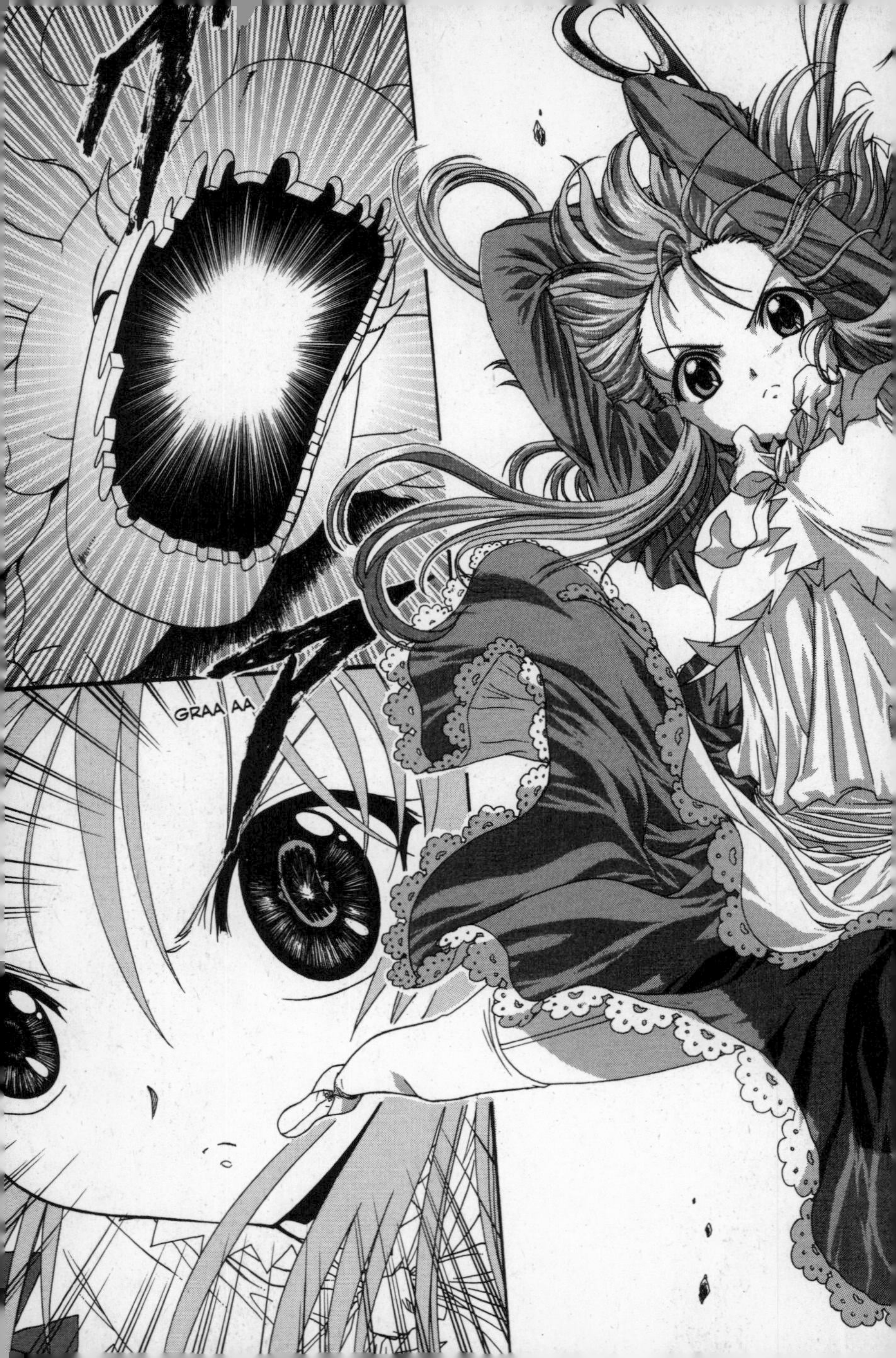
GRAA AA

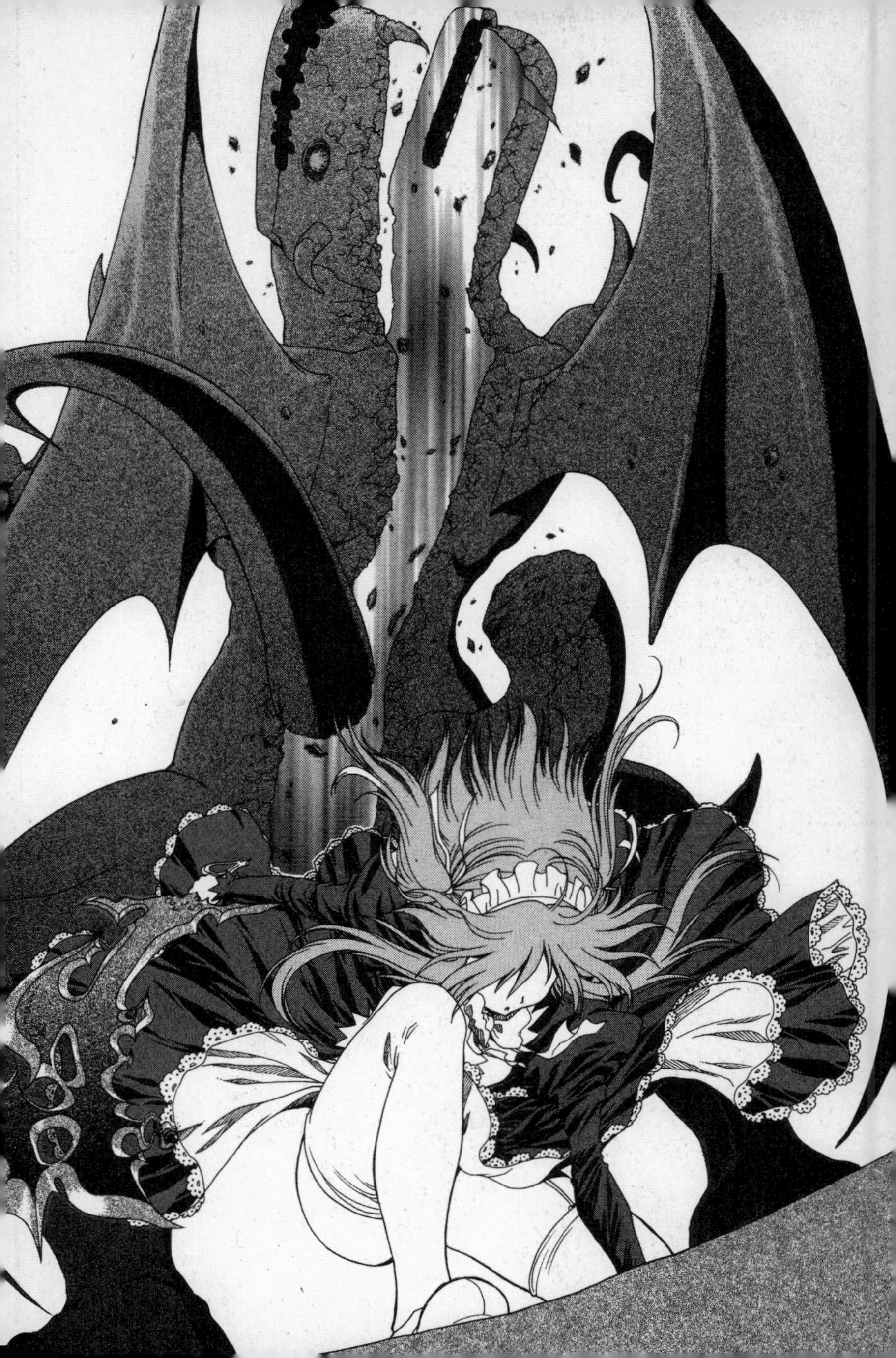

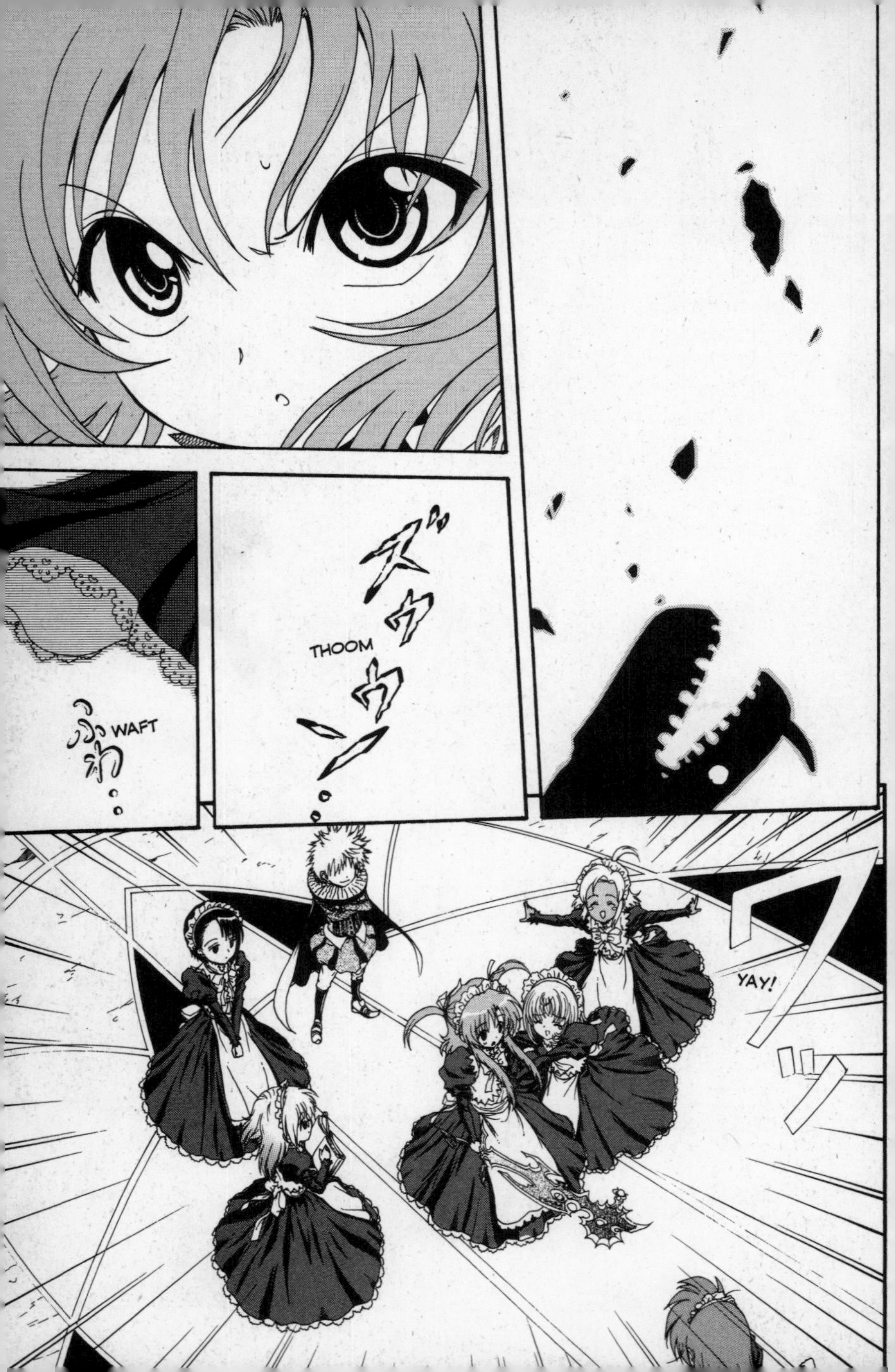
ズゥウン
THOOM
ふわ
WAFT
YAY!

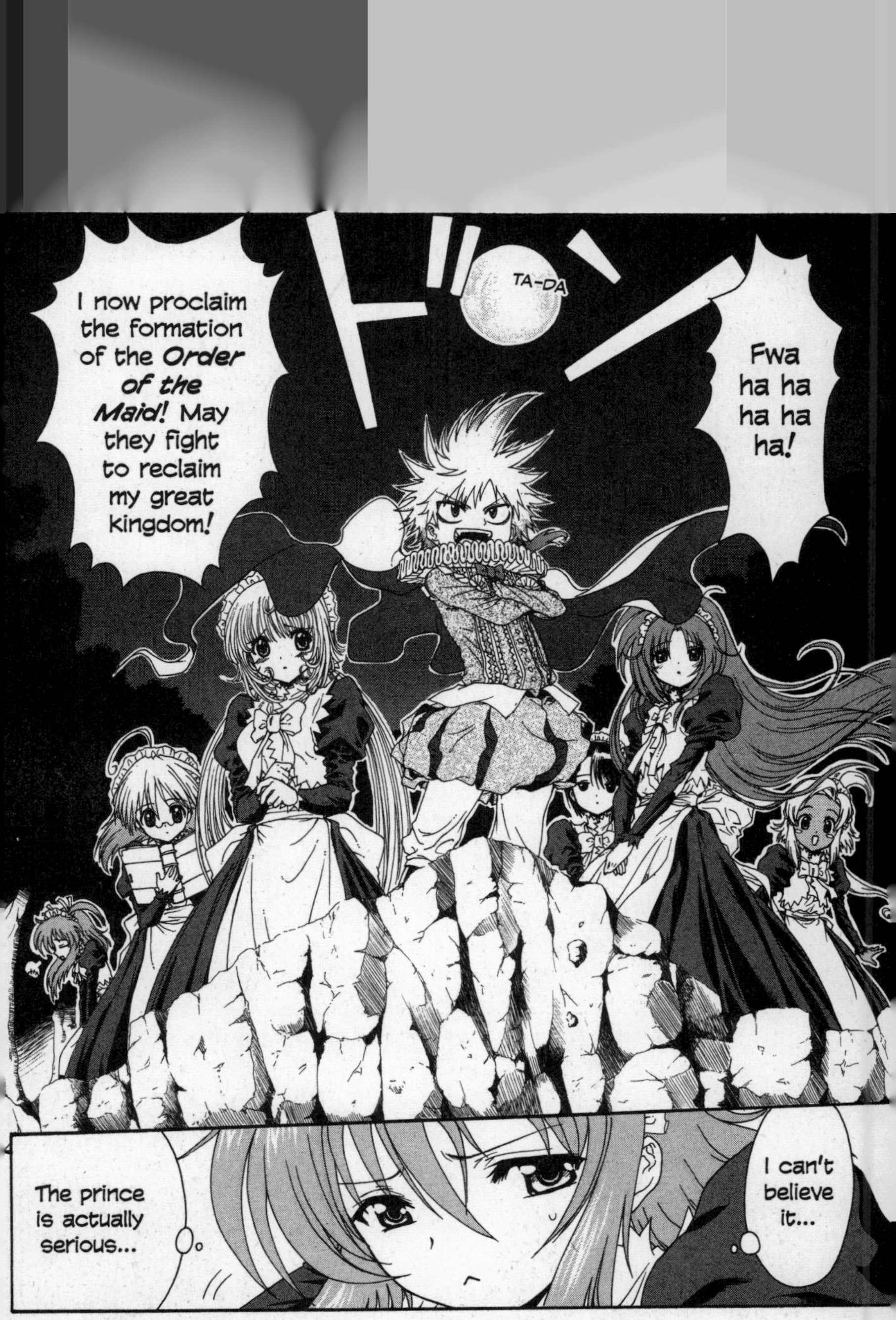
Fwa ha ha ha ha ha!
TA-DA
I now proclaim the formation of the *Order of the Maid!* May they fight to reclaim my great kingdom!
I can't believe it...
The prince is actually serious...

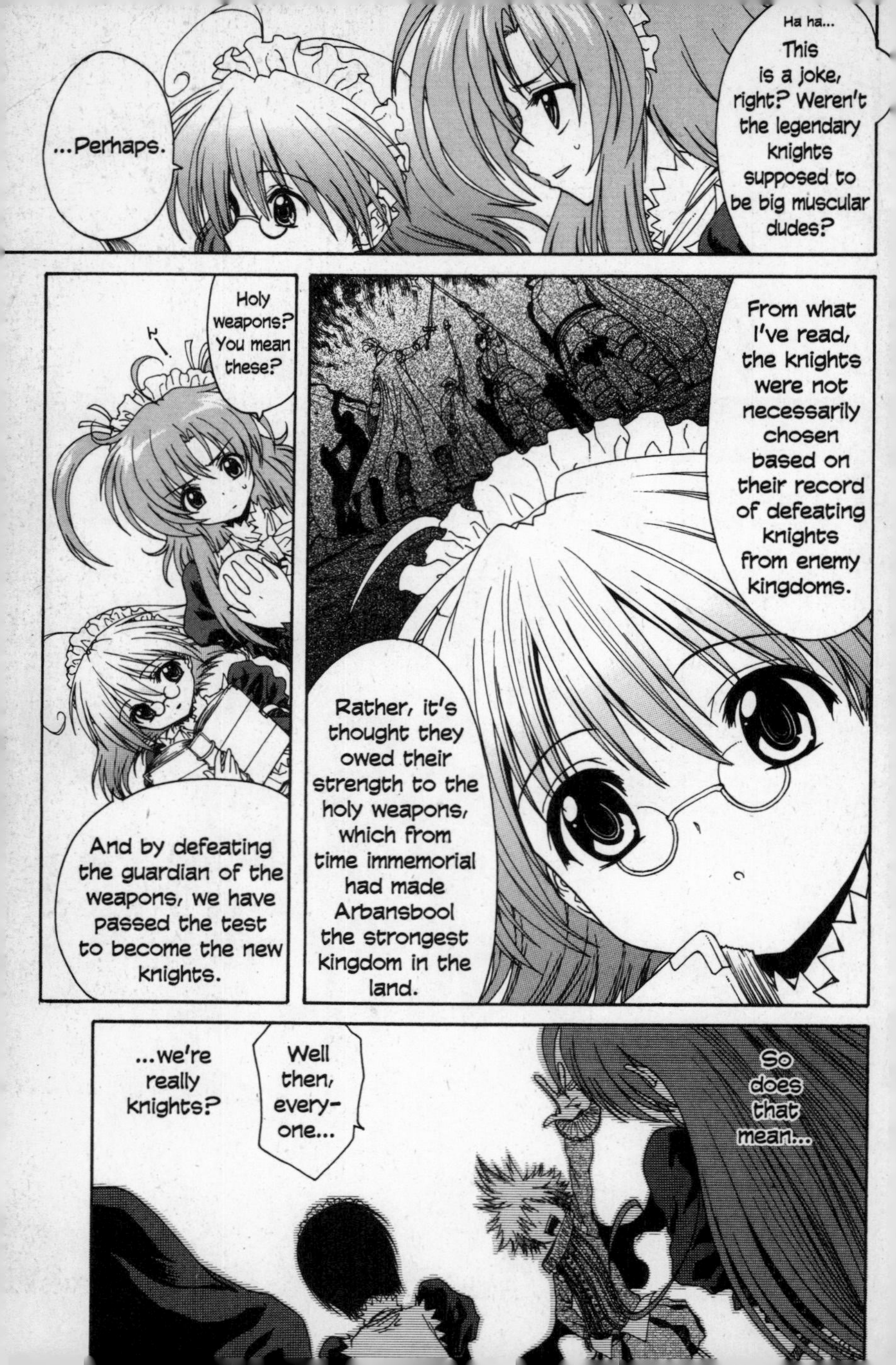
Ha ha... This is a joke, right? Weren't the legendary knights supposed to be big muscular dudes?
...Perhaps.
From what I've read, the knights were not necessarily chosen based on their record of defeating knights from enemy kingdoms.
Rather, it's thought they owed their strength to the holy weapons, which from time immemorial had made Arbansbool the strongest kingdom in the land.
Holy weapons? You mean these?
And by defeating the guardian of the weapons, we have passed the test to become the new knights.
So does that mean...
Well then, everyone...
...we're really knights?

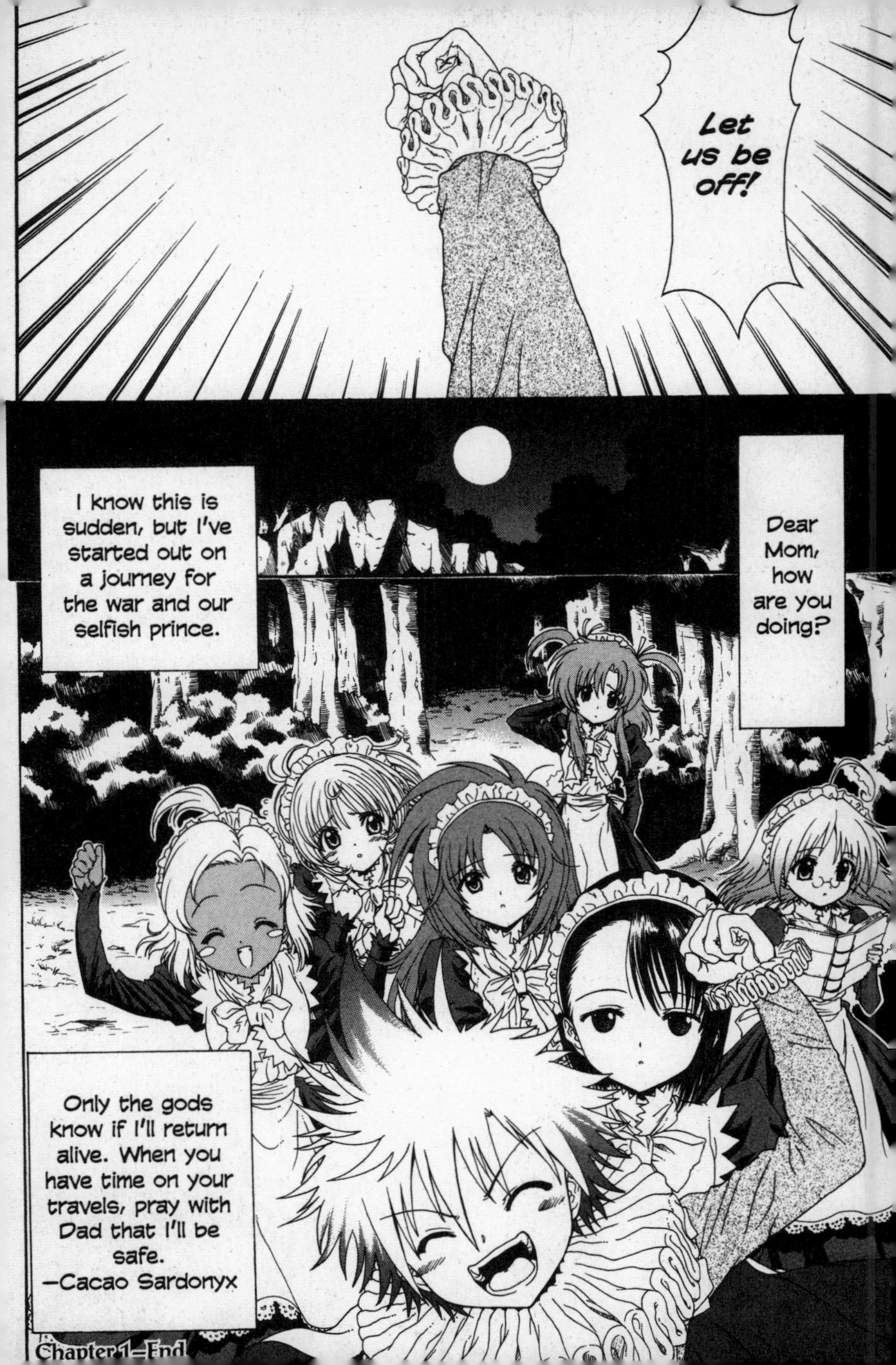
Let us be off!
Dear Mom, how are you doing?
I know this is sudden, but I've started out on a journey for the war and our selfish prince.
Only the gods know if I'll return alive. When you have time on your travels, pray with Dad that I'll be safe.
—Cacao Sardonyx
Chapter 1—End

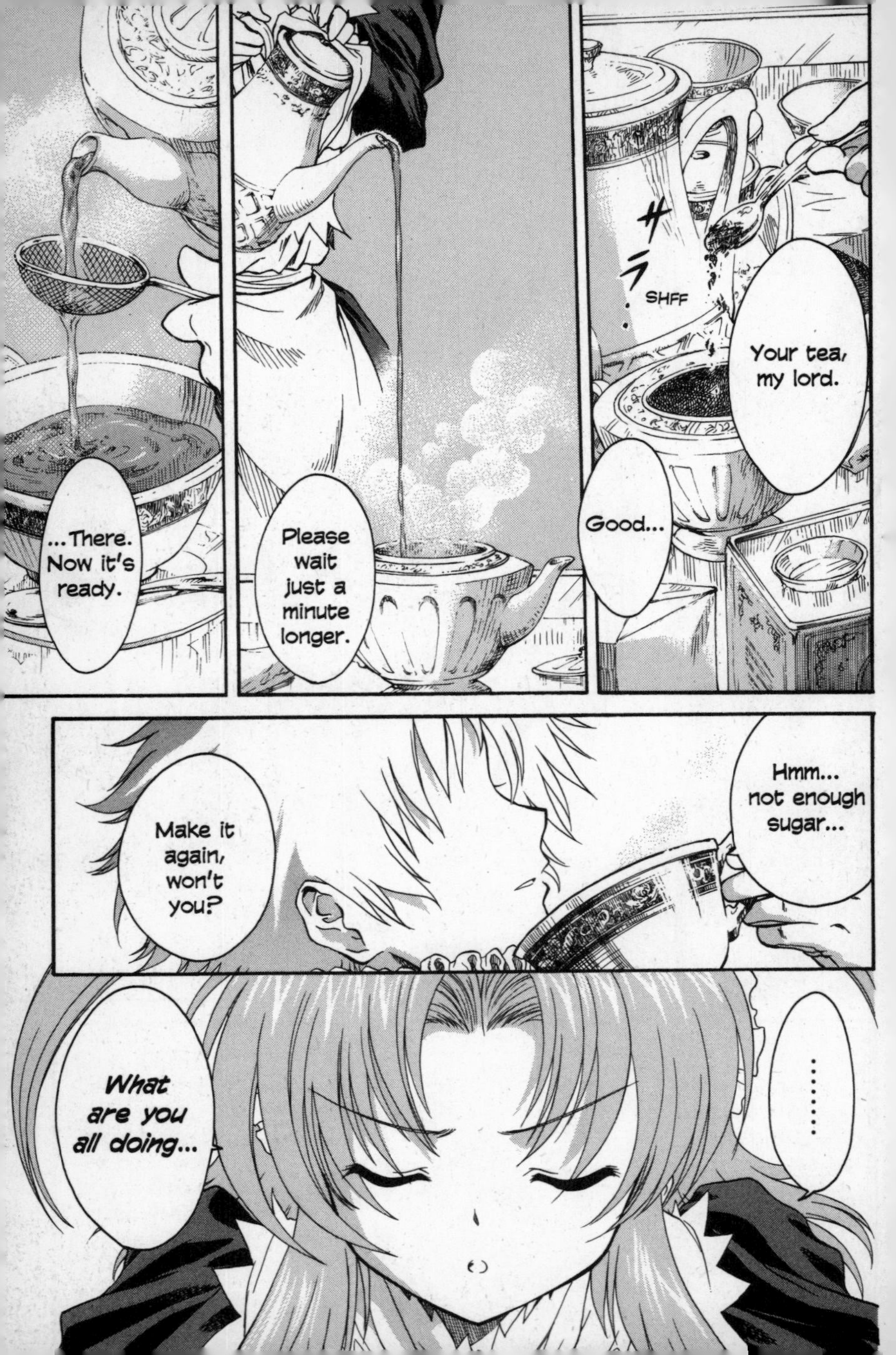

Your tea, my lord.
サラ
SHFF
Good...
Please wait just a minute longer.
...There. Now it's ready.
Hmm... not enough sugar...
Make it again, won't you?
......
What are you all doing...

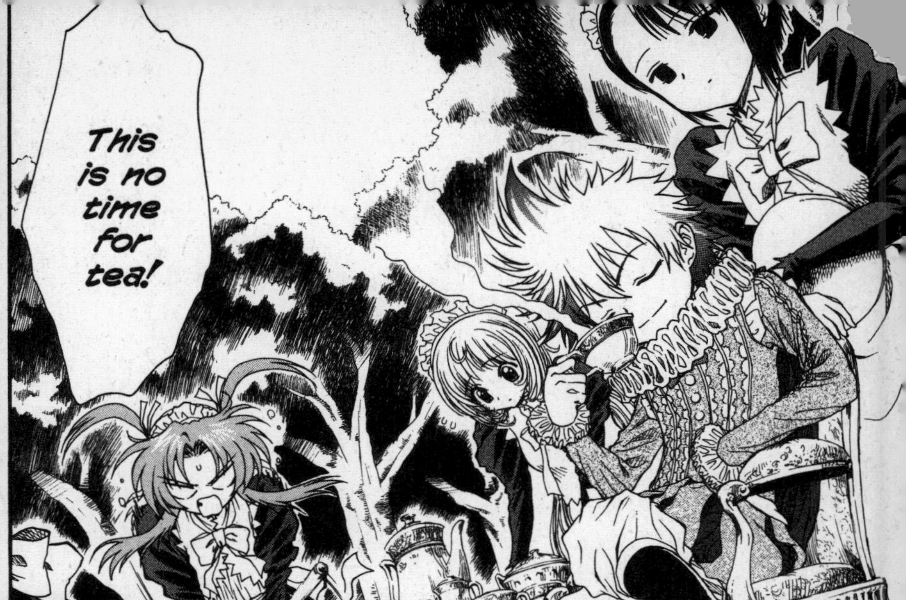
This is no time for tea!

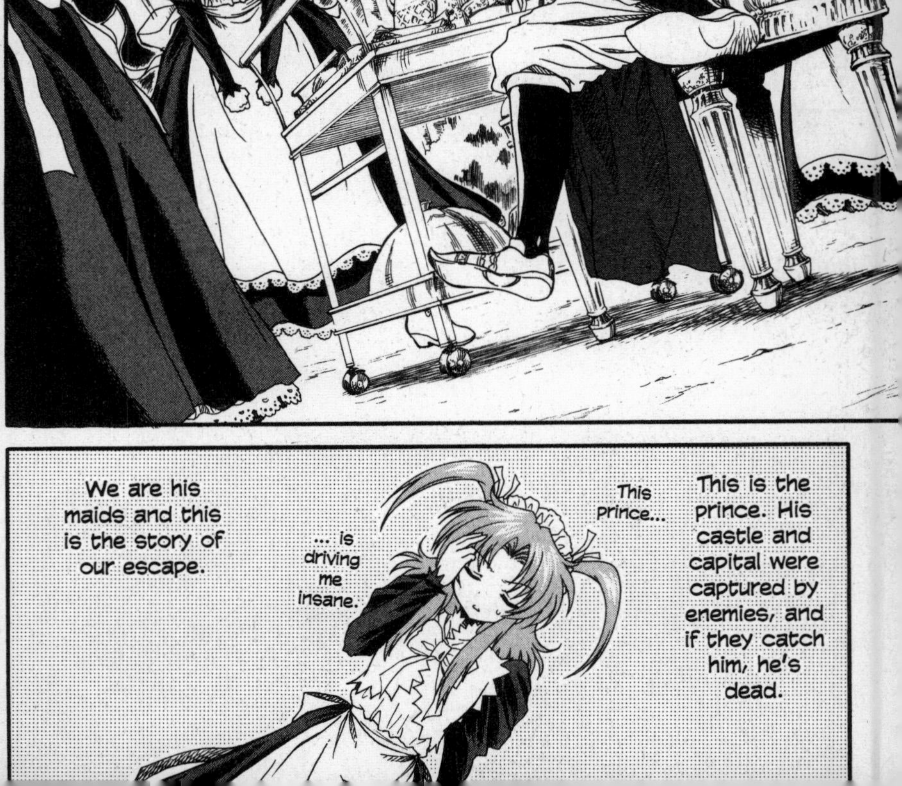
This is the prince. His castle and capital were captured by enemies, and if they catch him, he's dead.
This prince...
... is driving me insane.
We are his maids and this is the story of our escape.

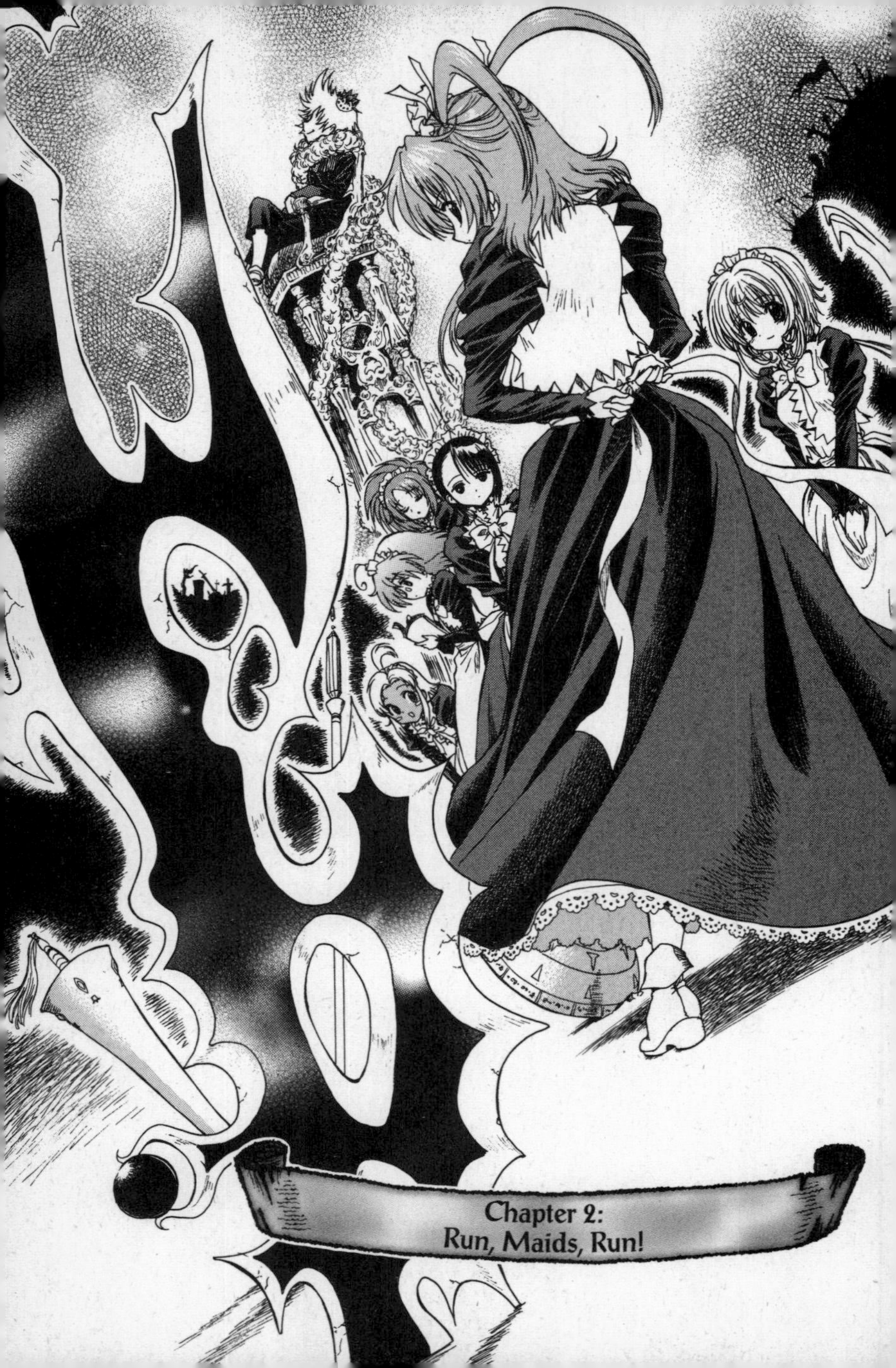
Chapter 2:
Run, Maids, Run!

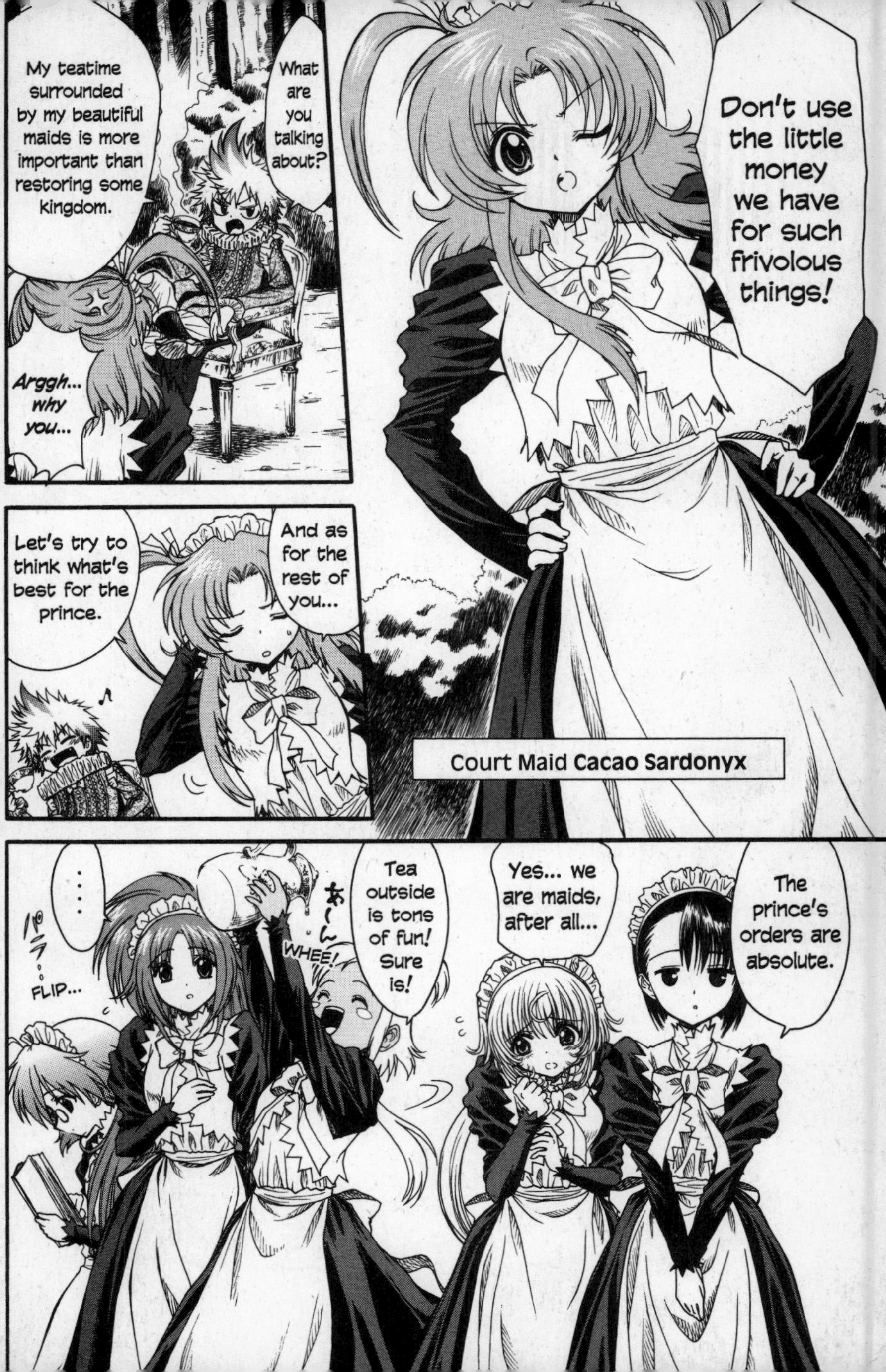

Don't use the little money we have for such frivolous things!
Court Maid Cacao Sardonyx
What are you talking about?
My teatime surrounded by my beautiful maids is more important than restoring some kingdom.
Arggh... why you...
And as for the rest of you...
Let's try to think what's best for the prince.
The prince's orders are absolute.
Yes... we are maids, after all...
Tea outside is tons of fun! Sure is!
WHEE!
....
FLIP...

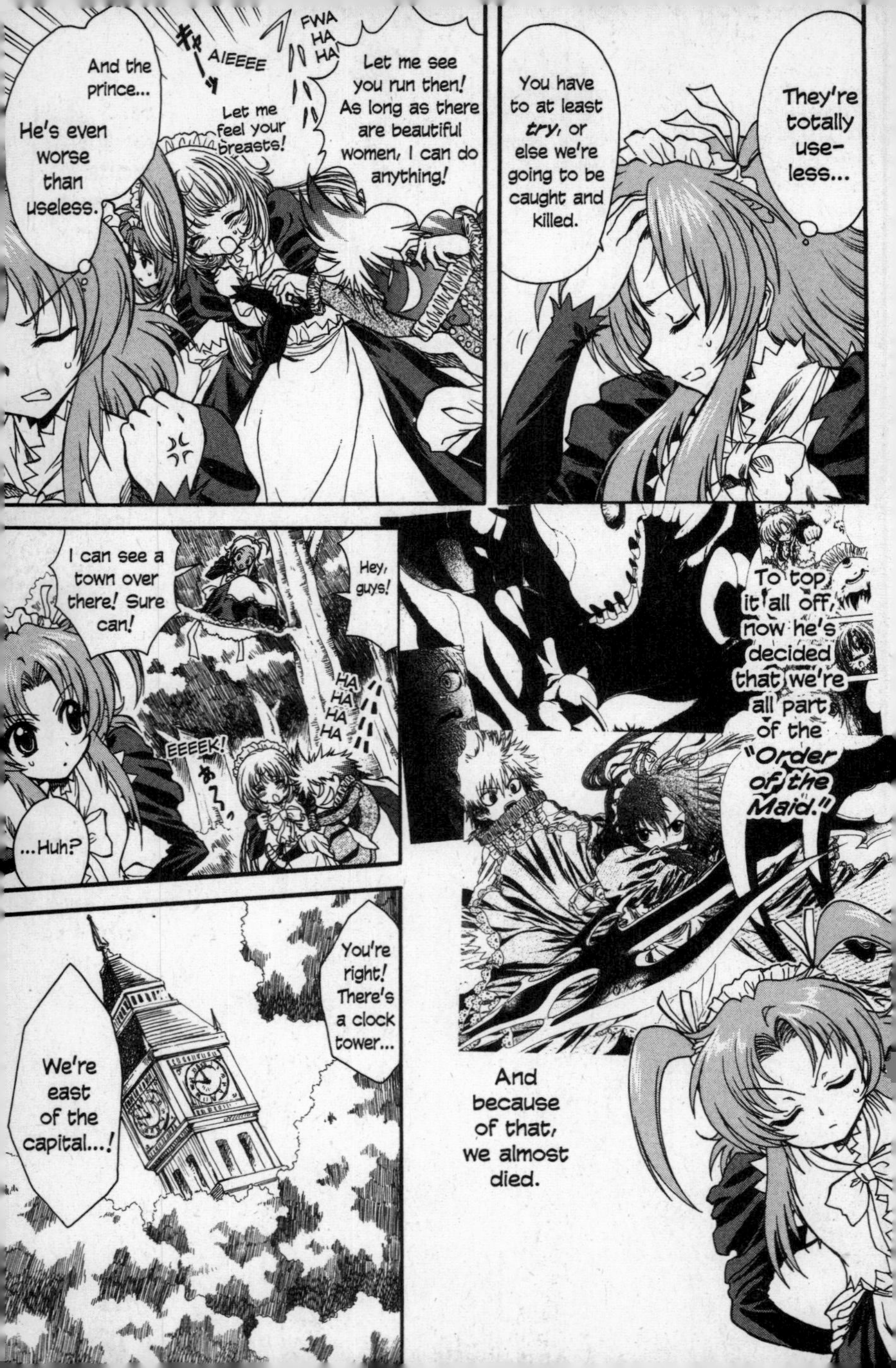
They're totally useless...
You have to at least *try*, or else we're going to be caught and killed.
Let me see you run then! As long as there are beautiful women, I can do anything!
FWA HA HA
AIEEEE
Let me feel your breasts!
And the prince...
He's even worse than useless.
To top it all off, now he's decided that we're all part of the "*Order of the Maid.*"
And because of that, we almost died.
Hey, guys!
I can see a town over there! Sure can!
HA HA HA HA
EEEEK!
...Huh?
You're right! There's a clock tower...
We're east of the capital...!

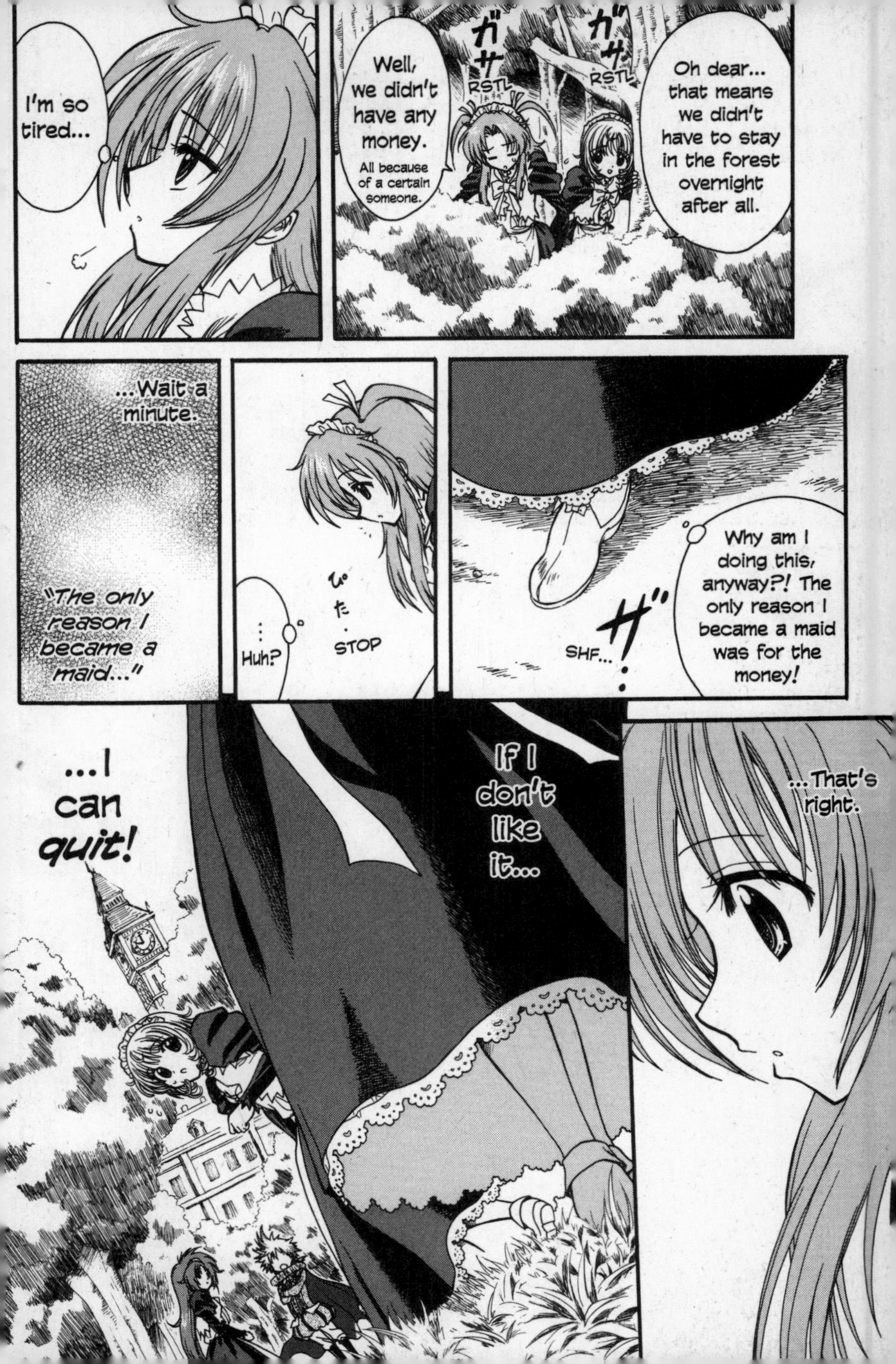
ガサ
RSTL
ガサ
RSTL
Oh dear... that means we didn't have to stay in the forest overnight after all.
Well, we didn't have any money.
All because of a certain someone.
I'm so tired...
Why am I doing this, anyway?! The only reason I became a maid was for the money!
ザ
SHF...
ぴた
STOP
...Huh?
...Wait a minute.
"The only reason I became a maid..."
...That's right.
If I don't like it...
...I can quit!

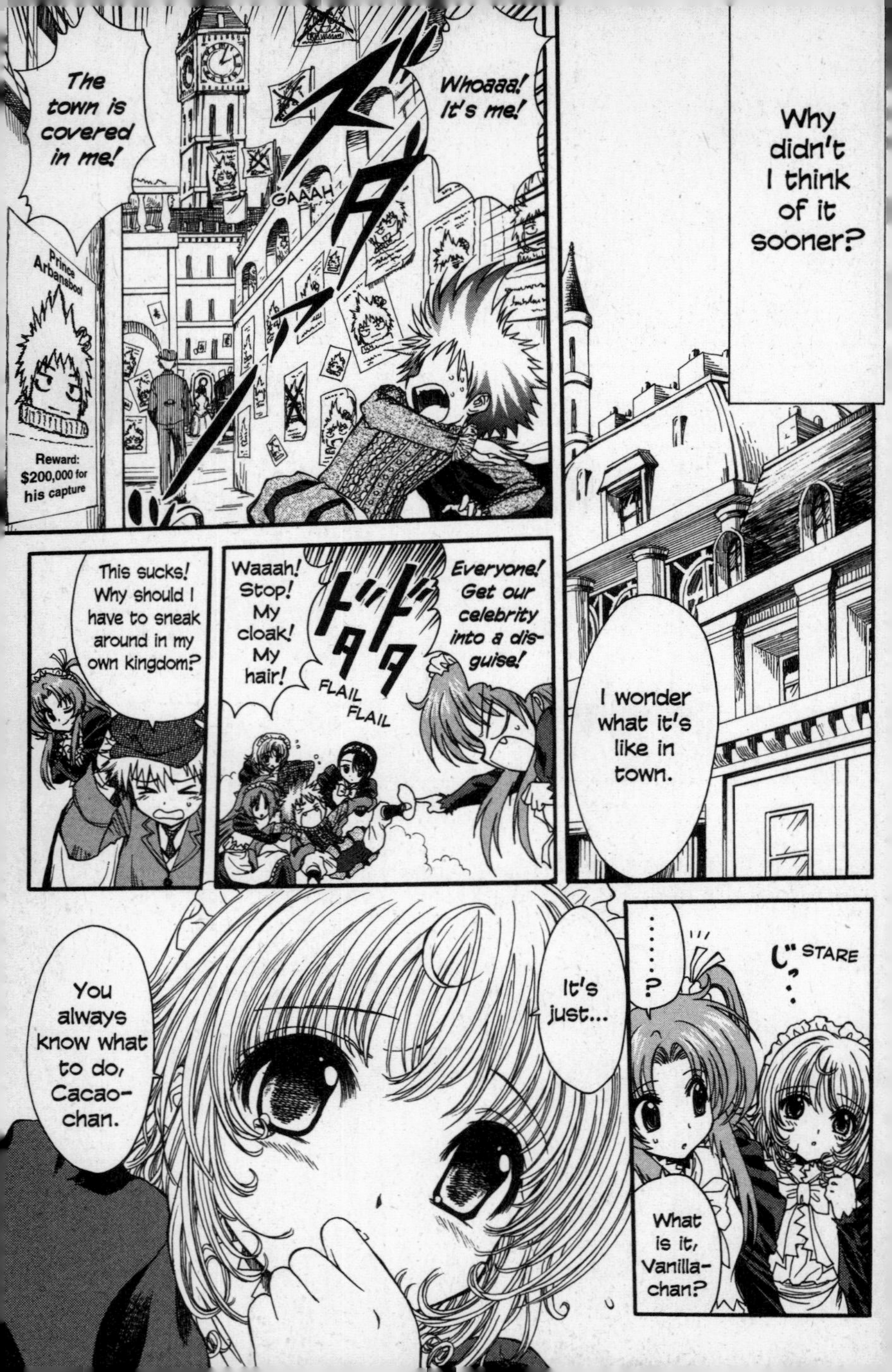
Why didn't I think of it sooner?
I wonder what it's like in town.
Whoaaa! It's me!
GAAAH
The town is covered in me!
Prince Arbansbool
Reward: $200,000 for his capture
Everyone! Get our celebrity into a disguise!
Waaah! Stop! My cloak! My hair!
FLAIL FLAIL
This sucks! Why should I have to sneak around in my own kingdom?
STARE
......?
What is it, Vanilla-chan?
It's just...
You always know what to do, Cacao-chan.

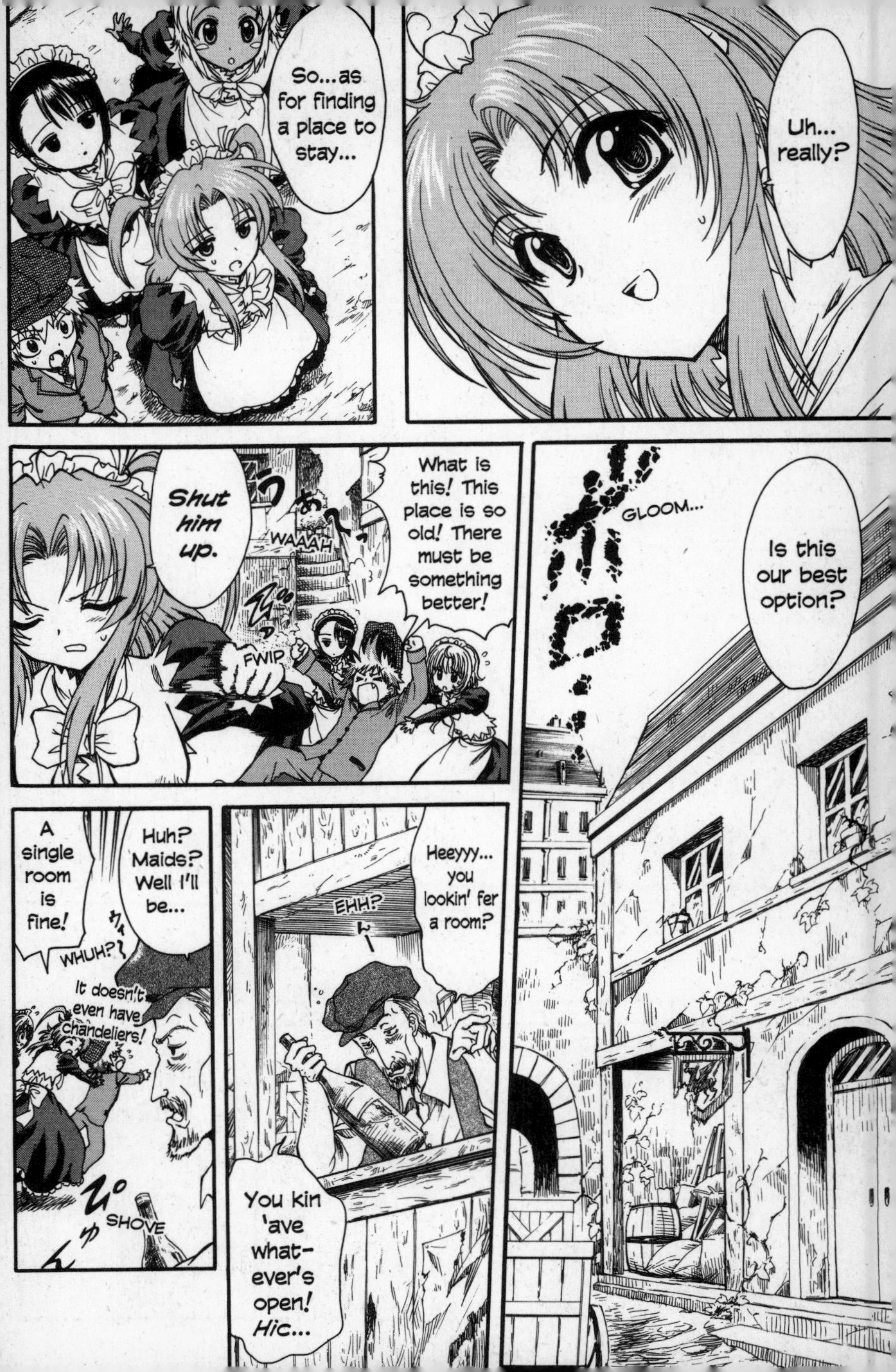

Uh... really?
So...as for finding a place to stay...
GLOOM...
Is this our best option?
What is this! This place is so old! There must be something better!
WAAAH
Shut him up.
FWIP
Heeyyy... you lookin' fer a room?
EHH?
You kin 'ave whatever's open! Hic...
Huh? Maids? Well I'll be...
A single room is fine!
WHUH?
It doesn't even have chandeliers!
SHOVE

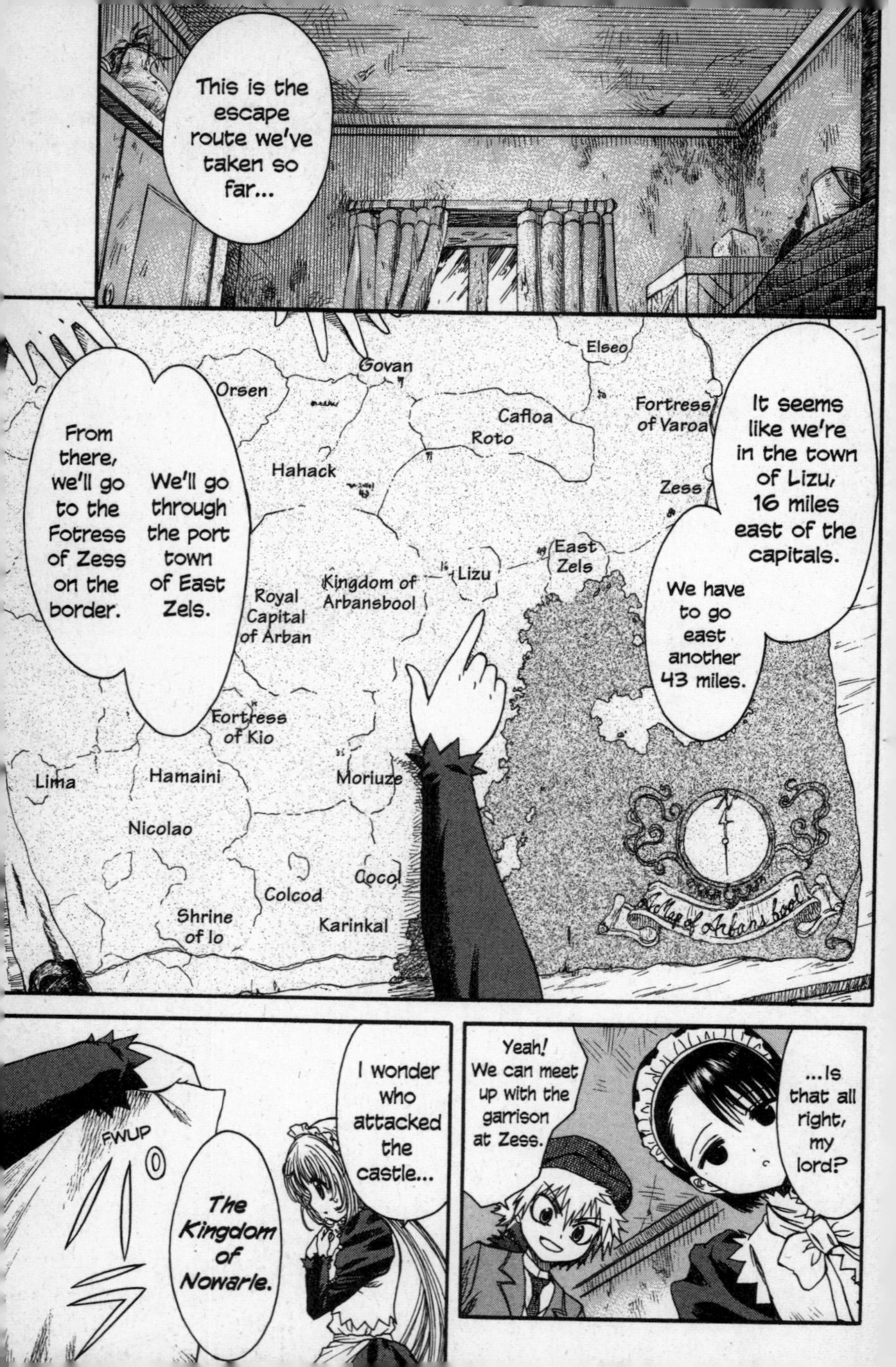

This is the escape route we've taken so far...
It seems like we're in the town of Lizu, 16 miles east of the capitals.
We have to go east another 43 miles.
We'll go through the port town of East Zels.
From there, we'll go to the Fotress of Zess on the border.
Elseo
Govan
Orsen
Fortress of Varoa
Cafloa
Roto
Hahack
Zess
East Zels
Lizu
Kingdom of Arbansbool
Royal Capital of Arban
Fortress of Kio
Lima
Hamaini
Moriuze
Nicolao
Cocol
Colcod
Shrine of Io
Karinkal
A Map of Arbansbool
...Is that all right, my lord?
Yeah! We can meet up with the garrison at Zess.
I wonder who attacked the castle...
The Kingdom of Nowarle.
FWUP

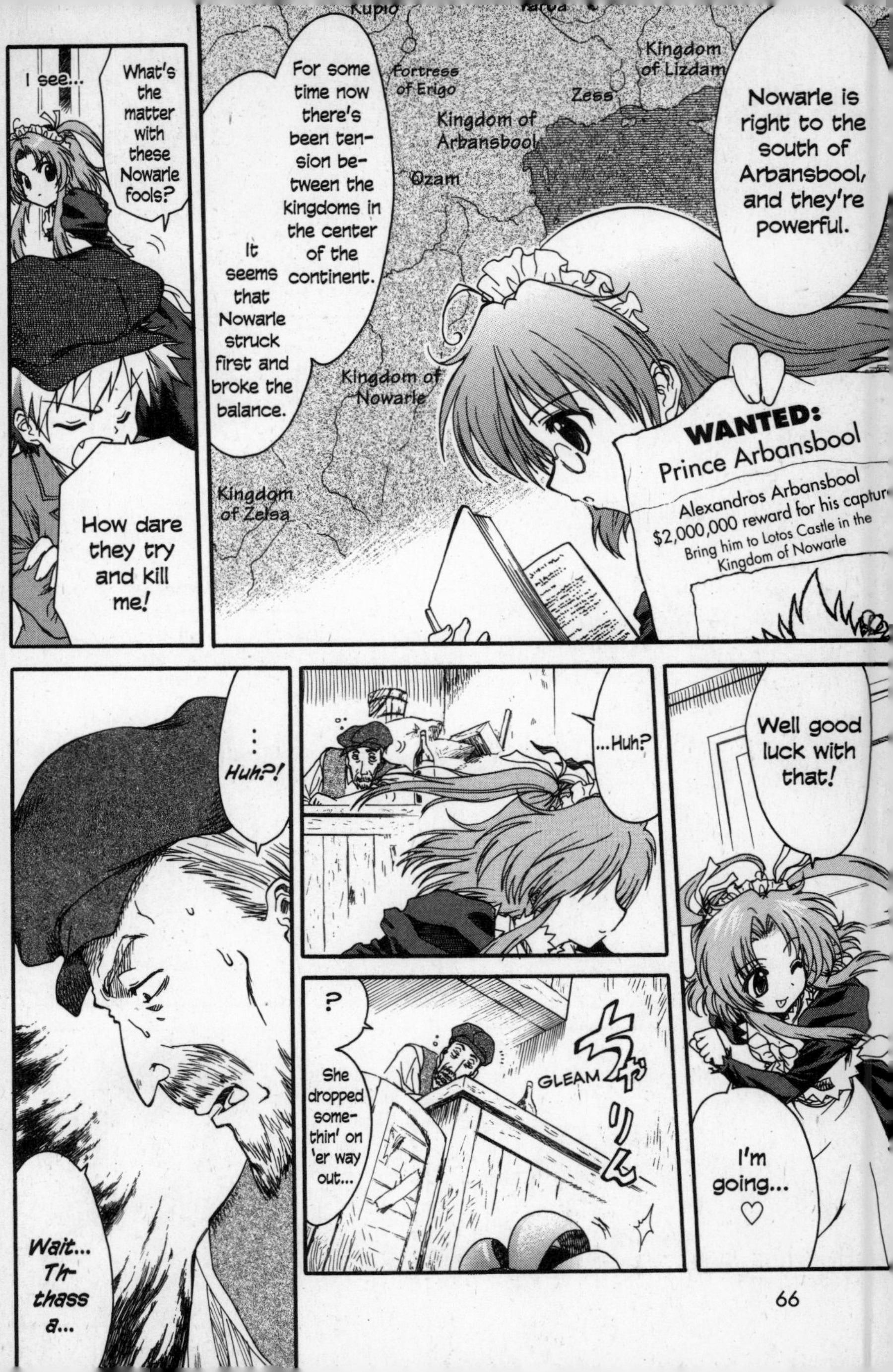
Nowarle is right to the south of Arbansbool, and they're powerful.
Kingdom of Lizdam
Zess
Fortress of Erigo
Kingdom of Arbansbool
Ozam
Kingdom of Nowarle
Kingdom of Zelsa
For some time now there's been tension between the kingdoms in the center of the continent.
It seems that Nowarle struck first and broke the balance.
WANTED:
Prince Arbansbool
Alexandros Arbansbool
$2,000,000 reward for his
Bring him to Lotos Castle in the Kingdom of Nowarle
What's the matter with these Nowarle fools?
I see...
How dare they try and kill me!
Well good luck with that!
I'm going... ♡
...Huh?
?
She dropped somethin' on 'er way out...
GLEAM
... Huh?!
Wait... Thrthass a...

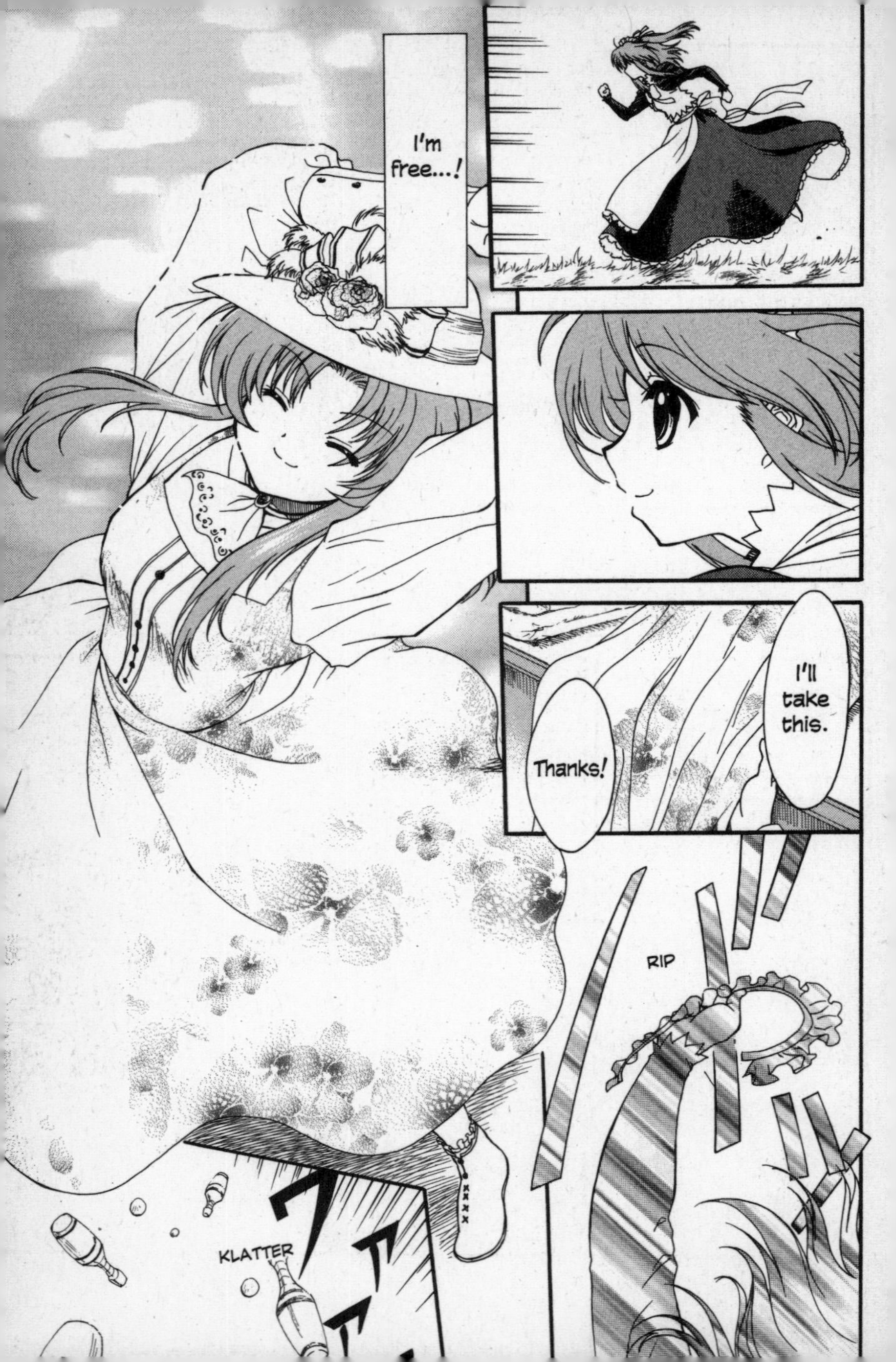

I'll take this.
Thanks!
RIP
I'm free...!
KLATTER

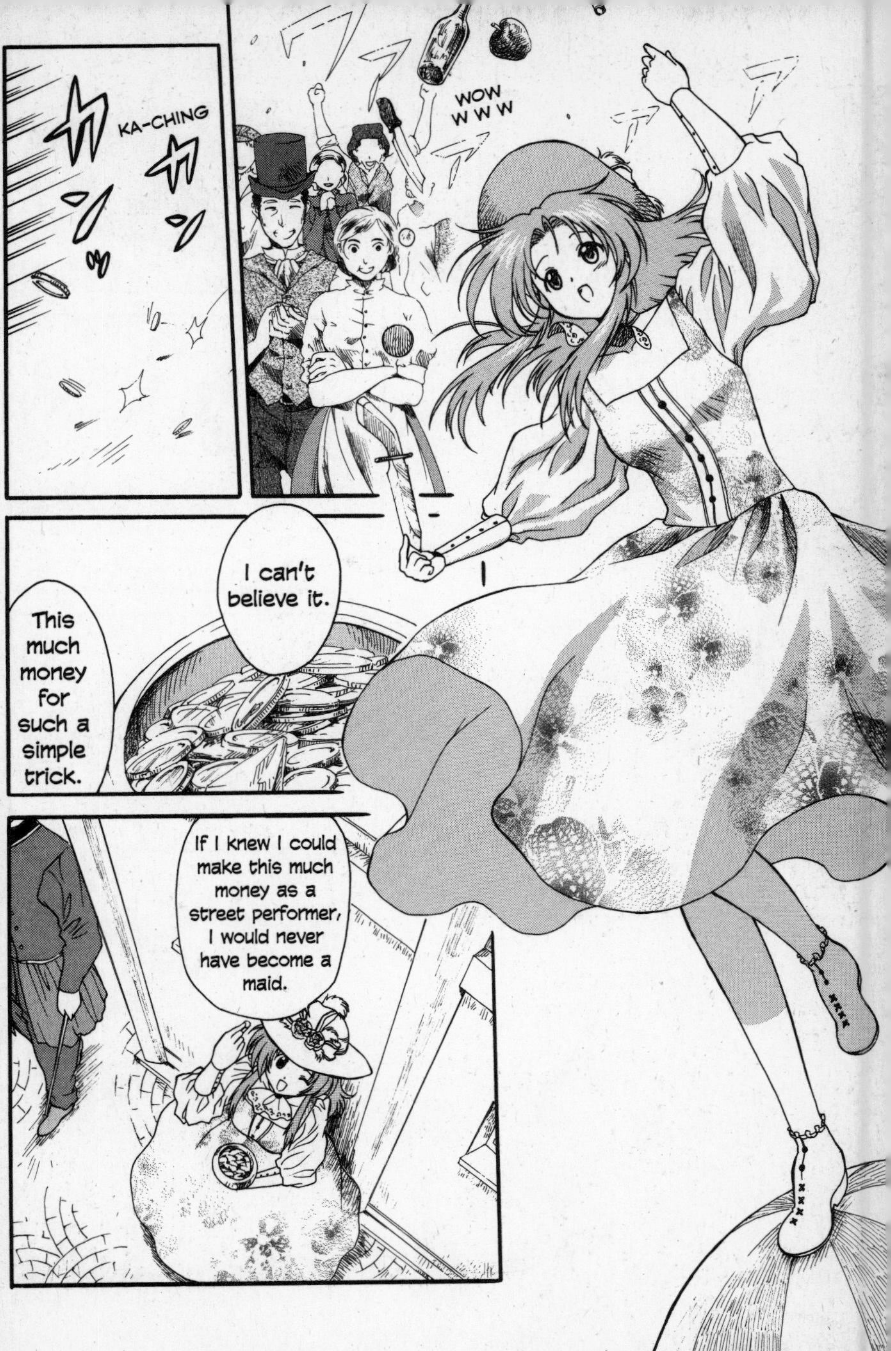
WOW W W W
KA-CHING
I can't believe it.
This much money for such a simple trick.
If I knew I could make this much money as a street performer, I would never have become a maid.

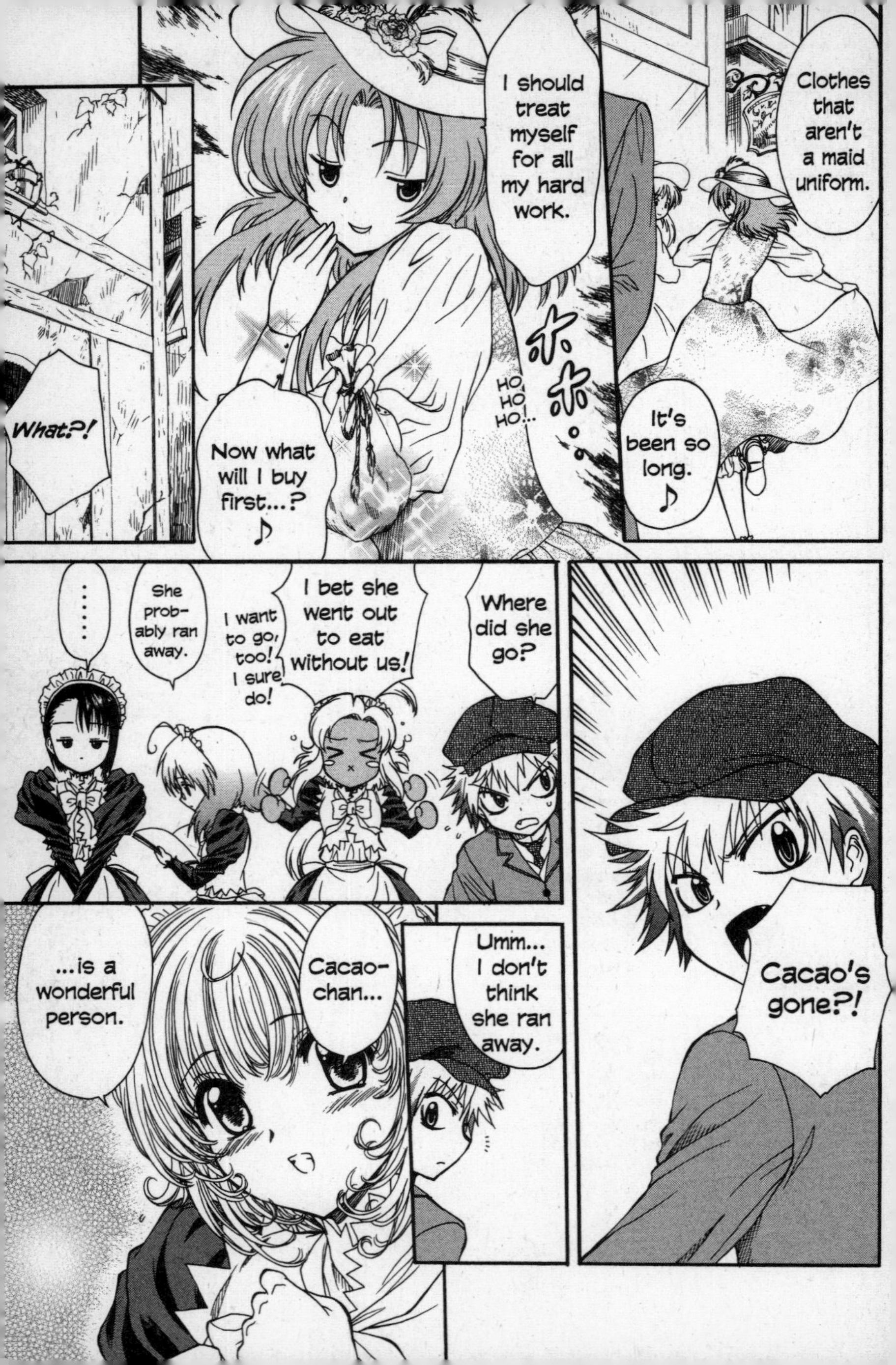
Clothes that aren't a maid uniform.
It's been so long. ♪
I should treat myself for all my hard work.
HO, HO HO...
Now what will I buy first...? ♪
What?!
Cacao's gone?!
Where did she go?
I bet she went out to eat without us!
I want to go, too! I sure do!
She probably ran away.
......
Umm... I don't think she ran away.
Cacao-chan...
...is a wonderful person.

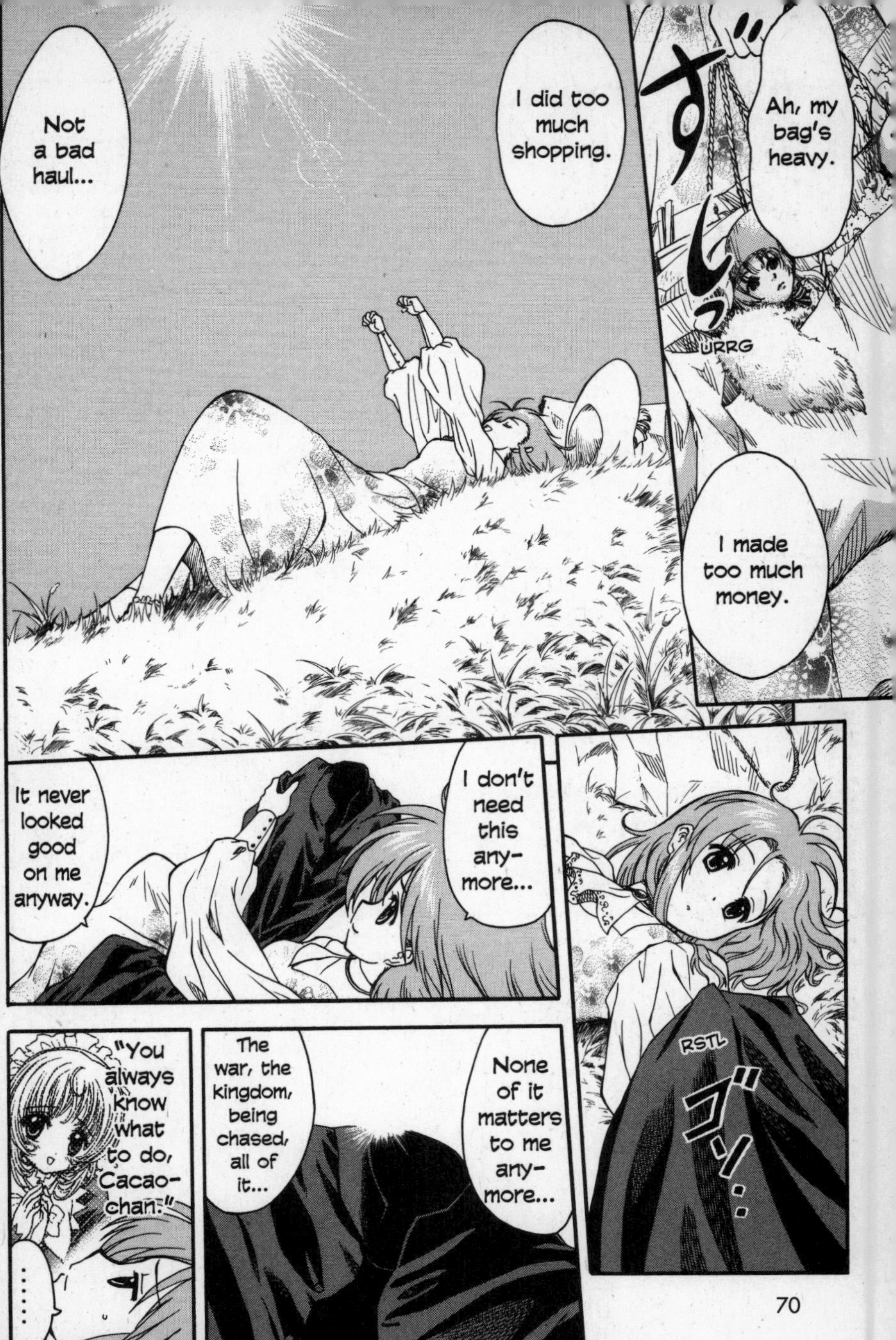
Ah, my bag's heavy.
URRG
I made too much money.
I did too much shopping.
Not a bad haul...
RSTL
I don't need this any-more...
It never looked good on me anyway.
None of it matters to me any-more...
The war, the kingdom, being chased, all of it...
"You always know what to do, Cacao-chan."
......

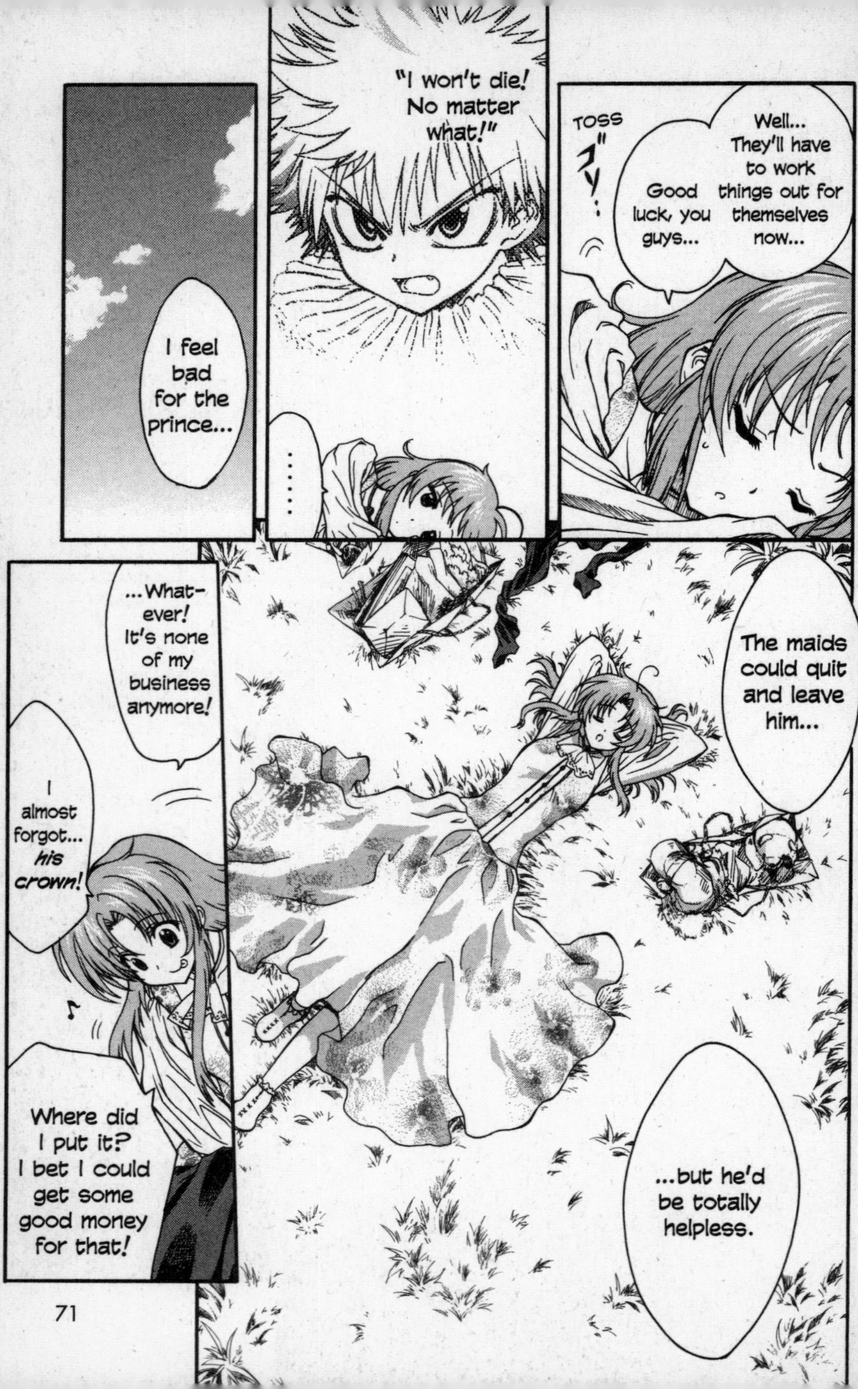
TOSS
Well... They'll have to work things out for themselves now...
Good luck, you guys...
"I won't die! No matter what!"
......
I feel bad for the prince...
The maids could quit and leave him...
...but he'd be totally helpless.
...What-ever! It's none of my business anymore!
I almost forgot... *his crown!*
Where did I put it? I bet I could get some good money for that!

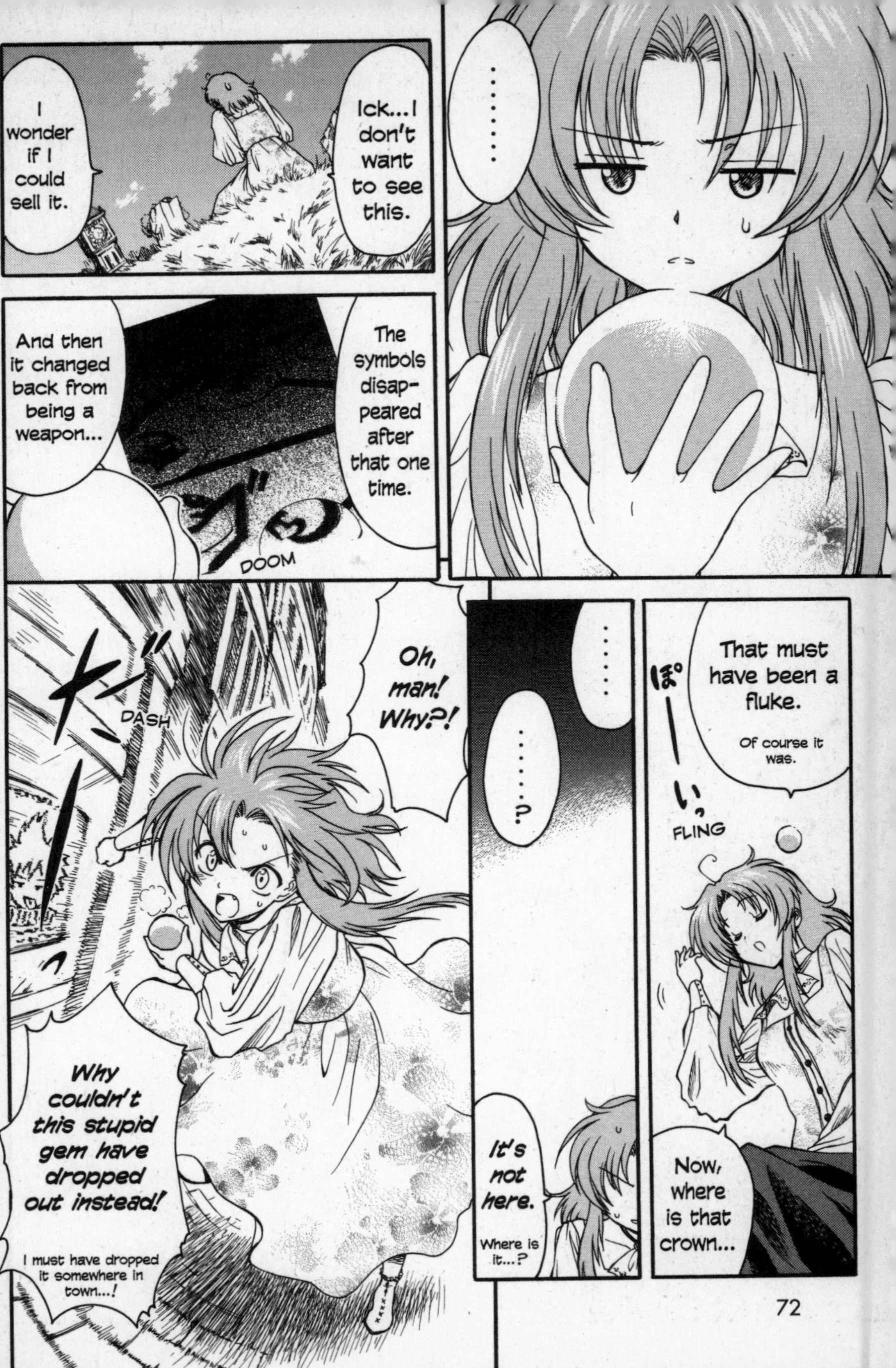
......
Ick...I don't want to see this.
I wonder if I could sell it.
The symbols disappeared after that one time.
And then it changed back from being a weapon...
DOOM
That must have been a fluke.
Of course it was.
ぽーい
FLING
Now, where is that crown...
......
......?
It's not here.
Where is it...?
Oh, man! Why?!
DASH
Why couldn't this stupid gem have dropped out instead!
I must have dropped it somewhere in town...!

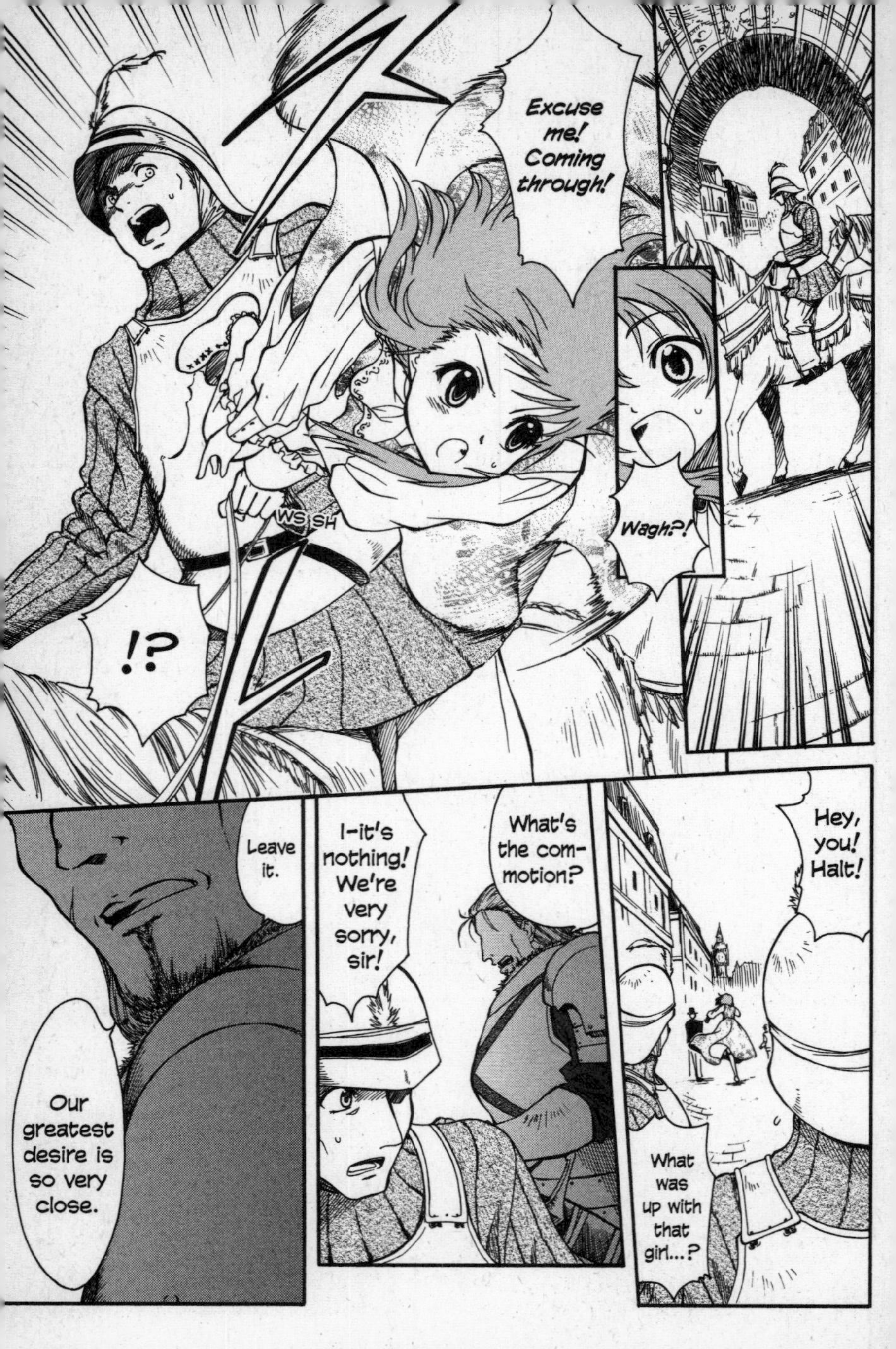
Wagh?!
Excuse me! Coming through!
WSSH
!?
Hey, you! Halt!
What was up with that girl...?
What's the com-motion?
I-it's nothing! We're very sorry, sir!
Leave it.
Our greatest desire is so very close.

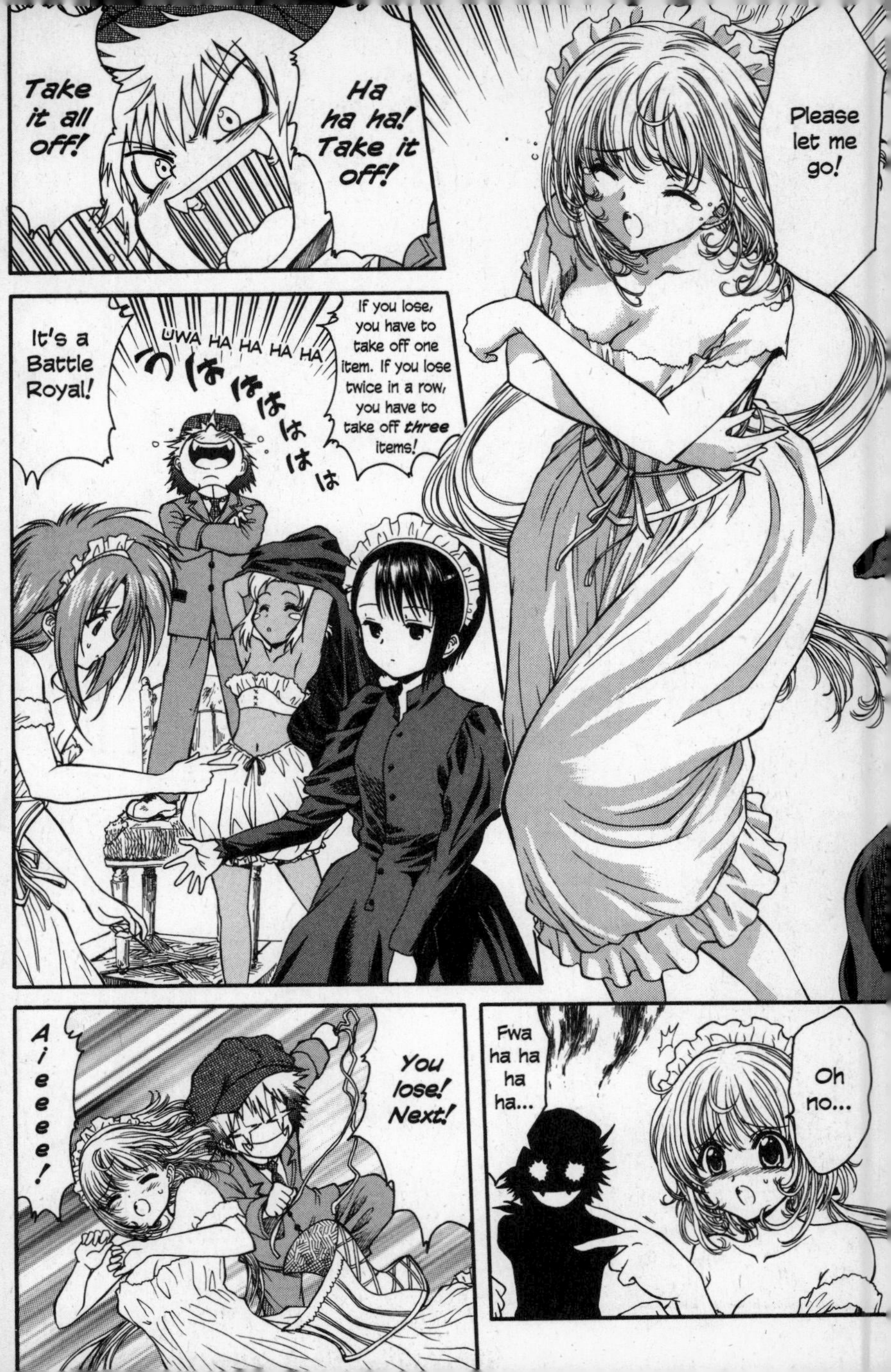
Please let me go!
Ha ha ha! Take it off!
Take it all off!
If you lose, you have to take off one item. If you lose twice in a row, you have to take off *three* items!
UWA HA HA HA HA
It's a Battle Royal!
Oh no...
Fwa ha ha ha ha...
You lose! Next!
Aieeeee!

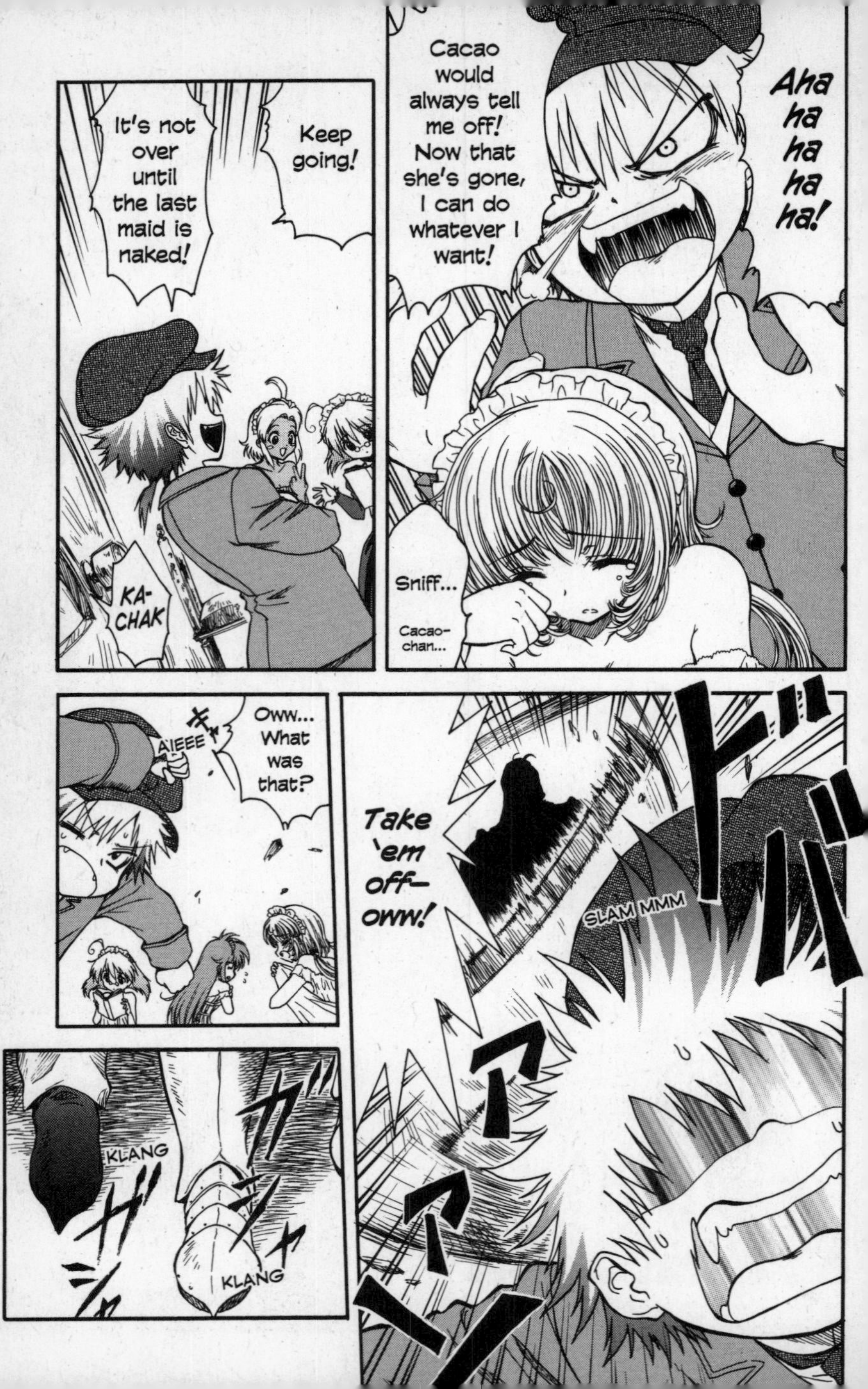
Cacao would always tell me off! Now that she's gone, I can do whatever I want!
Aha ha ha ha ha!
Sniff...
Cacao-chan...
Keep going!
It's not over until the last maid is naked!
KA-CHAK
Take 'em off-oww!
SLAM MMM
AIEEE
Oww... What was that?
KLANG
KLANG

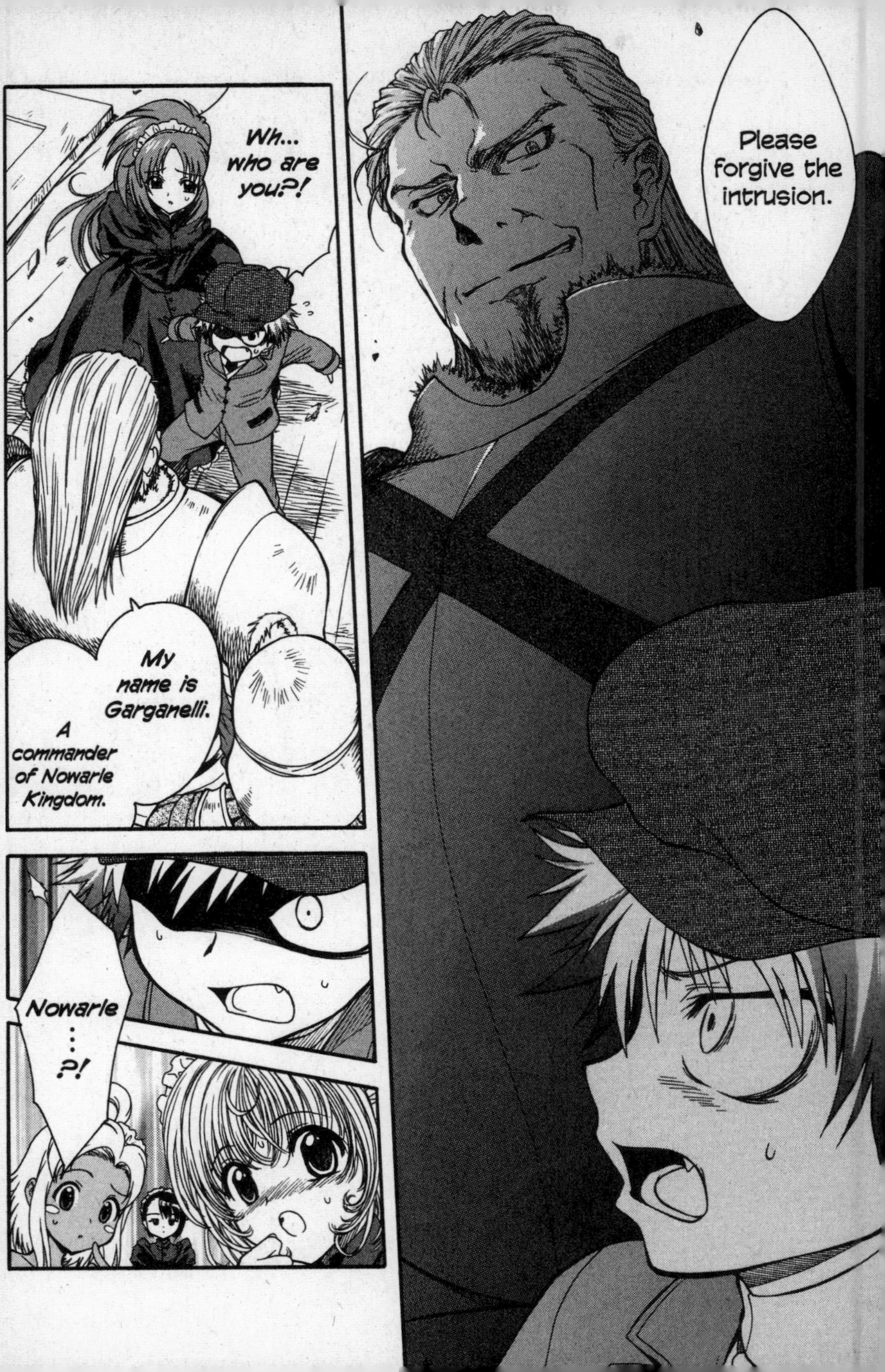
Please forgive the intrusion.
Wh... who are you?!
My name is Garganelli.
A commander of Nowarle Kingdom.
Nowarle ...?!

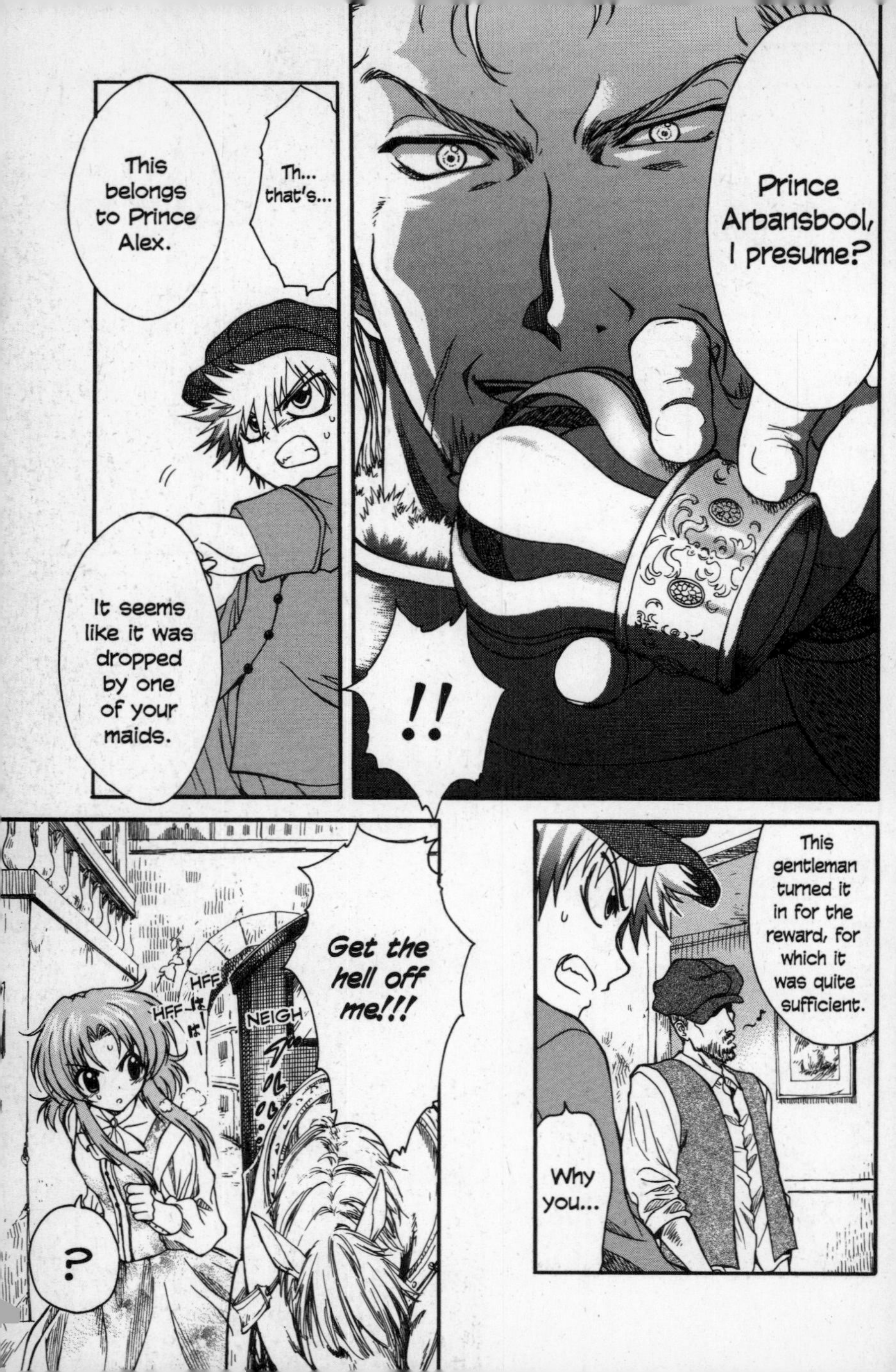
Prince Arbansbool, I presume?
!!
Th... that's...
This belongs to Prince Alex.
It seems like it was dropped by one of your maids.
This gentleman turned it in for the reward, for which it was quite sufficient.
Why you...
Get the hell off me!!!
NEIGH
HFF HFF
?

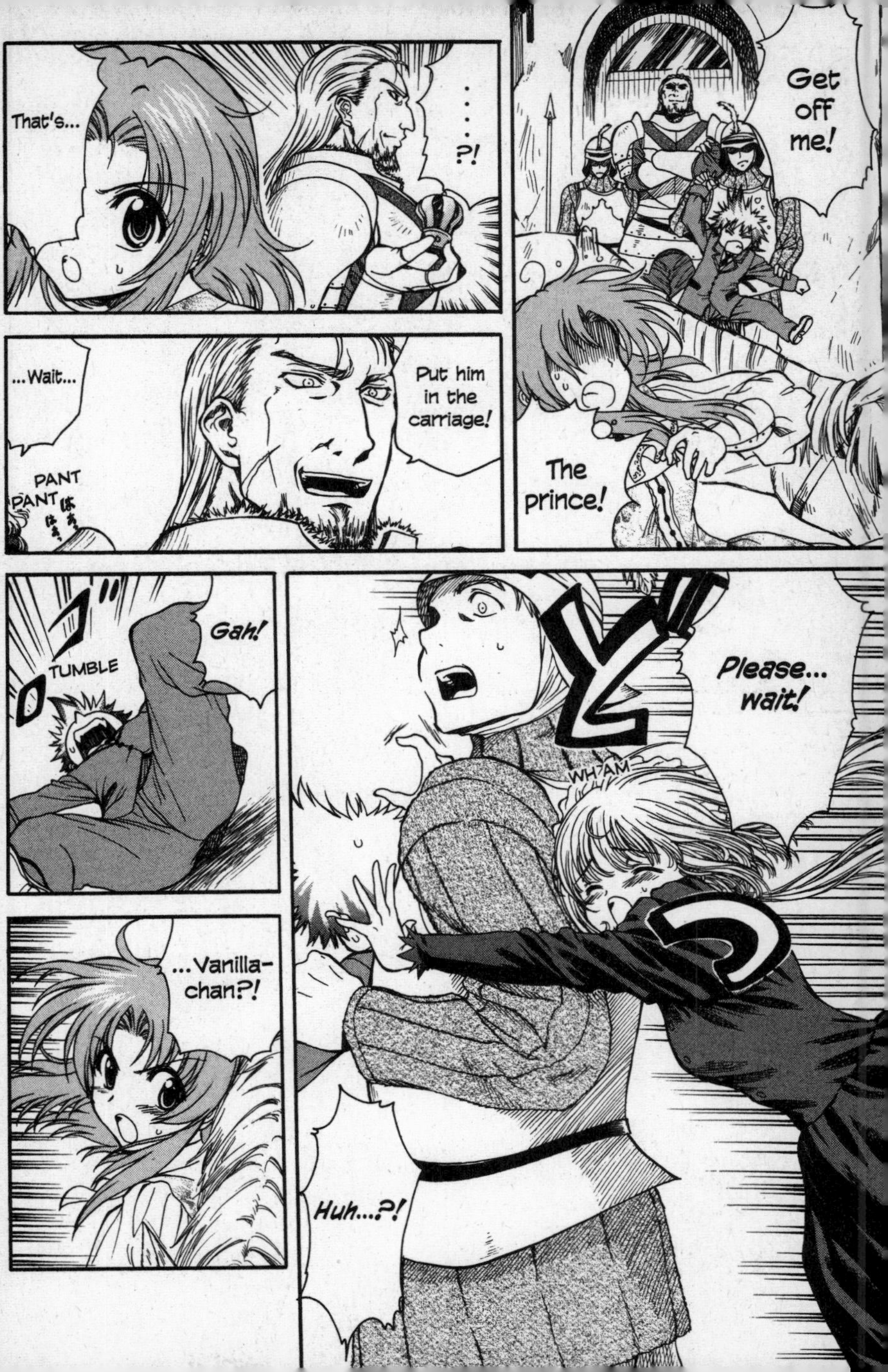

Get off me!
The prince!
....?!
That's...
Put him in the carriage!
...Wait...
PANT PANT
Please... wait!
WHAM
Huh...?!
Gah!
TUMBLE
...Vanilla-chan?!

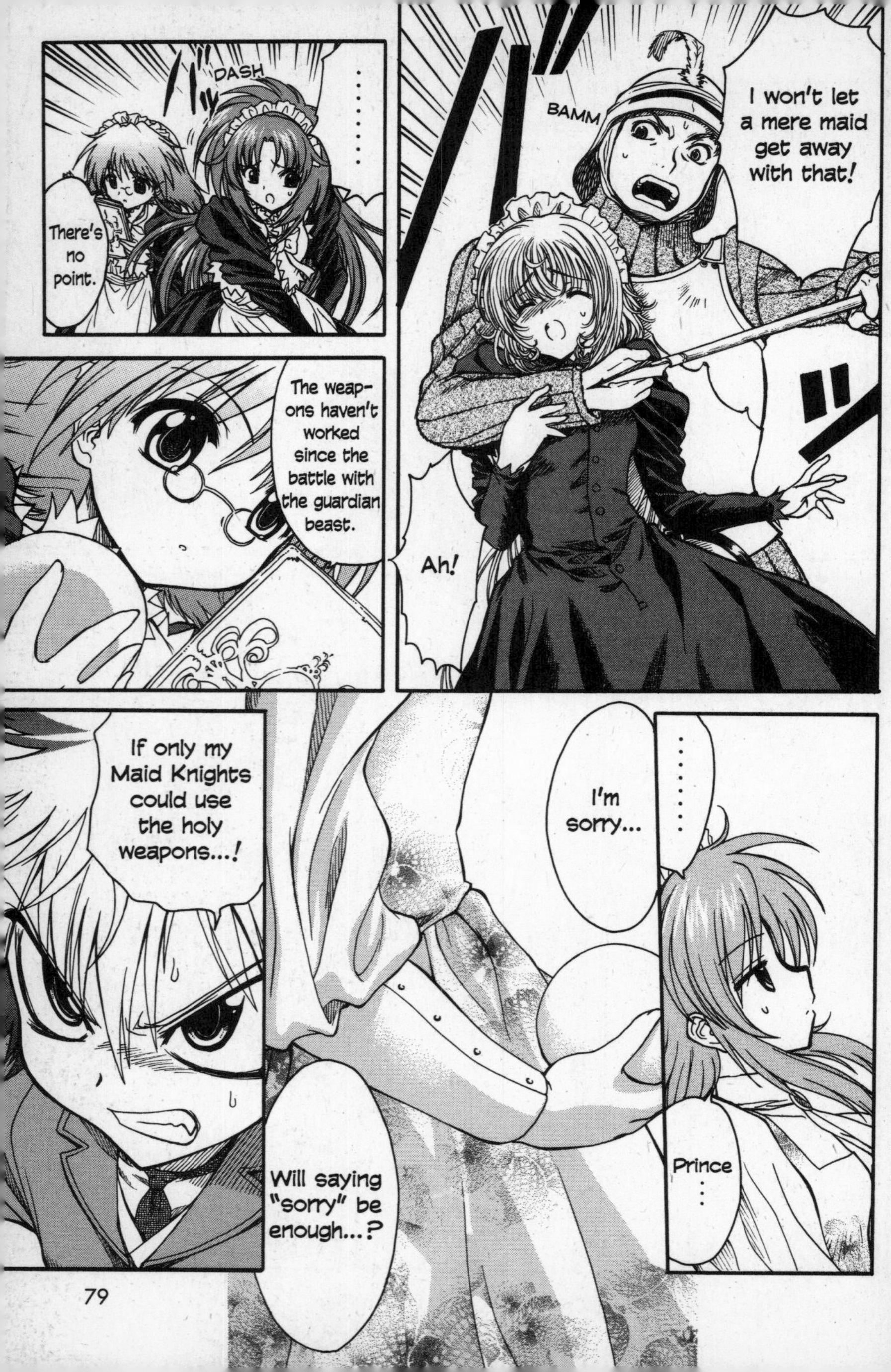
BAMM
I won't let a mere maid get away with that!
Ah!
DASH
......
There's no point.
The weap-ons haven't worked since the battle with the guardian beast.
......
Prince ...
I'm sorry...
Will saying "sorry" be enough...?
If only my Maid Knights could use the holy weapons...!

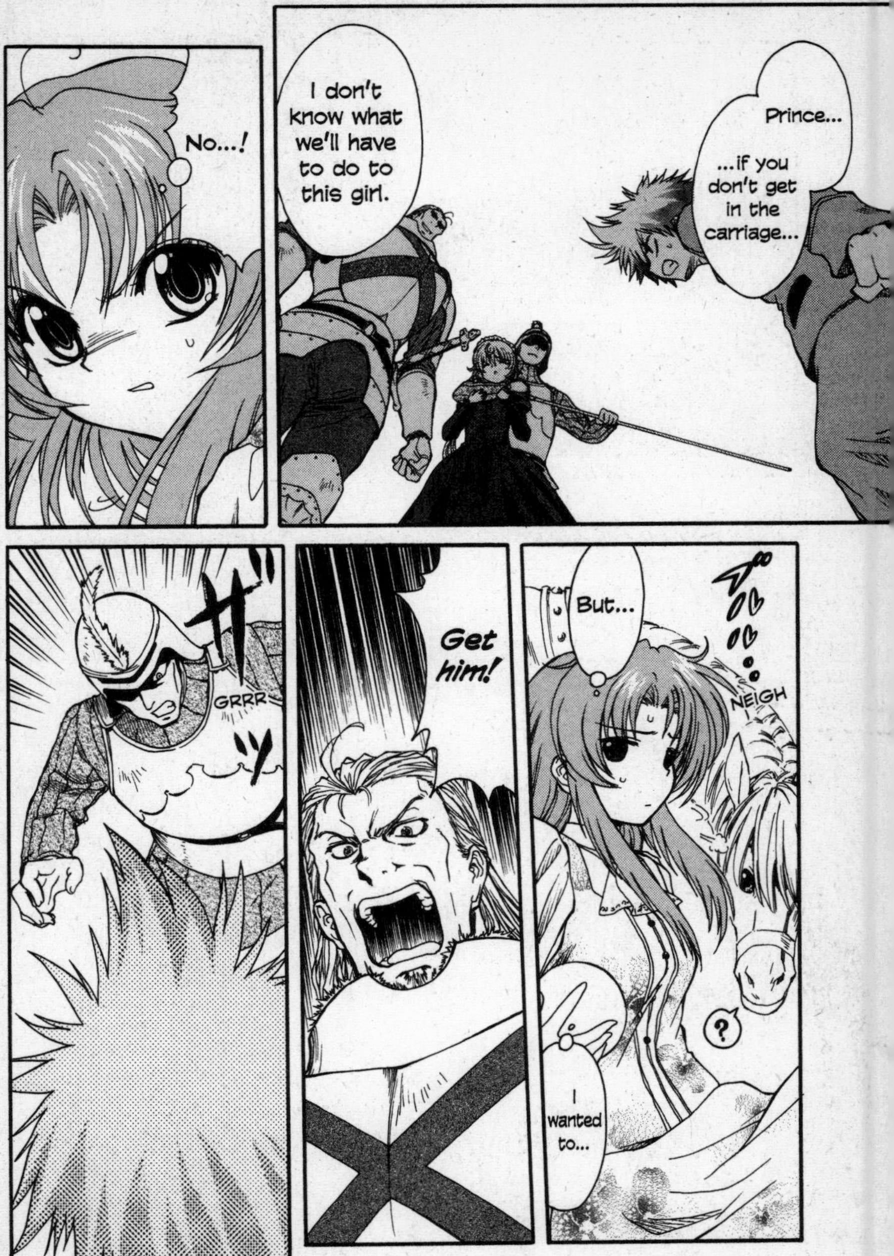

Prince...
...if you don't get in the carriage...
I don't know what we'll have to do to this girl.
No...!
But...
NEIGH
?
I wanted to...
Get him!
GRRR

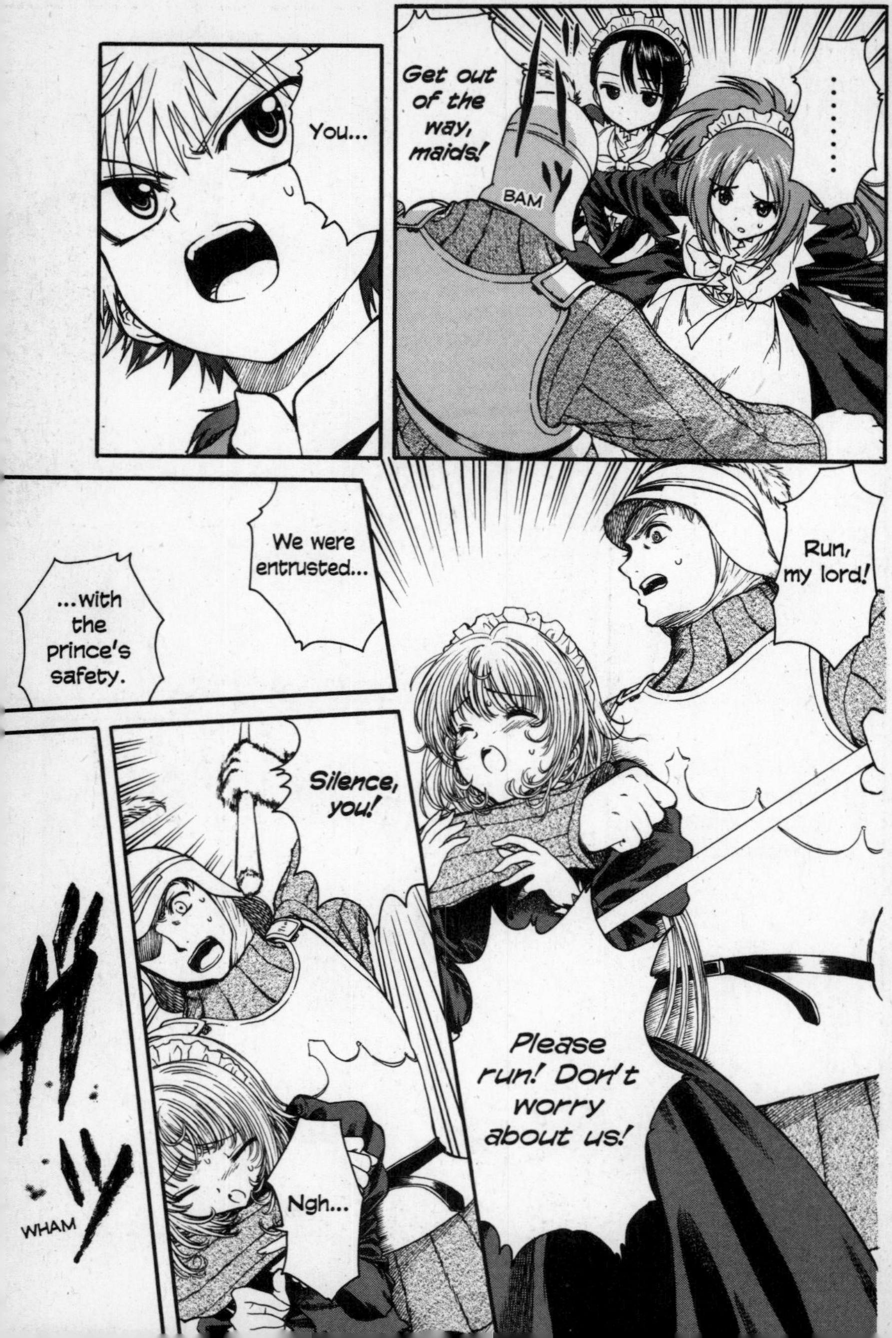
Get out of the way, maids!
BAM
......
You...
Run, my lord!
We were entrusted...
...with the prince's safety.
Please run! Don't worry about us!
Silence, you!
Ngh...
WHAM

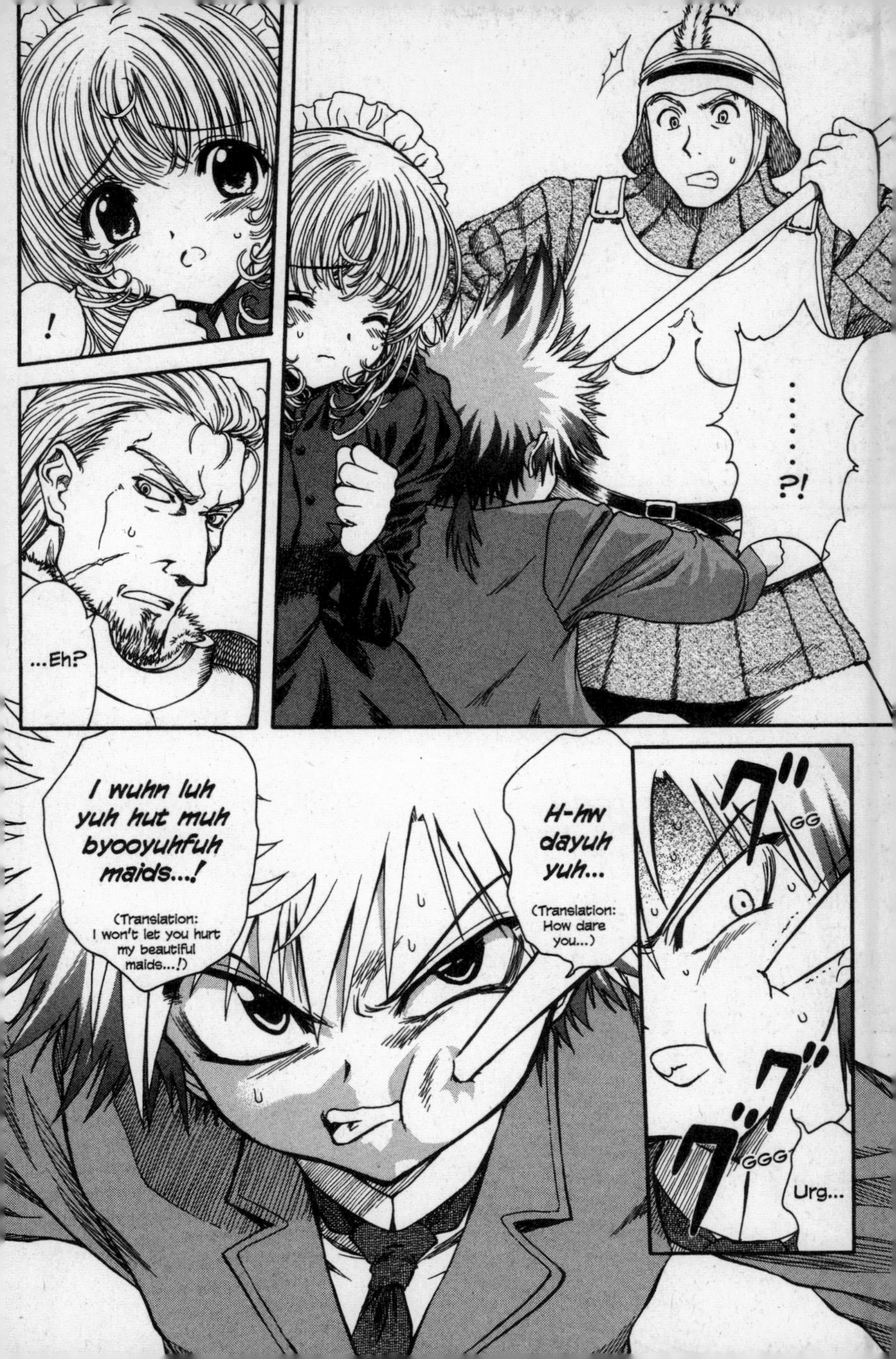

......?!
!
...Eh?
GG
GGG
Urg...
H-hw dayuh yuh...
(Translation: How dare you...)
I wuhn luh yuh hut muh byooyuhfuh maids...!
(Translation: I won't let you hurt my beautiful maids...!)

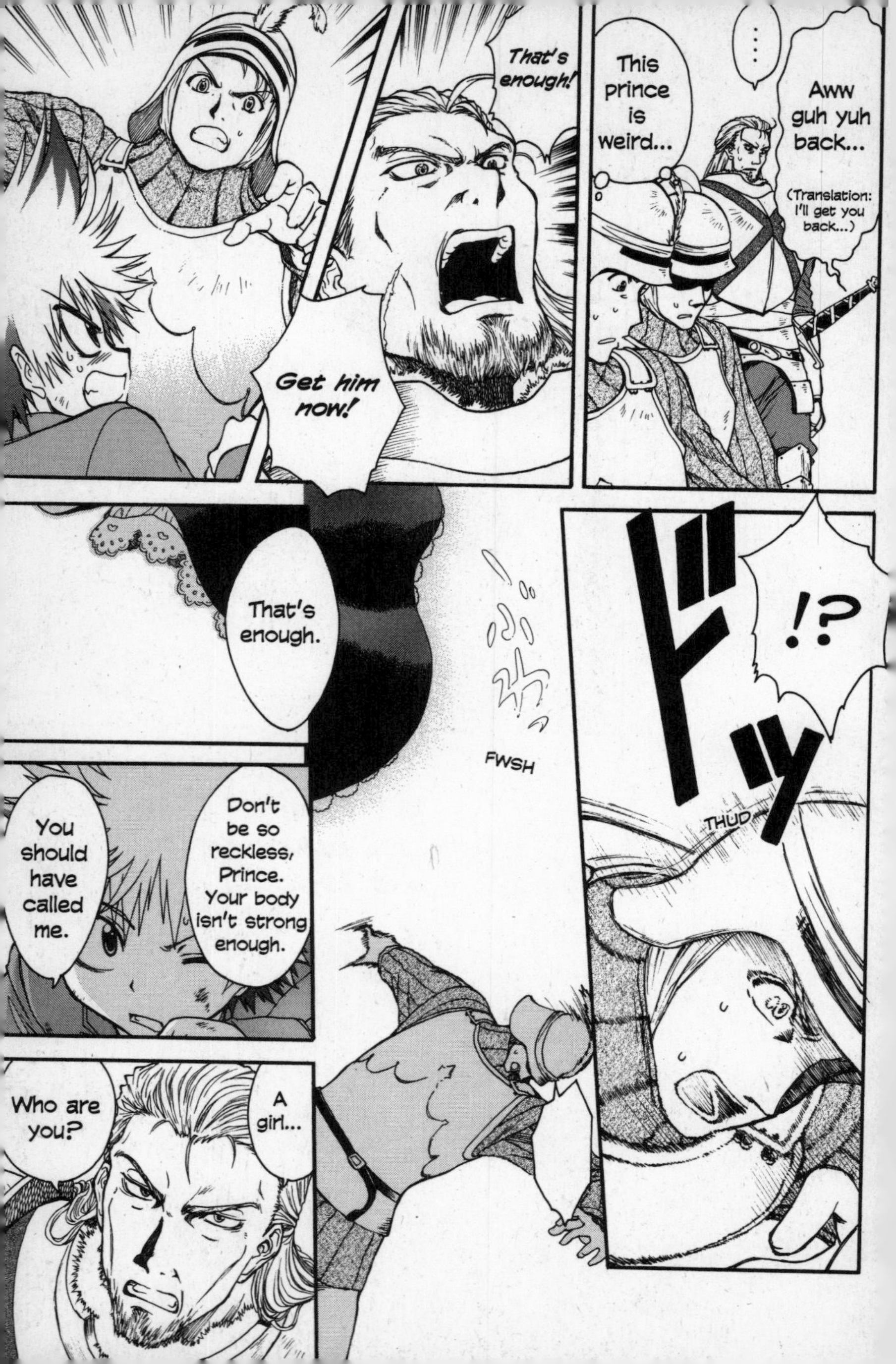
....
Aww guh yuh back...
(Translation: I'll get you back...)
This prince is weird...
That's enough!
Get him now!
!?
ドッ
THUD
FWSH
That's enough.
Don't be so reckless, Prince. Your body isn't strong enough.
You should have called me.
A girl...
Who are you?

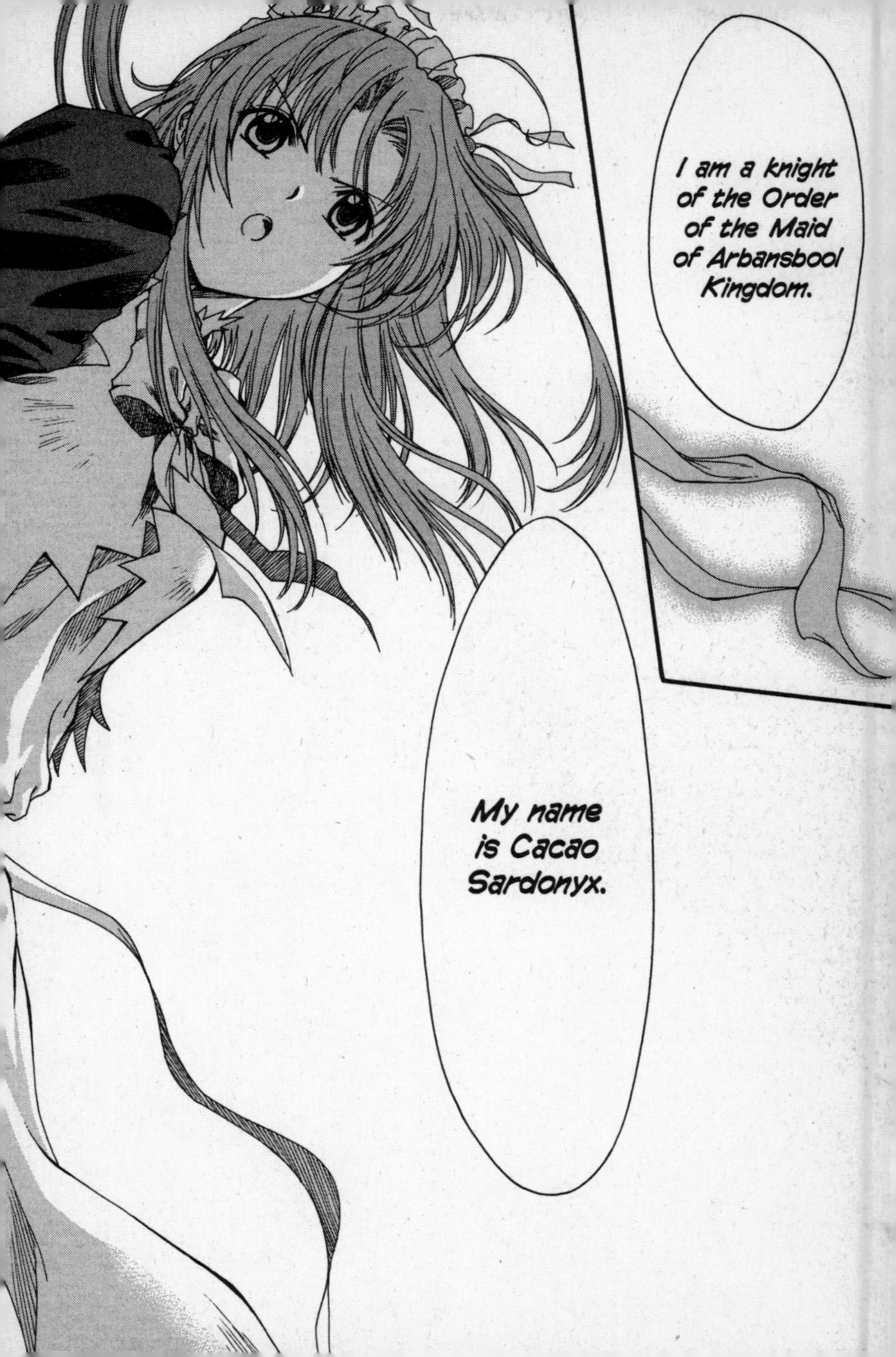
I am a knight of the Order of the Maid of Arbansbool Kingdom.
My name is Cacao Sardonyx.

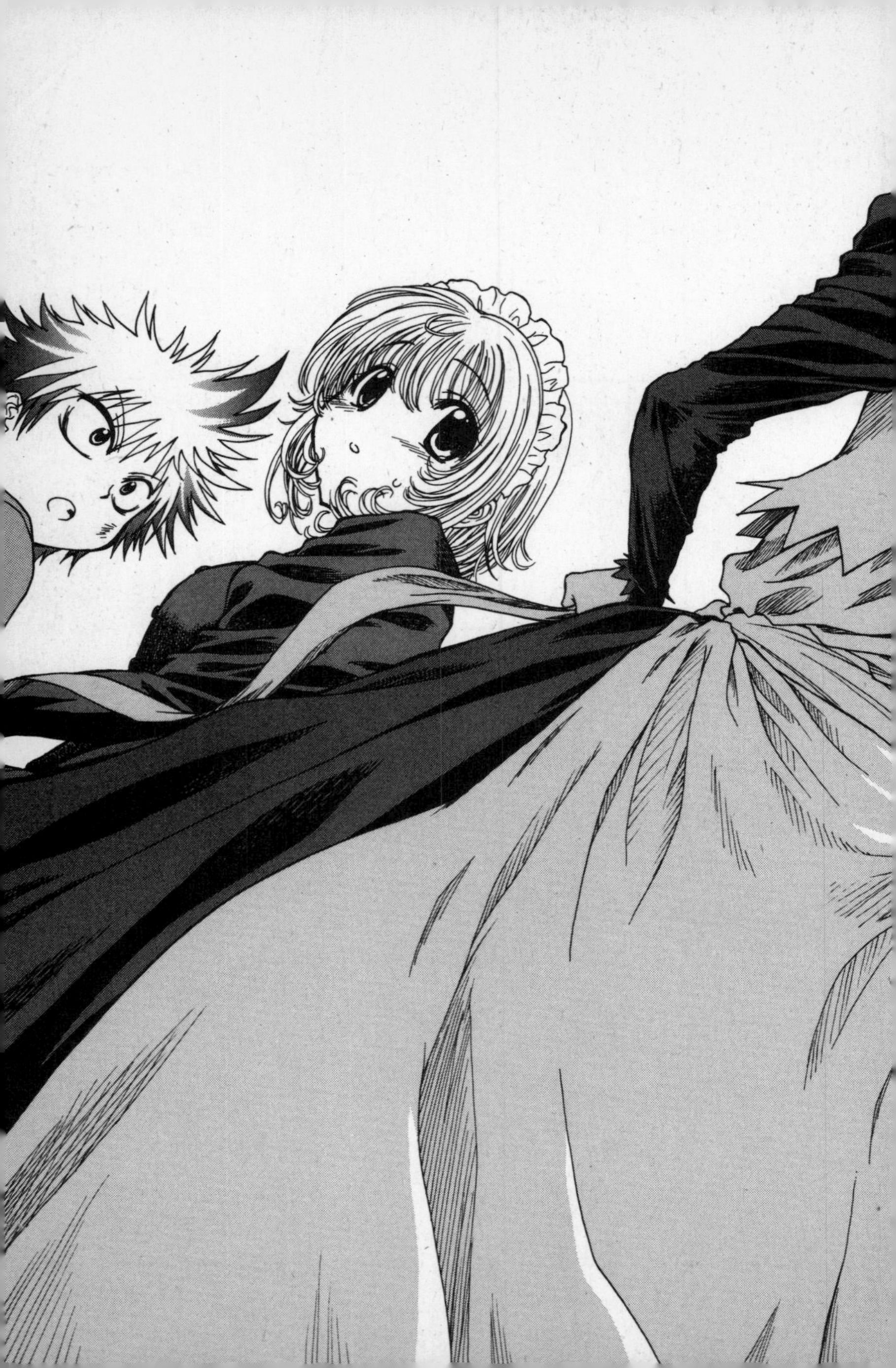

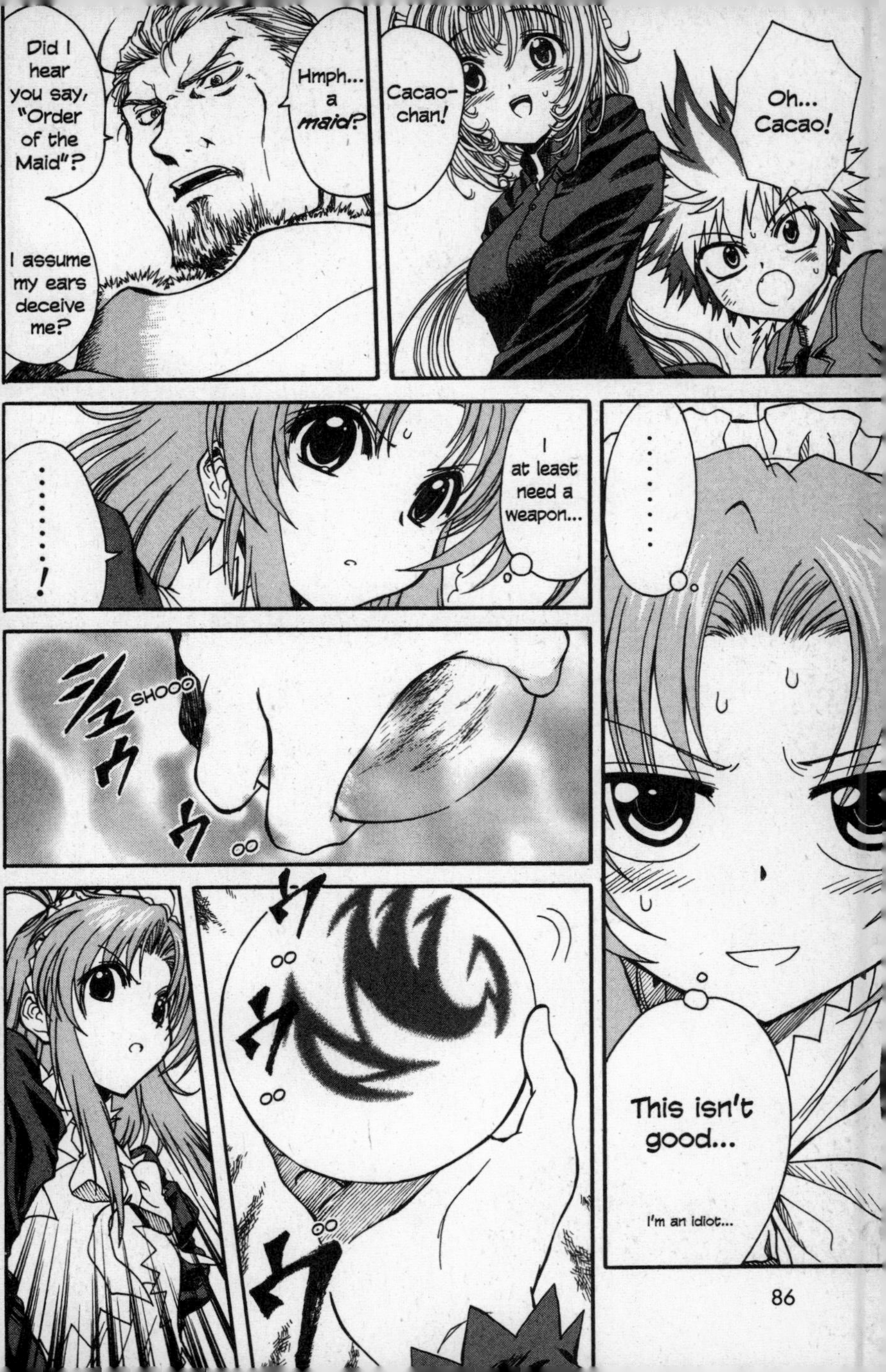
Oh... Cacao!
Cacao-chan!
Hmph... a *maid*?
Did I hear you say, "Order of the Maid"?
I assume my ears deceive me?
....
This isn't good...
I'm an idiot...
I at least need a weapon...
......!
SHOOO

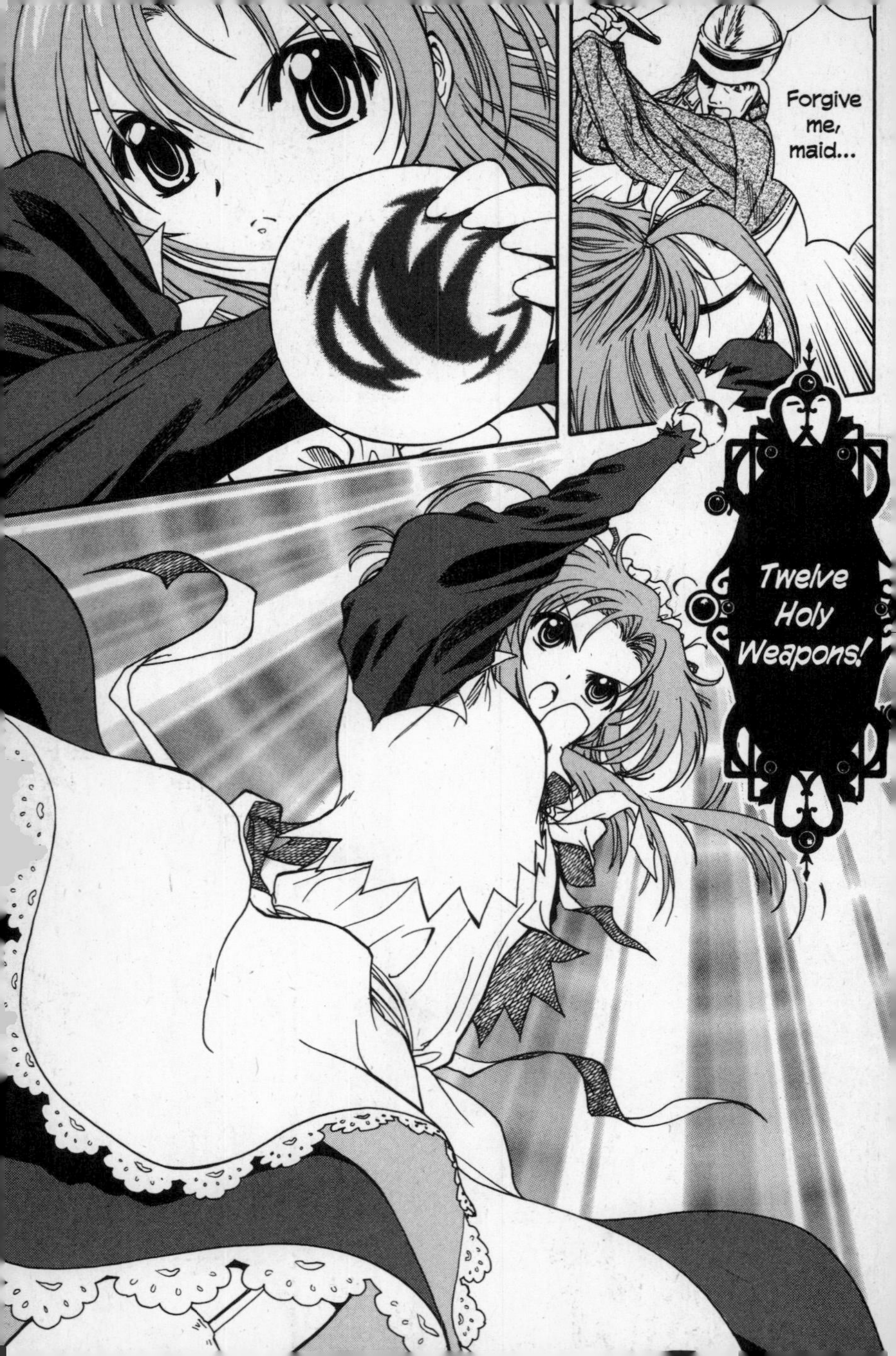
Forgive me, maid...
Twelve Holy Weapons!

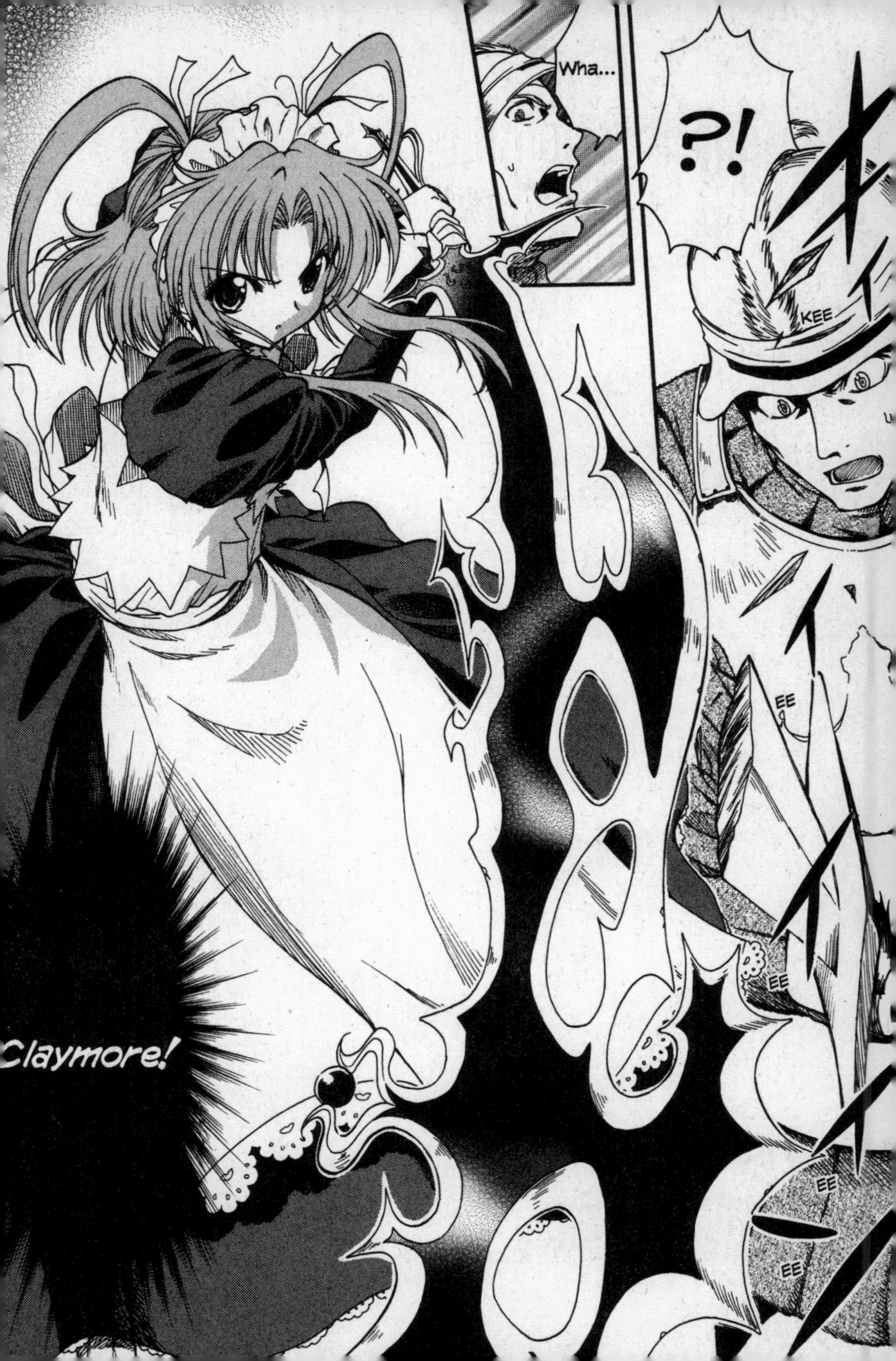
?!
KEE
EE
EE
EE
EE
Wha...
Claymore!

!?
What the...
URK
Gwah!
BAM
PLOP
PLOP
!?
What is this?!
Just a little money I earned.
There are some coaches down the street.
Buy or borrow one, and get out of here!
Wow! You're great!
I'll give you my autograph and a kiss to show my gratitude!
DASH
Ugh...
I don't need that.

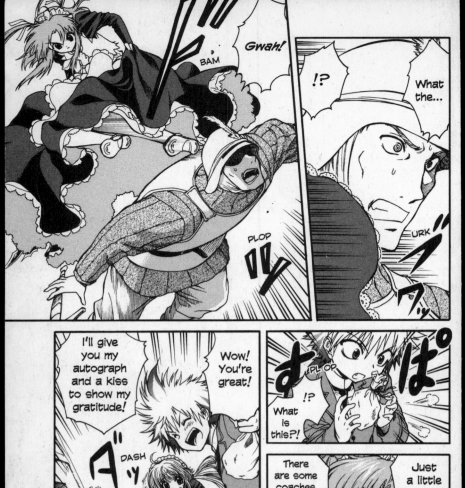

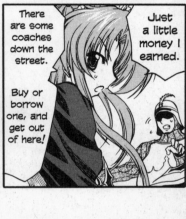

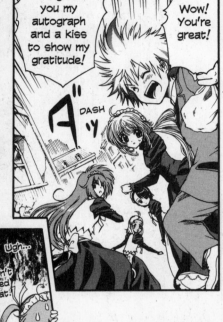

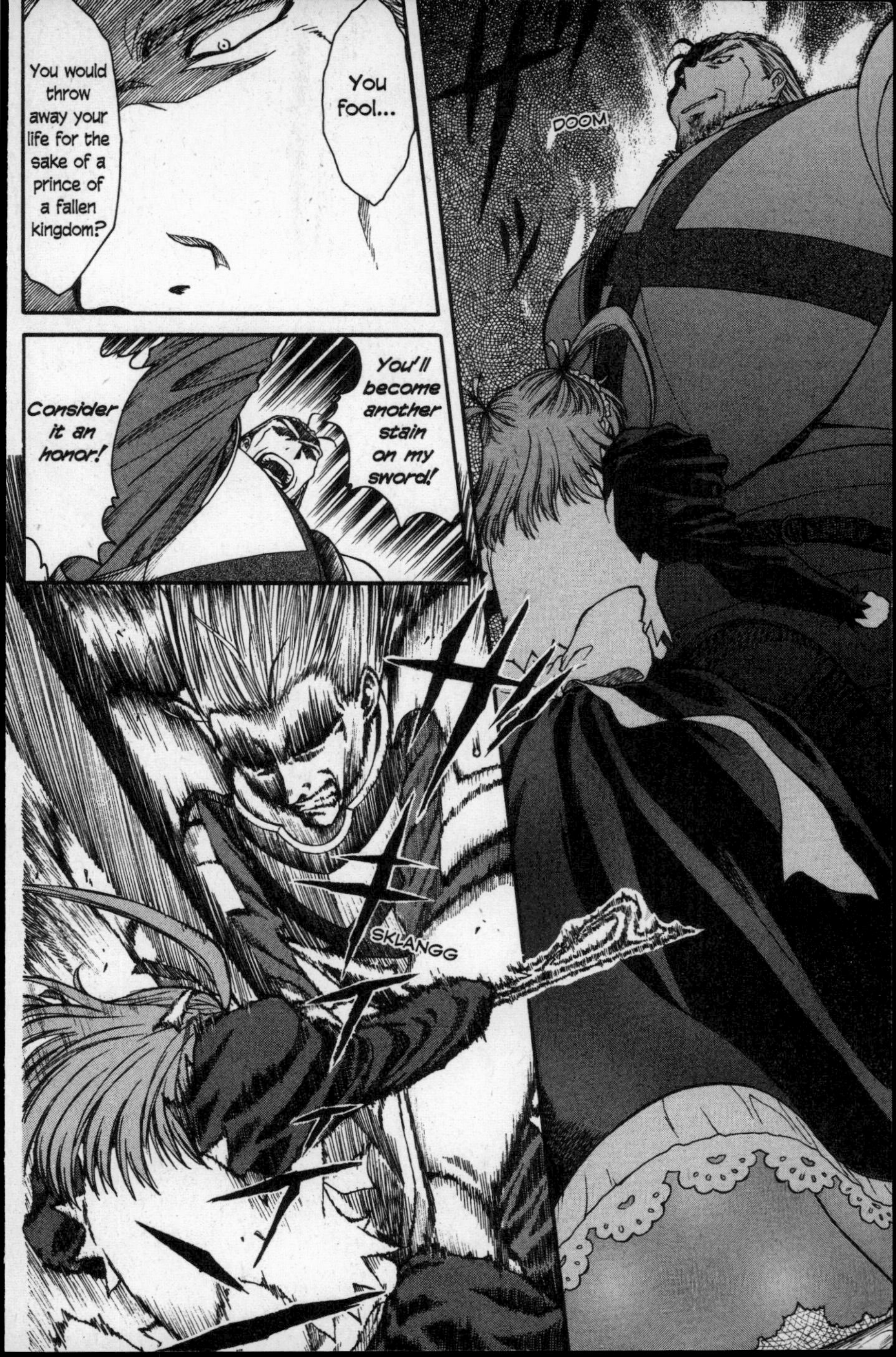
DOOM
You fool...
You would throw away your life for the sake of a prince of a fallen kingdom?
You'll become another stain on my sword!
Consider it an honor!
SKLANGG

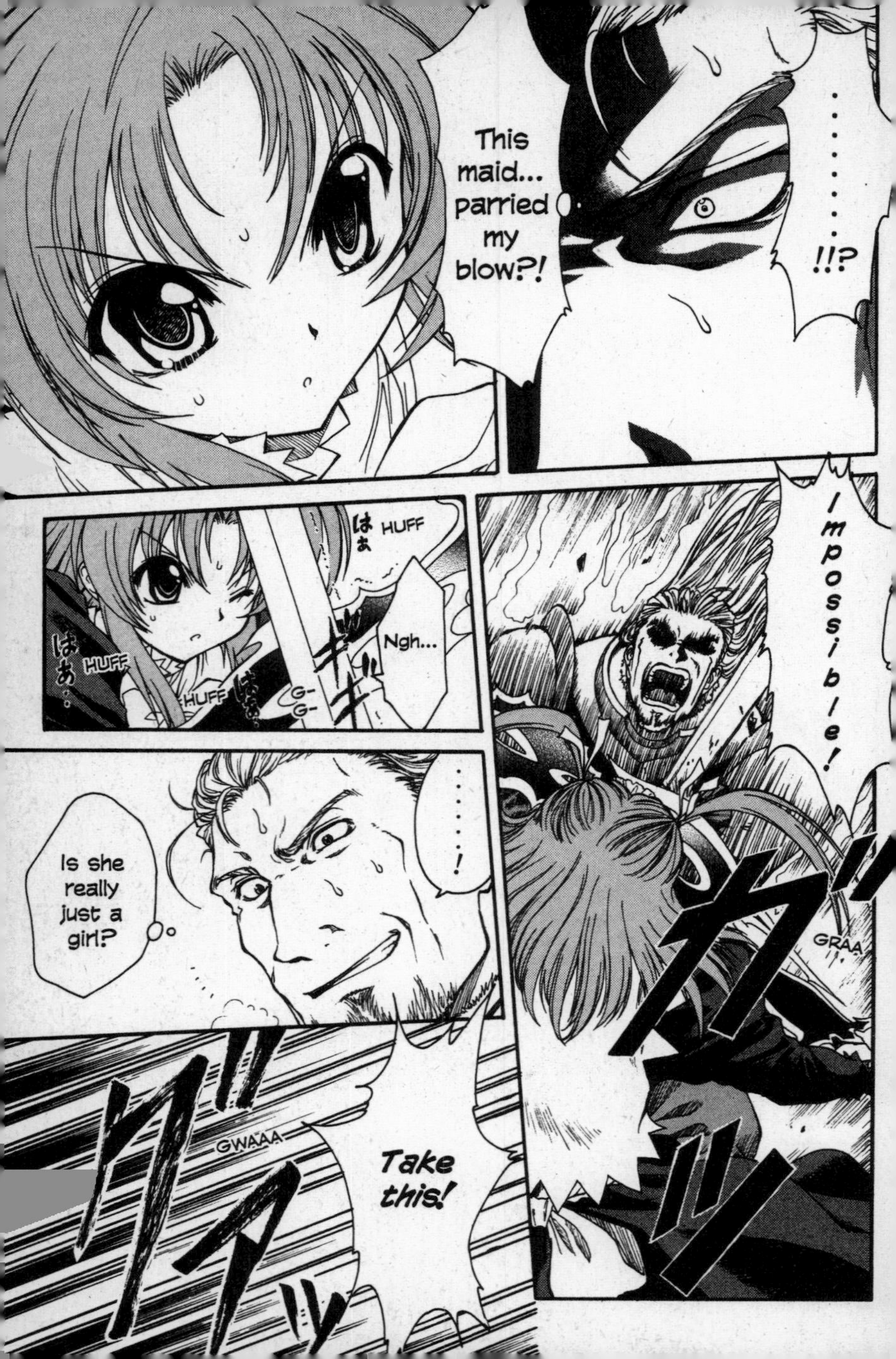
......!!?
This maid... parried my blow?!
Impossible!
GRAA
はぁ HUFF
Ngh...
G- G-
はぁ HUFF
HUFF
......!
Is she really just a girl?
GWAAA
Take this!

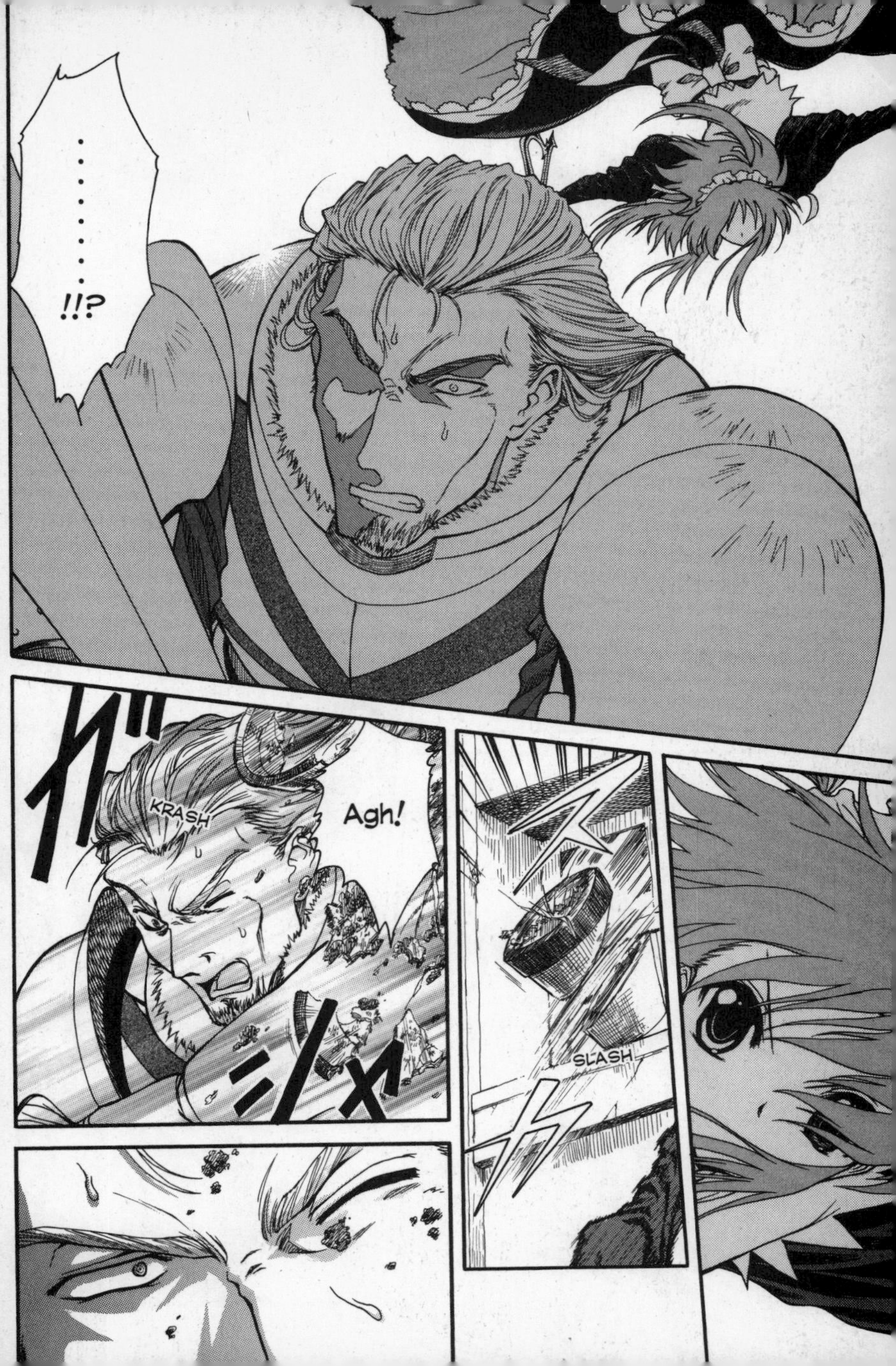
......
!!?
SLASH
Agh!
KRASH

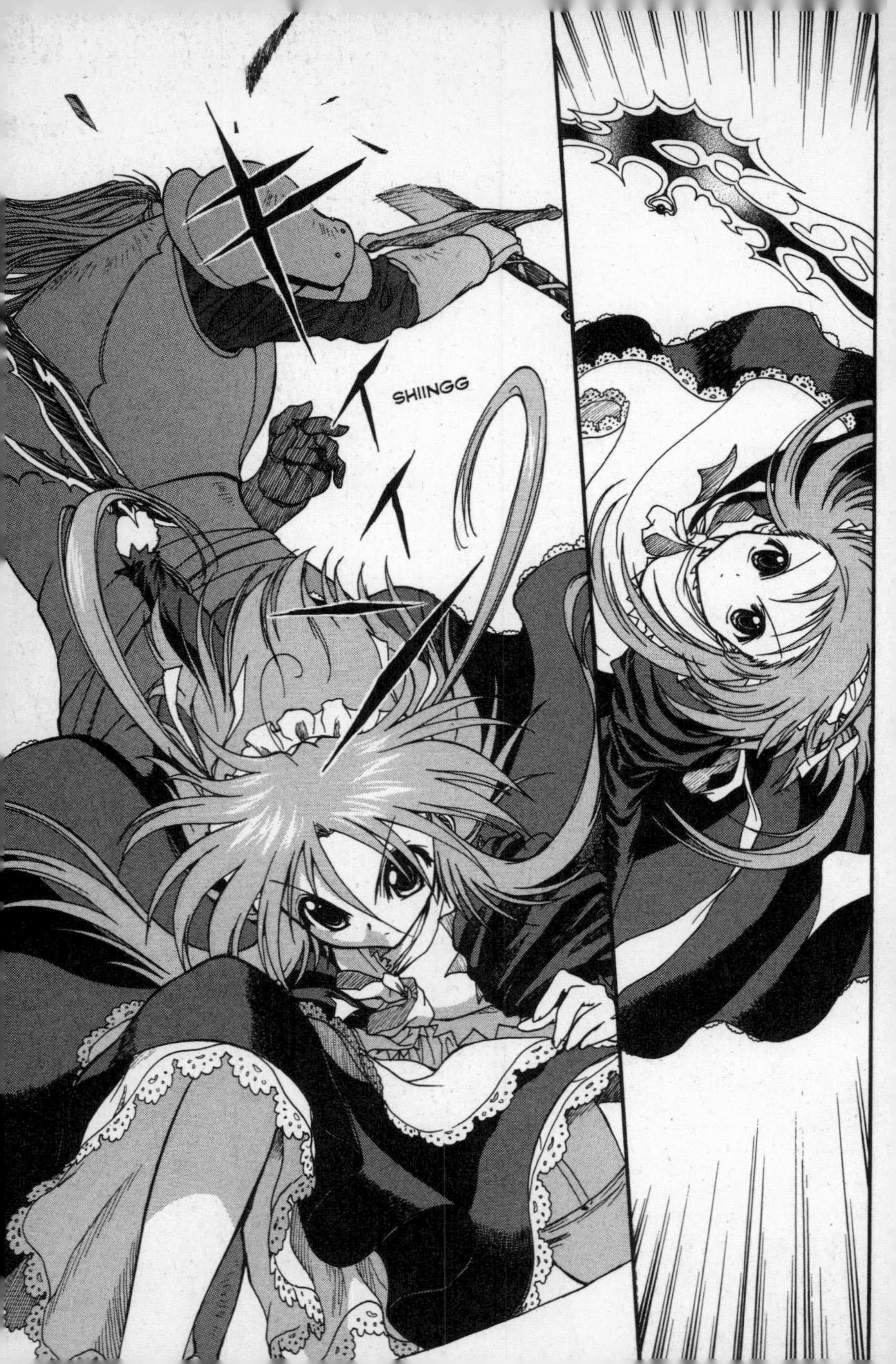
SHIINGG

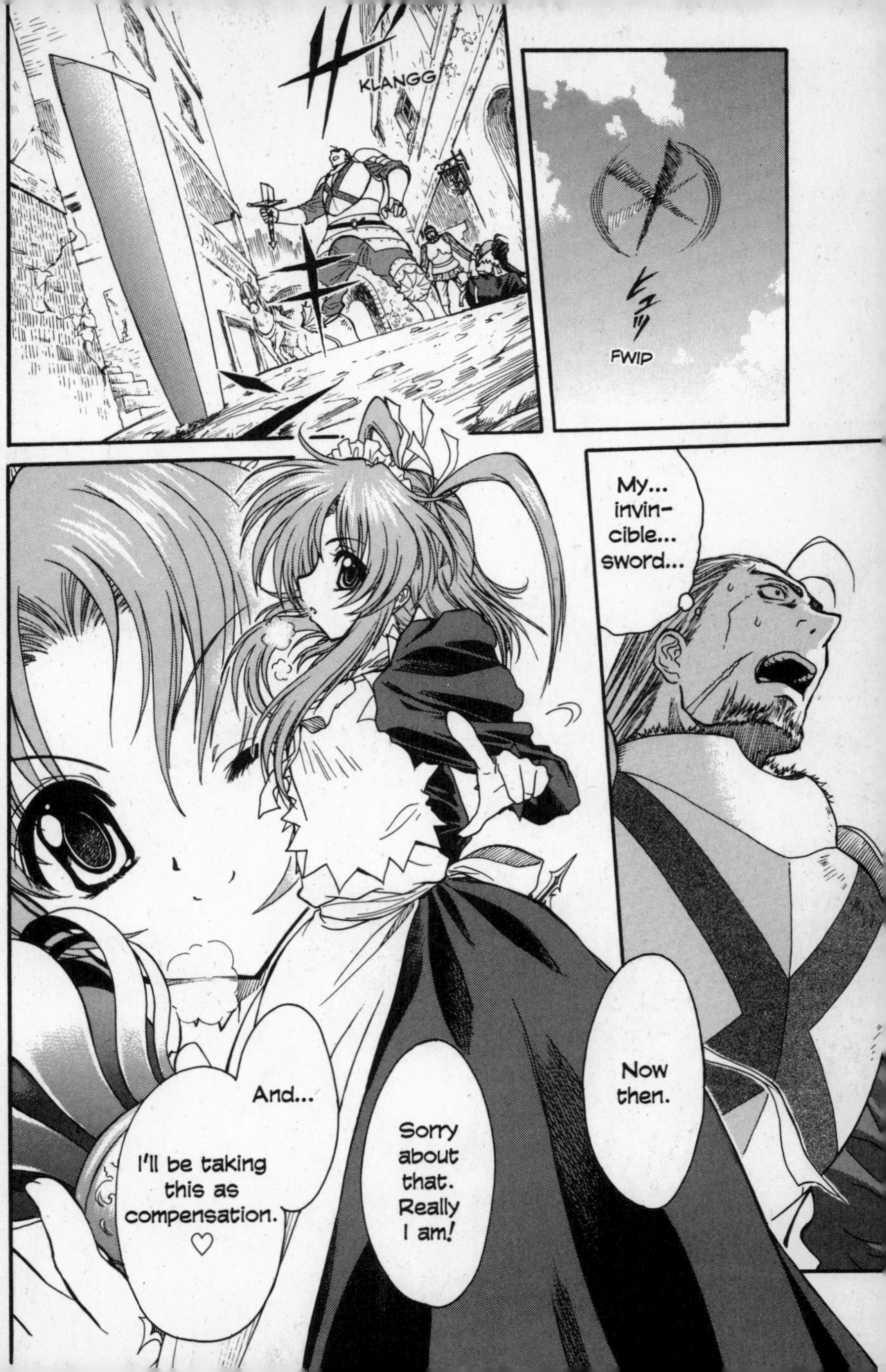
ヒュッ
FWIP
KLANGG
My... invincible... sword...
Now then.
Sorry about that. Really I am!
And...
I'll be taking this as compensation. ♡

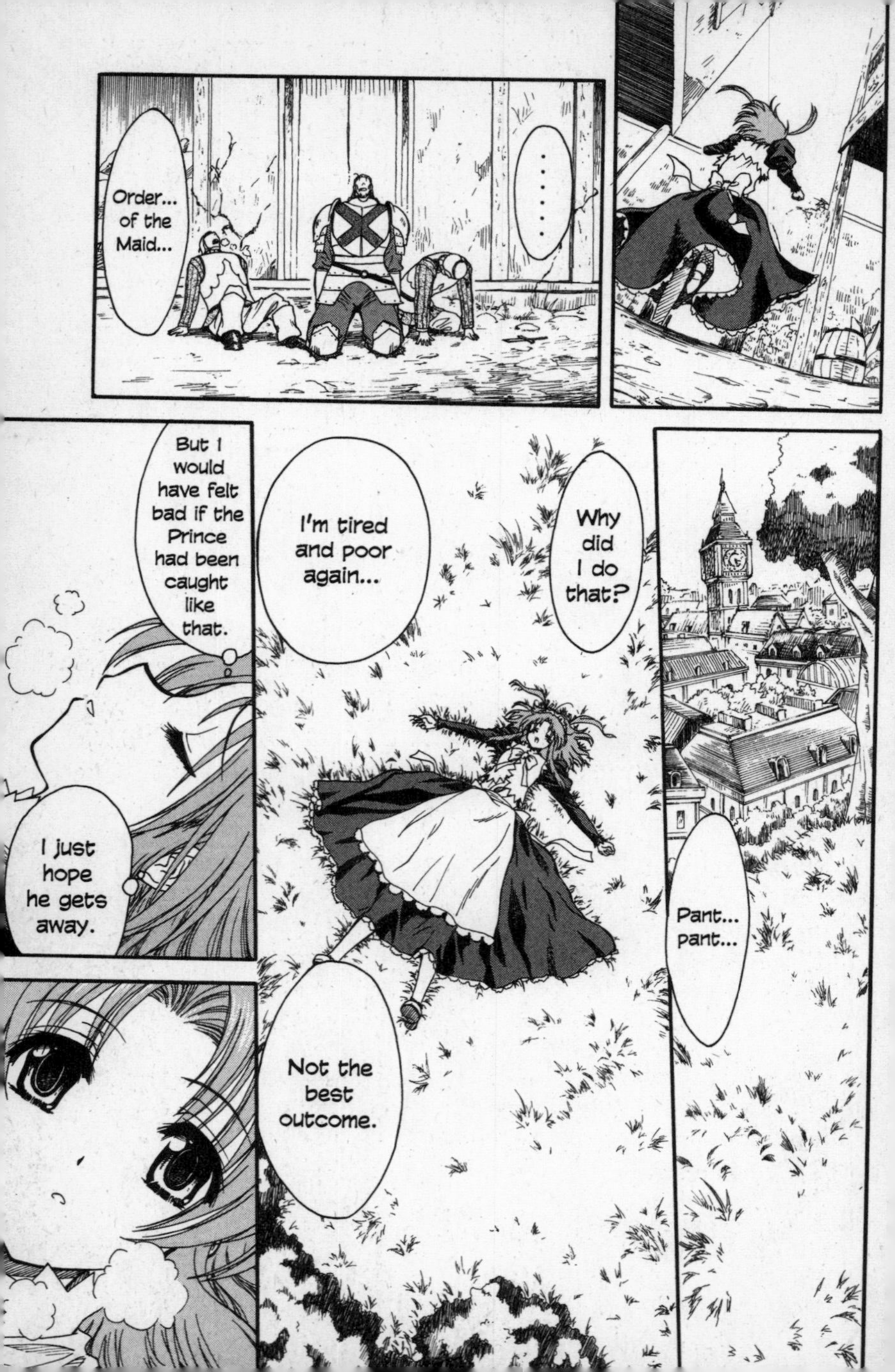
.....
Order... of the Maid...
Pant... pant...
Why did I do that?
I'm tired and poor again...
Not the best outcome.
But I would have felt bad if the Prince had been caught like that.
I just hope he gets away.

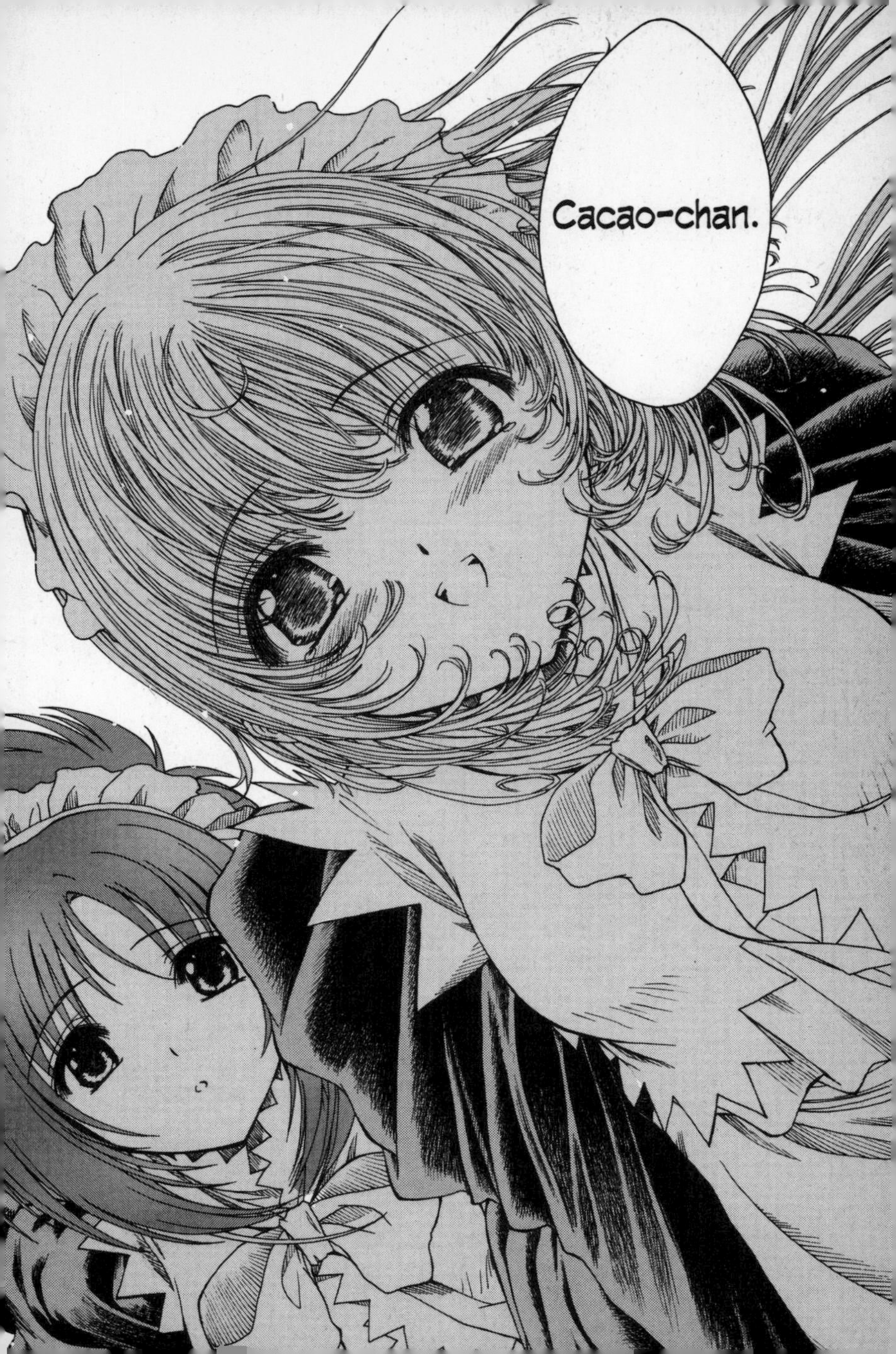
Cacao-chan.

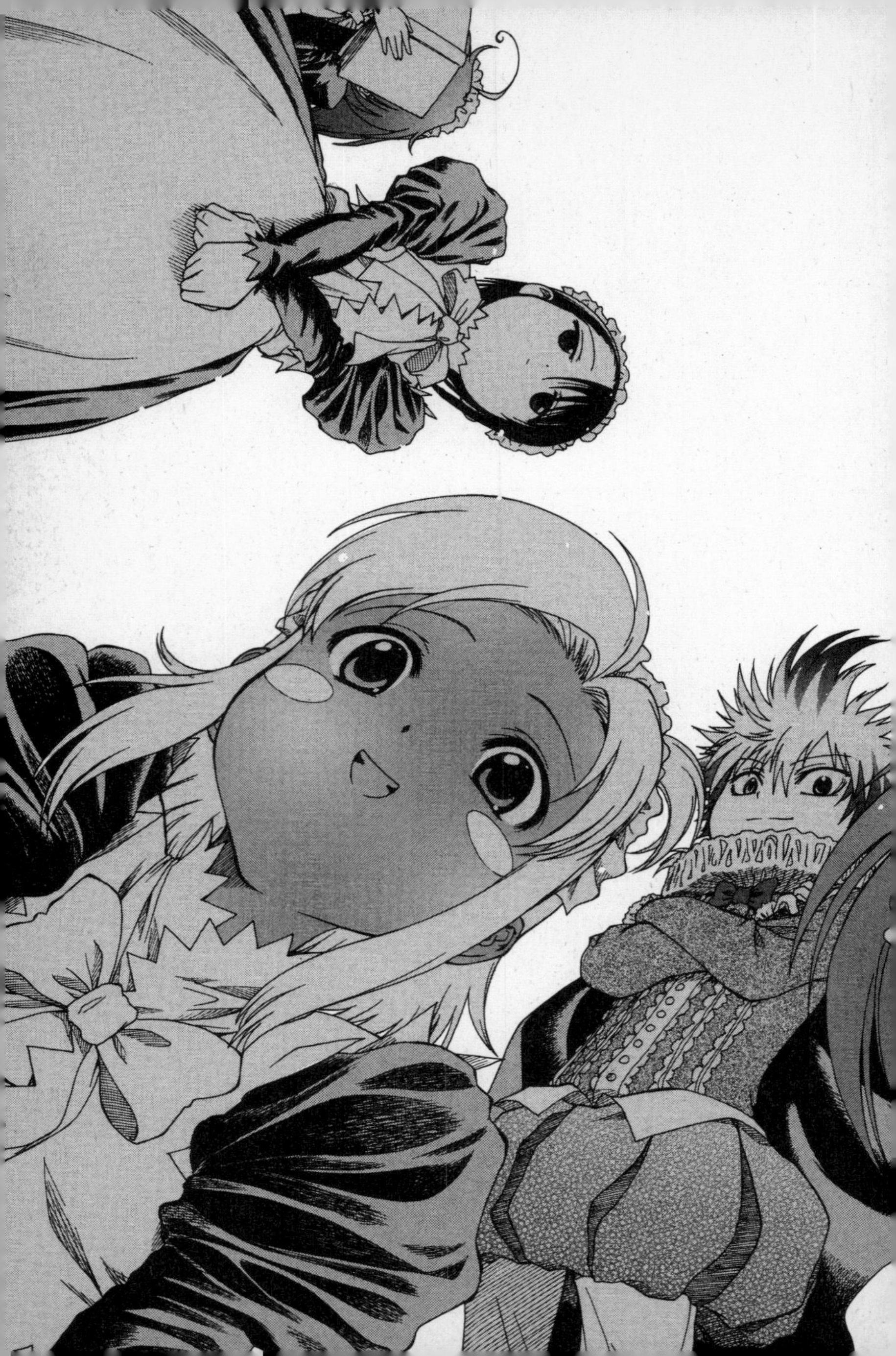

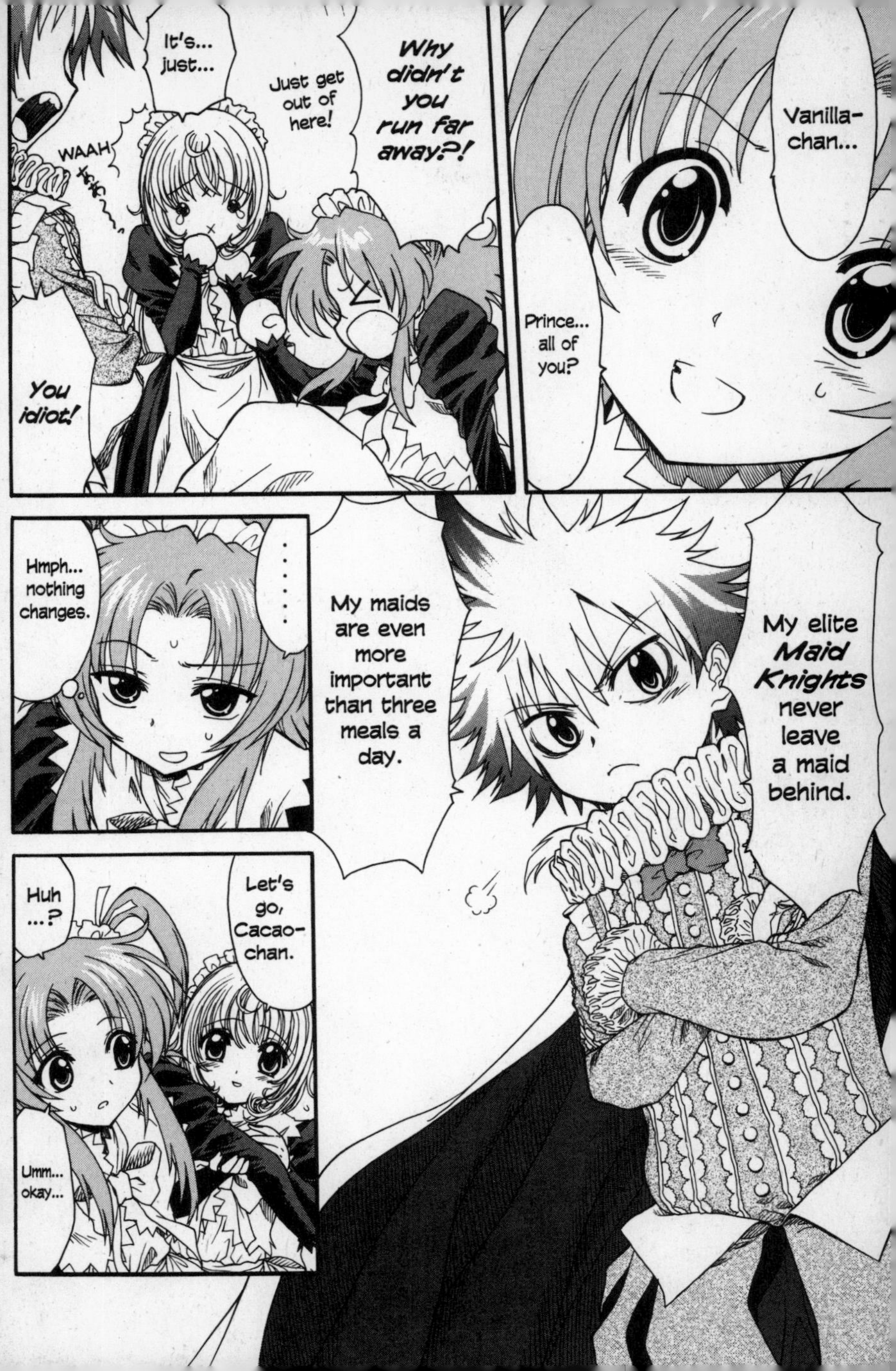
Vanilla-chan...
Prince... all of you?
Why didn't you run far away?!
Just get out of here!
It's... just...
WAAH
You idiot!
My elite Maid Knights never leave a maid behind.
My maids are even more important than three meals a day.
......
Hmph... nothing changes.
Let's go, Cacao-chan.
Huh ...?
Umm... okay...

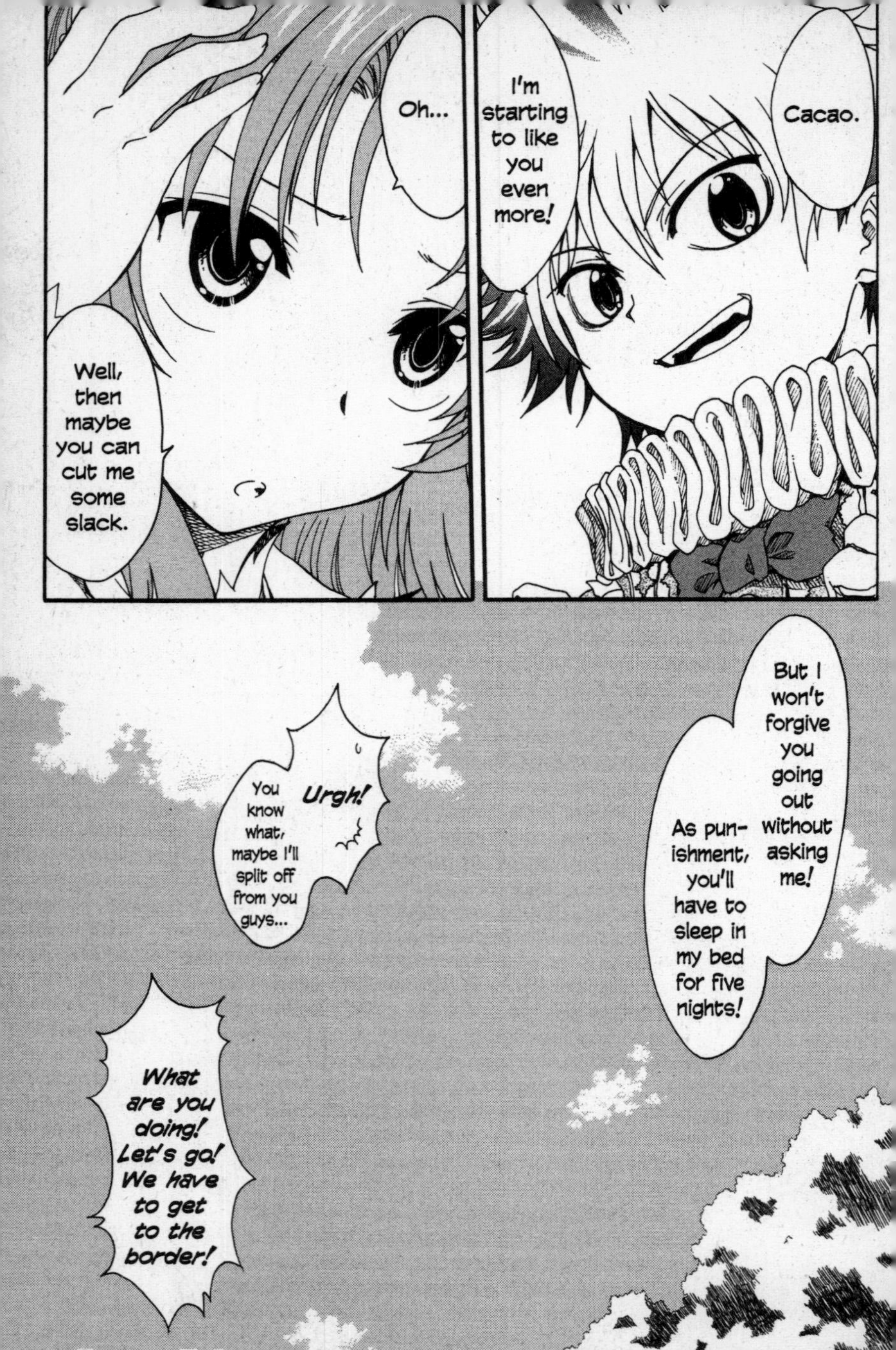
Cacao.
I'm starting to like you even more!
Oh...
Well, then maybe you can cut me some slack.
But I won't forgive you going out without asking me!
As punishment, you'll have to sleep in my bed for five nights!
Urgh!
You know what, maybe I'll split off from you guys...
What are you doing! Let's go! We have to get to the border!

Chapter 2—End

Try saying "ni."

The Japanese word for "two" is "ni"...
Yeah?
Did you know, you can't help smiling when you say it?
...Really...
にー NI!
にー NI!
There it is! Just a little!
Don't cover your mouth!
I see it!
Get her to say it!
Good idea!
Say "Ni"!
NI.
Prince
I kinda guessed that would happen.
Only in a manga...

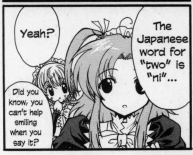

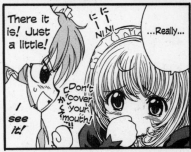

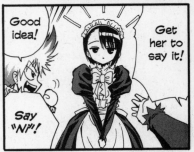

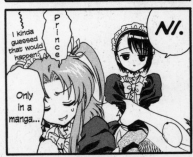

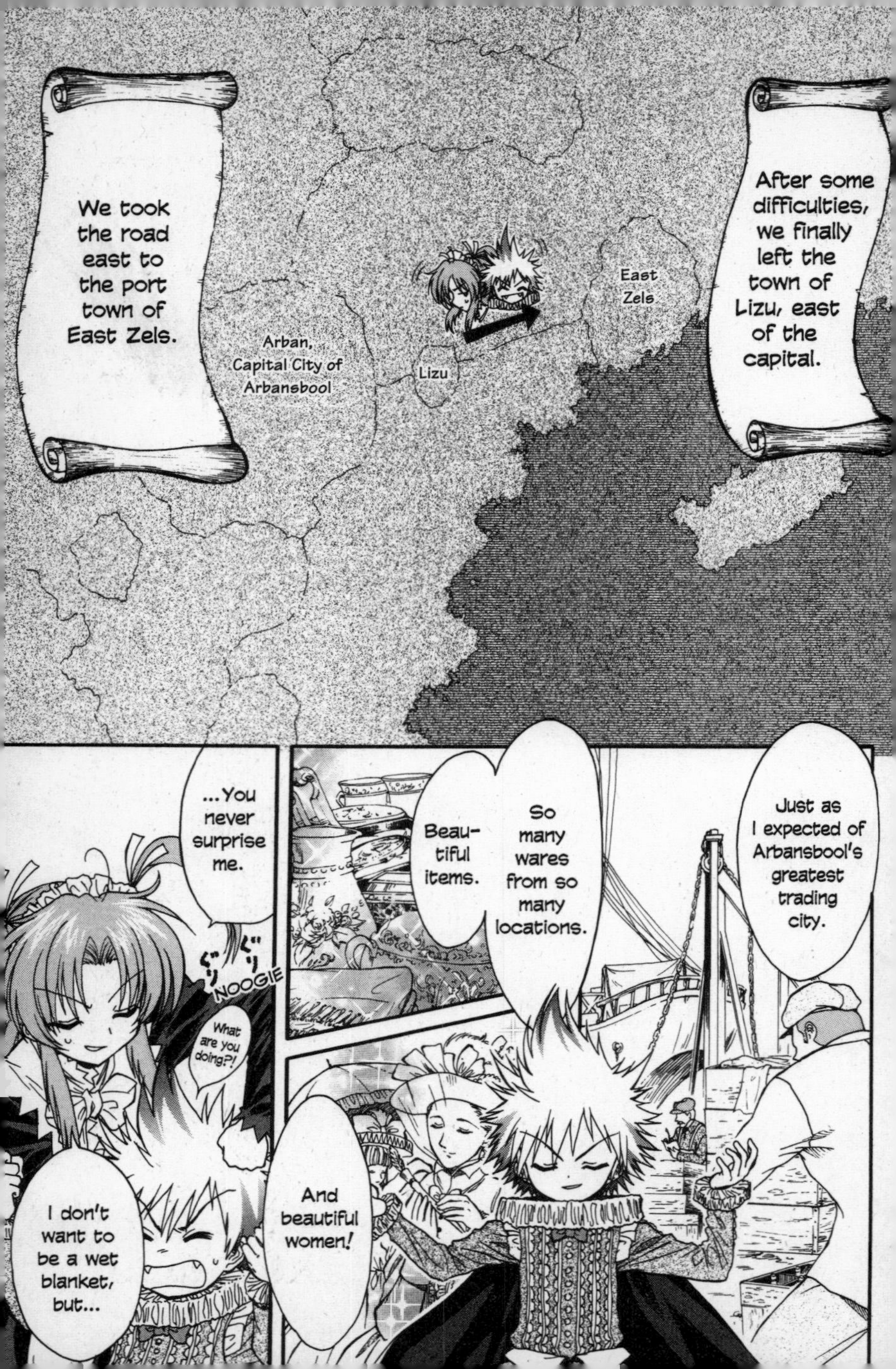
After some difficulties, we finally left the town of Lizu, east of the capital.
East Zels
Lizu
Arban, Capital City of Arbansbool
We took the road east to the port town of East Zels.
Just as I expected of Arbansbool's greatest trading city.
So many wares from so many locations.
Beau-tiful items.
And beautiful women!
...You never surprise me.
NOOGIE
What are you doing?!
I don't want to be a wet blanket, but...

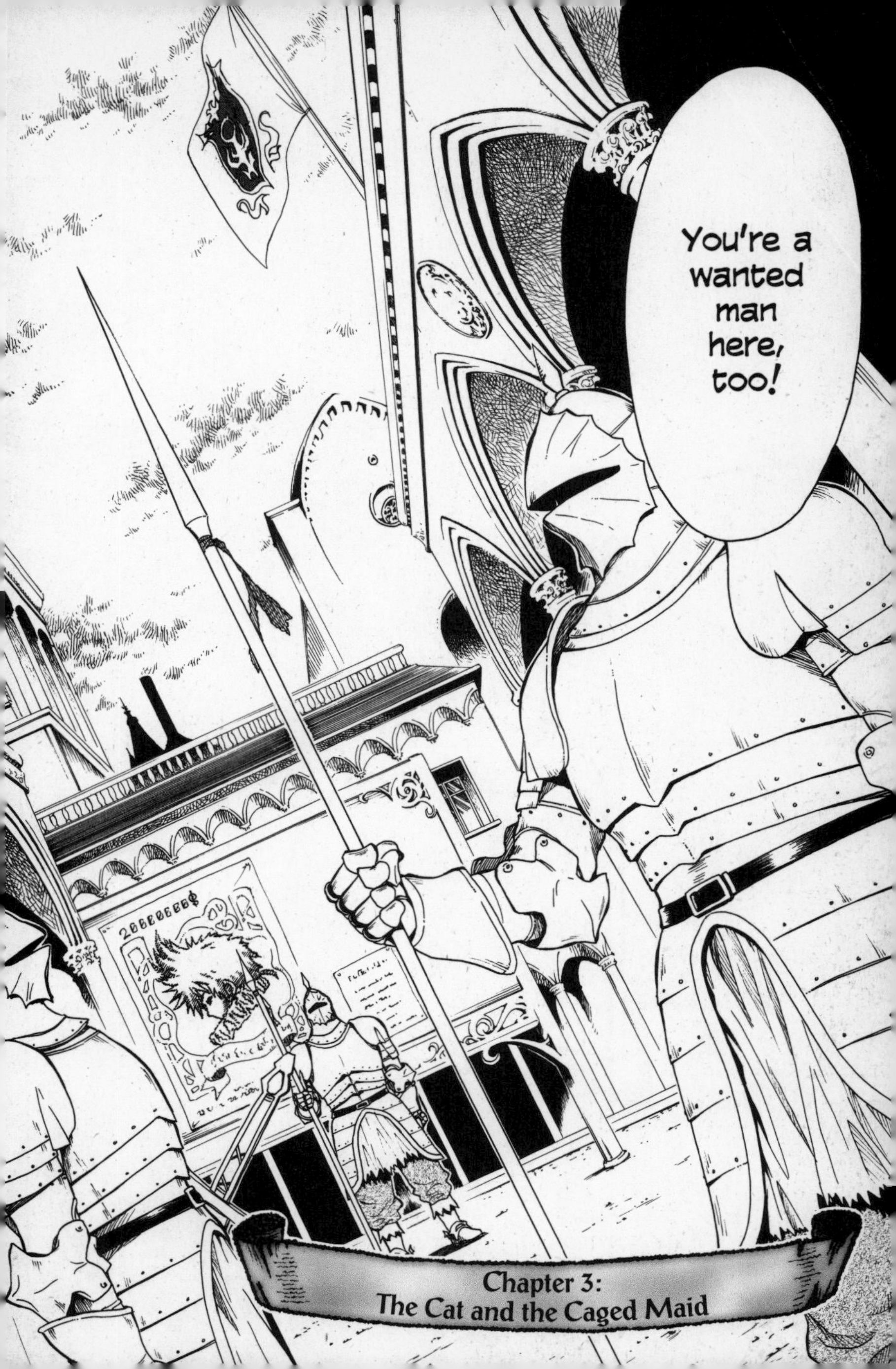
You're a wanted man here, too!
Chapter 3: The Cat and the Caged Maid

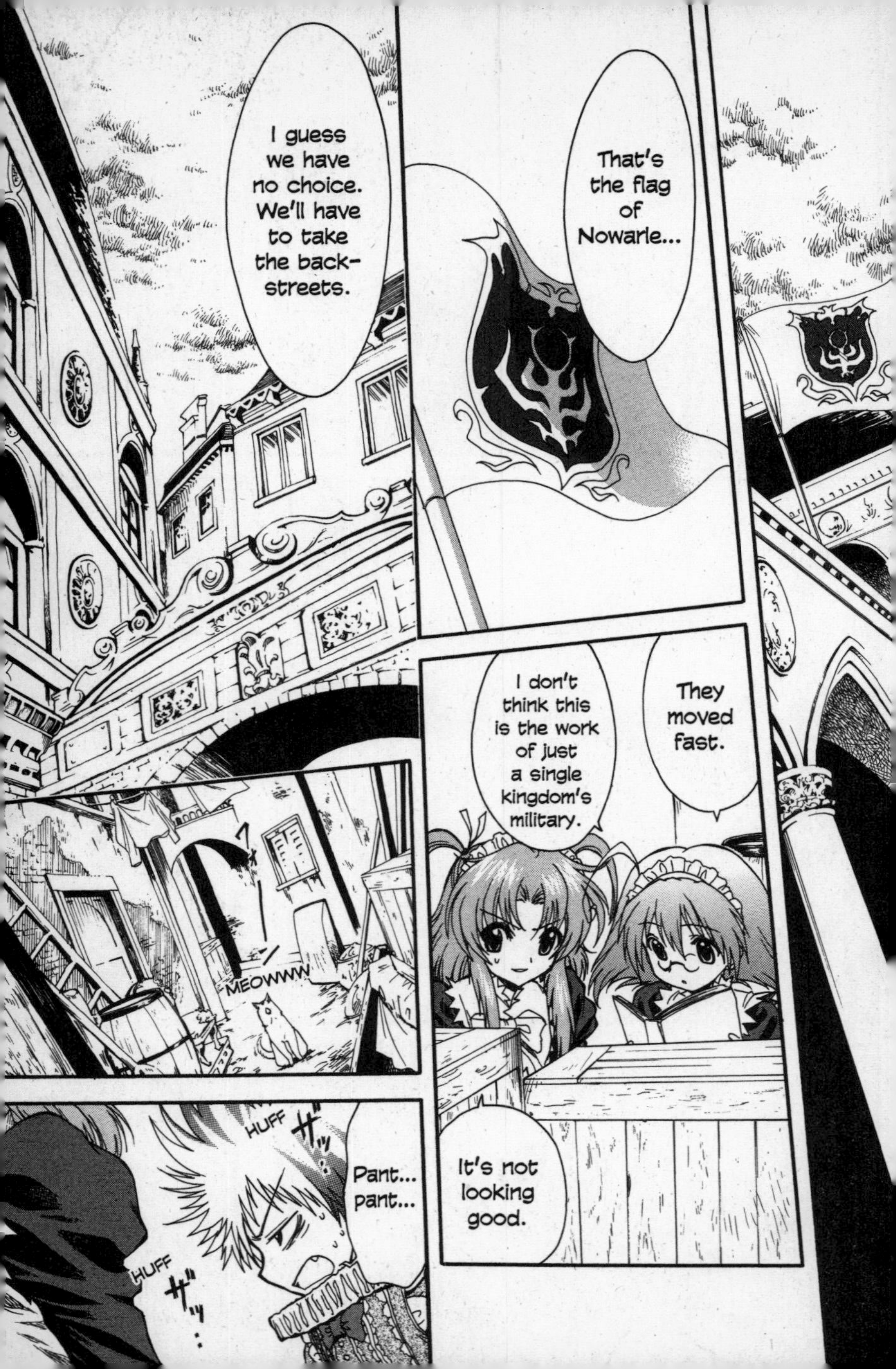
That's the flag of Nowarle...
I guess we have no choice. We'll have to take the back-streets.
They moved fast.
I don't think this is the work of just a single kingdom's military.
It's not looking good.
MEOWWW
HUFF
Pant... pant...
HUFF

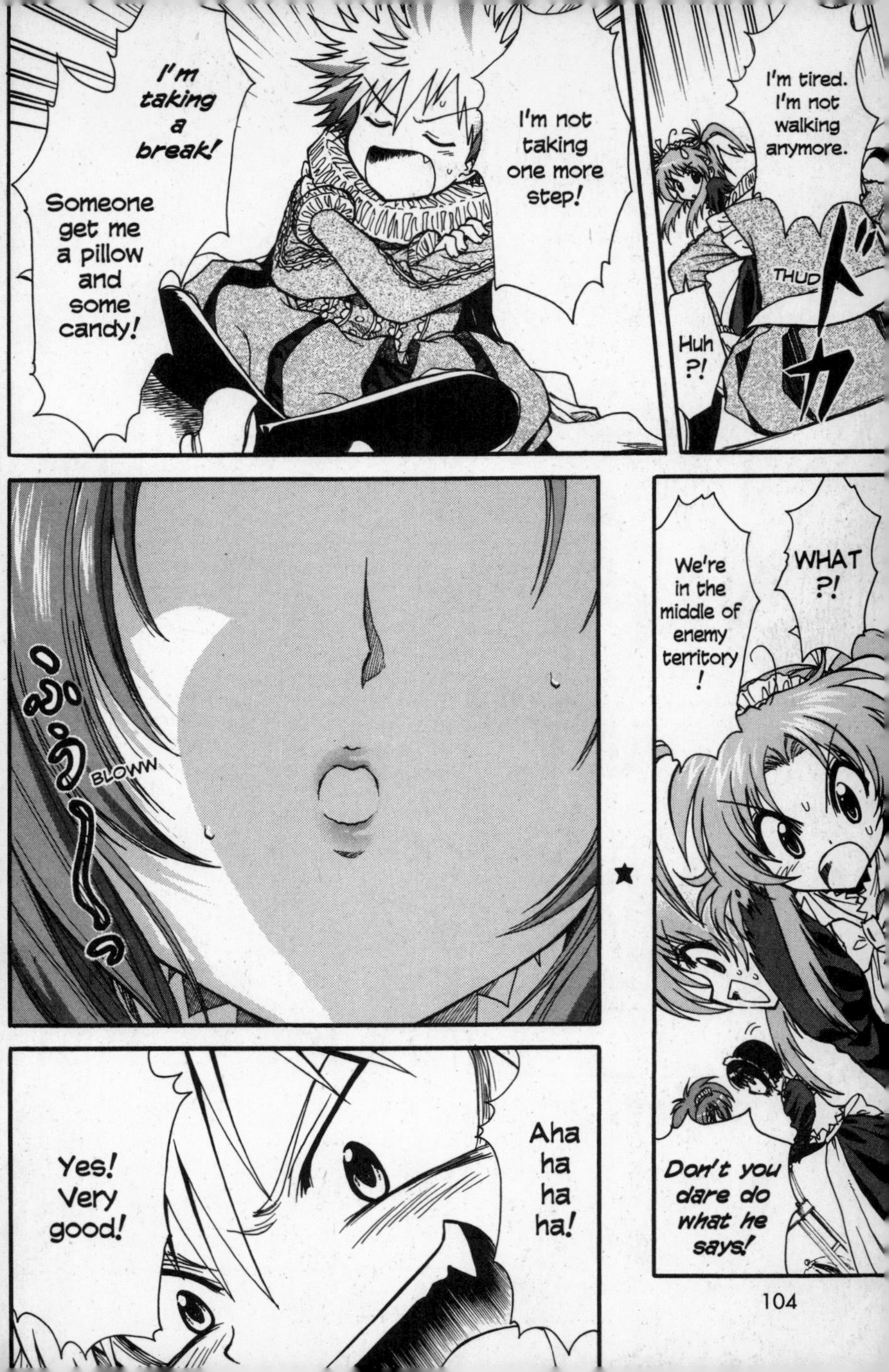
I'm tired. I'm not walking anymore.
THUD
Huh?!
I'm not taking one more step!
I'm taking a break!
Someone get me a pillow and some candy!
WHAT?!
We're in the middle of enemy territory!
Don't you dare do what he says!
BLOWW
Aha ha ha ha!
Yes! Very good!

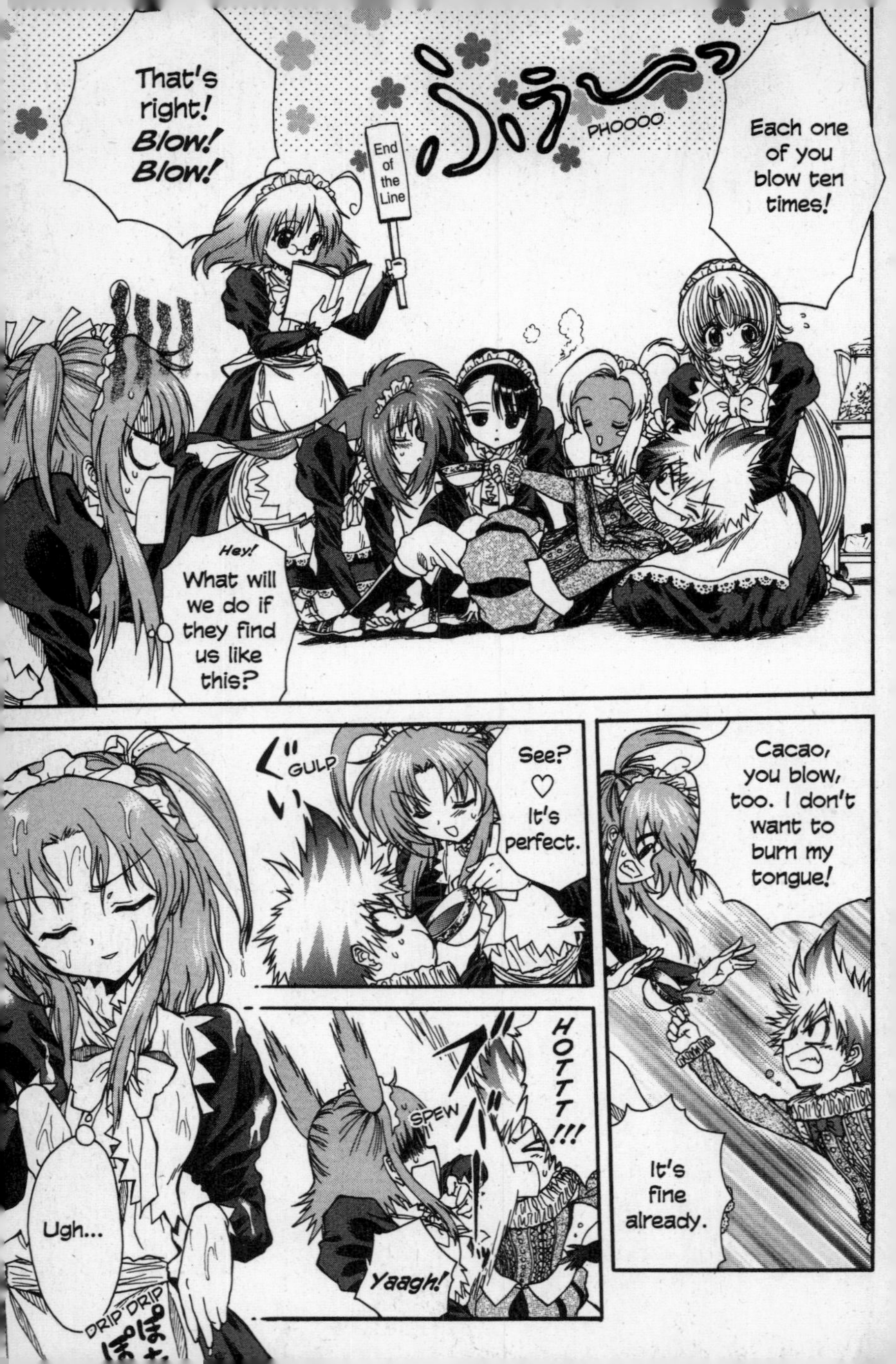
Each one of you blow ten times!
PHOOOO
That's right! Blow! Blow!
End of the Line
Hey!
What will we do if they find us like this?
Cacao, you blow, too. I don't want to burn my tongue!
It's fine already.
See? ♡ It's perfect.
GULP
HOTTT!!!
SPEW
Yaagh!
Ugh...
DRIP DRIP

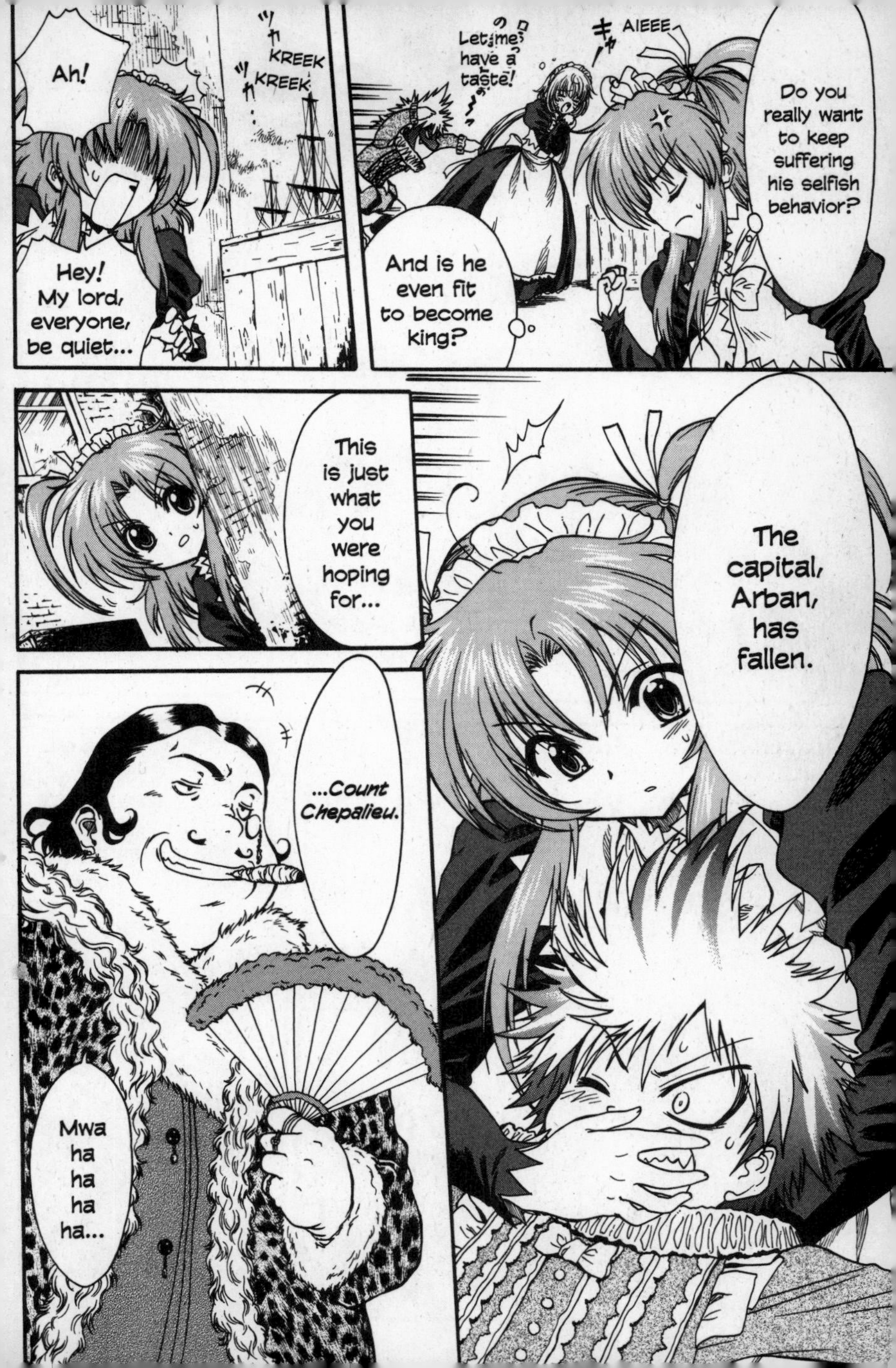

Do you really want to keep suffering his selfish behavior?
And is he even fit to become king?
AIEEE
Let me have a taste!
Ah!
KREEK
KREEK
Hey! My lord, everyone, be quiet...
The capital, Arban, has fallen.
This is just what you were hoping for...
...Count Chepalieu.
Mwa ha ha ha ha ha...

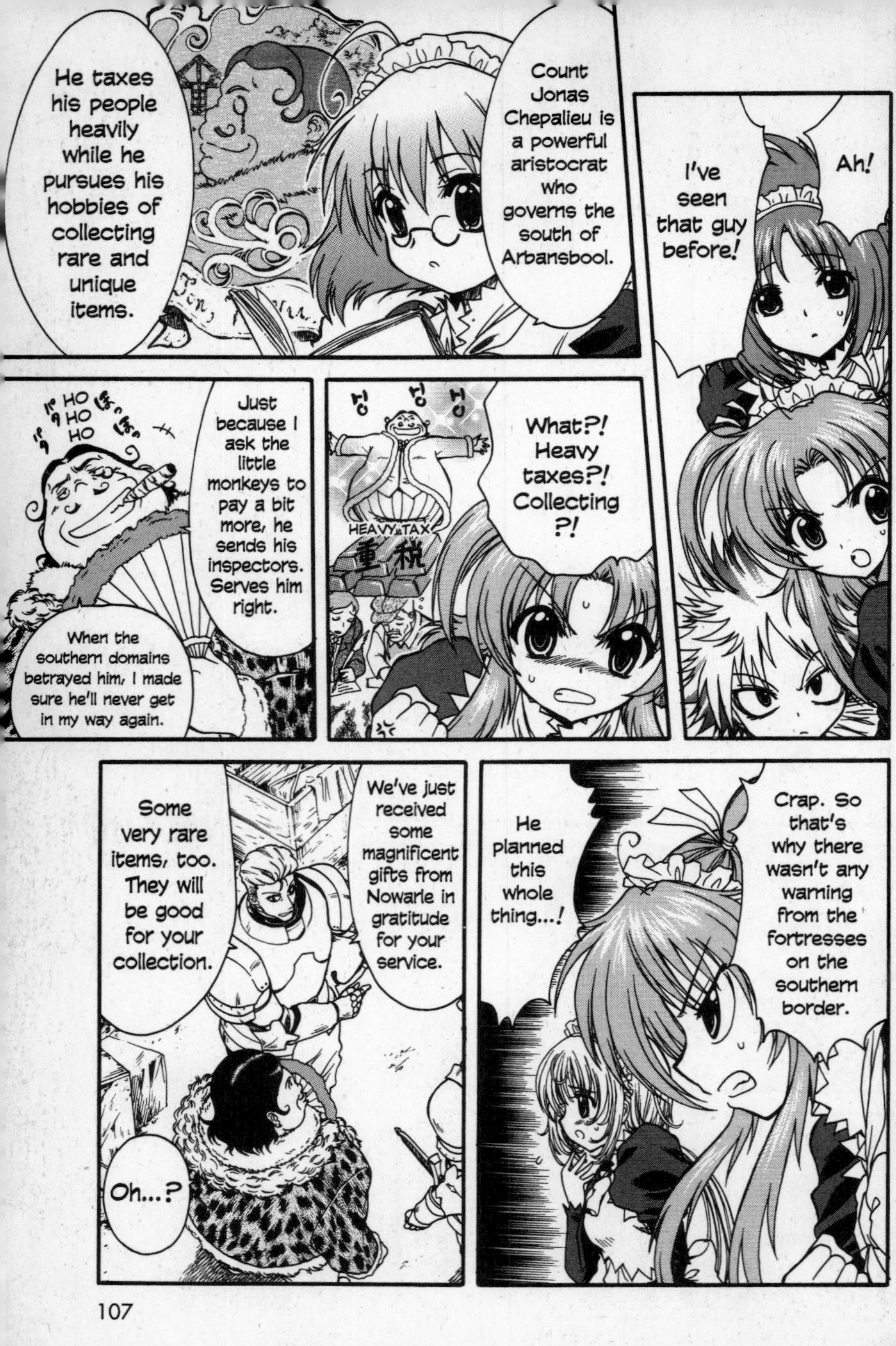
Count Jonas Chepalieu is a powerful aristocrat who governs the south of Arbansbool.
He taxes his people heavily while he pursues his hobbies of collecting rare and unique items.
Ah!
I've seen that guy before!
What?! Heavy taxes?! Collecting?!
HEAVY TAX
重税
HO HO HO
Just because I ask the little monkeys to pay a bit more, he sends his inspectors. Serves him right.
When the southern domains betrayed him, I made sure he'll never get in my way again.
Crap. So that's why there wasn't any warning from the fortresses on the southern border.
He planned this whole thing...!
We've just received some magnificent gifts from Nowarle in gratitude for your service.
Some very rare items, too. They will be good for your collection.
Oh...?

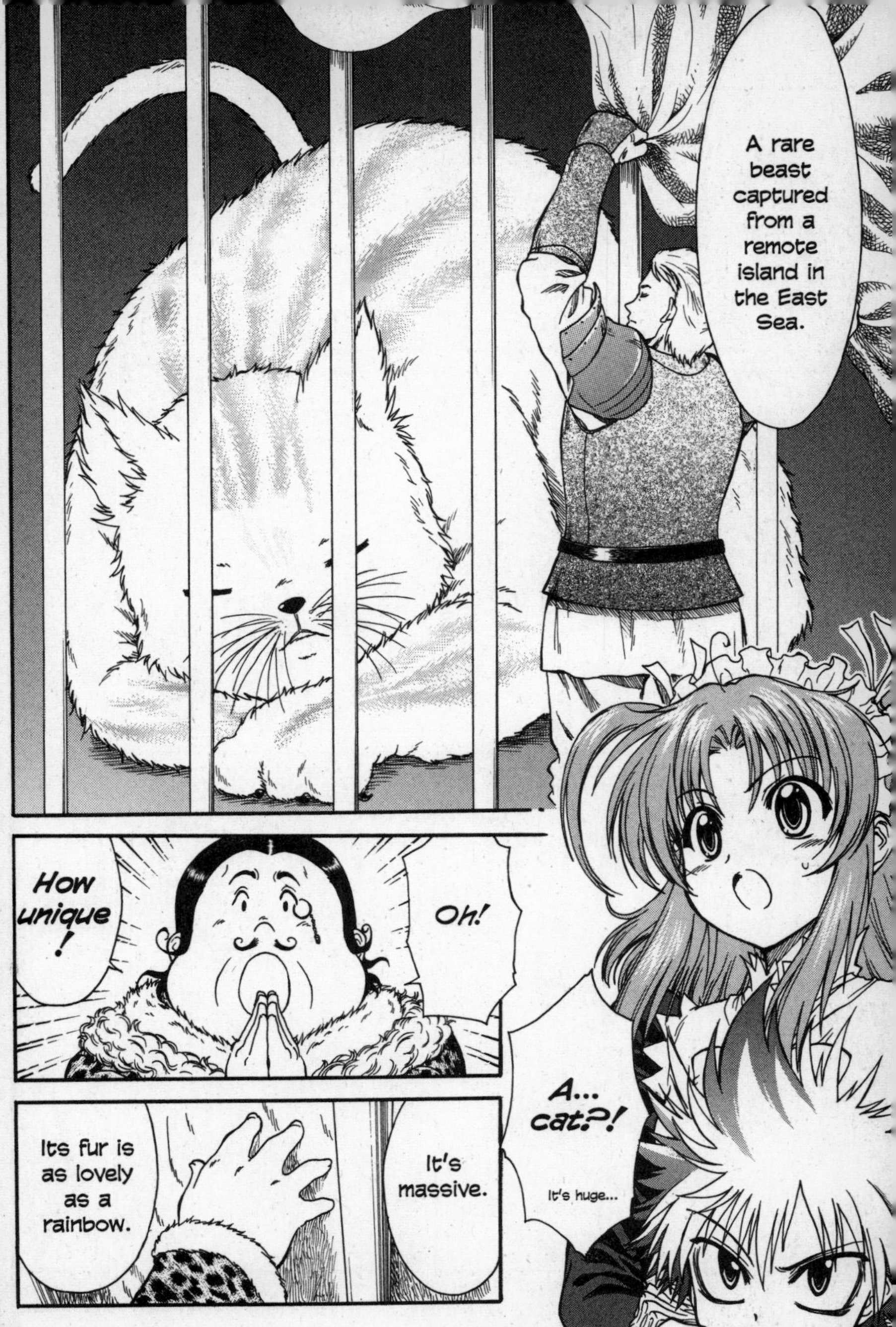
A rare beast captured from a remote island in the East Sea.
A... cat?!
It's huge...
Oh!
How unique!
It's massive.
Its fur is as lovely as a rainbow.

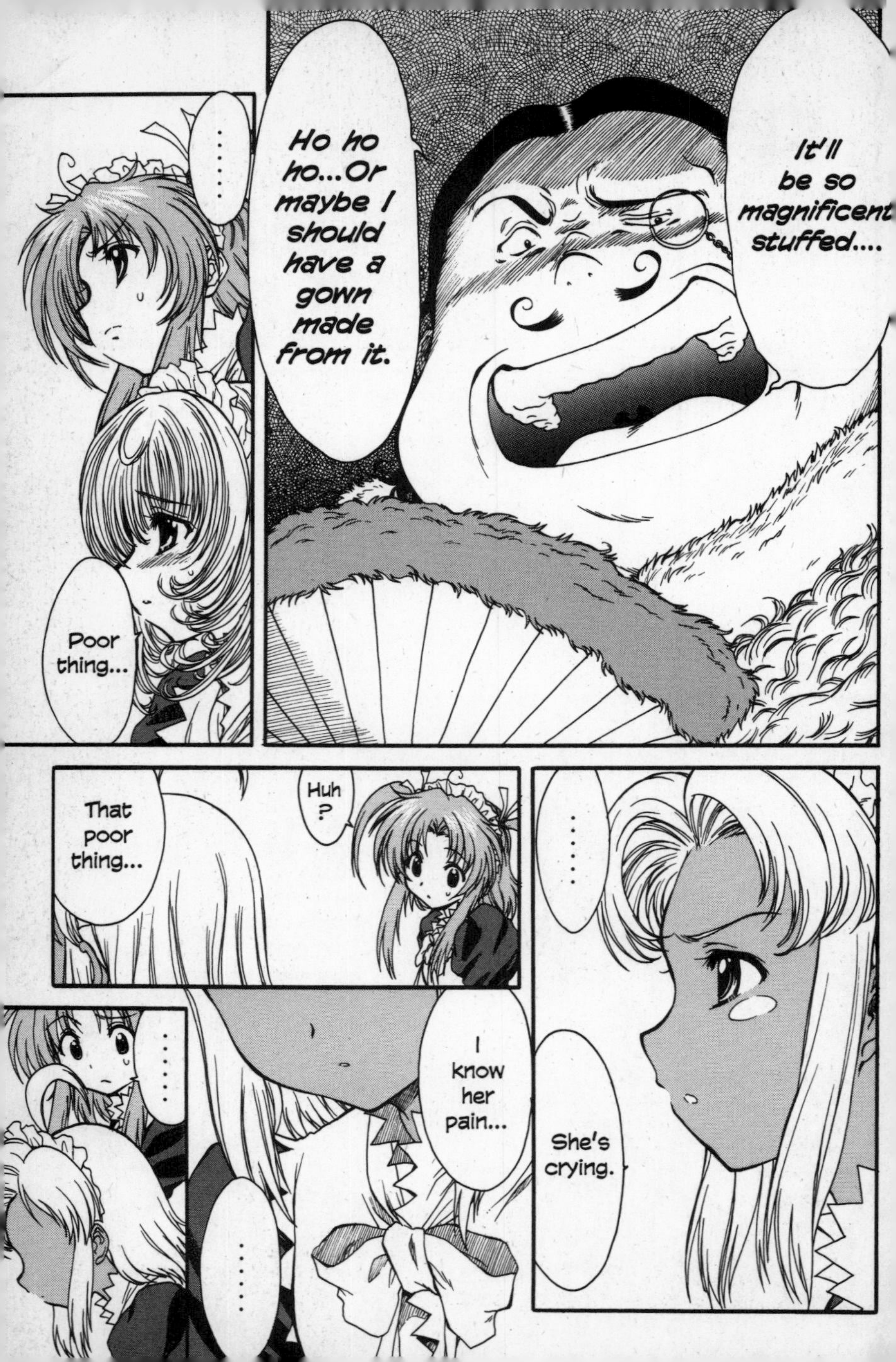
It'll be so magnificent stuffed....
Ho ho ho...Or maybe I should have a gown made from it.
......
Poor thing...
......
She's crying.
That poor thing...
Huh?
I know her pain...
......
......

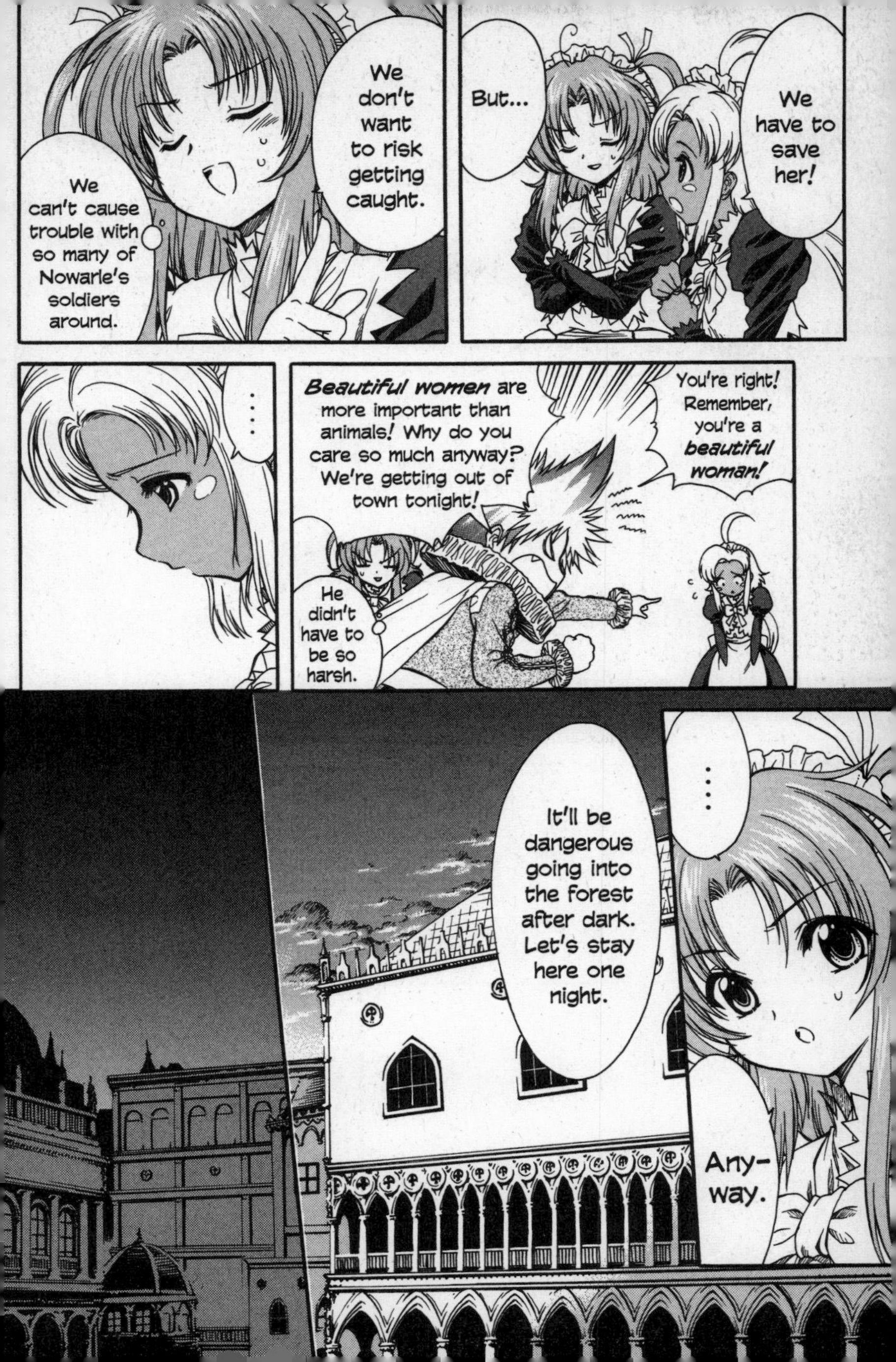
We have to save her!
But...
We don't want to risk getting caught.
We can't cause trouble with so many of Nowarle's soldiers around.
You're right! Remember, you're a *beautiful woman!*
Beautiful women are more important than animals! Why do you care so much anyway? We're getting out of town tonight!
He didn't have to be so harsh.
....
....
It'll be dangerous going into the forest after dark. Let's stay here one night.
Any-way.

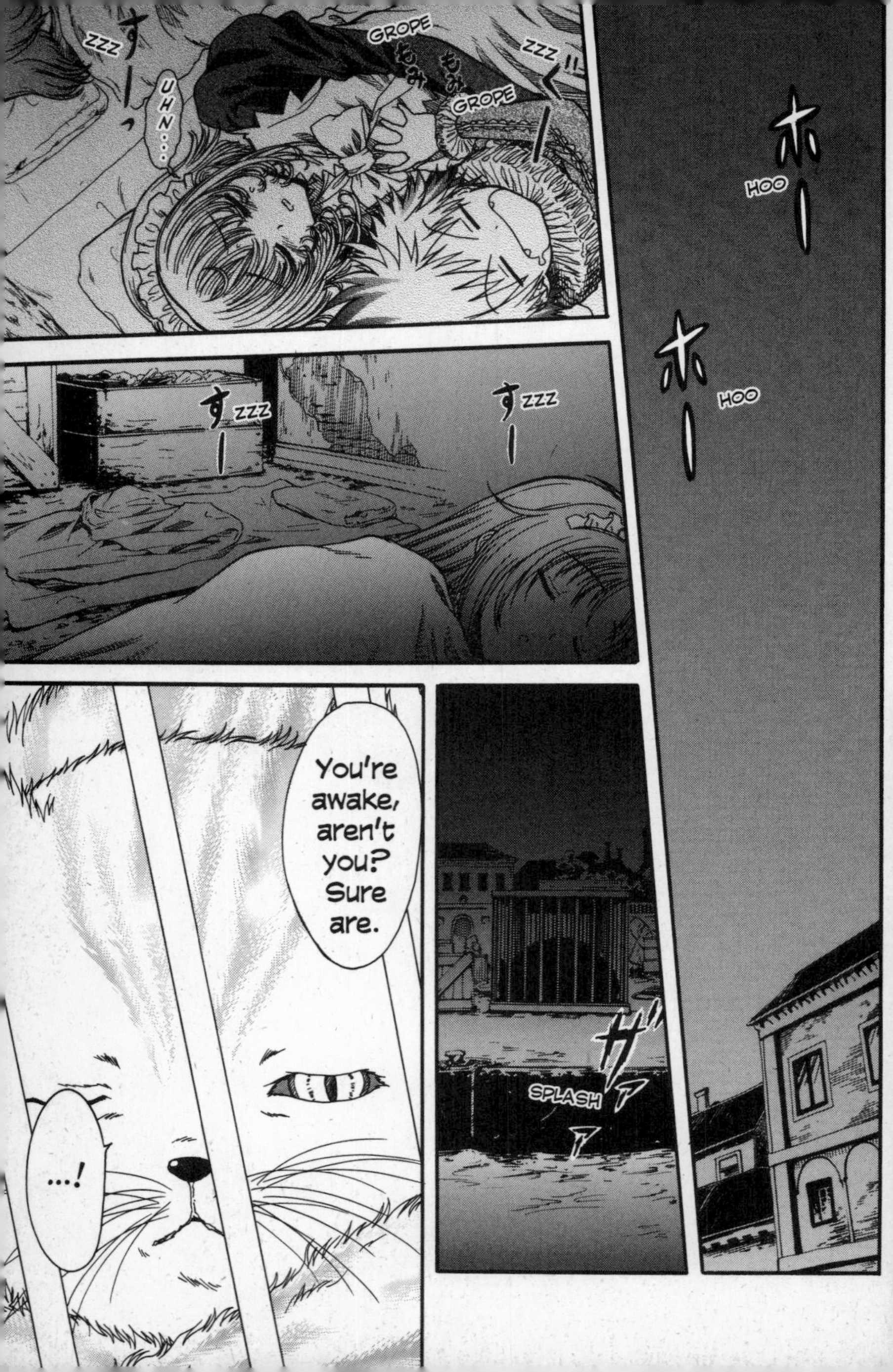
HOO
HOO
ZZZ
GROPE
GROPE
UHN...
ZZZ
ZZZ
ZZZ
SPLASH
You're awake, aren't you? Sure are.
...!

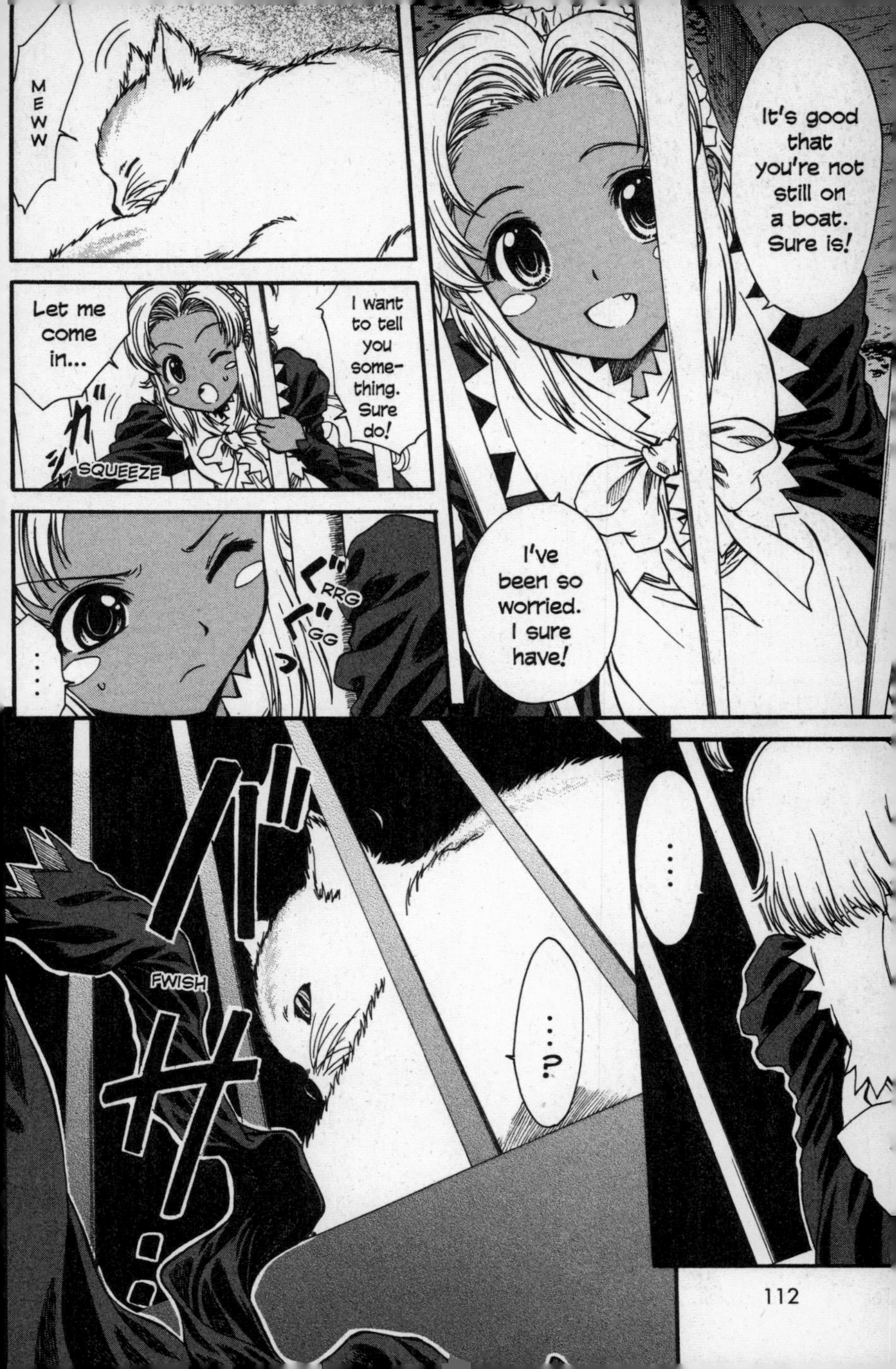
It's good that you're not still on a boat. Sure is!
I've been so worried. I sure have!
MEWW
I want to tell you something. Sure do!
Let me come in...
SQUEEZE
RRG
GG
....
....
...?
FWISH

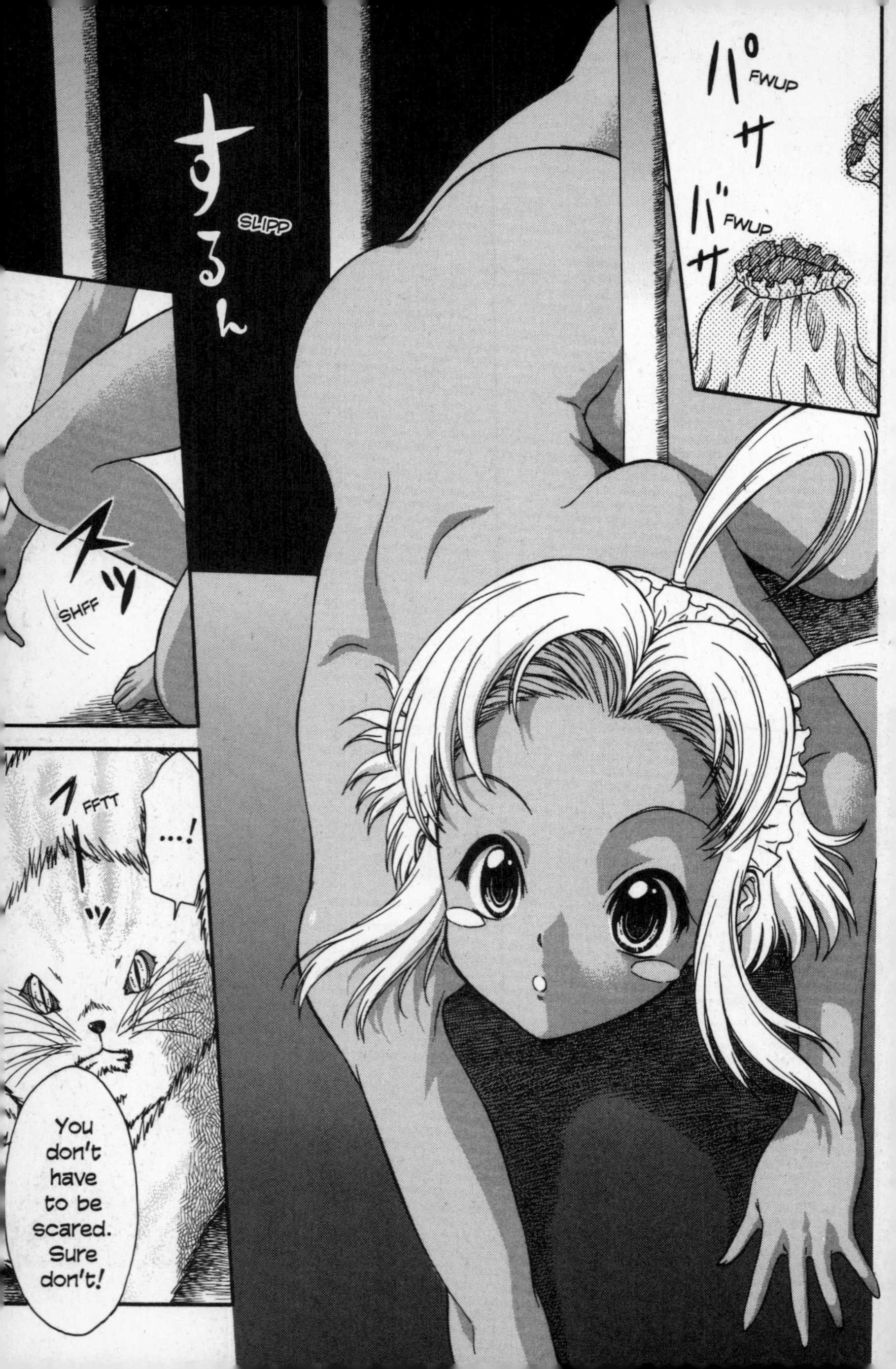

パサバサ
FWUP
FWUP
するん
SLIPP
スッ
SHFF
フトッ
FFTT
...!
You don't have to be scared. Sure don't!

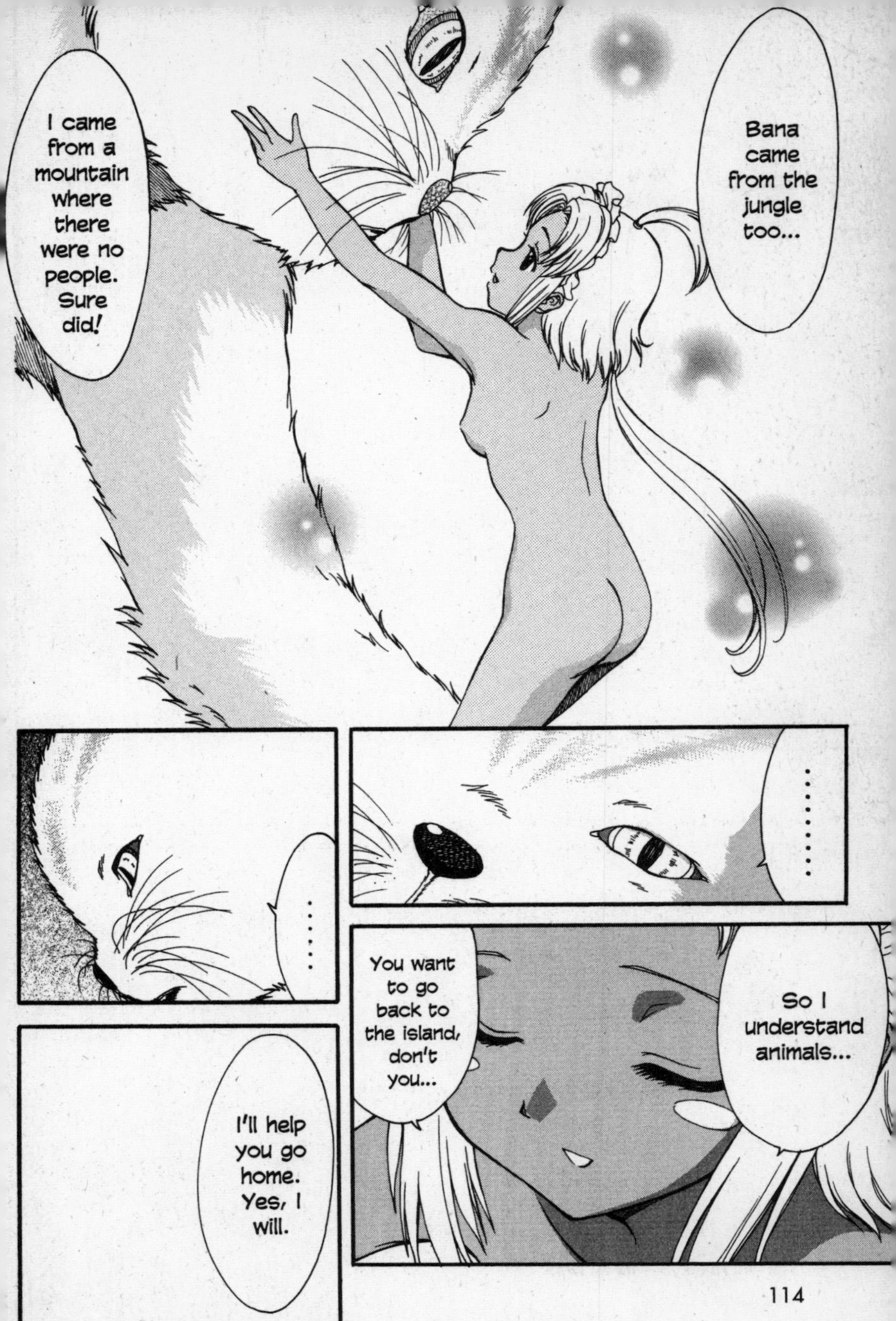
Bana came from the jungle too...
I came from a mountain where there were no people. Sure did!
....
......
So I understand animals...
You want to go back to the island, don't you...
I'll help you go home. Yes, I will.

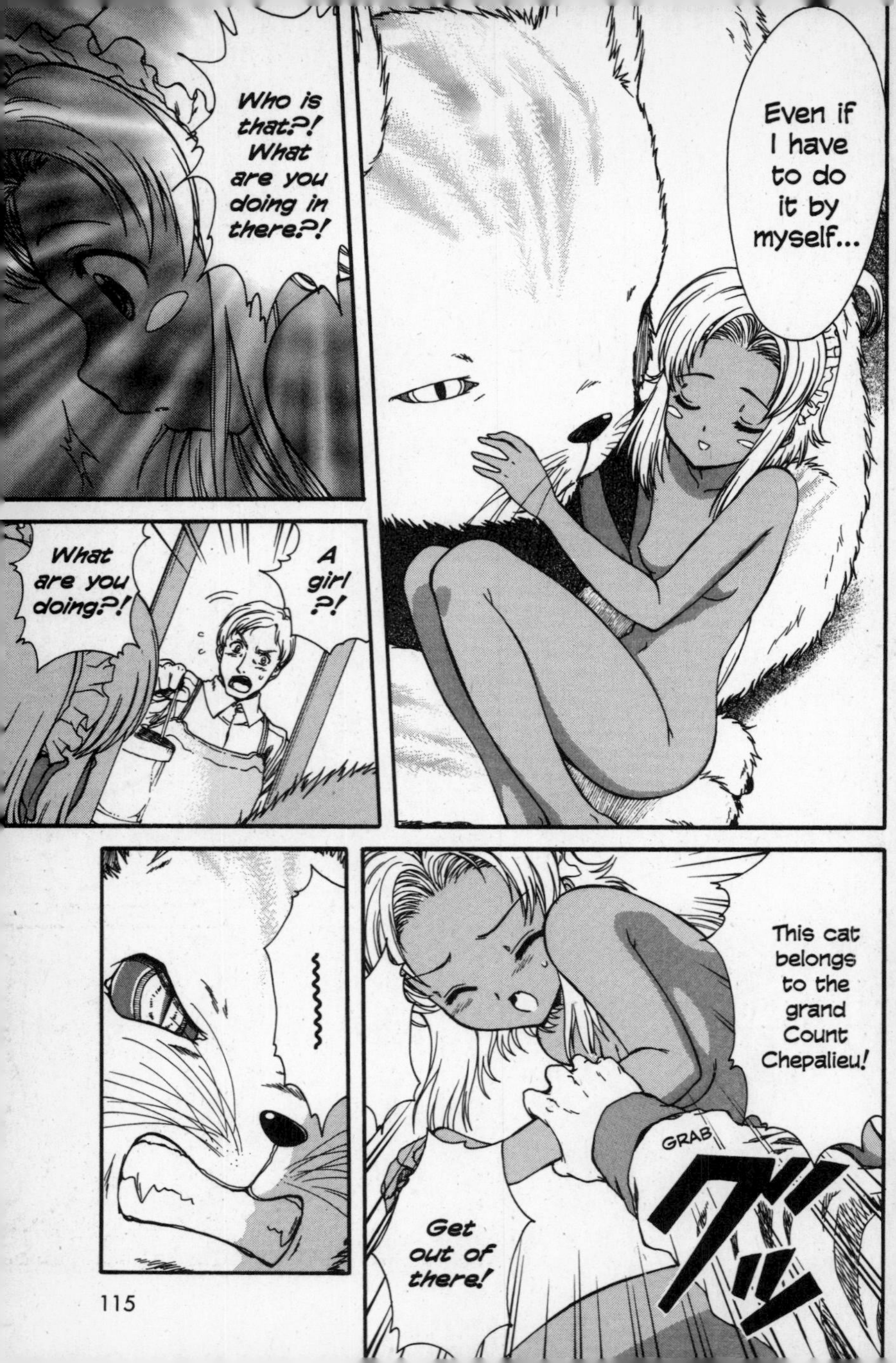
Even if I have to do it by myself...
Who is that?! What are you doing in there?!
A girl ?!
What are you doing?!
This cat belongs to the grand Count Chepalieu!
GRAB
Get out of there!

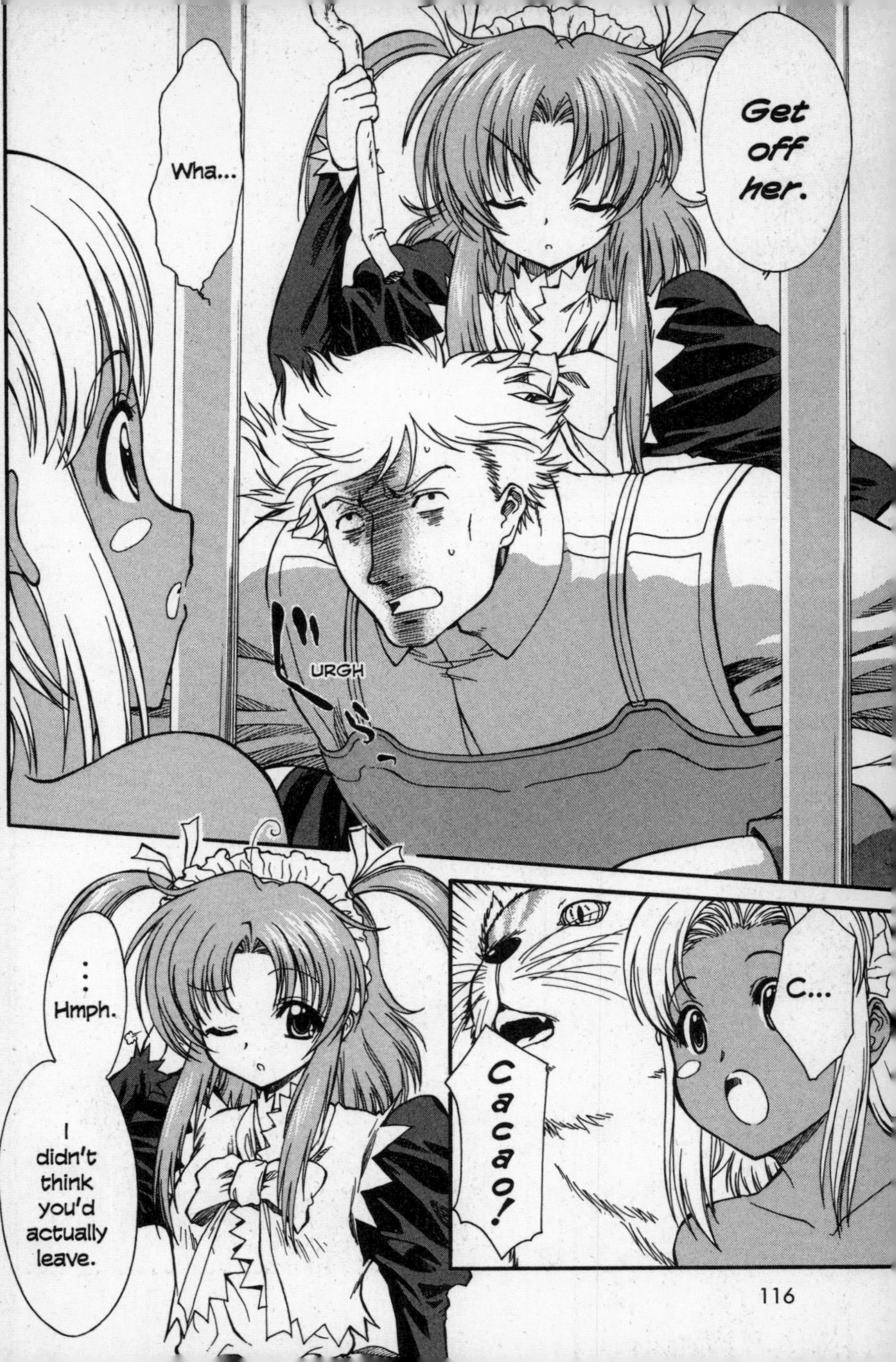
Get off her.
Wha...
URGH
C...
Cacao!
... Hmph.
I didn't think you'd actually leave.

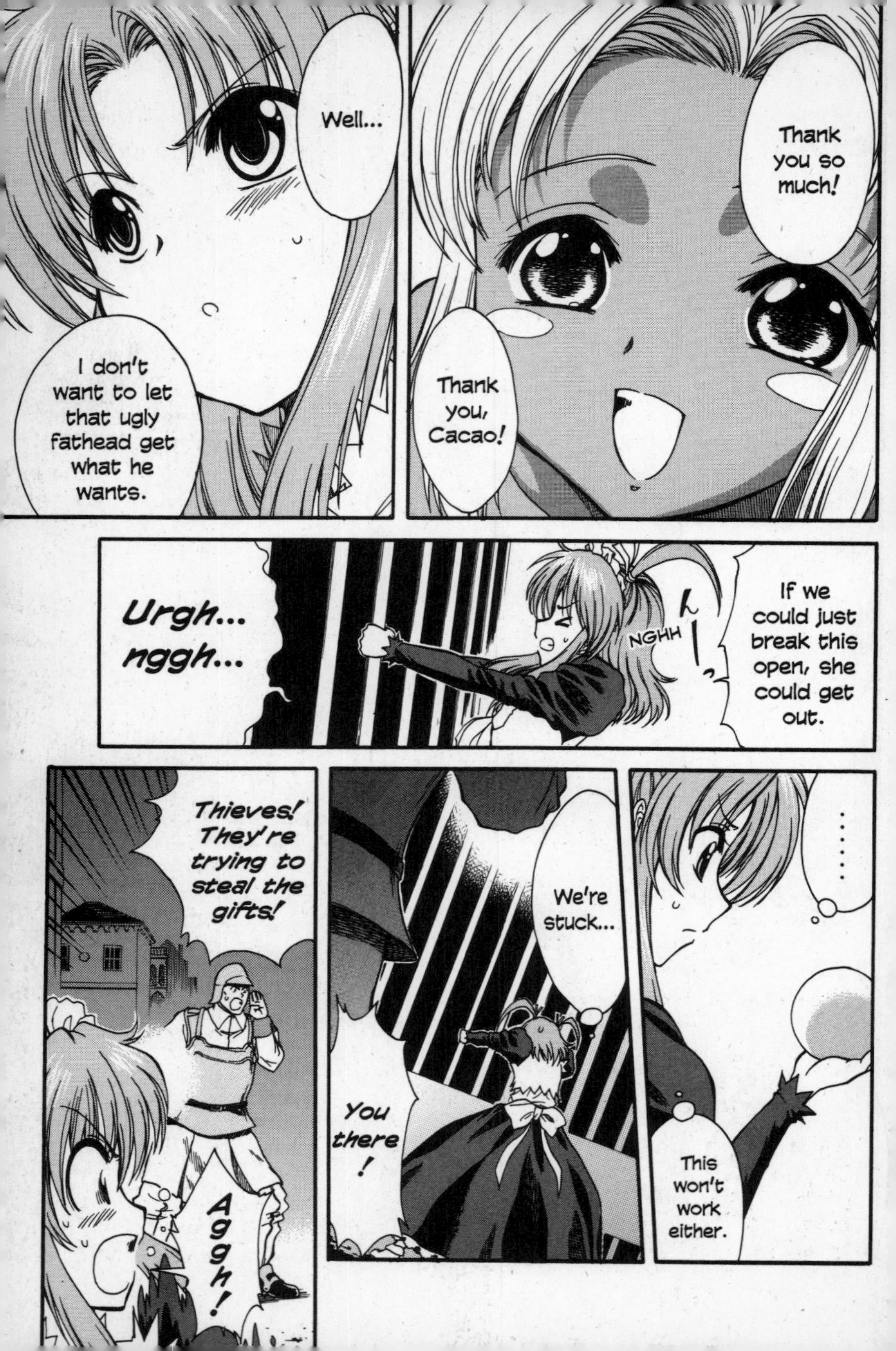
Thank you so much!
Thank you, Cacao!
Well...
I don't want to let that ugly fathead get what he wants.
If we could just break this open, she could get out.
NGHH
Urgh... nggh...
......
This won't work either.
We're stuck...
You there!
Thieves! They're trying to steal the gifts!
Aggh!

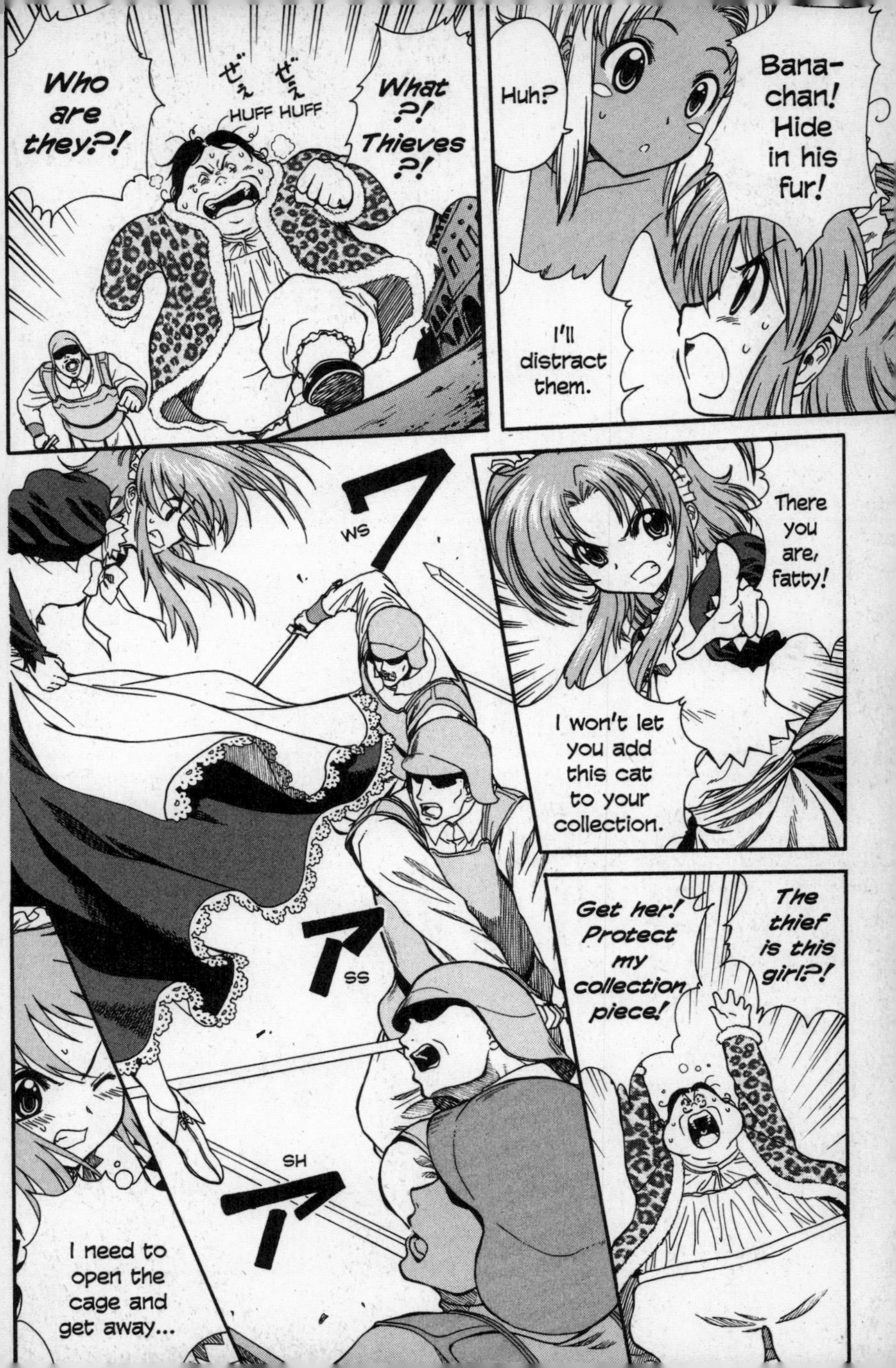

Bana-chan! Hide in his fur!
Huh?
I'll distract them.
What?! Thieves?!
ぜぇ ぜぇ
HUFF HUFF
Who are they?!
There you are, fatty!
I won't let you add this cat to your collection.
The thief is this girl?!
Get her! Protect my collection piece!
WS
SS
SH
I need to open the cage and get away...

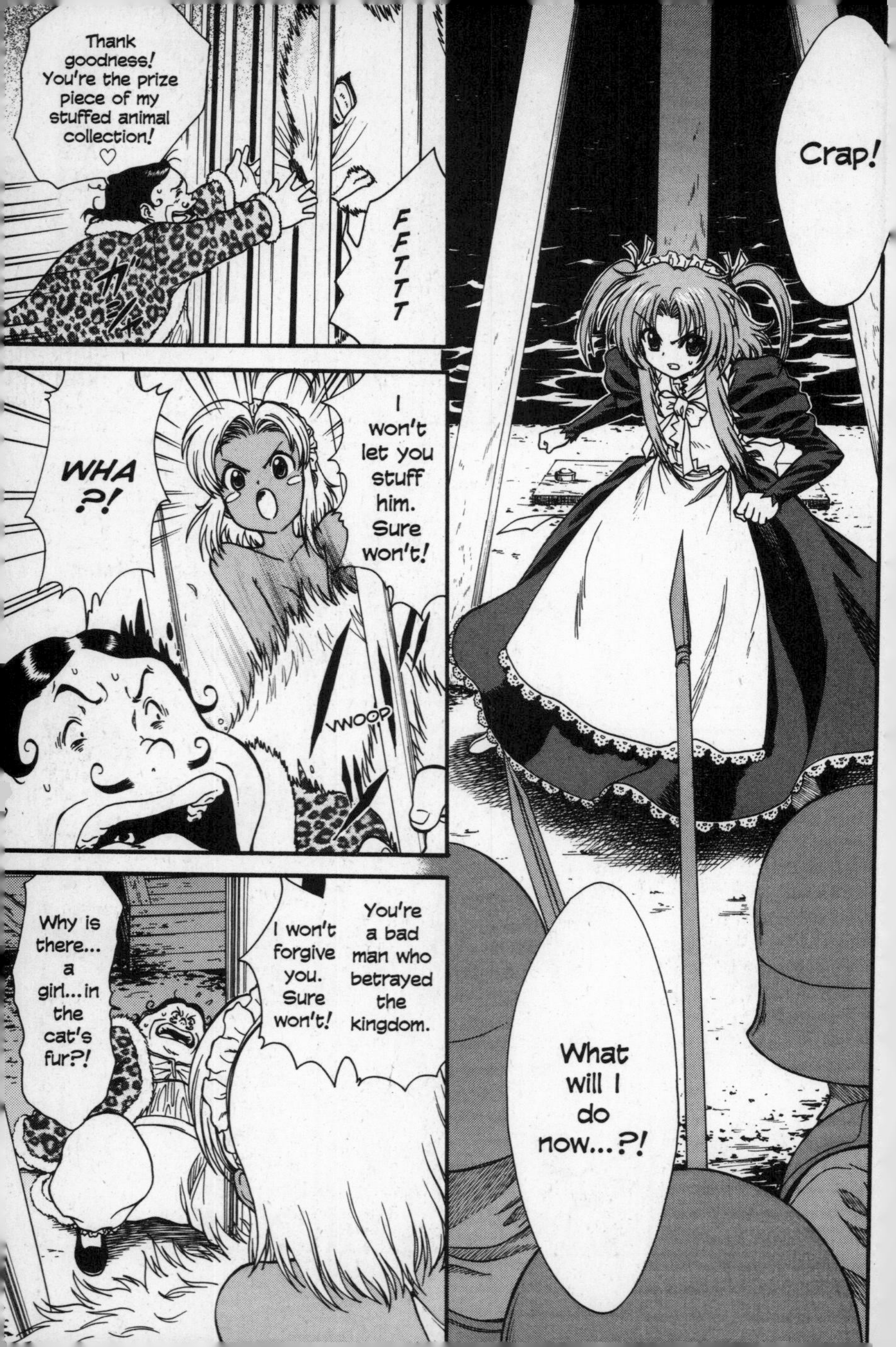

Crap!
What will I do now...?!
Thank goodness! You're the prize piece of my stuffed animal collection! ♡
FFTTTT
I won't let you stuff him. Sure won't!
WHA?!
VWOOP
You're a bad man who betrayed the kingdom.
I won't forgive you. Sure won't!
Why is there... a girl...in the cat's fur?!

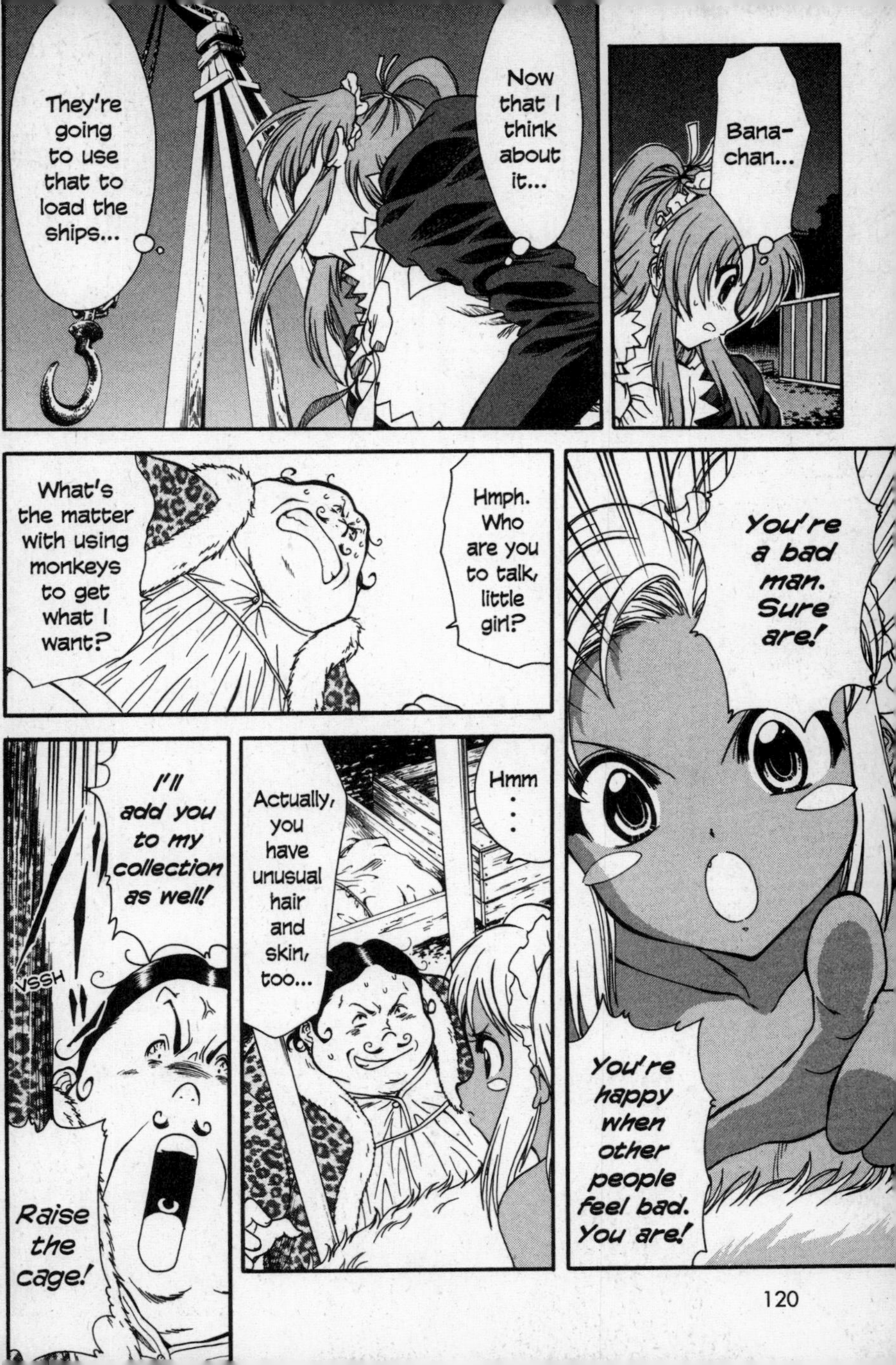

Bana-chan...
Now that I think about it...
They're going to use that to load the ships...
You're a bad man. Sure are!
You're happy when other people feel bad. You are!
Hmph. Who are you to talk, little girl?
What's the matter with using monkeys to get what I want?
Hmm...
Actually, you have unusual hair and skin, too...
I'll add you to my collection as well!
VSSH
Raise the cage!

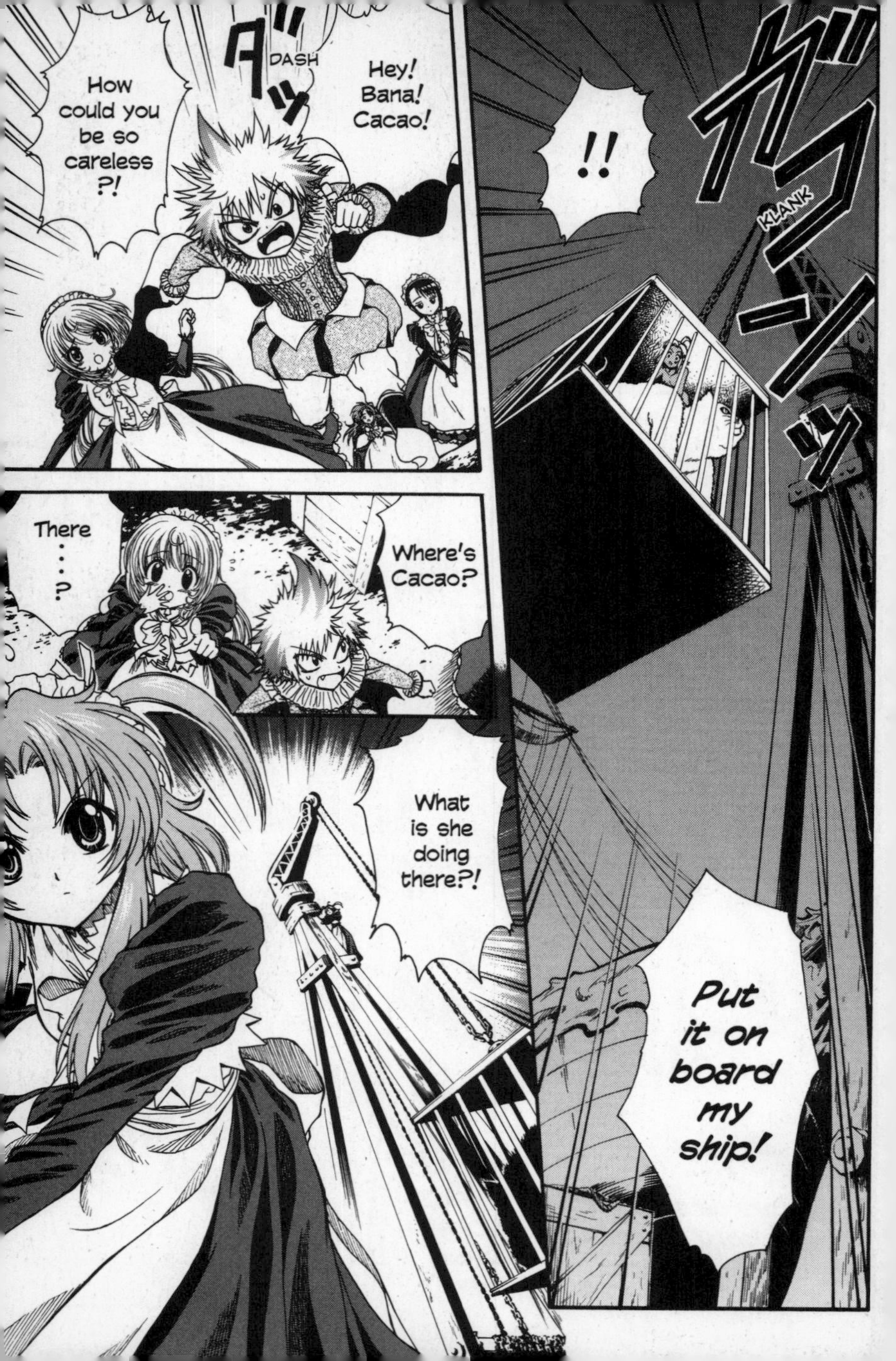
!!
KLANK
Put it on board my ship!
DASH
Hey! Bana! Cacao!
How could you be so careless ?!
Where's Cacao?
There . . . ?
What is she doing there?!

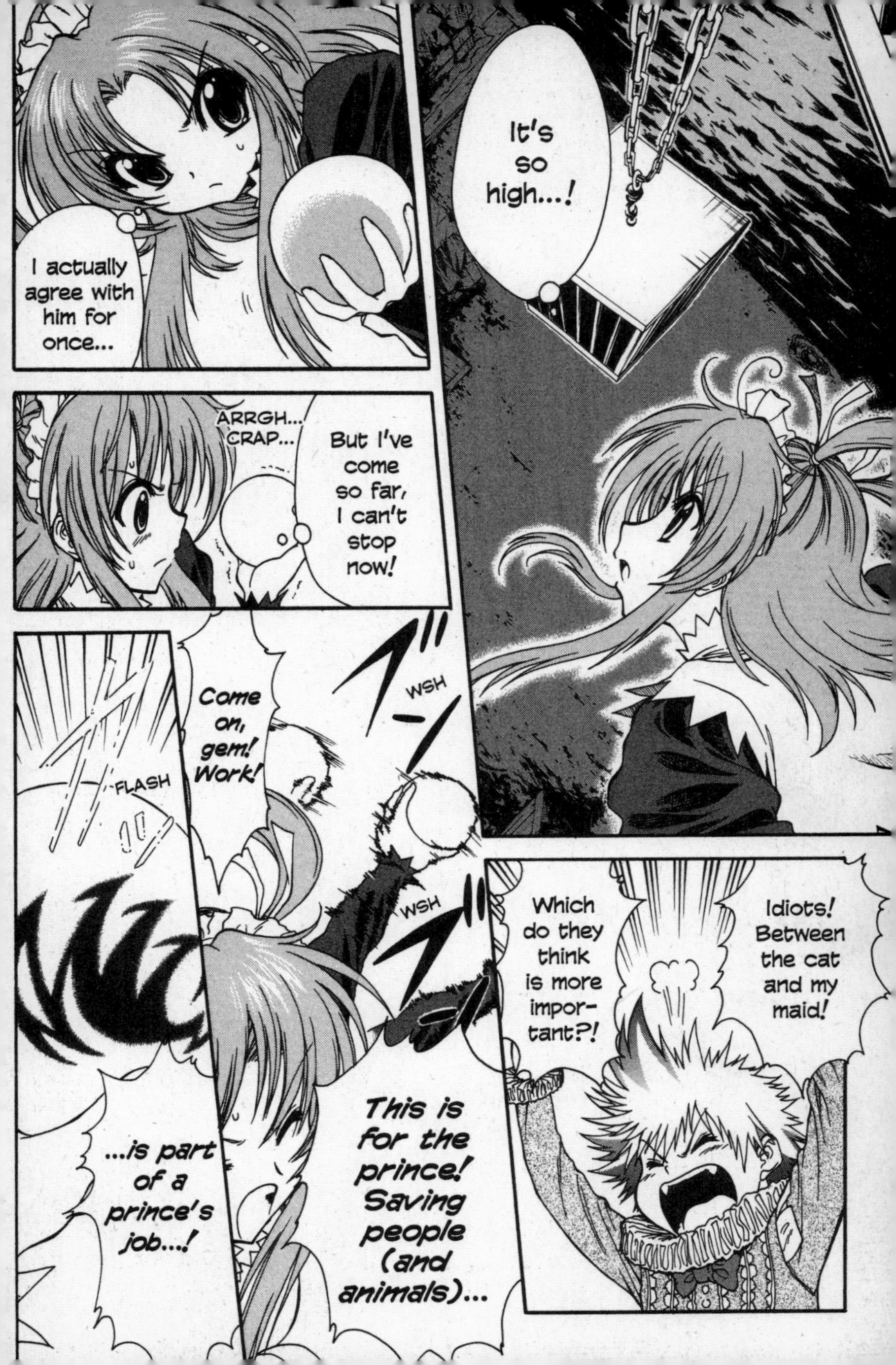
It's so high...!
I actually agree with him for once...
But I've come so far, I can't stop now!
ARRGH... CRAP...
Idiots! Between the cat and my maid!
Which do they think is more important?!
WSH
Come on, gem! Work!
WSH
This is for the prince! Saving people (and animals)...
FLASH
...is part of a prince's job...!

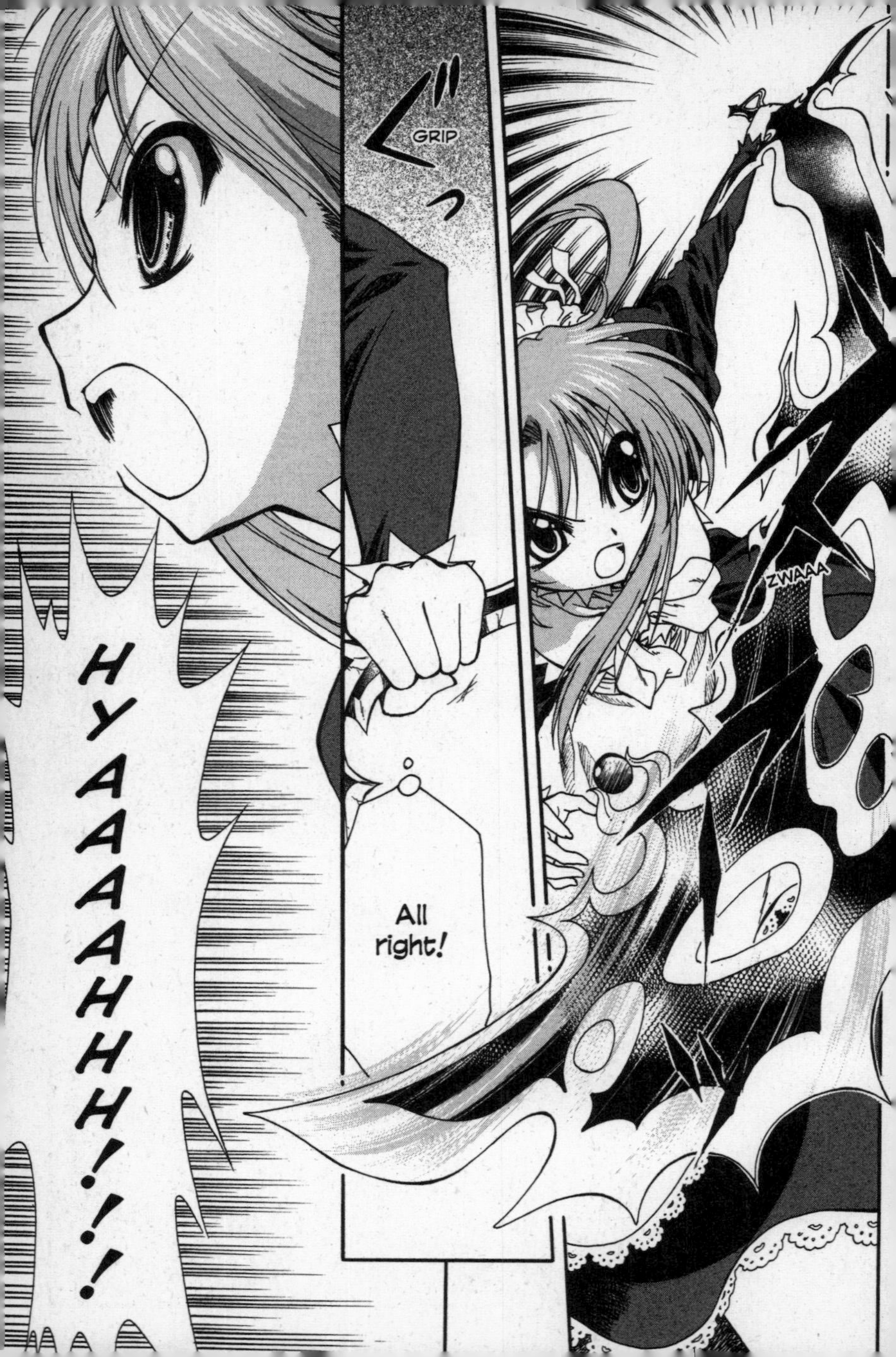
ZWAAA
GRIP
All right!
HYAAAAHHH!!!

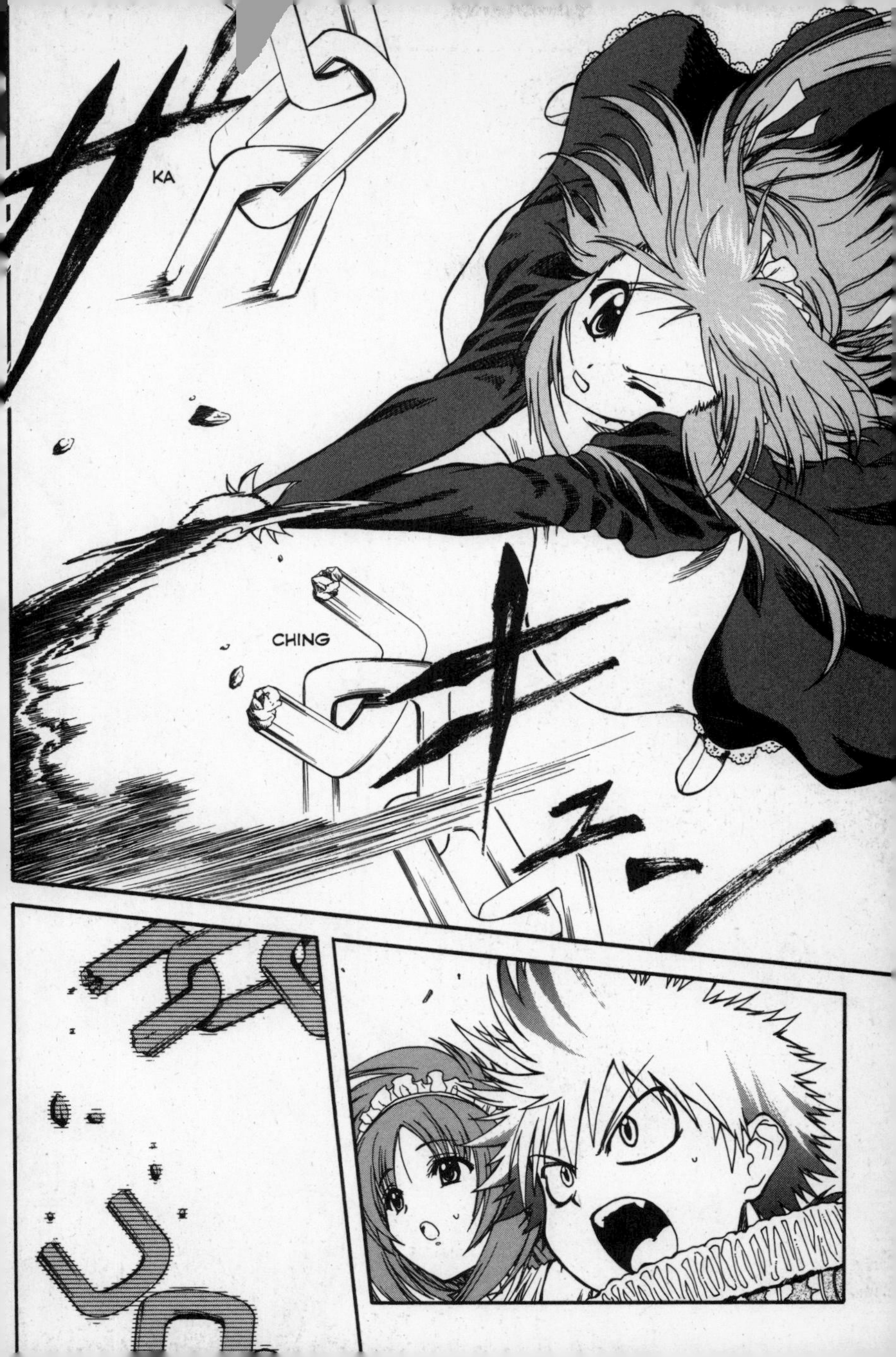
KA
CHING

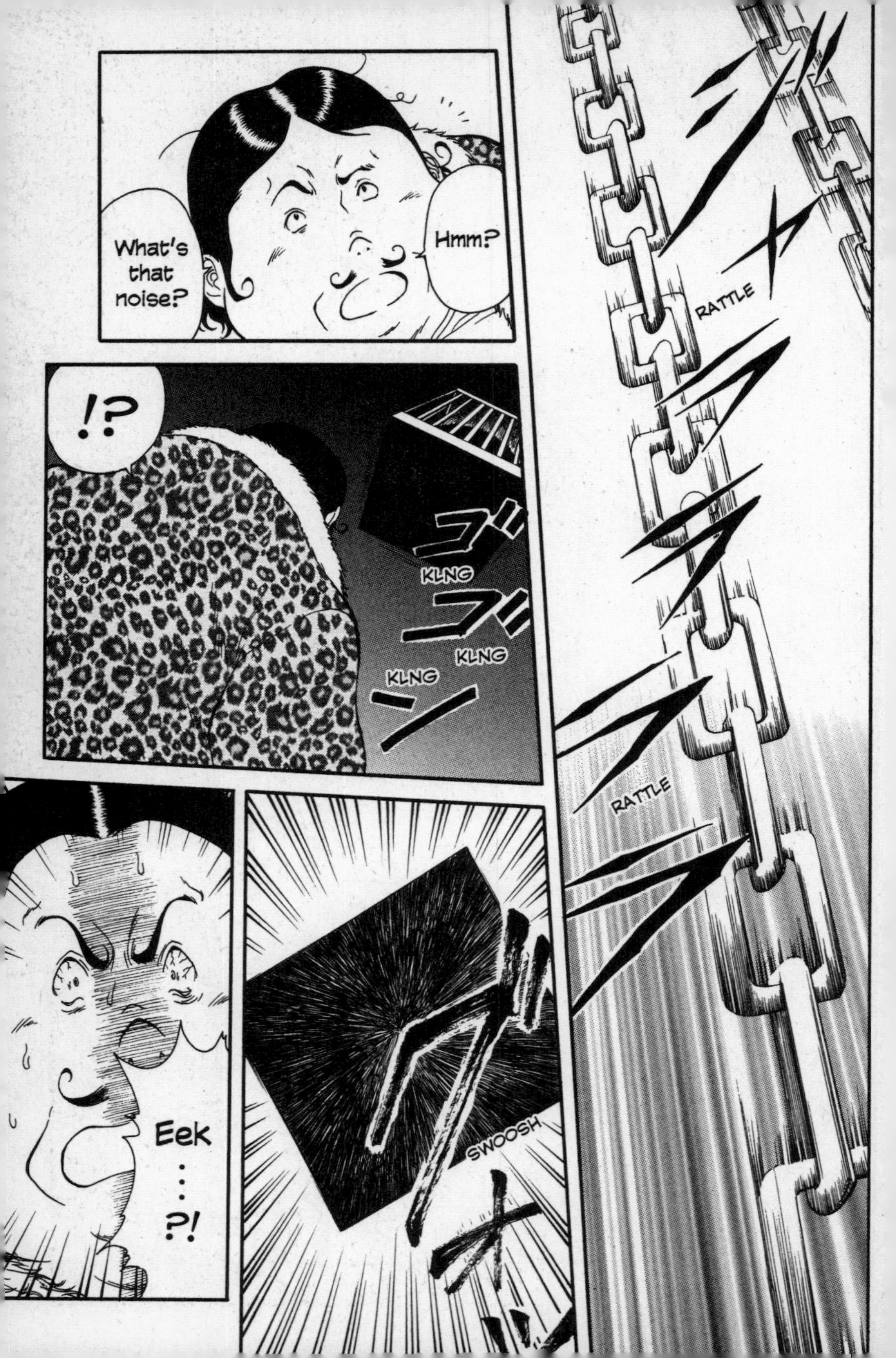
RATTLE
RATTLE
Hmm?
What's that noise?
!?
KLNG
KLNG
KLNG
SWOOSH
Eek ... ?!

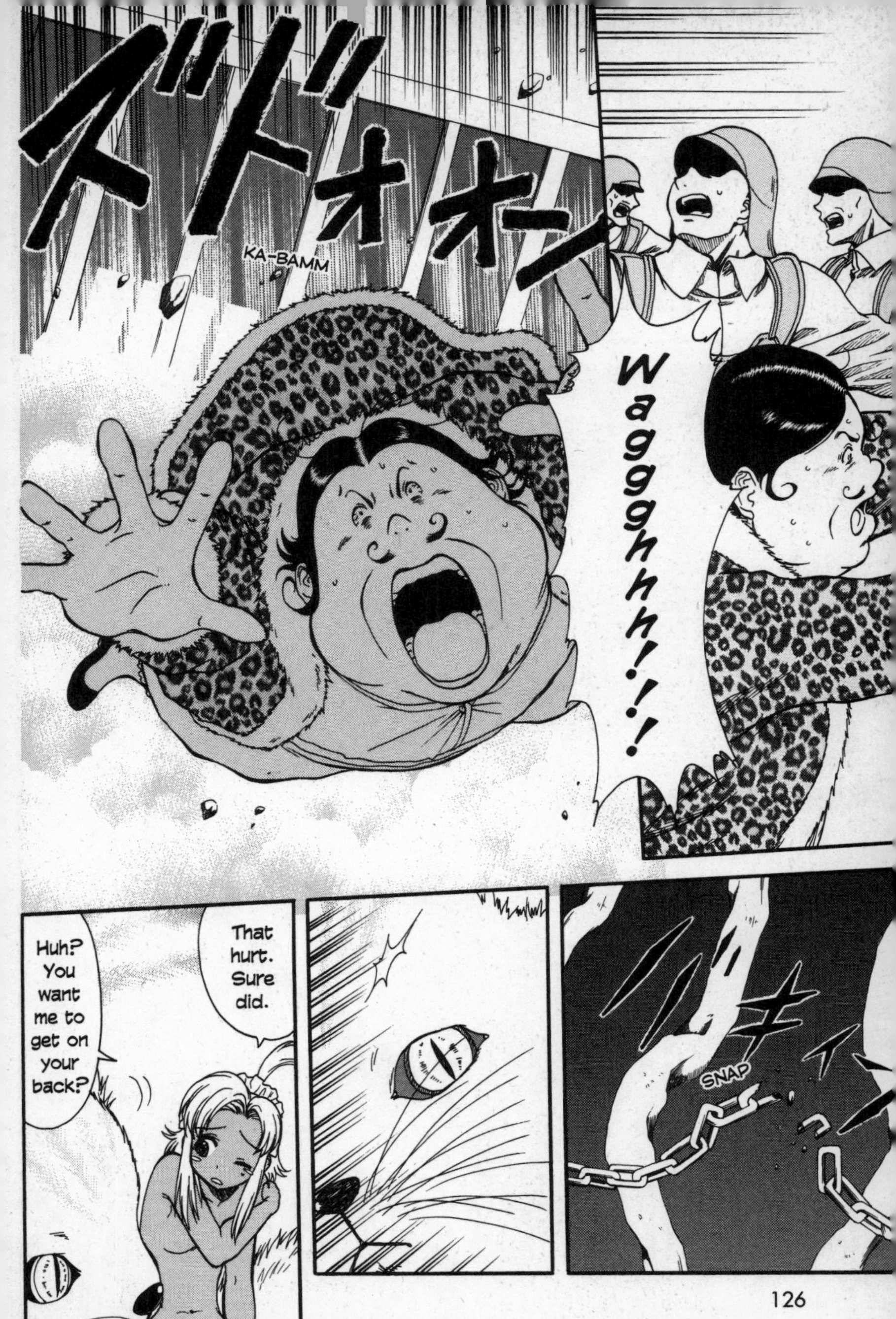
KA-BAMM
Waggghhhh!!!
SNAP
That hurt. Sure did.
Huh? You want me to get on your back?

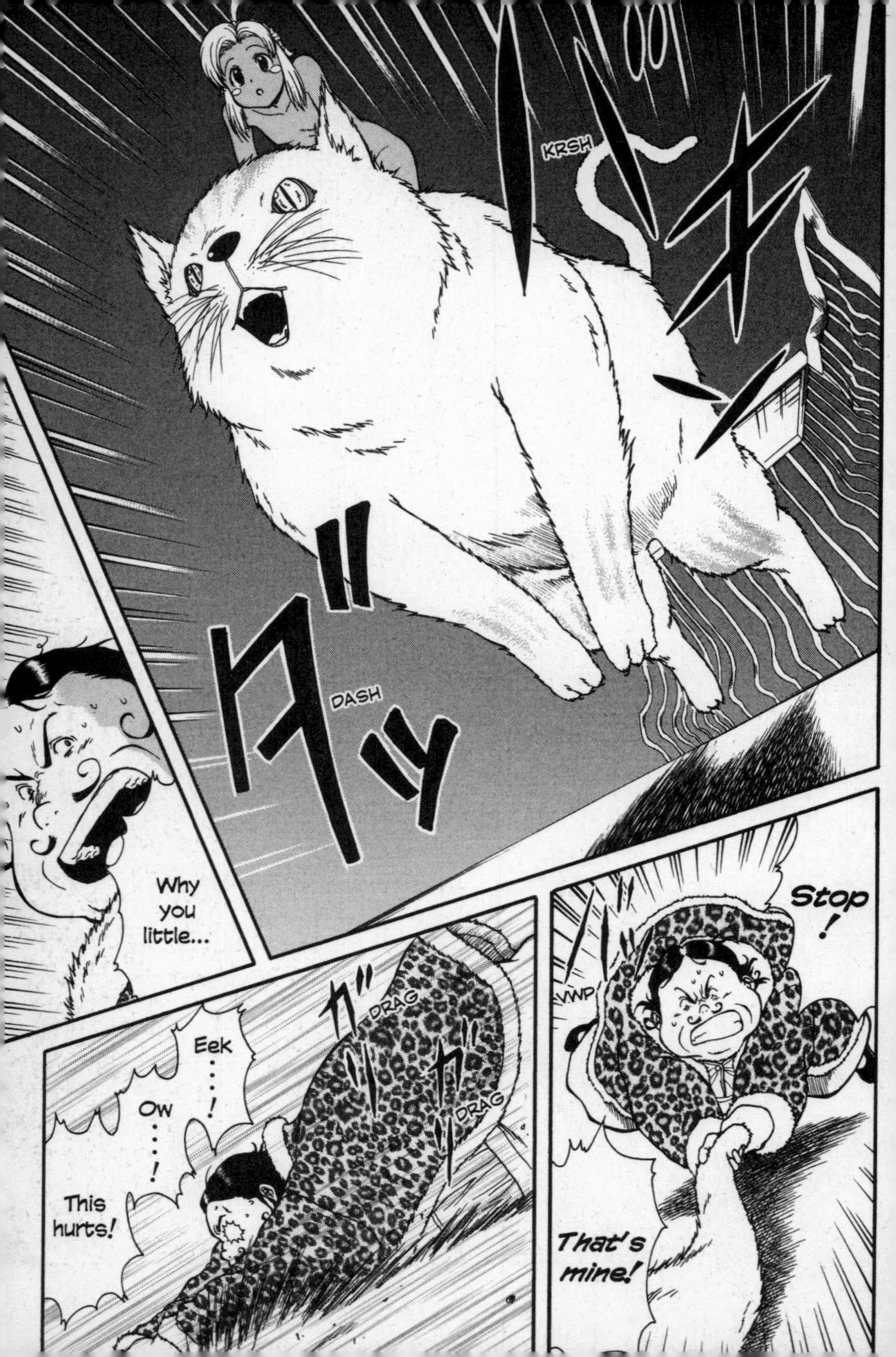
KRSH
DASH
Why you little...
Stop!
VWP
That's mine!
DRAG
DRAG
Eek...!
Ow...!
This hurts!

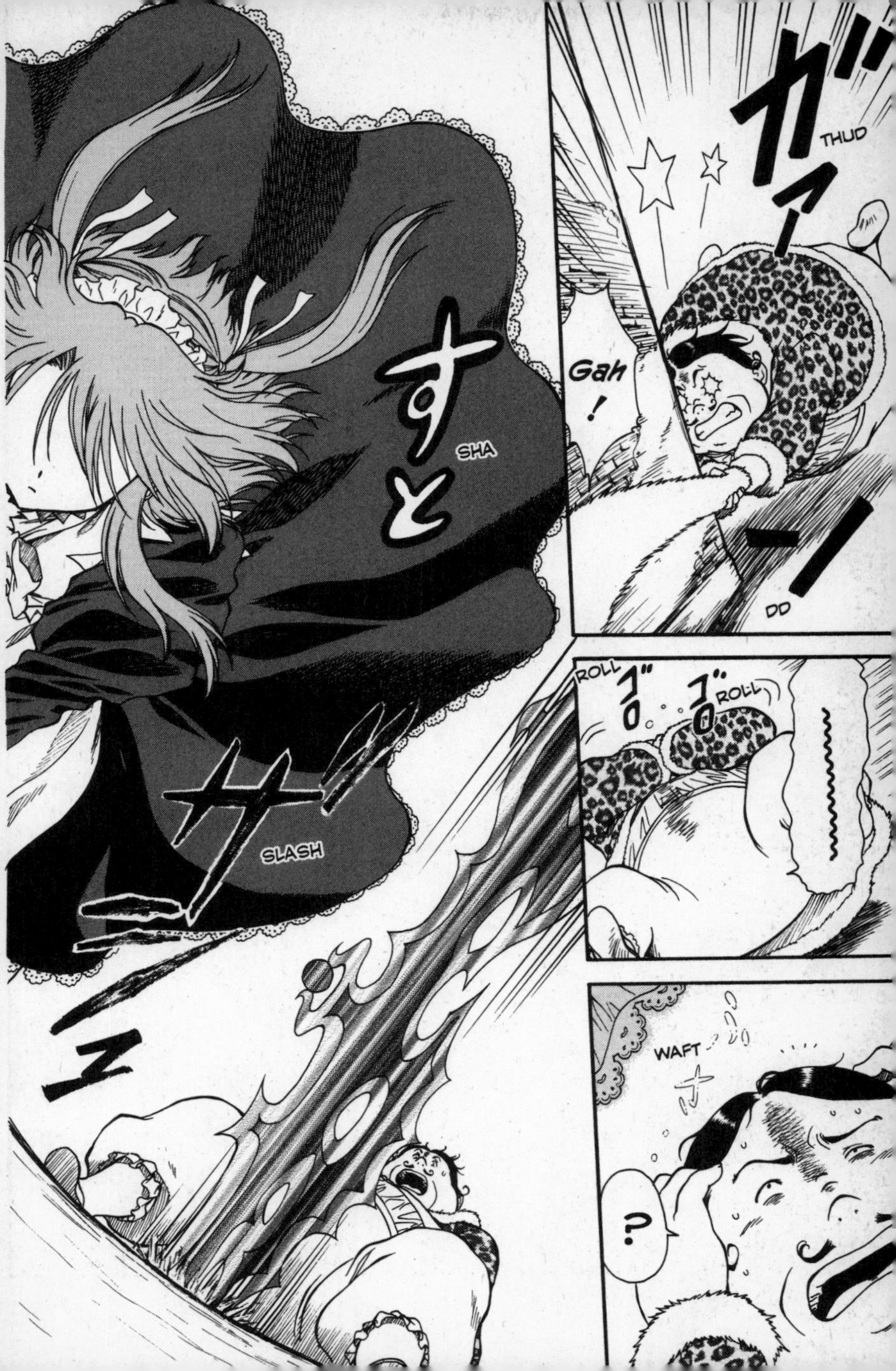

THUD
Gah!
DD
ROLL
ROLL
WAFT
?
SHA
SLASH

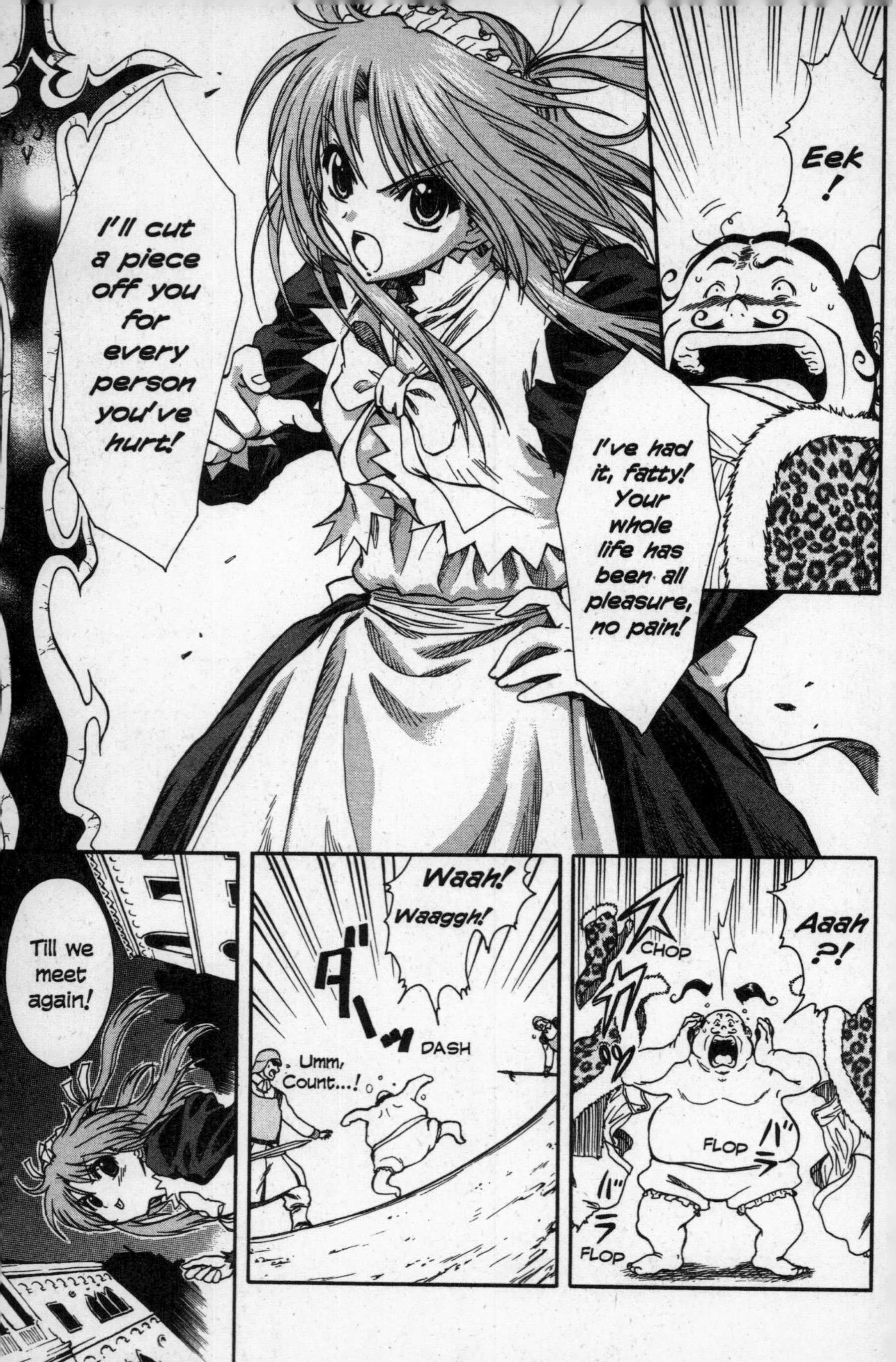

Eek!
I've had it, fatty! Your whole life has been all pleasure, no pain!
I'll cut a piece off you for every person you've hurt!
Aaah?!
CHOP
FLOP
FLOP
Waah!
Waaggh!
DASH
Umm, Count...!
Till we meet again!

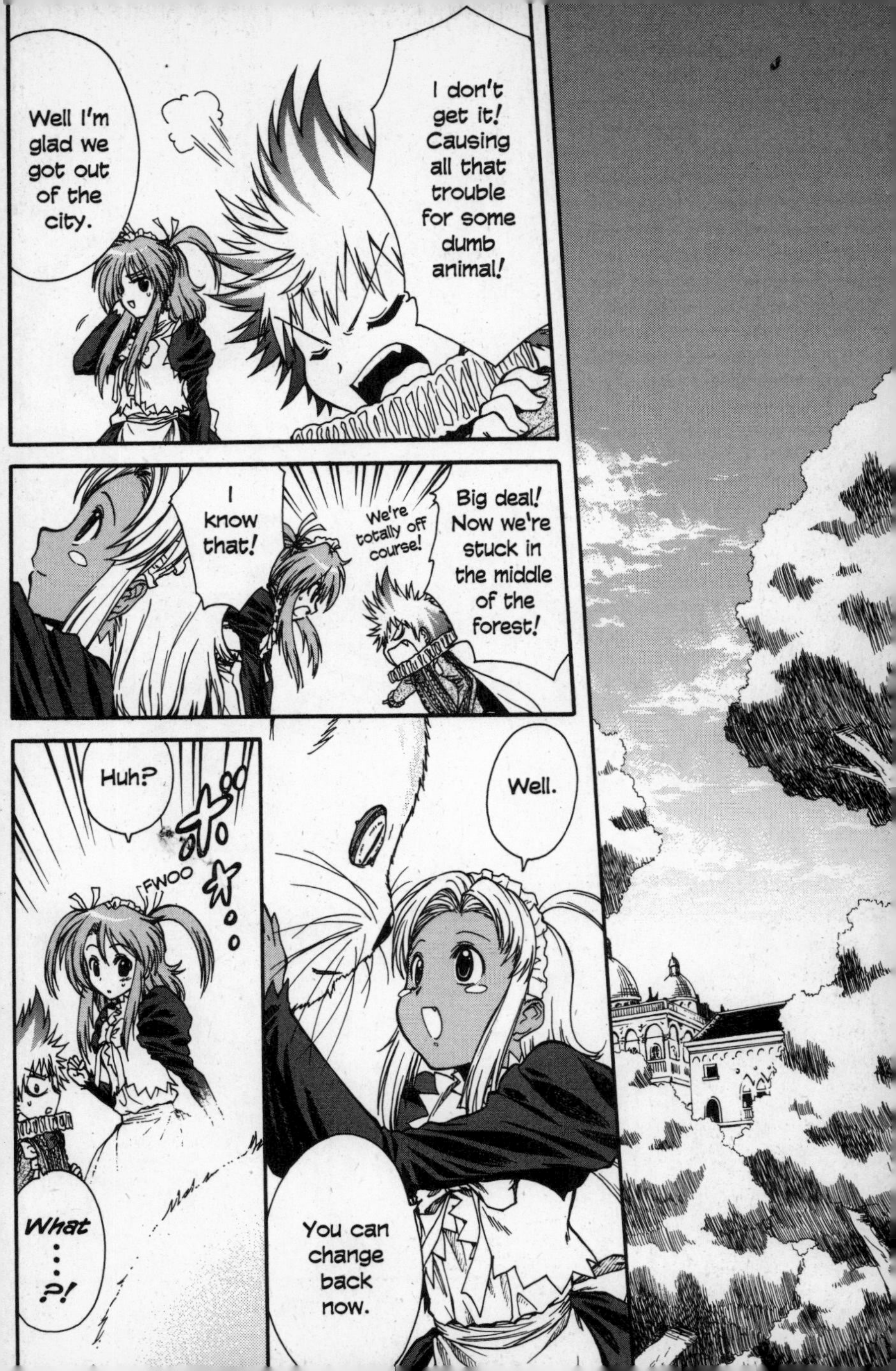
I don't get it! Causing all that trouble for some dumb animal!
Well I'm glad we got out of the city.
Big deal! Now we're stuck in the middle of the forest!
We're totally off course!
I know that!
Well.
You can change back now.
Huh?
FWOO
What...?!

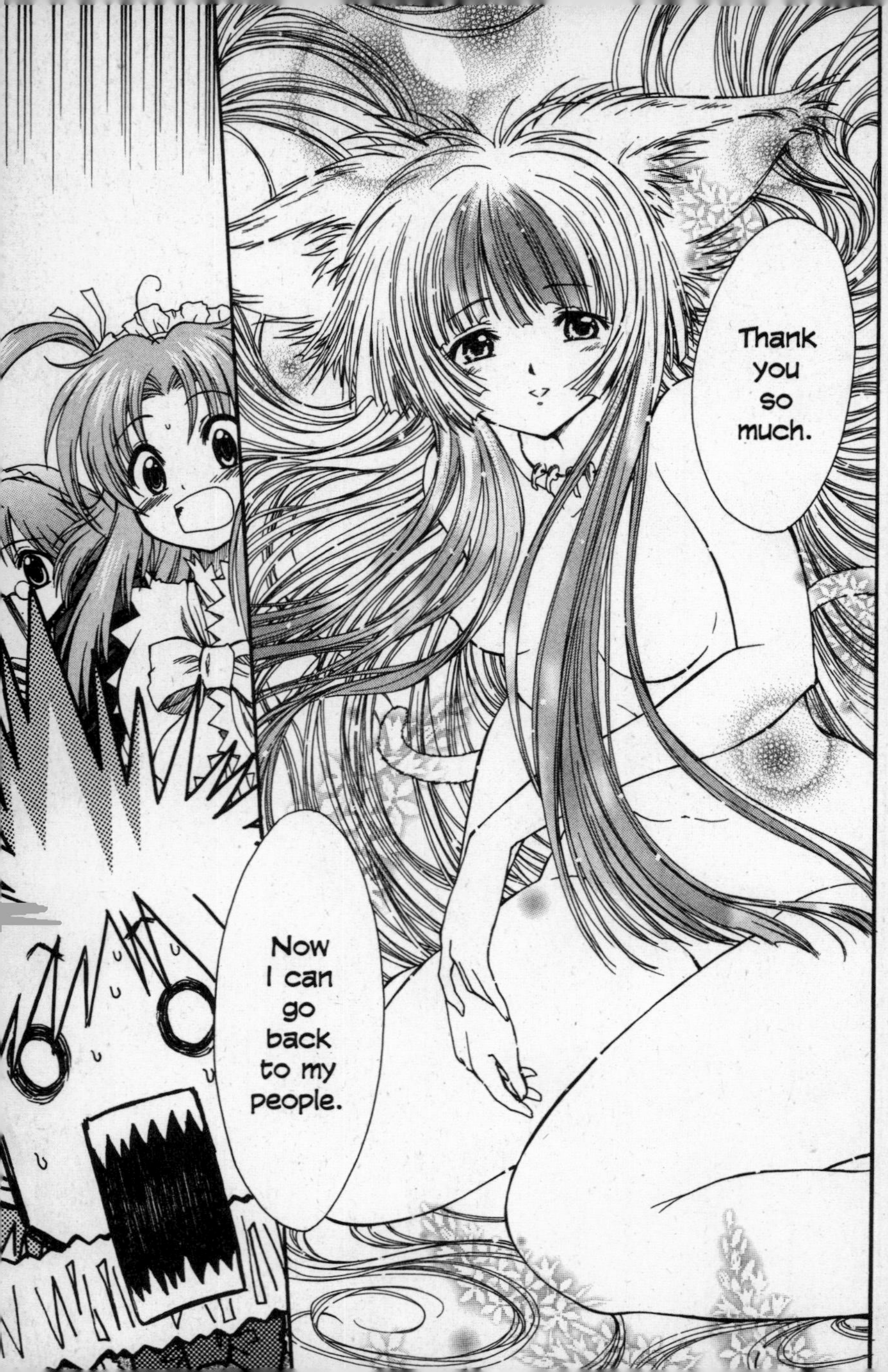
Thank you so much.
Now I can go back to my people.

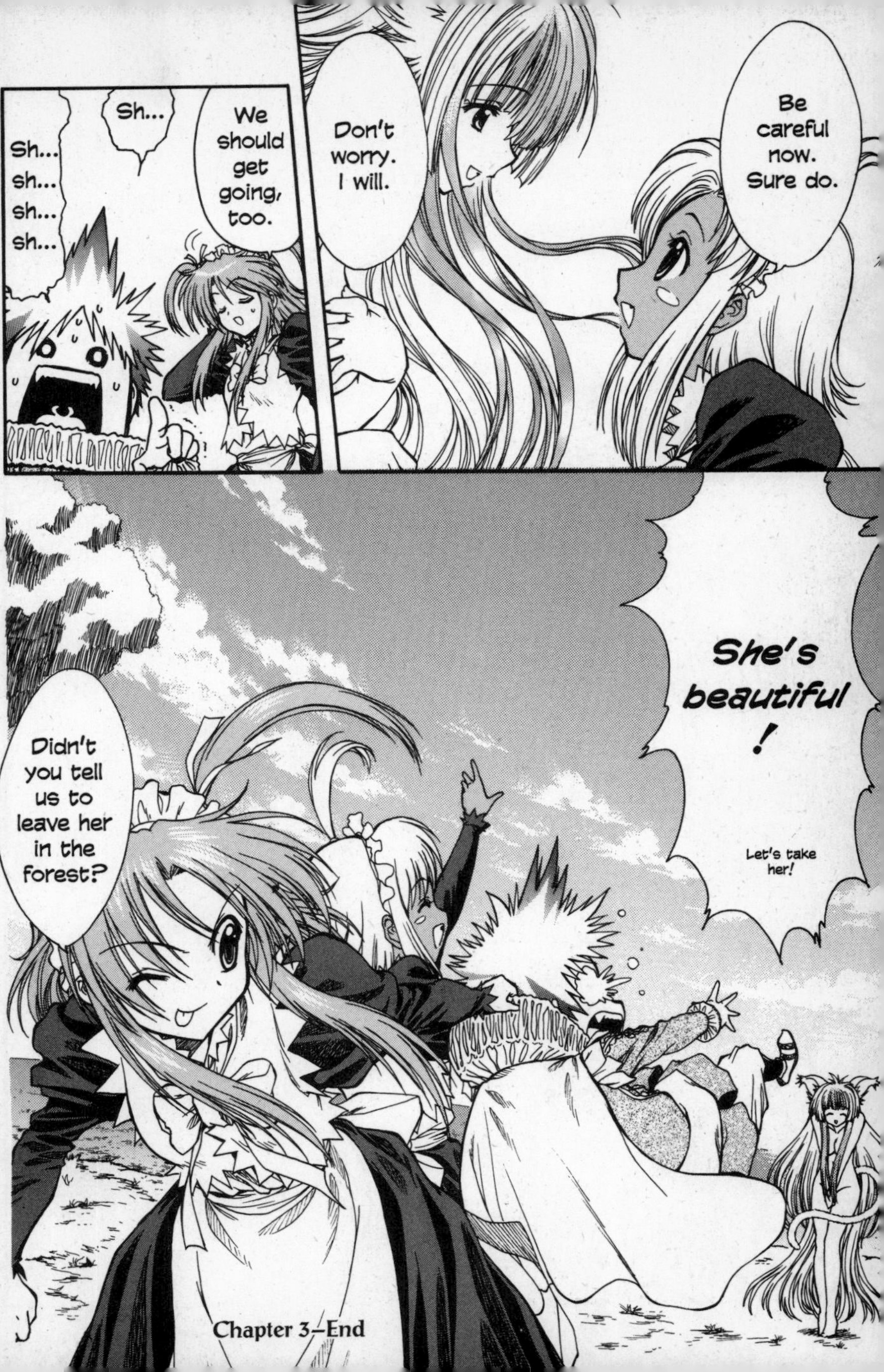
Be careful now. Sure do.
Don't worry. I will.
We should get going, too.
Sh...
Sh... sh... sh... sh...
She's beautiful!
Let's take her!
Didn't you tell us to leave her in the forest?
Chapter 3—End

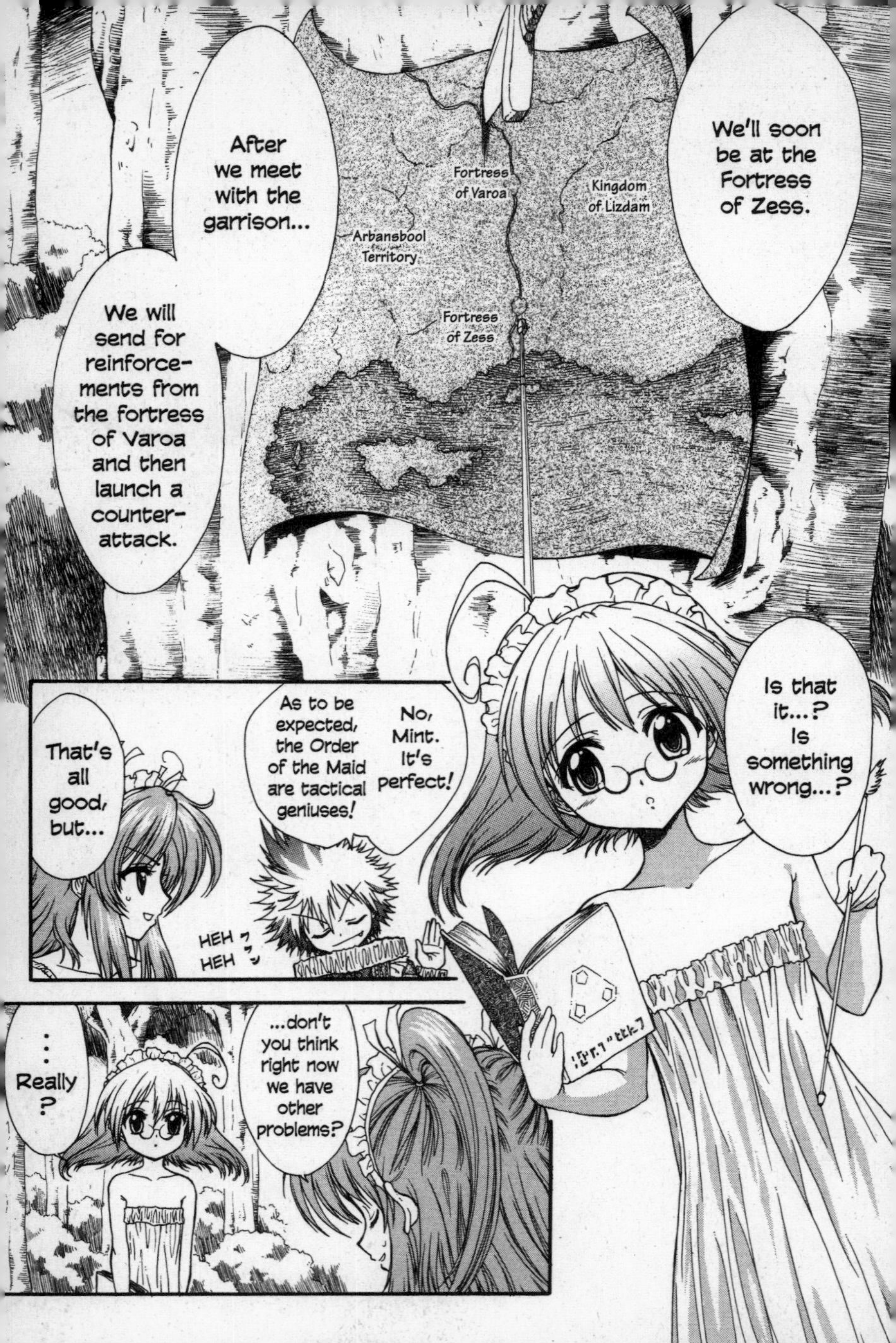
We'll soon be at the Fortress of Zess.
Fortress of Varoa
Kingdom of Lizdam
Arbansbool Territory
Fortress of Zess
After we meet with the garrison...
We will send for reinforcements from the fortress of Varoa and then launch a counter-attack.
Is that it...? Is something wrong...?
No, Mint. It's perfect!
As to be expected, the Order of the Maid are tactical geniuses!
HEH HEH
That's all good, but...
...don't you think right now we have other problems?
... Really?

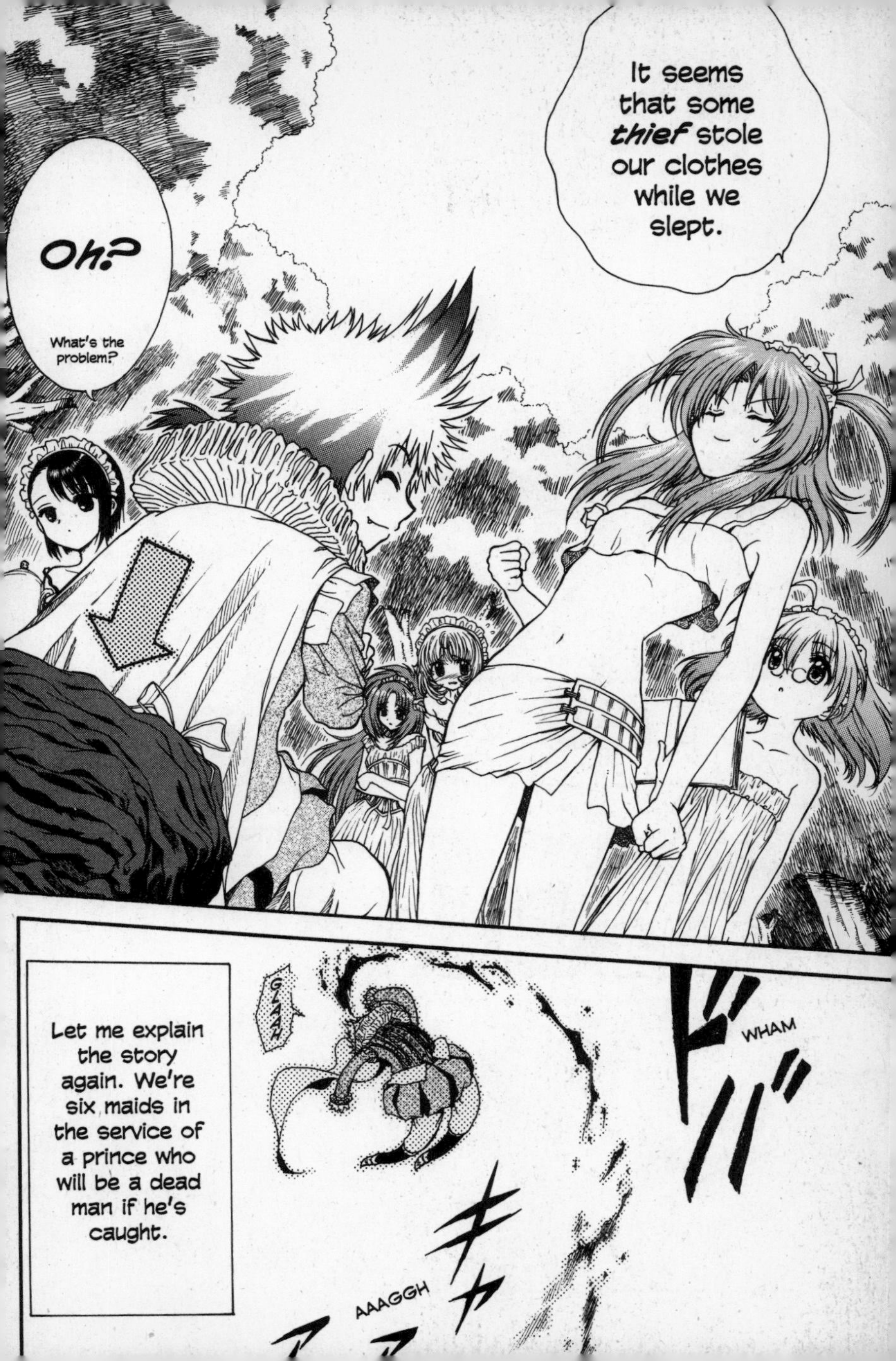
It seems that some *thief* stole our clothes while we slept.
Oh?
What's the problem?
WHAM
GLAAH
Let me explain the story again. We're six maids in the service of a prince who will be a dead man if he's caught.
AAAGGH

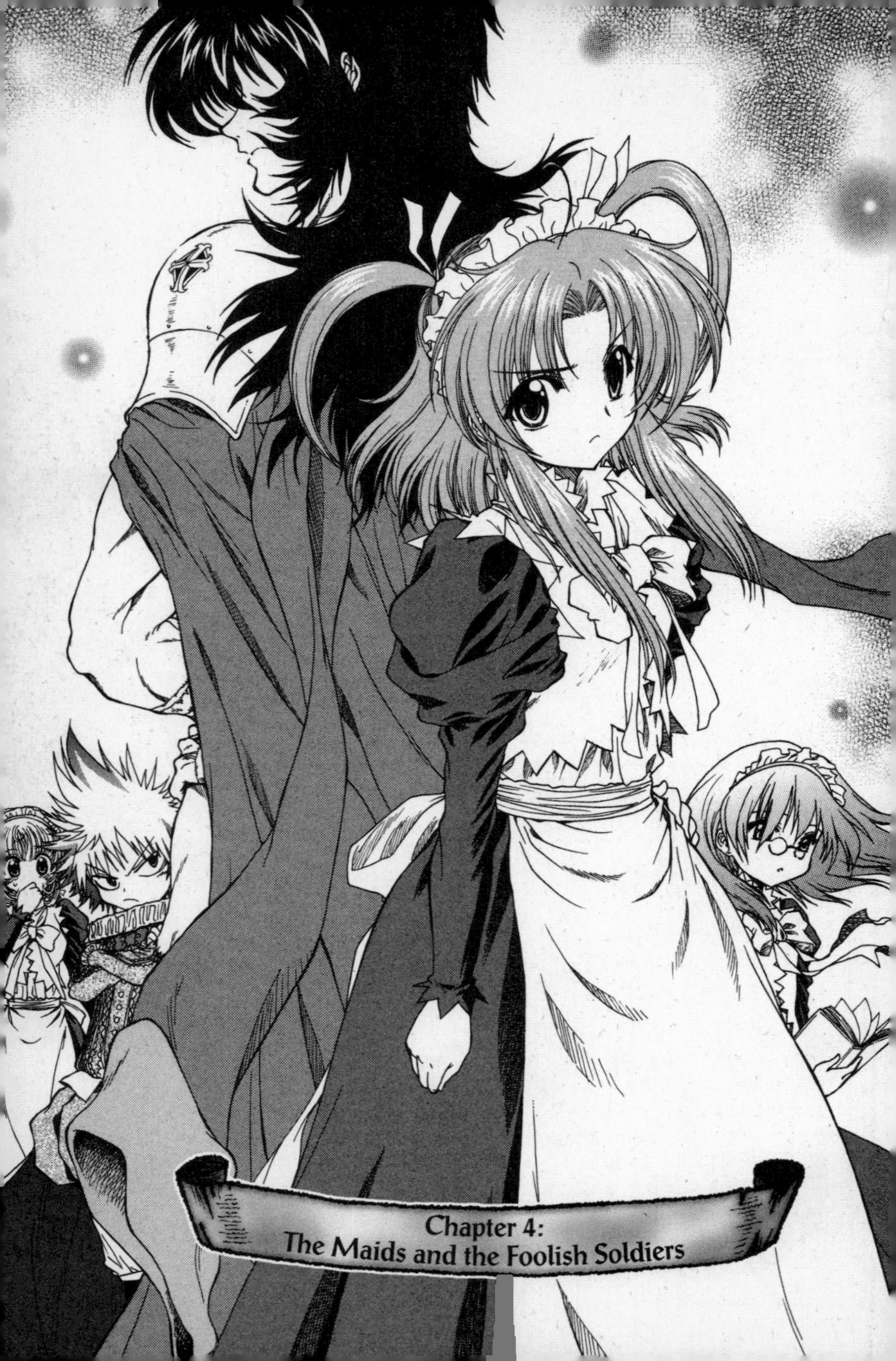
Chapter 4:
The Maids and the Foolish Soldiers

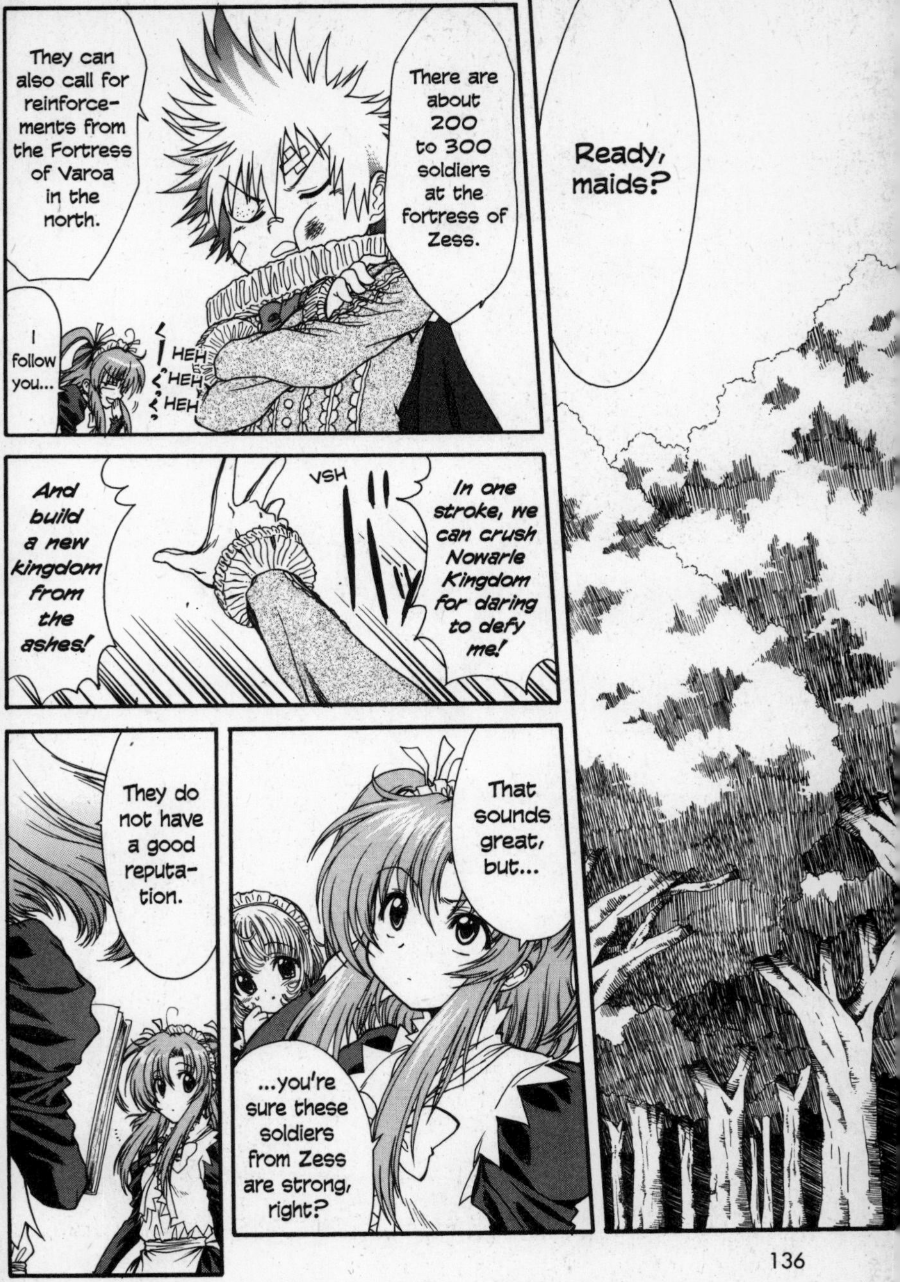

Ready, maids?
There are about 200 to 300 soldiers at the fortress of Zess.
They can also call for reinforcements from the Fortress of Varoa in the north.
HEH HEH HEH
I follow you...
VSH
In one stroke, we can crush Nowarle Kingdom for daring to defy me!
And build a new kingdom from the ashes!
That sounds great, but...
...you're sure these soldiers from Zess are strong, right?
They do not have a good reputation.

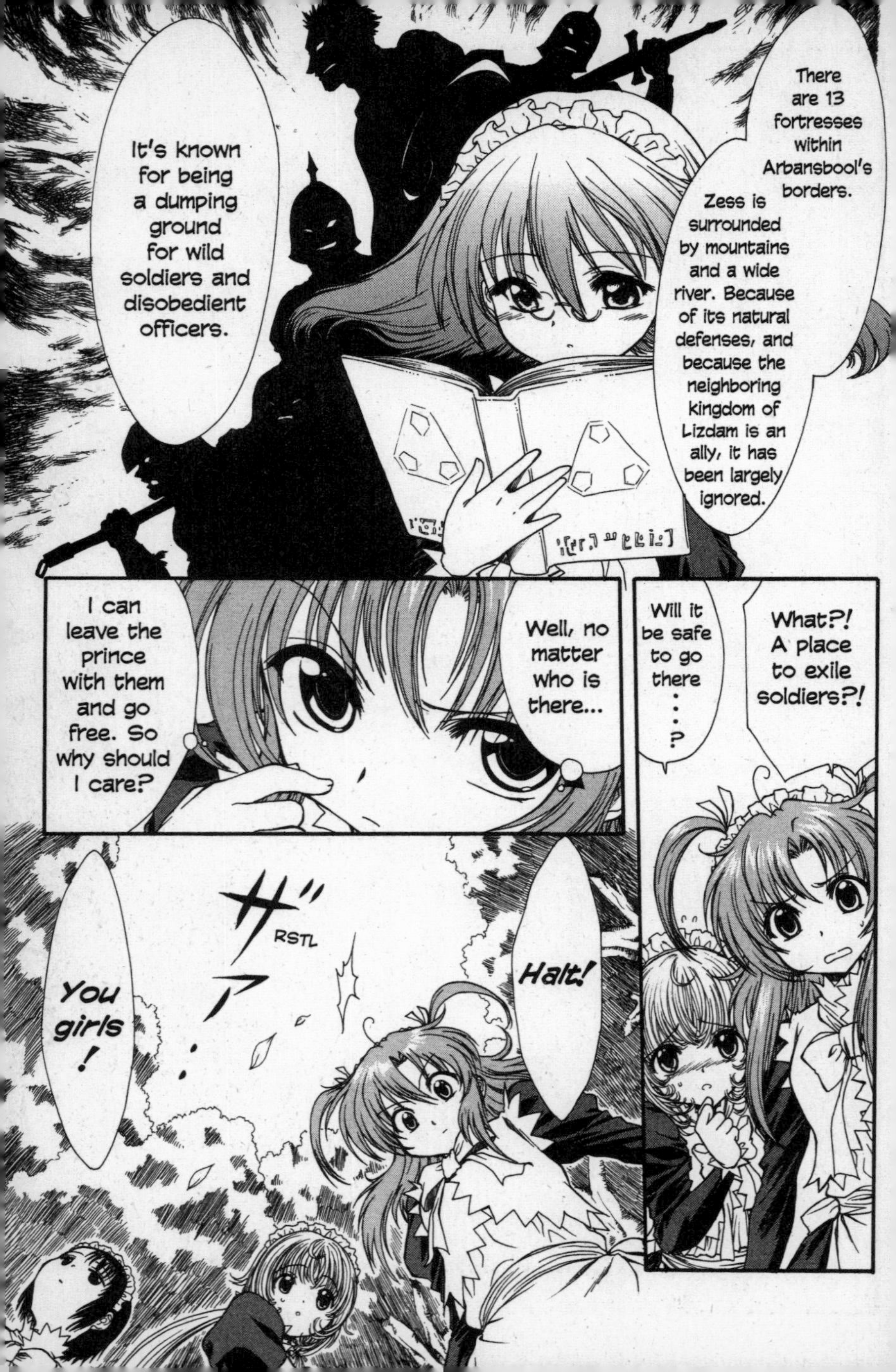
There are 13 fortresses within Arbansbool's borders.
Zess is surrounded by mountains and a wide river. Because of its natural defenses, and because the neighboring kingdom of Lizdam is an ally, it has been largely ignored.
It's known for being a dumping ground for wild soldiers and disobedient officers.
What?! A place to exile soldiers?!
Will it be safe to go there...?
Well, no matter who is there...
I can leave the prince with them and go free. So why should I care?
Halt!
RSTL
You girls!

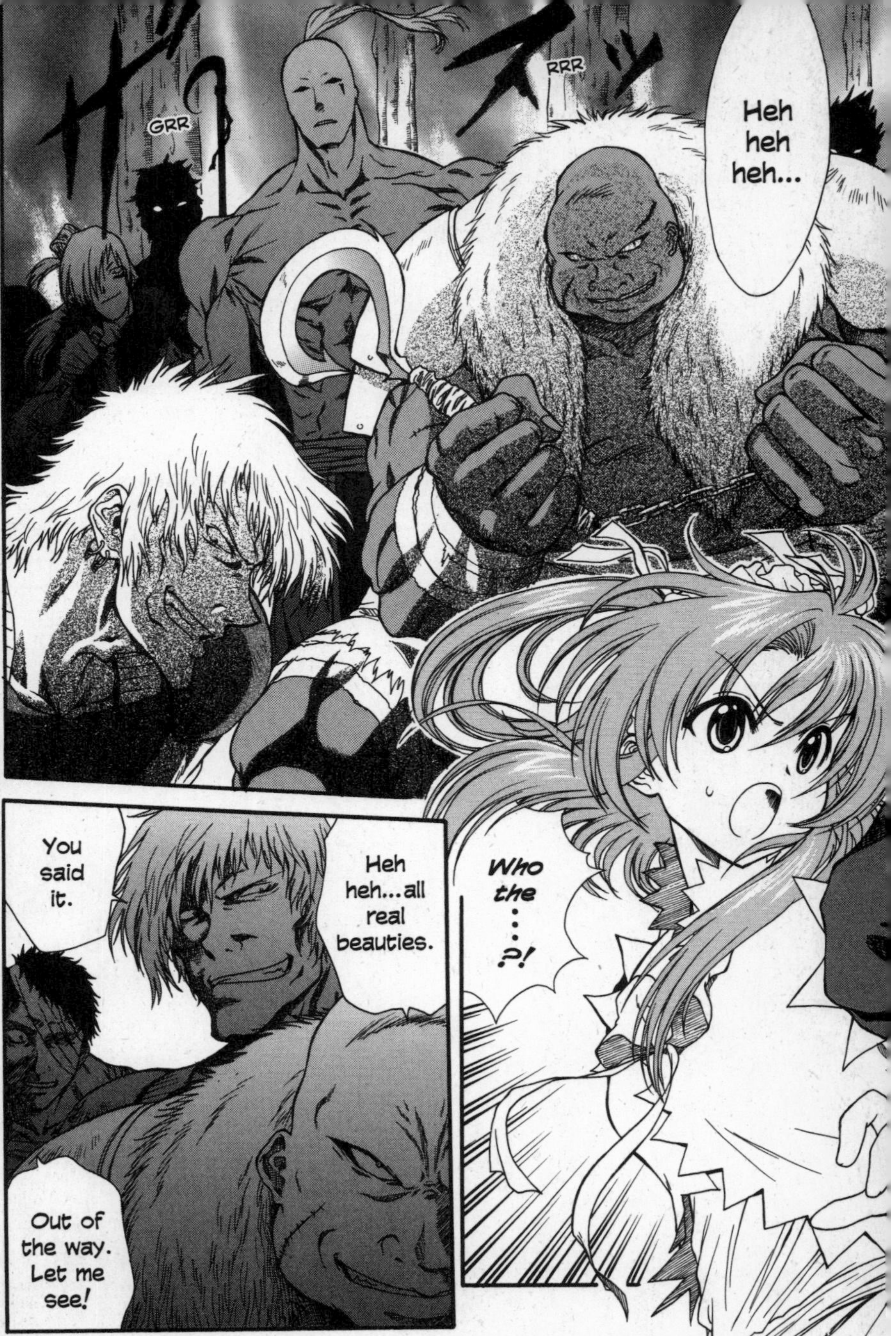
Heh heh heh...
RRR
GRR
Who the...?!
Heh heh...all real beauties.
You said it.
Out of the way. Let me see!

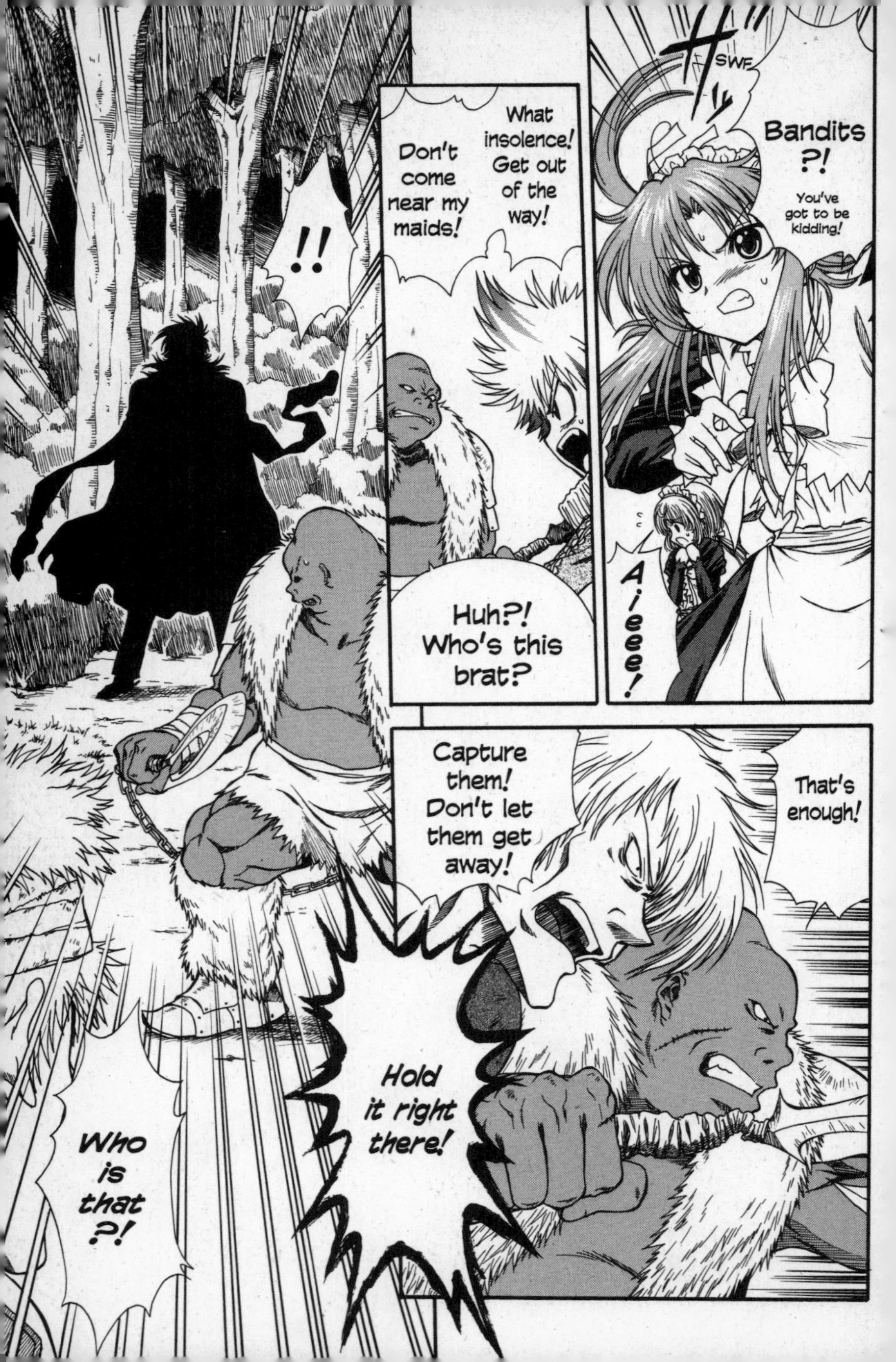
SWF
Bandits ?!
You've got to be kidding!
Aieee!
What insolence! Get out of the way!
Don't come near my maids!
Huh?! Who's this brat?
That's enough!
Capture them! Don't let them get away!
!!
Hold it right there!
Who is that ?!

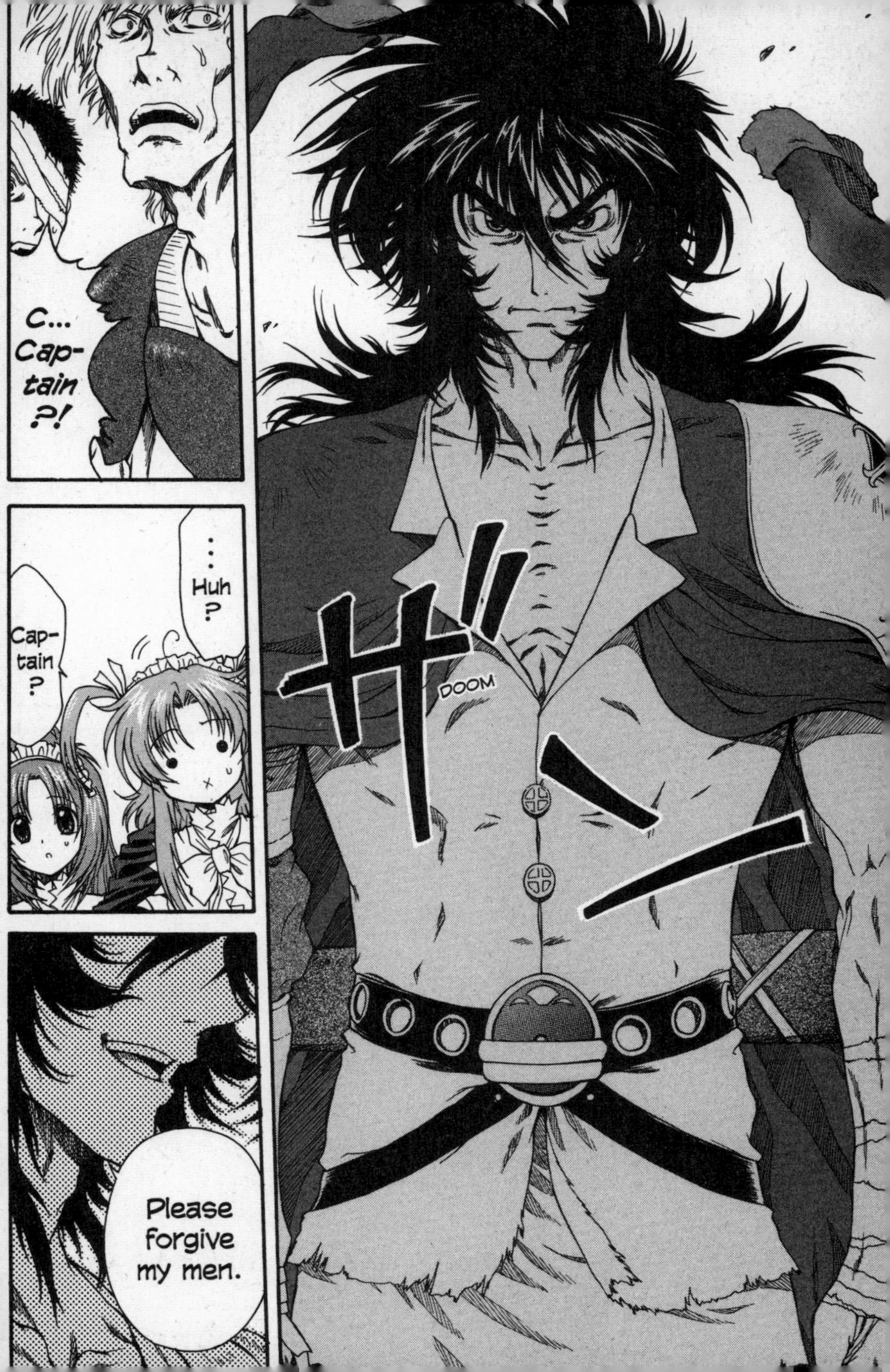
ザン
DOOM
C... Captain?!
...Huh?
Captain?
Please forgive my men.

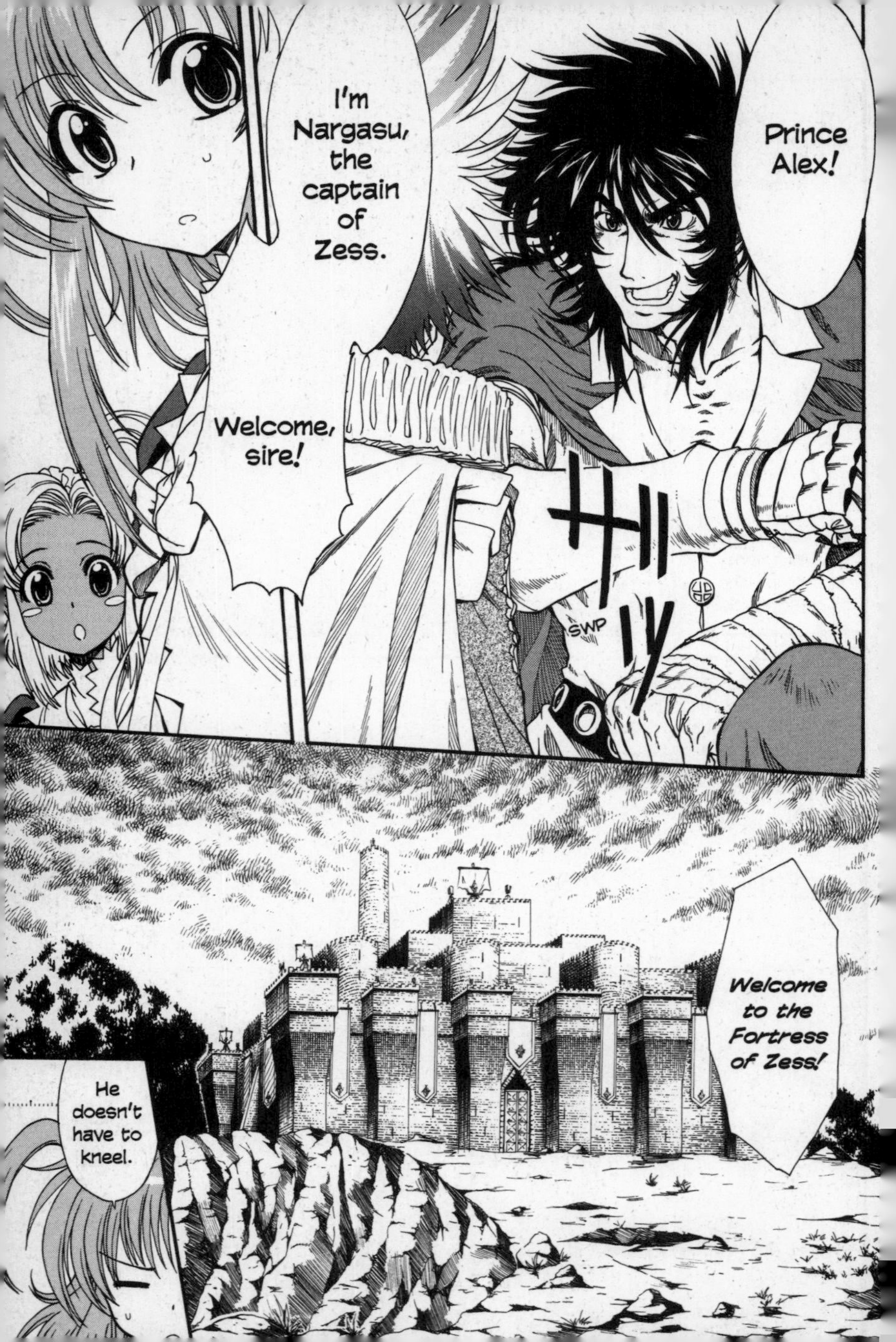
Prince Alex!
I'm Nargasu, the captain of Zess.
Welcome, sire!
SWP
Welcome to the Fortress of Zess!
He doesn't have to kneel.

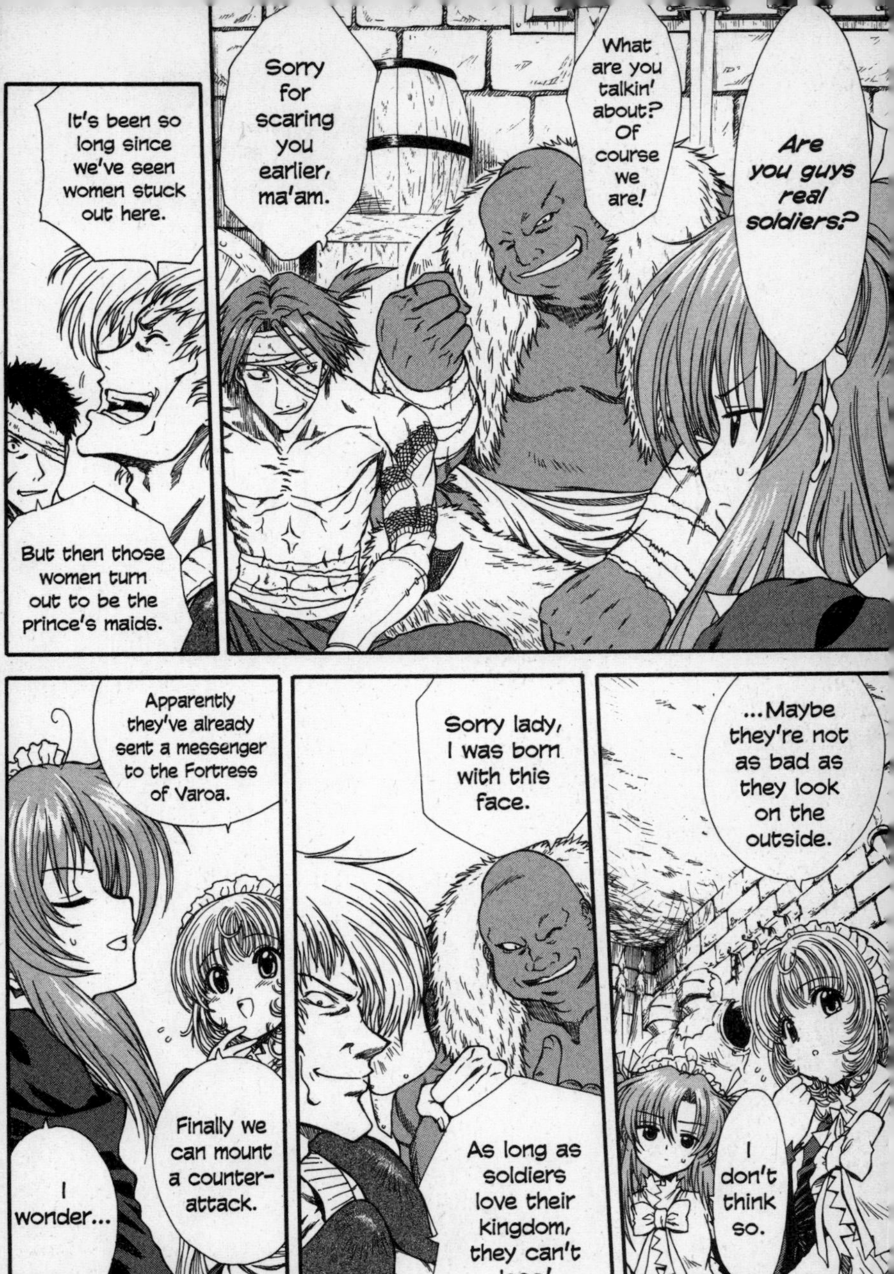
Are you guys real soldiers?
What are you talkin' about? Of course we are!
Sorry for scaring you earlier, ma'am.
It's been so long since we've seen women stuck out here.
But then those women turn out to be the prince's maids.
...Maybe they're not as bad as they look on the outside.
I don't think so.
Sorry lady, I was born with this face.
As long as soldiers love their kingdom, they can't lose!
Apparently they've already sent a messenger to the Fortress of Varoa.
Finally we can mount a counter-attack.
I wonder...

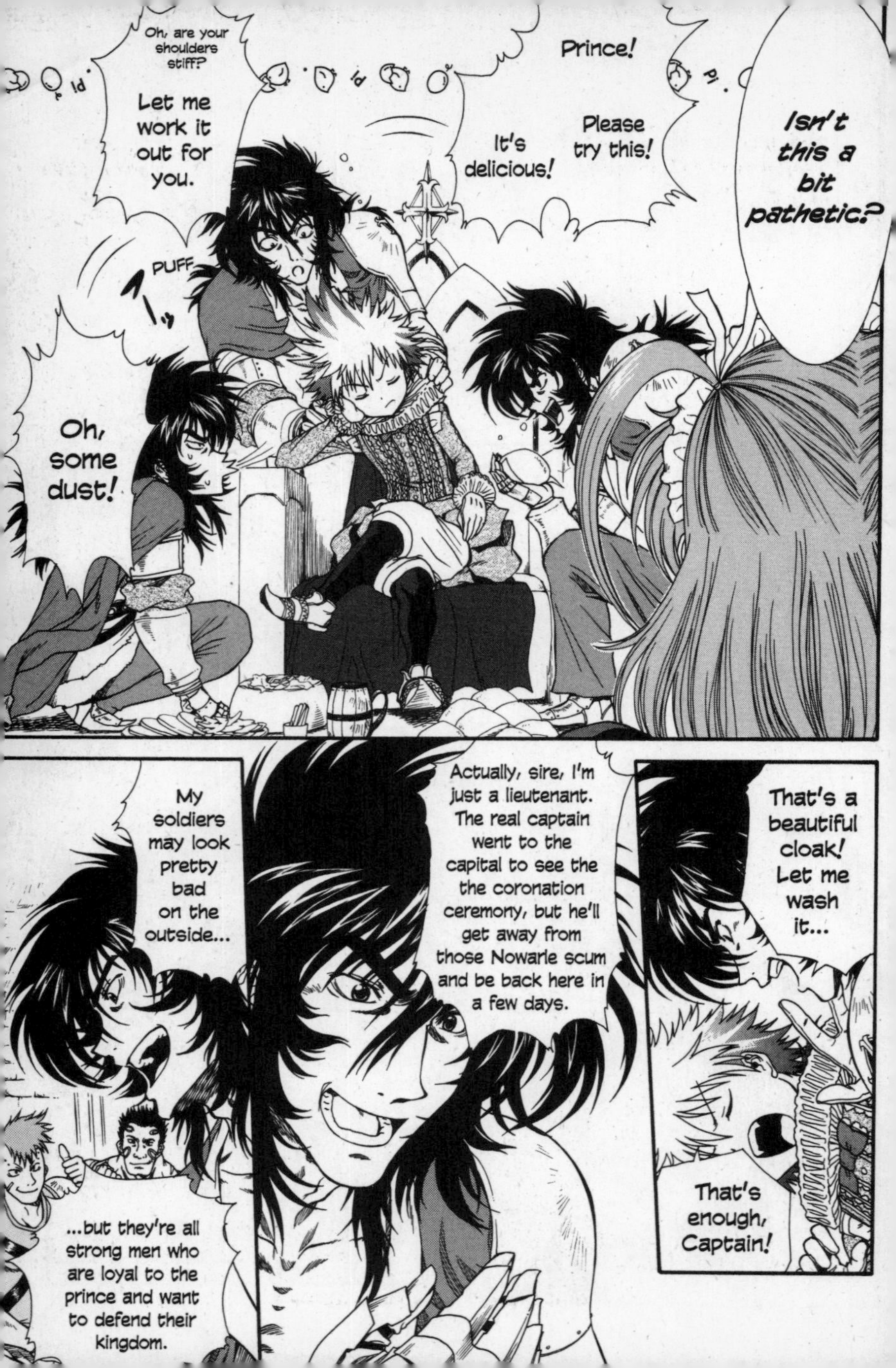

Isn't this a bit pathetic?
Prince!
Please try this!
It's delicious!
Oh, are your shoulders stiff?
Let me work it out for you.
PUFF
Oh, some dust!
That's a beautiful cloak! Let me wash it...
That's enough, Captain!
Actually, sire, I'm just a lieutenant. The real captain went to the capital to see the the coronation ceremony, but he'll get away from those Nowarle scum and be back here in a few days.
My soldiers may look pretty bad on the outside...
...but they're all strong men who are loyal to the prince and want to defend their kingdom.

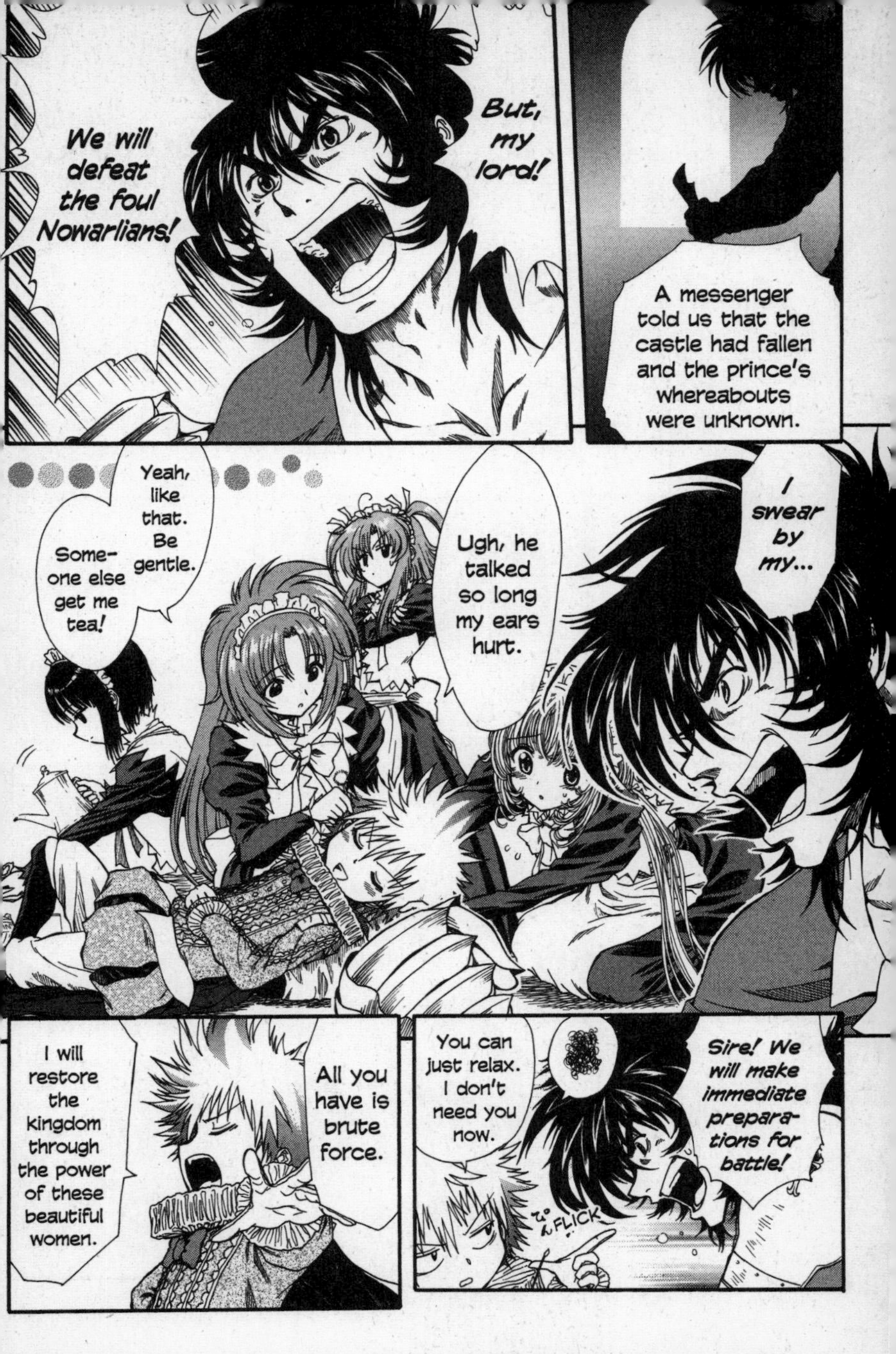
A messenger told us that the castle had fallen and the prince's whereabouts were unknown.
But, my lord!
We will defeat the foul Nowarlians!
I swear by my...
Ugh, he talked so long my ears hurt.
Yeah, like that. Be gentle.
Some-one else get me tea!
Sire! We will make immediate prepara-tions for battle!
You can just relax. I don't need you now.
FLICK
All you have is brute force.
I will restore the kingdom through the power of these beautiful women.

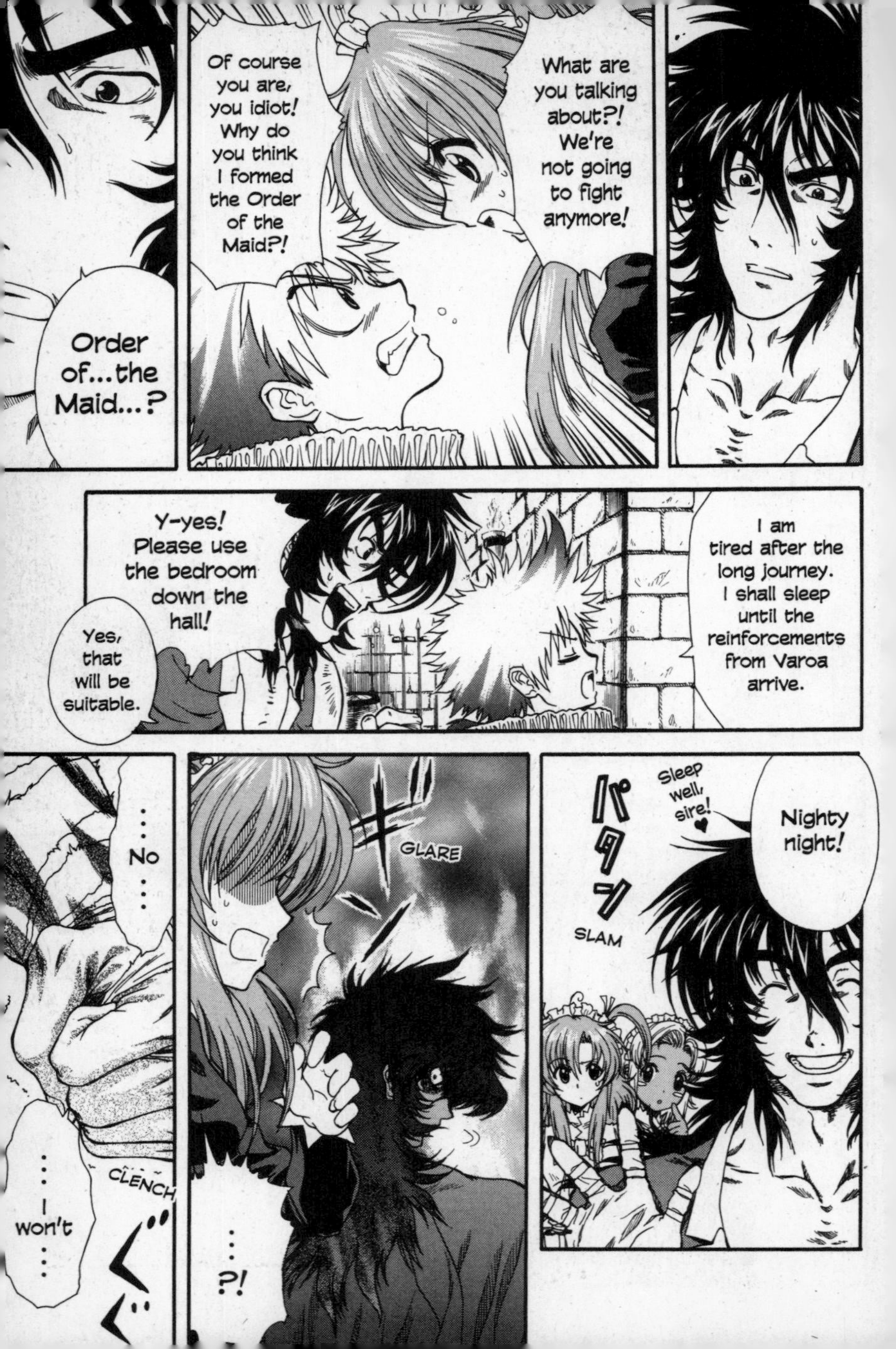

What are you talking about?! We're not going to fight anymore!
Of course you are, you idiot! Why do you think I formed the Order of the Maid?!
Order of...the Maid...?
I am tired after the long journey. I shall sleep until the reinforcements from Varoa arrive.
Y-yes! Please use the bedroom down the hall!
Yes, that will be suitable.
Nighty night!
Sleep well, sire! ♥
パタン
SLAM
GLARE
...?!
...No...
...I won't...
CLENCH

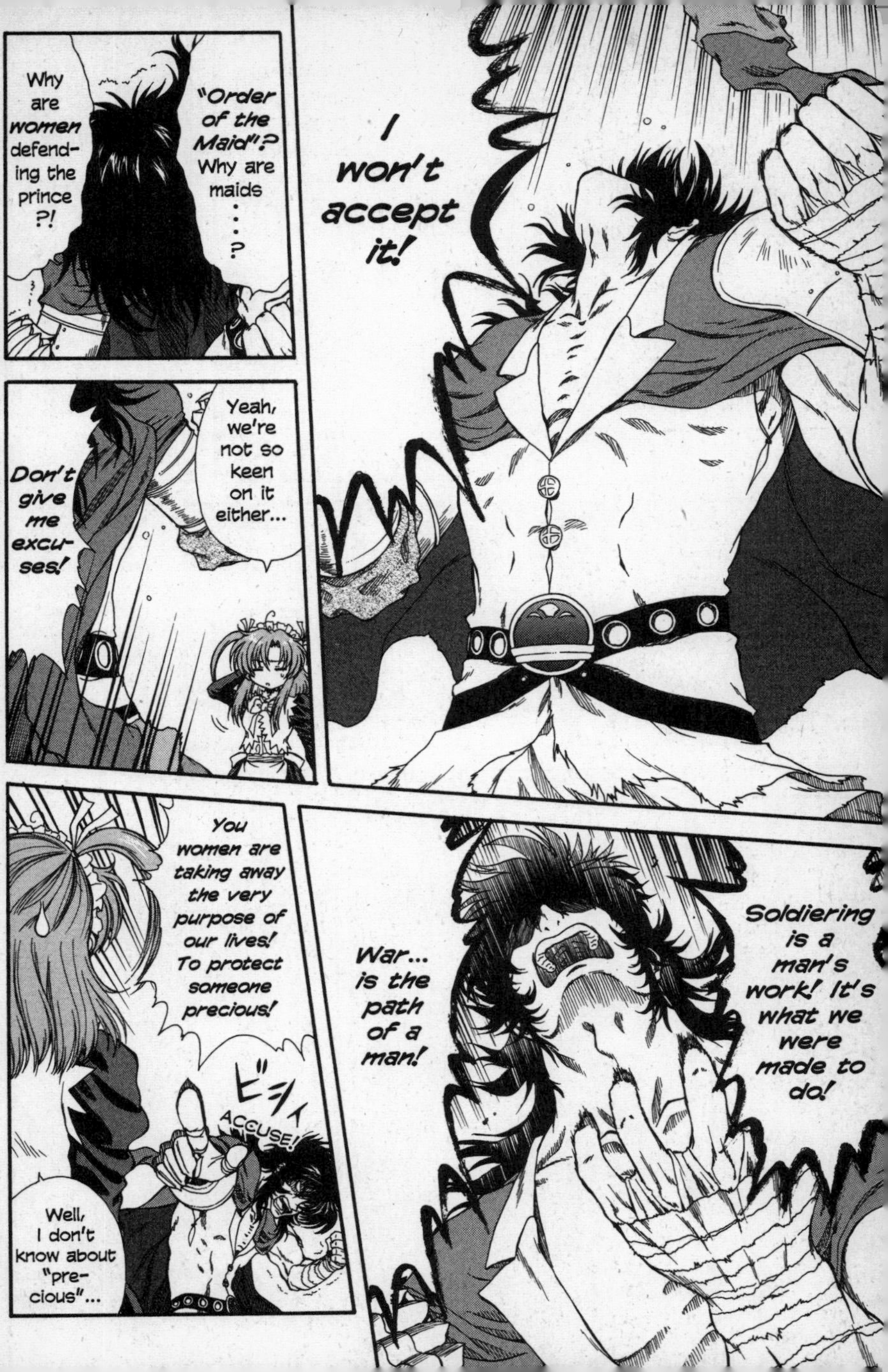

I won't accept it!
"Order of the Maid"? Why are maids . . . ?
Why are women defending the prince ?!
Yeah, we're not so keen on it either...
Don't give me excuses!
Soldiering is a man's work! It's what we were made to do!
War... is the path of a man!
You women are taking away the very purpose of our lives! To protect someone precious!
ビシィ
ACCUSE!
Well, I don't know about "precious"...

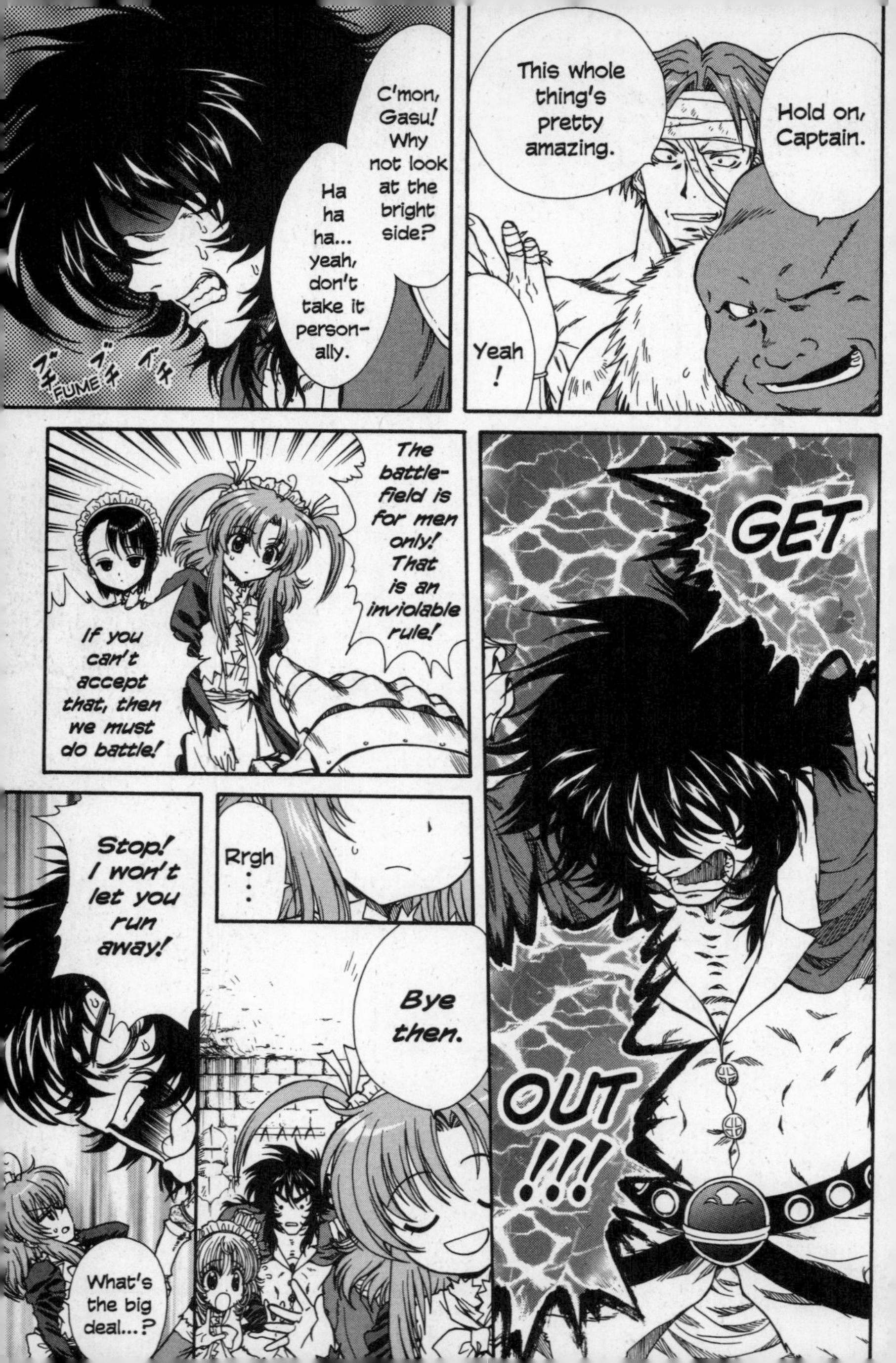
Hold on, Captain.
This whole thing's pretty amazing.
Yeah!
C'mon, Gasu! Why not look at the bright side?
Ha ha ha... yeah, don't take it personally.
FUME
GET OUT!!!
The battlefield is for men only! That is an inviolable rule!
If you can't accept that, then we must do battle!
Rrgh...
Bye then.
Stop! I won't let you run away!
What's the big deal...?

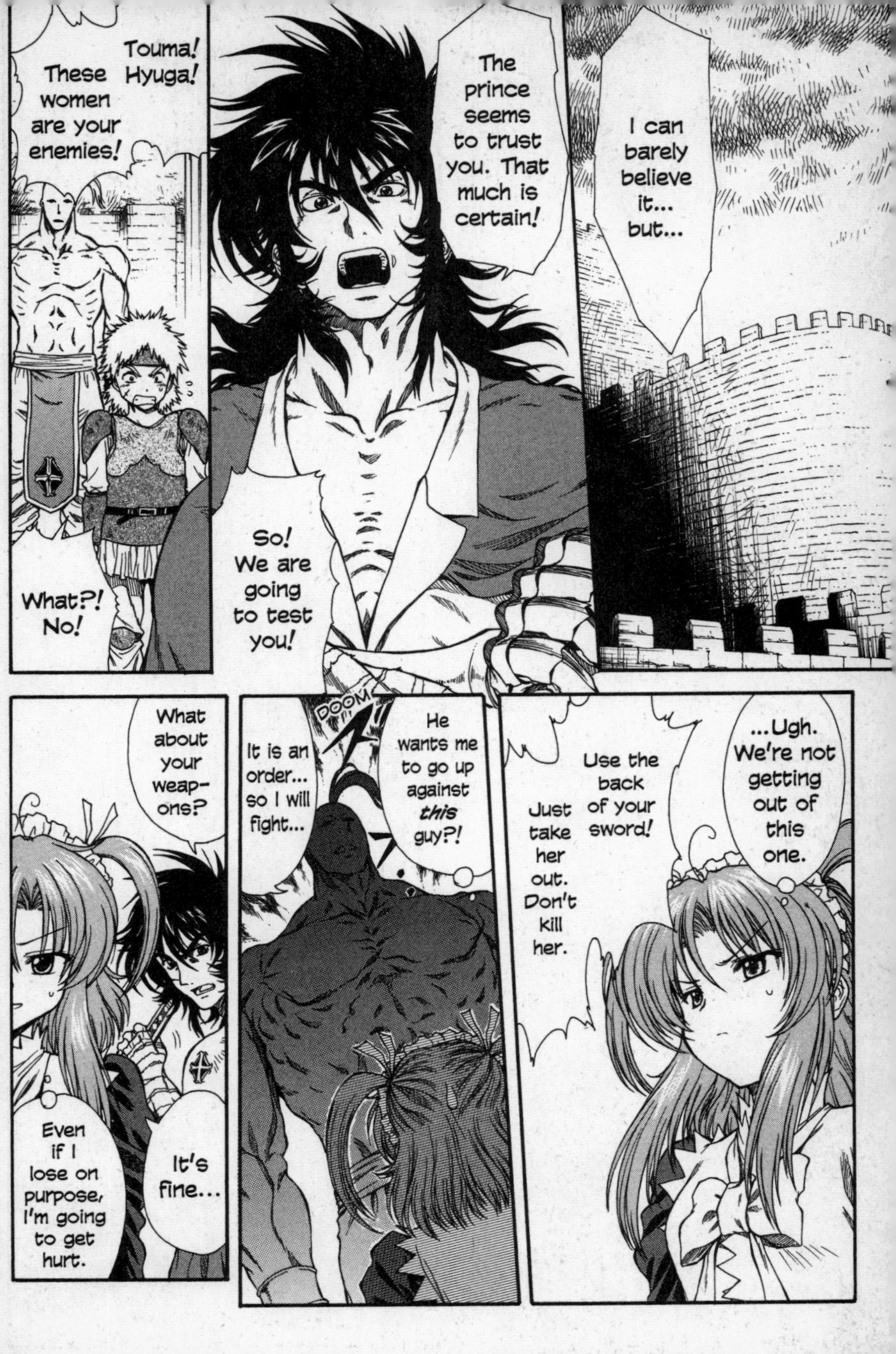
I can barely believe it... but...
The prince seems to trust you. That much is certain!
So! We are going to test you!
Touma! Hyuga!
These women are your enemies!
What?! No!
...Ugh. We're not getting out of this one.
Use the back of your sword!
Just take her out. Don't kill her.
He wants me to go up against *this* guy?!
DOOM
It is an order... so I will fight...
What about your weap-ons?
It's fine...
Even if I lose on purpose, I'm going to get hurt.

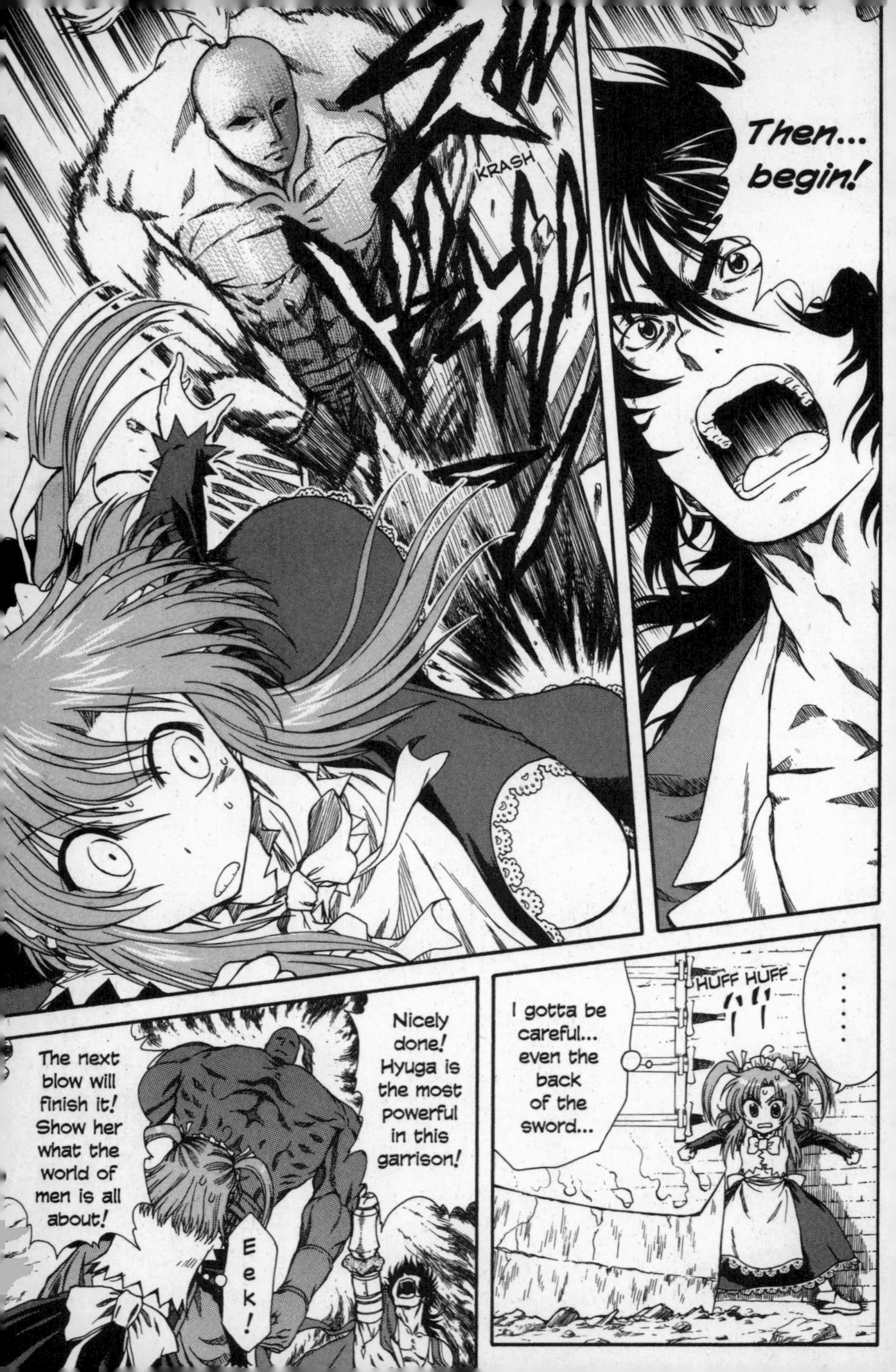
Then... begin!
KRASH
......
HUFF HUFF
I gotta be careful... even the back of the sword...
Nicely done! Hyuga is the most powerful in this garrison!
The next blow will finish it! Show her what the world of men is all about!
Eek!

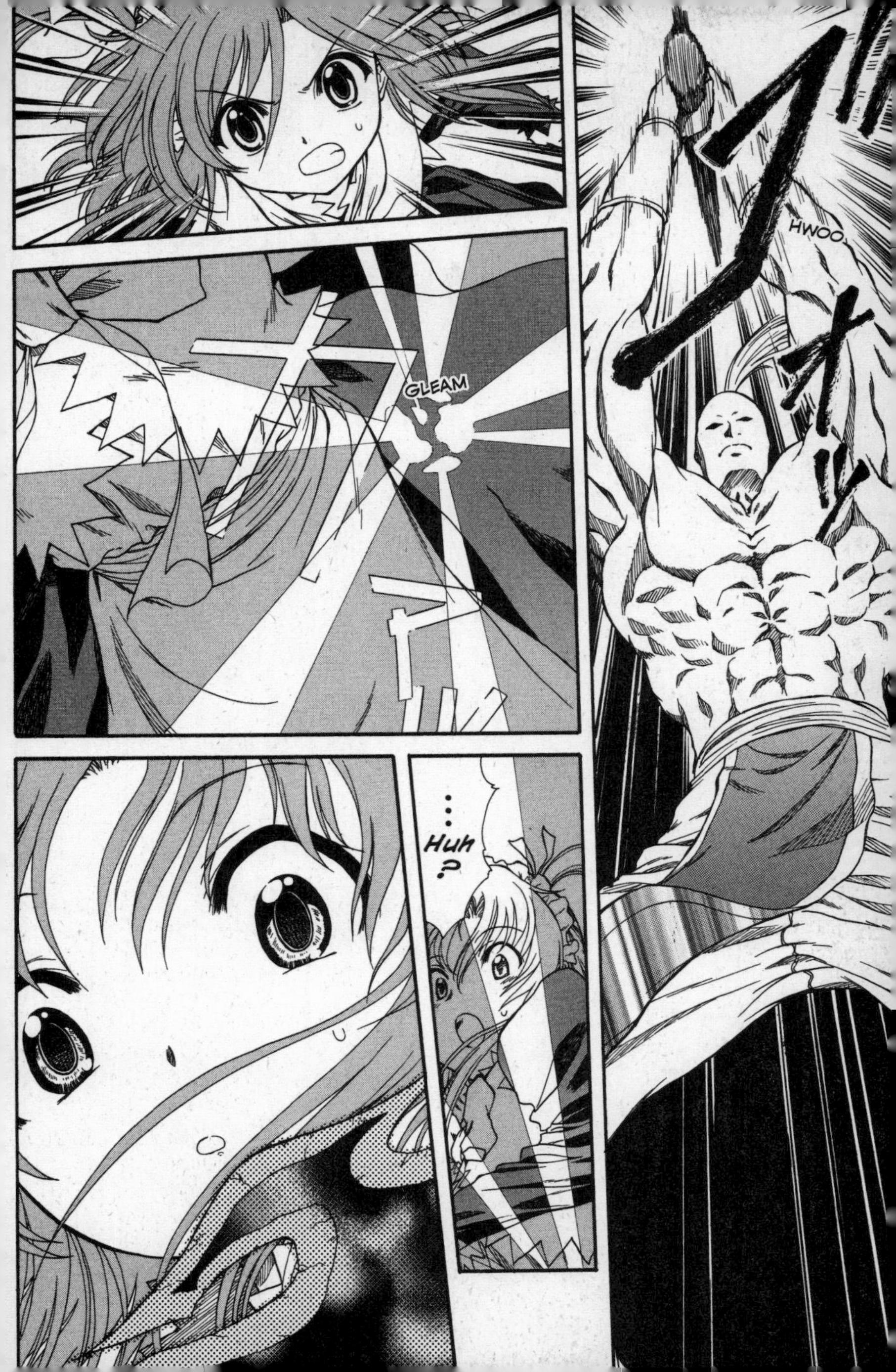
HWOO
GLEAM
...Huh?

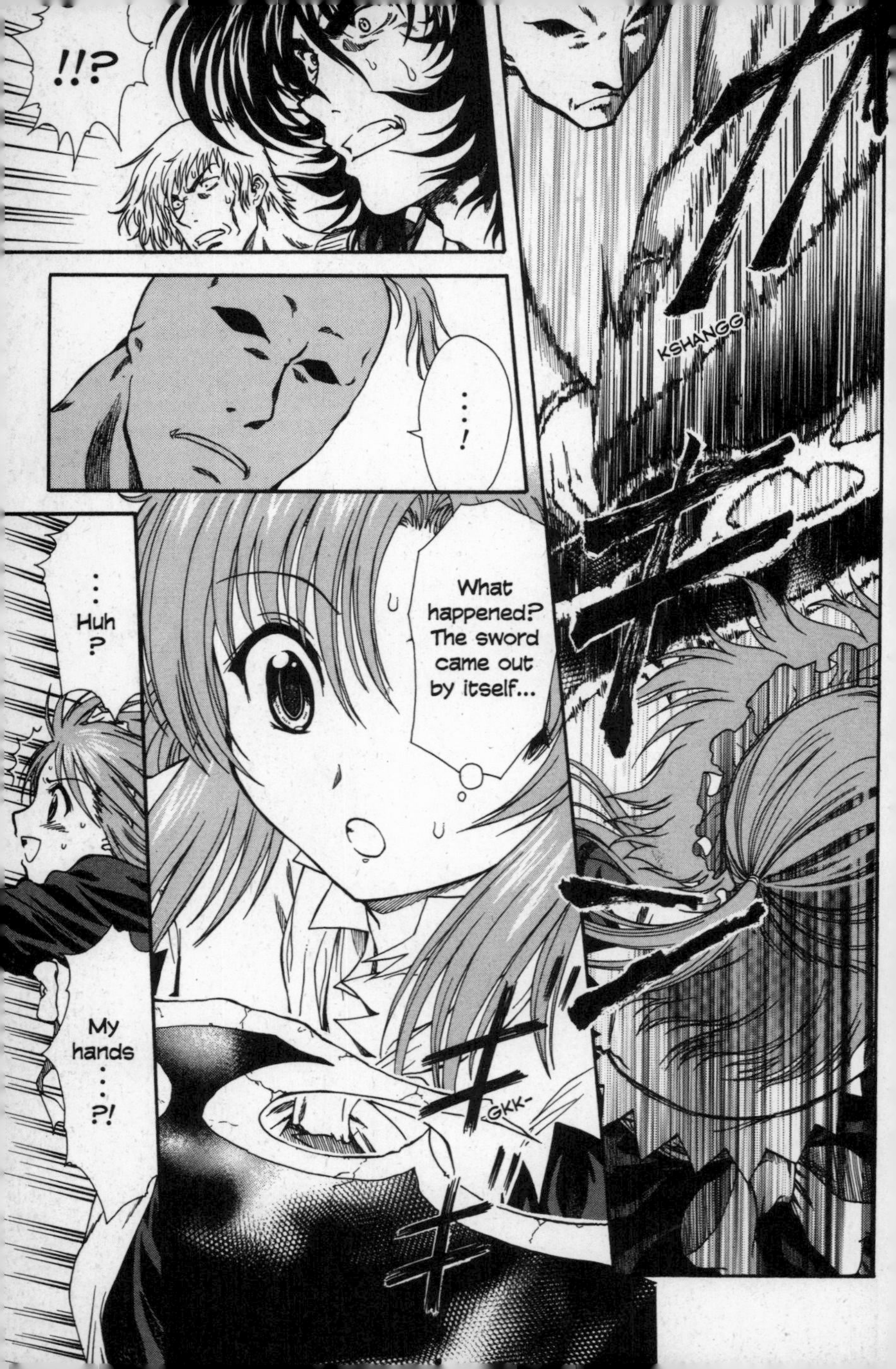
KSHANGG
!!?
...!
What happened? The sword came out by itself...
GKK-
...Huh?
My hands...?!

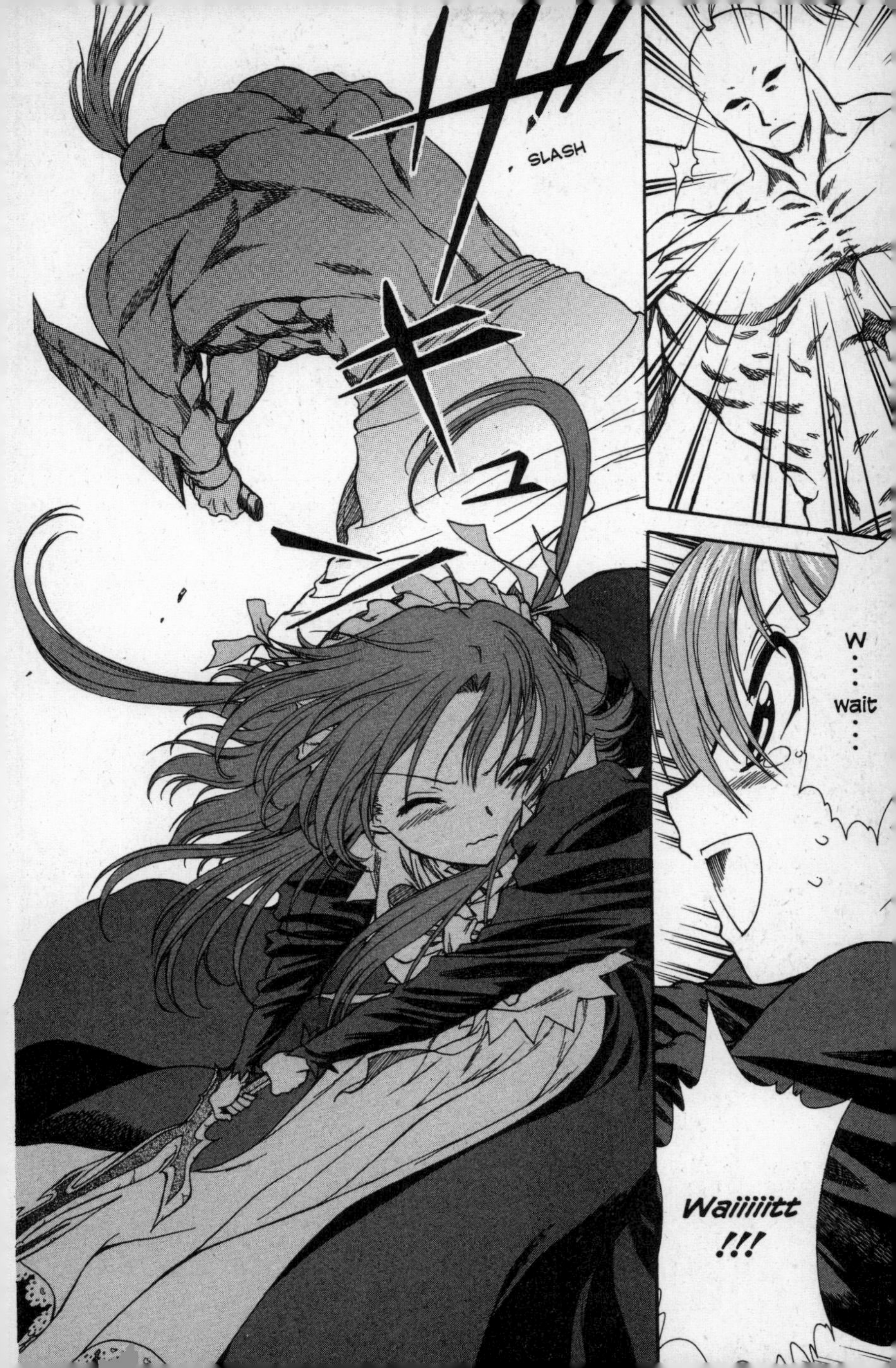
W... wait...
Waiiiiitt !!!
SLASH

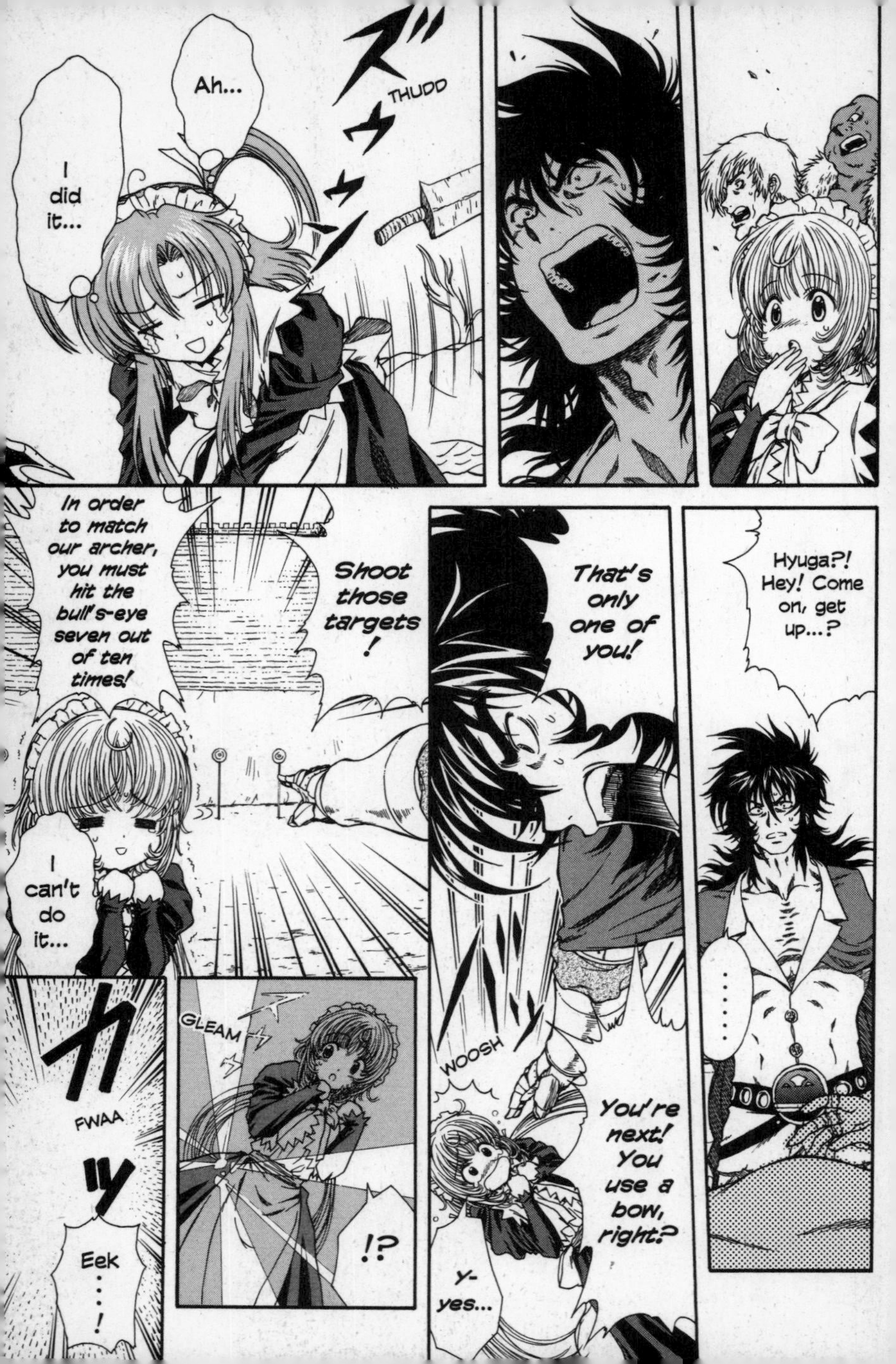
THUDD
Ah...
I did it...
Hyuga?! Hey! Come on, get up...?
......
That's only one of you!
WOOSH
You're next! You use a bow, right?
Y-yes...
Shoot those targets!
In order to match our archer, you must hit the bull's-eye seven out of ten times!
I can't do it...
GLEAM
!?
FWAA
Eek...!

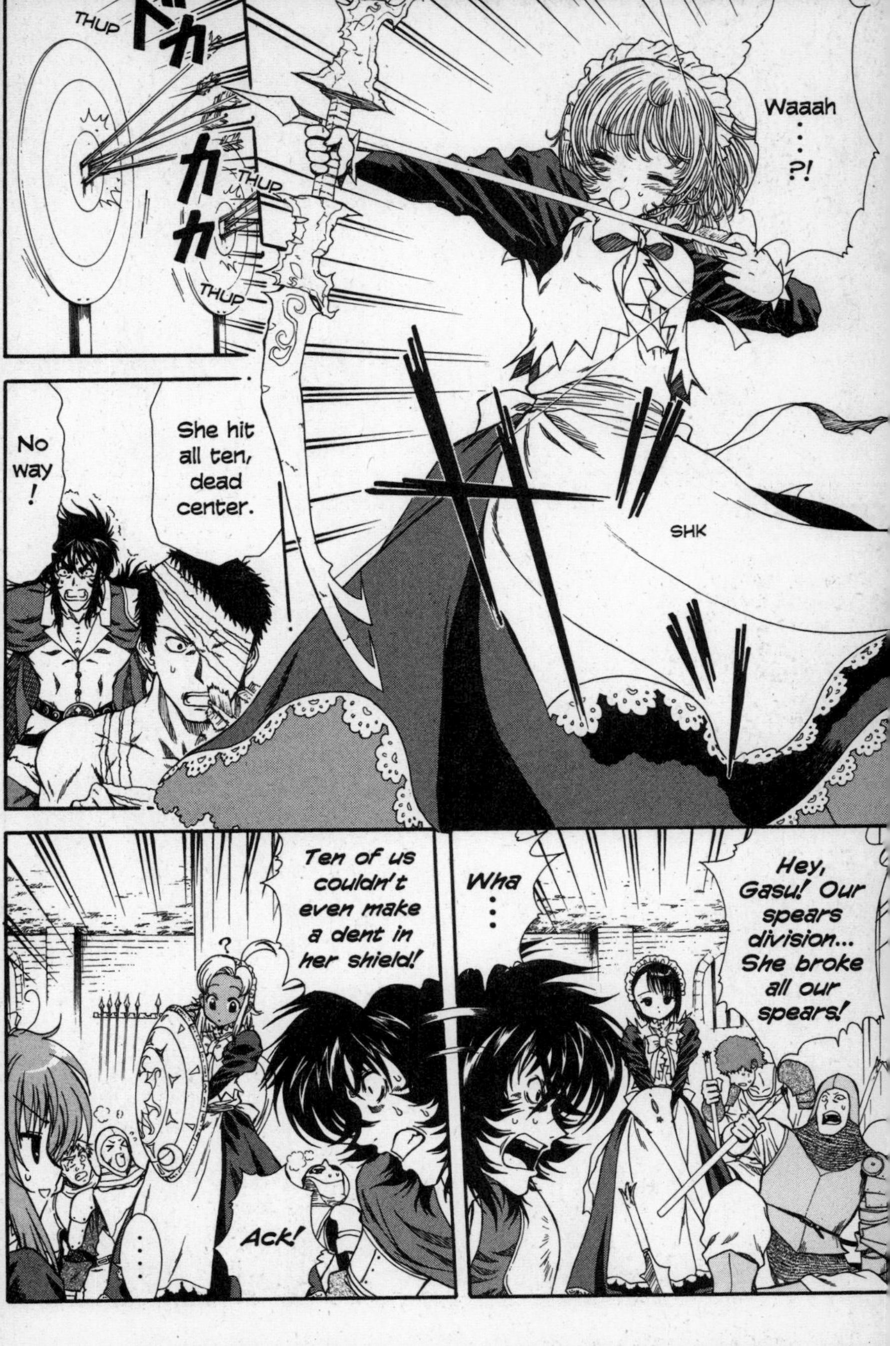

Waaah ...?!
SHK
THUP
ドカカ
THUP
THUP
She hit all ten, dead center.
No way!
Hey, Gasu! Our spears division... She broke all our spears!
Wha...
Ten of us couldn't even make a dent in her shield!
Ack!
....

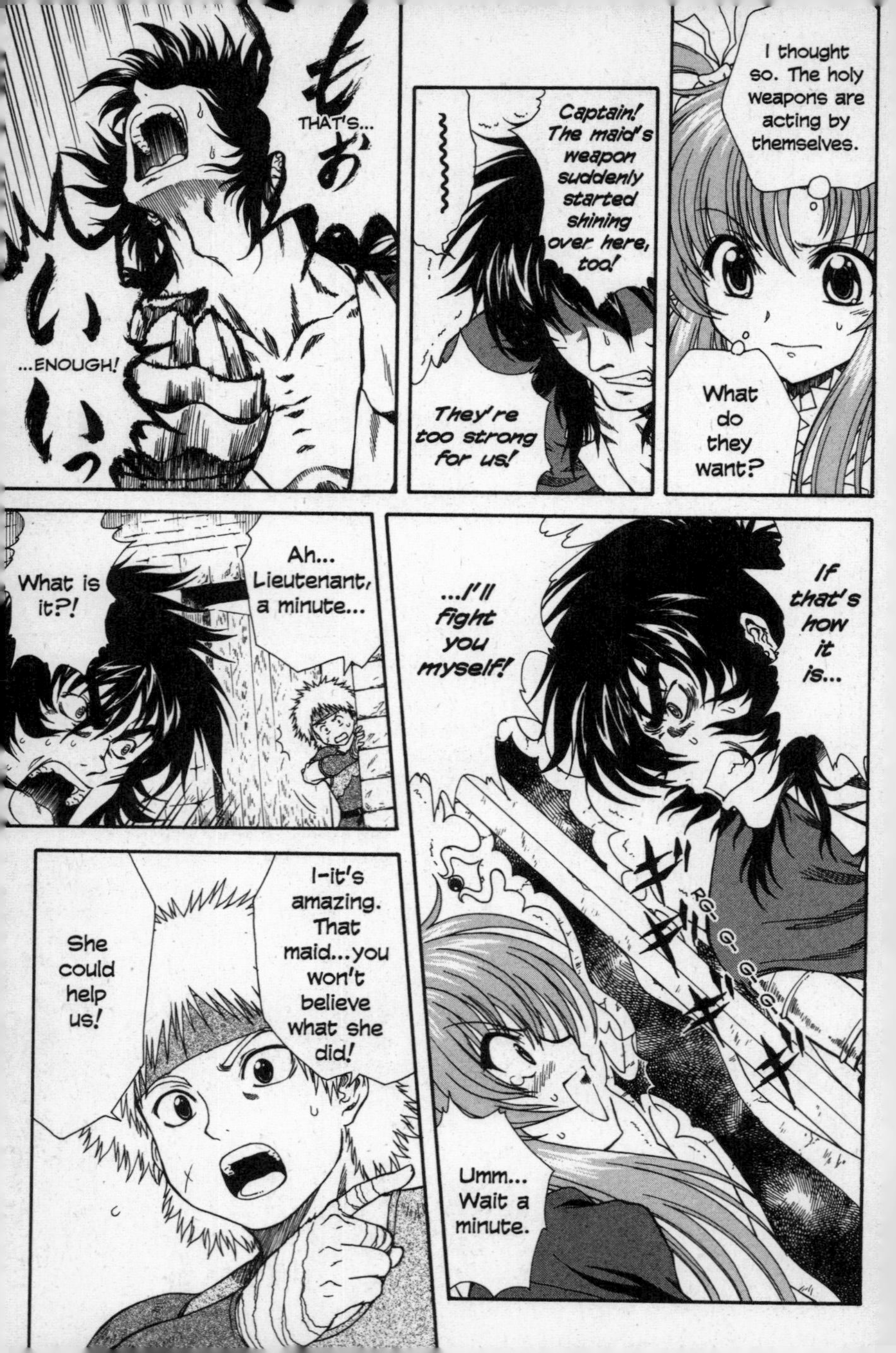
I thought so. The holy weapons are acting by themselves.
What do they want?
Captain! The maid's weapon suddenly started shining over here, too!
They're too strong for us!
THAT'S...
もおいいっ
...ENOUGH!
If that's how it is...
...I'll fight you myself!
RG- G- G-G-
Umm... Wait a minute.
Ah... Lieutenant, a minute...
What is it?!
I-it's amazing. That maid...you won't believe what she did!
She could help us!

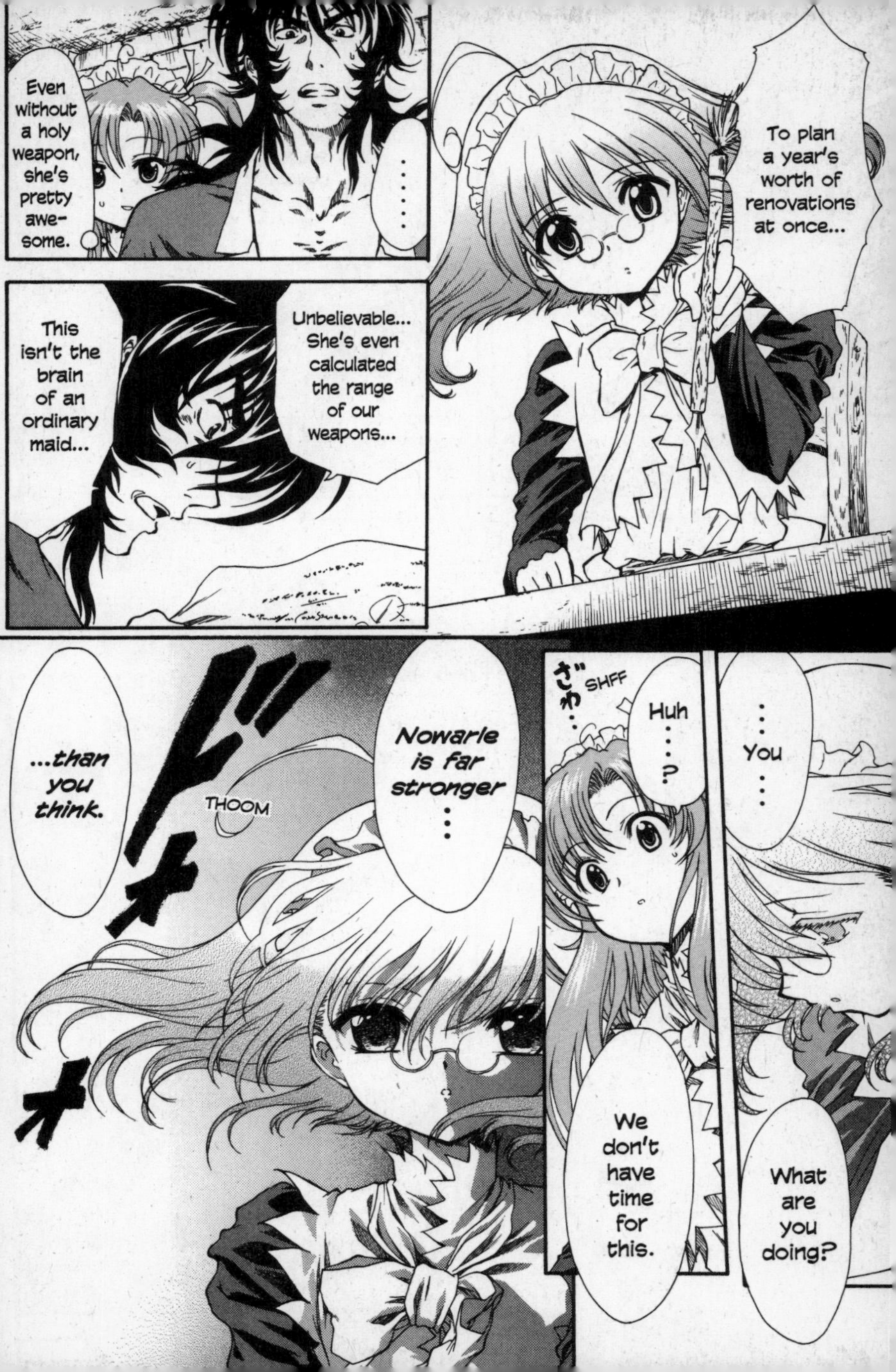

To plan a year's worth of renovations at once...
......
Even without a holy weapon, she's pretty awe-some.
Unbelievable... She's even calculated the range of our weapons...
This isn't the brain of an ordinary maid...
...You...
Huh...?
ざわ... SHFF
What are you doing?
We don't have time for this.
Nowarle is far stronger...
ドド THOOM
...than you think.

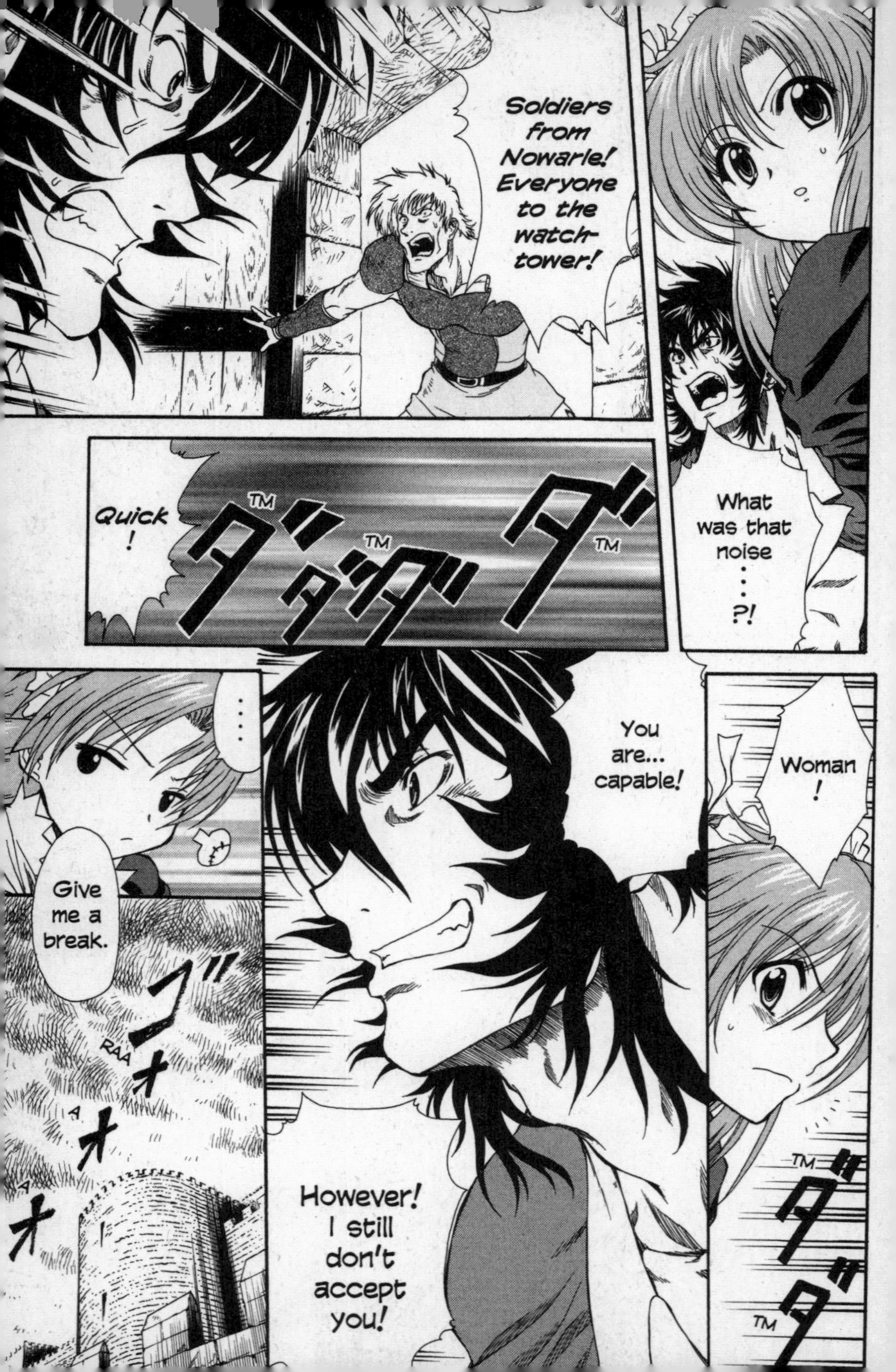
What was that noise...?!
Soldiers from Nowarle! Everyone to the watch-tower!
Quick!
Woman!
You are... capable!
However! I still don't accept you!
....
Give me a break.
RAA

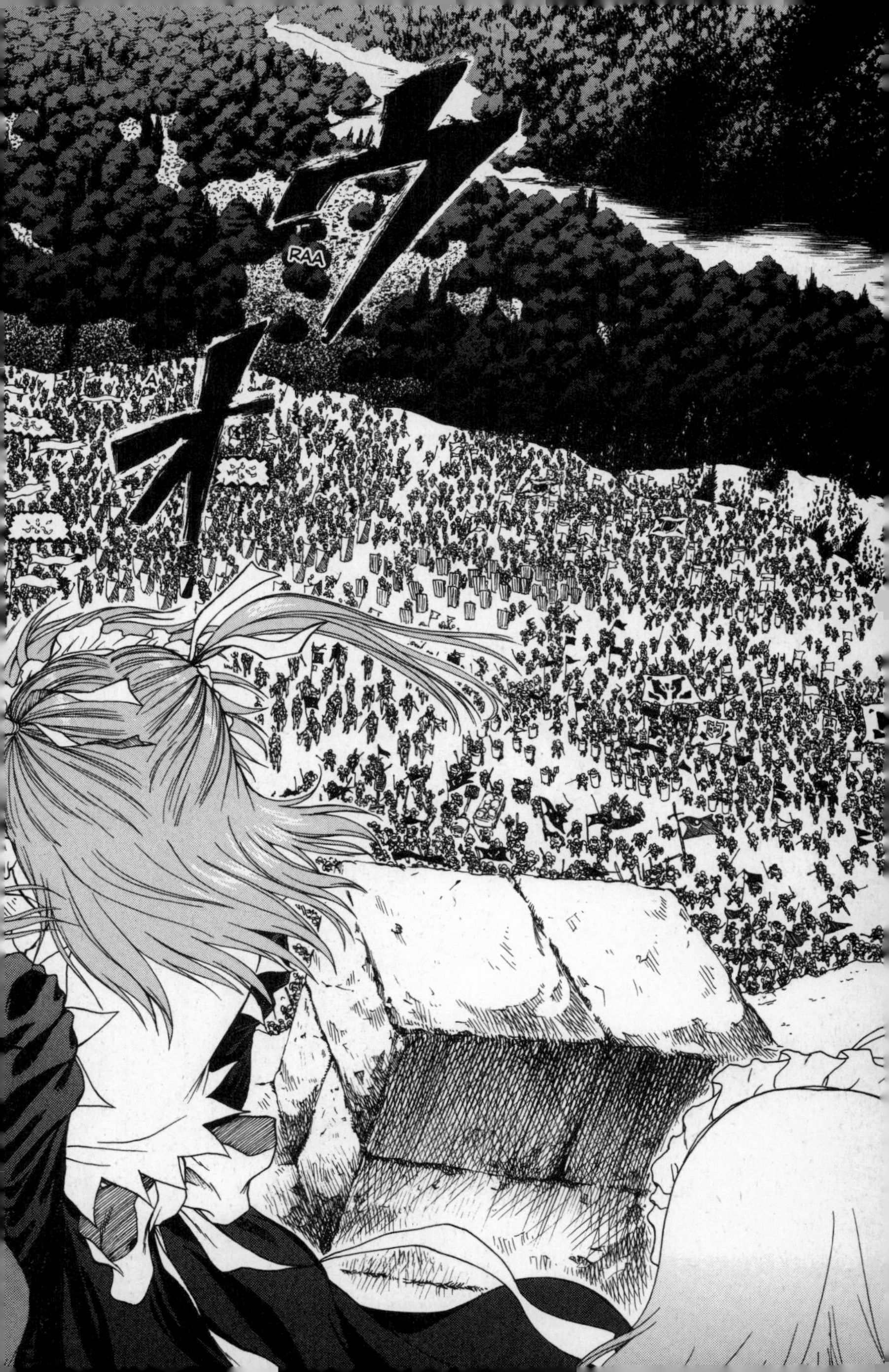

RAA
A

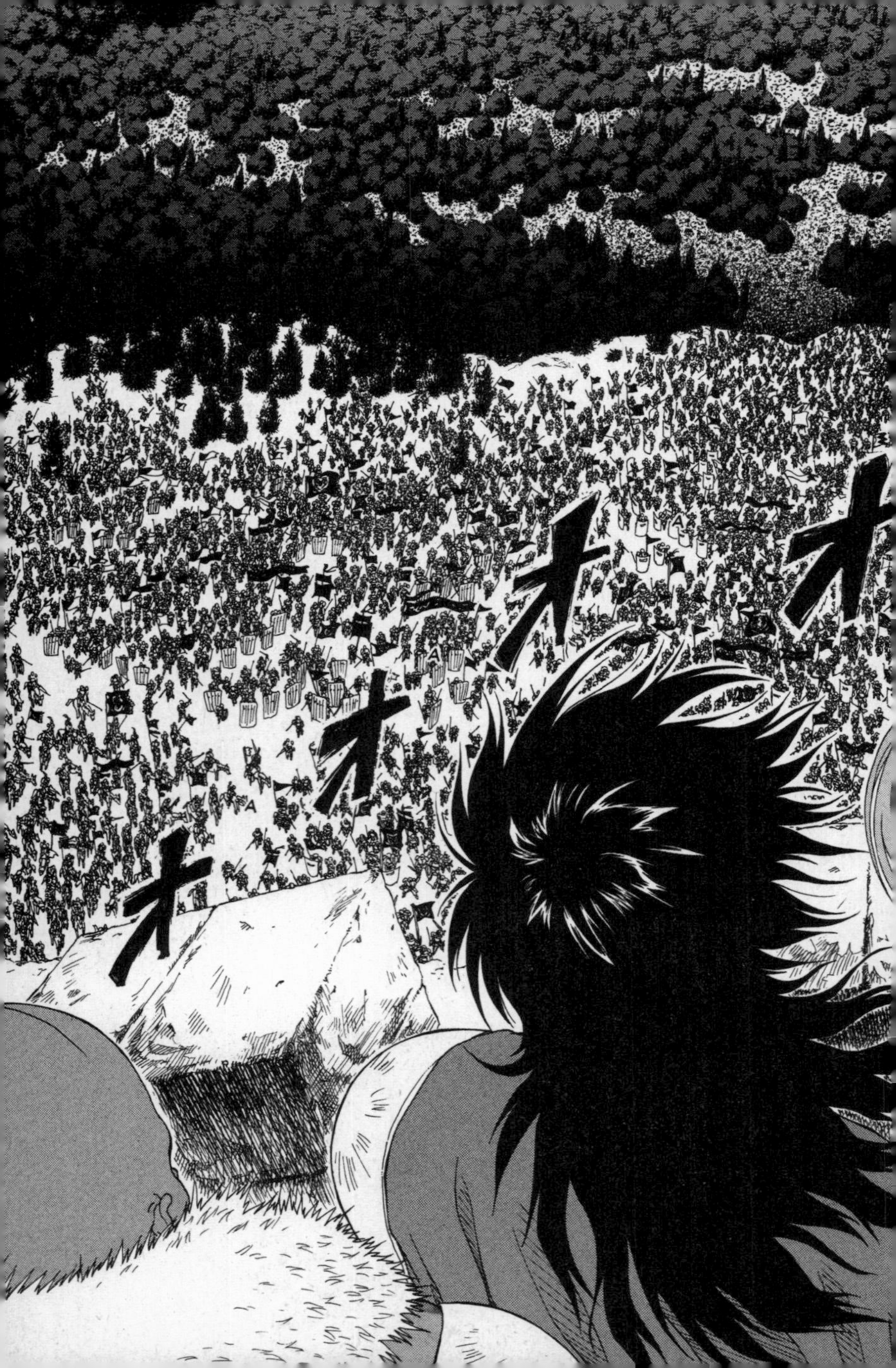
オオオオ

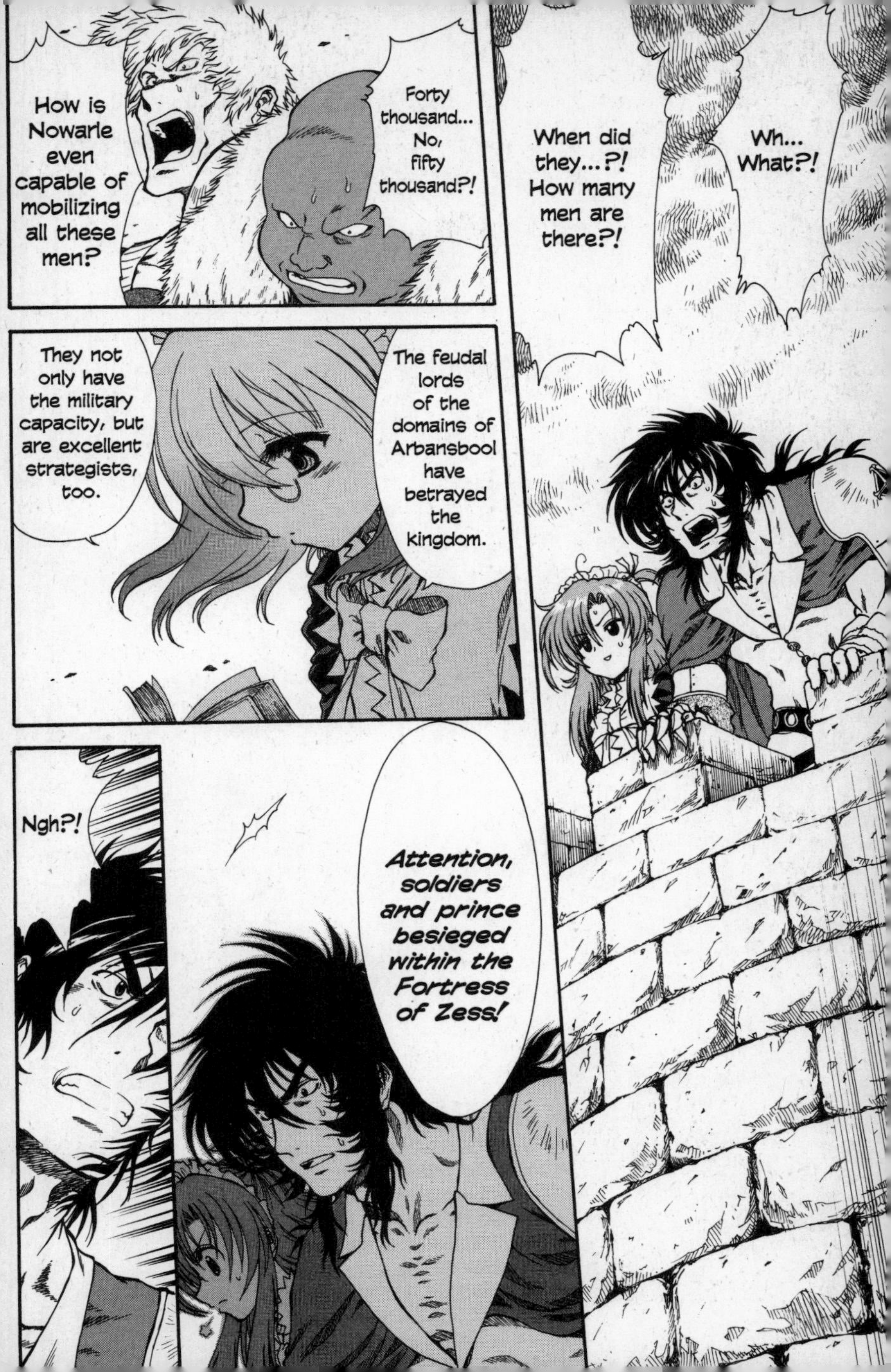
Wh... What?!
When did they...?! How many men are there?!
Forty thousand... No, fifty thousand?!
How is Nowarle even capable of mobilizing all these men?
The feudal lords of the domains of Arbansbool have betrayed the kingdom.
They not only have the military capacity, but are excellent strategists, too.
Attention, soldiers and prince besieged within the Fortress of Zess!
Ngh?!

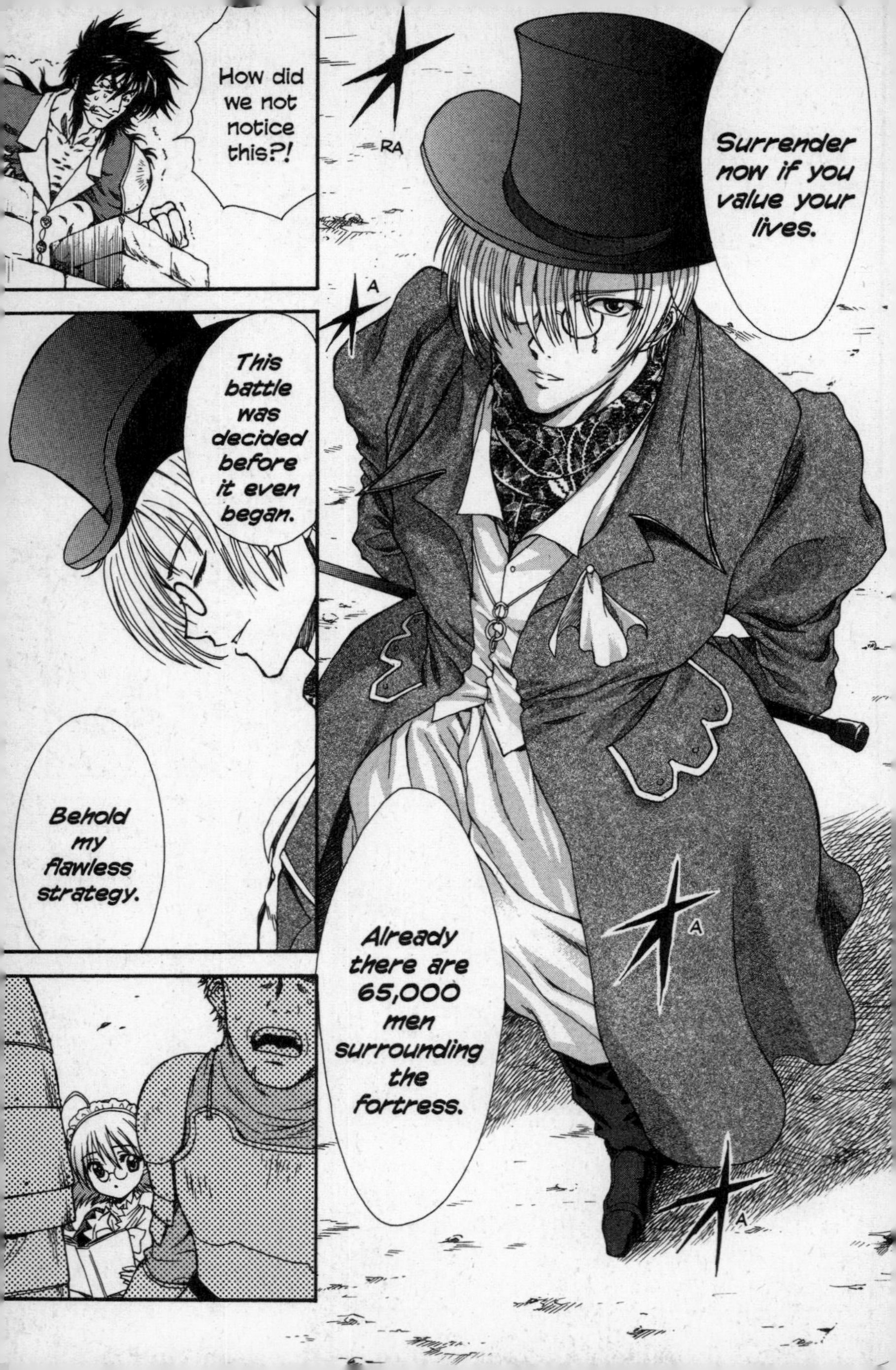
Surrender now if you value your lives.
RA
A
A
Already there are 65,000 men surrounding the fortress.
A
How did we not notice this?!
This battle was decided before it even began.
Behold my flawless strategy.

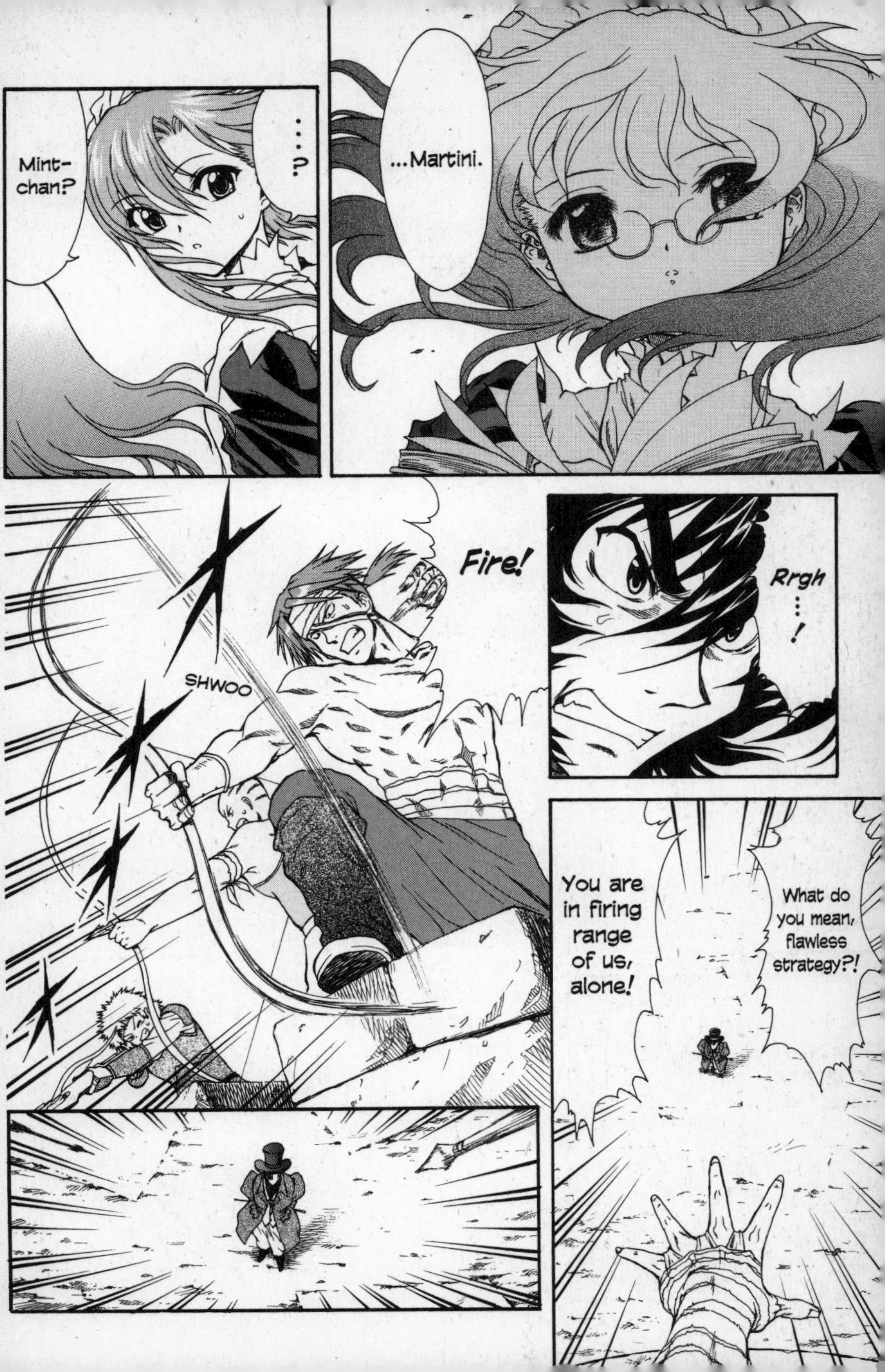
...Martini.
...?
Mint-chan?
Rrgh...!
Fire!
SHWOO
What do you mean, flawless strategy?!
You are in firing range of us, alone!

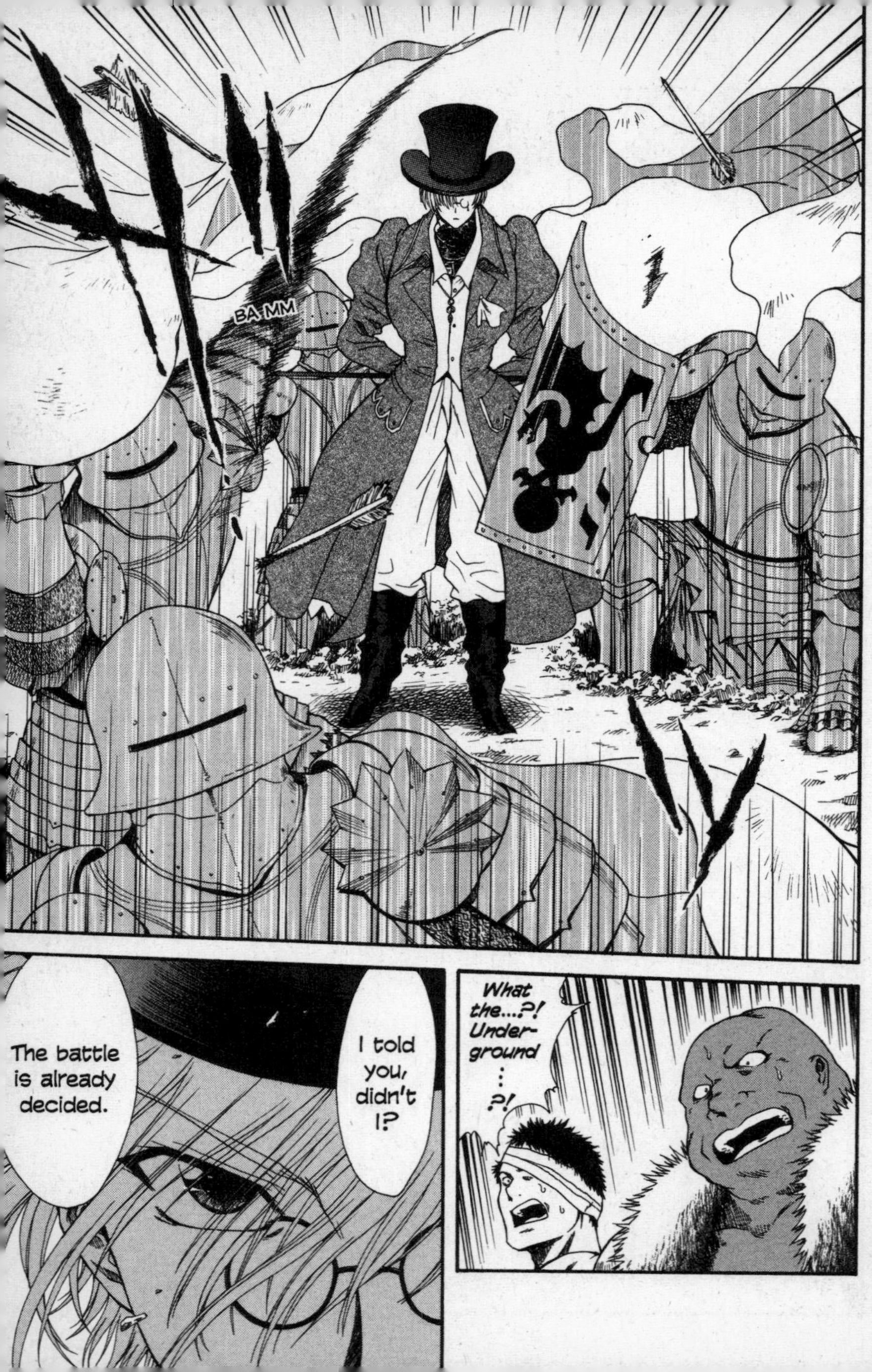
BA MM
What the...?! Underground...?!
I told you, didn't I?
The battle is already decided.

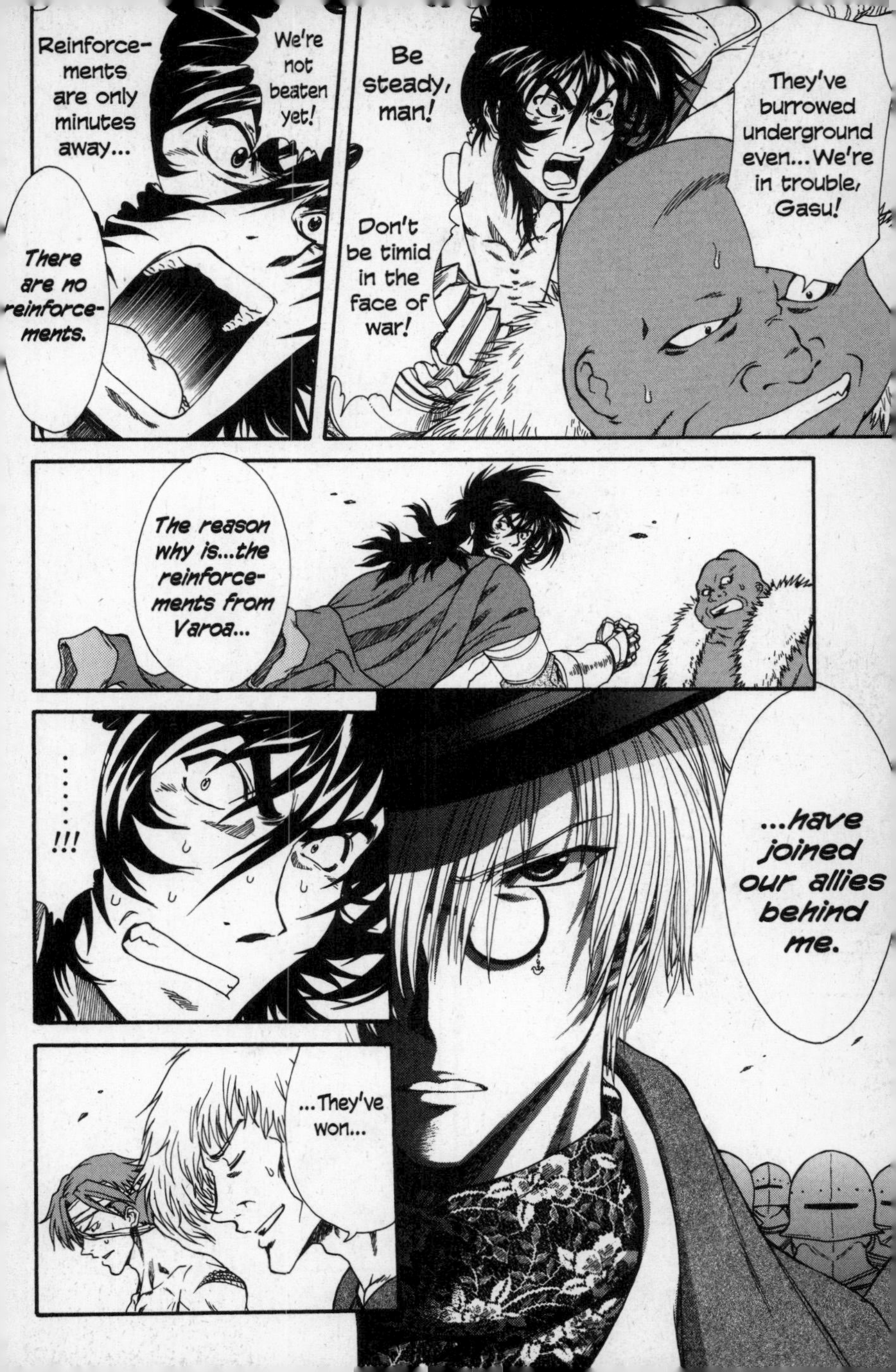
They've burrowed underground even... We're in trouble, Gasu!
Be steady, man!
Don't be timid in the face of war!
We're not beaten yet!
Reinforcements are only minutes away...
There are no reinforcements.
The reason why is...the reinforcements from Varoa...
...have joined our allies behind me.
......!!!
...They've won...

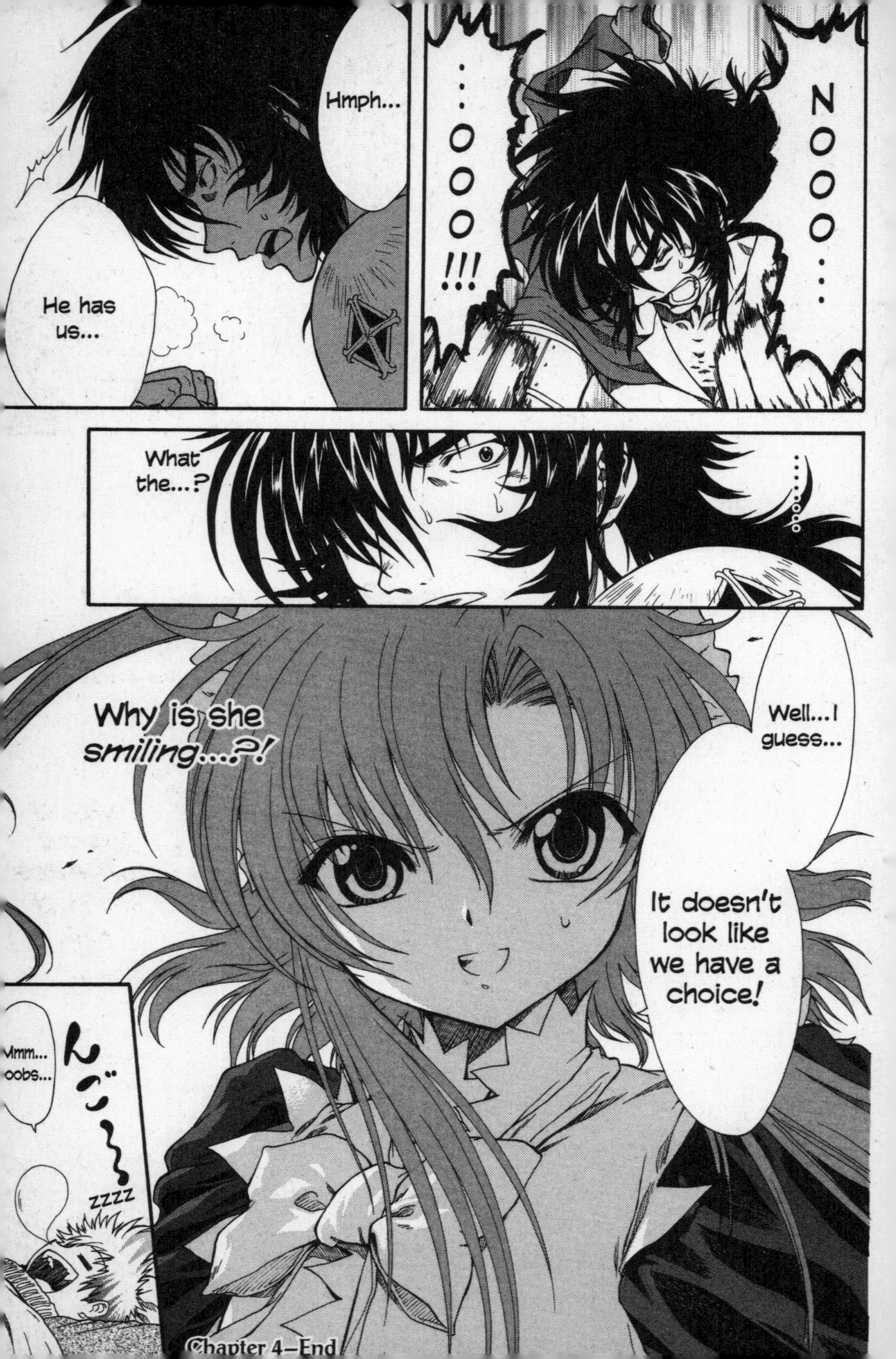
NOOOO...
...OOOO!!!
Hmph...
He has us...
......
What the...?
Well...I guess...
It doesn't look like we have a choice!
Why is she smiling...?!
Mmm... oobs...
zzzz

Chapter 4—End

Twelve people?

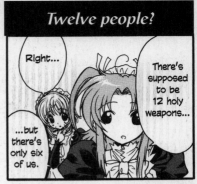

There's supposed to be 12 holy weapons...
Right...
...but there's only six of us.
What kind of "Order of the Maid" is this anyway?
I may as well quit.
Heh heh... that's what you think! I'll get six more!
DADUM
You're going to get more?!
Hmph...
See here, prince!!
You're going to make twelve people sacrifice themselves to your selfish desires?
Two hundred people!
200 Maid Parade
DADUM
SWP
Forget it.

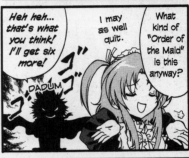

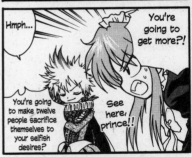

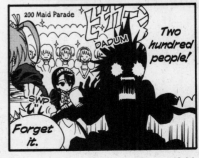

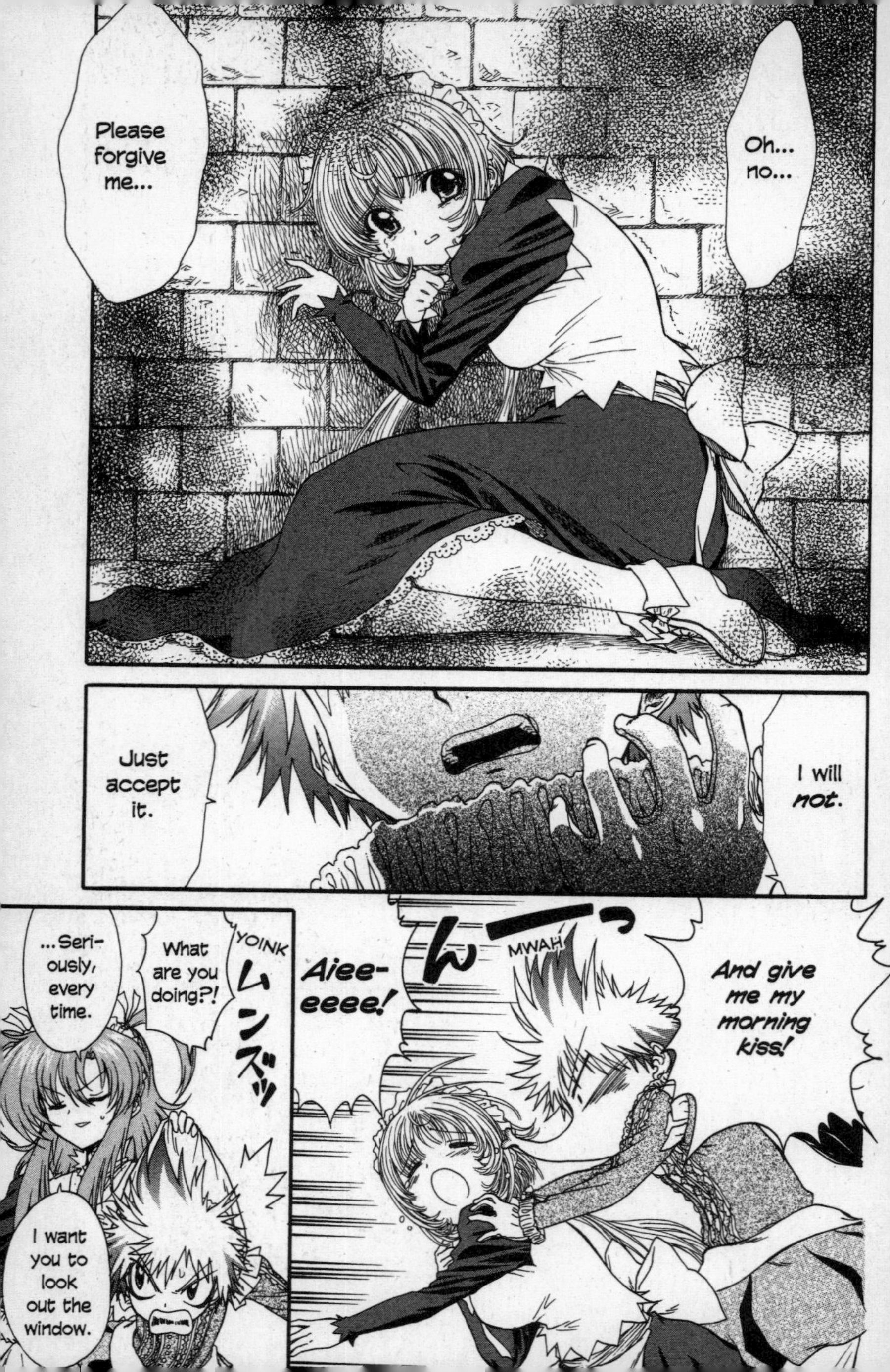
Oh... no...
Please forgive me...
I will *not*.
Just accept it.
And give me my morning kiss!
んーっ
MWAH
Aiee-eeee!
ムンズッ
YOINK
What are you doing?!
...Seri-ously, every time.
I want you to look out the window.

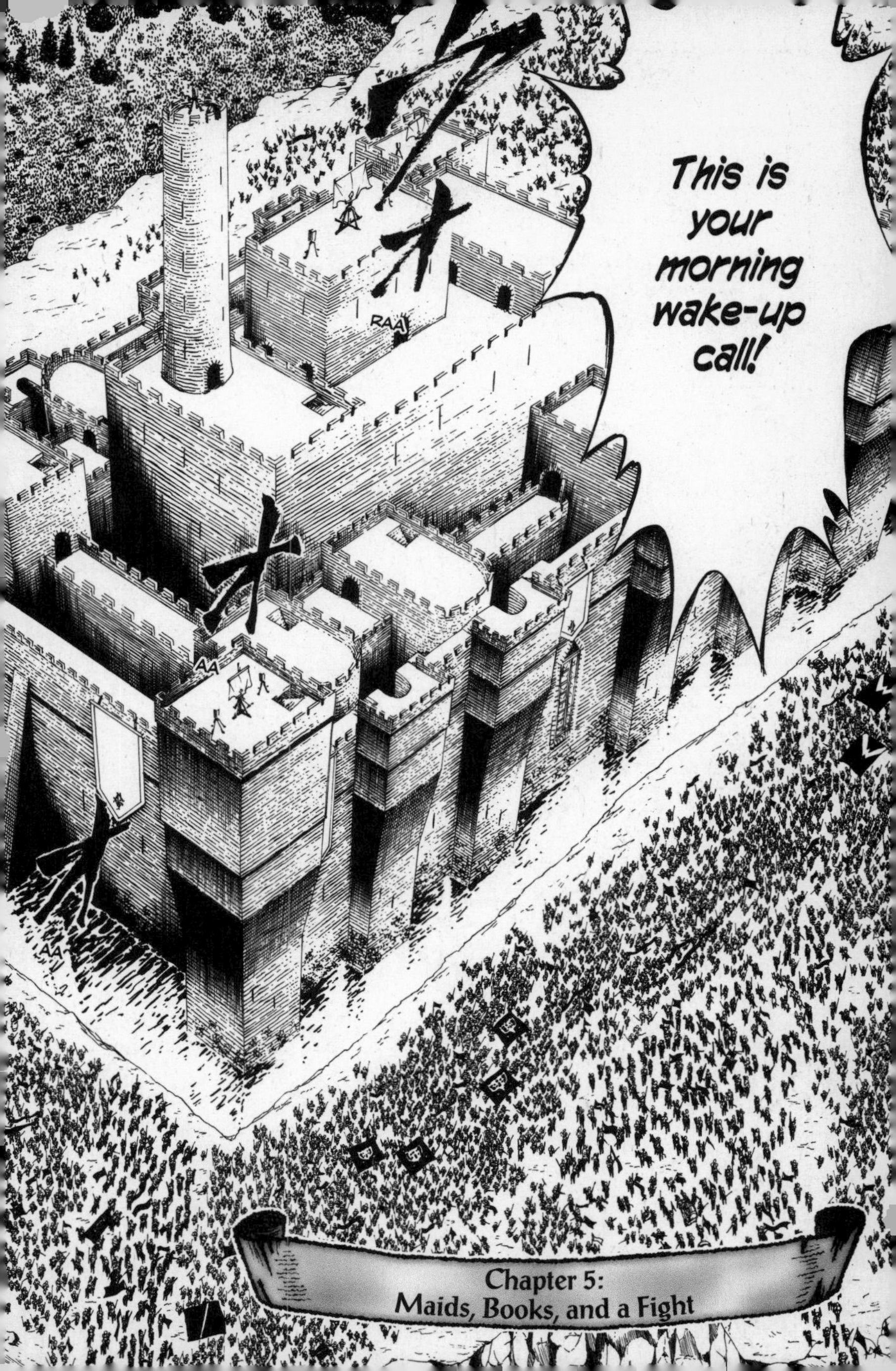
This is your morning wake-up call!
RAA
AA
AA
Chapter 5:
Maids, Books, and a Fight

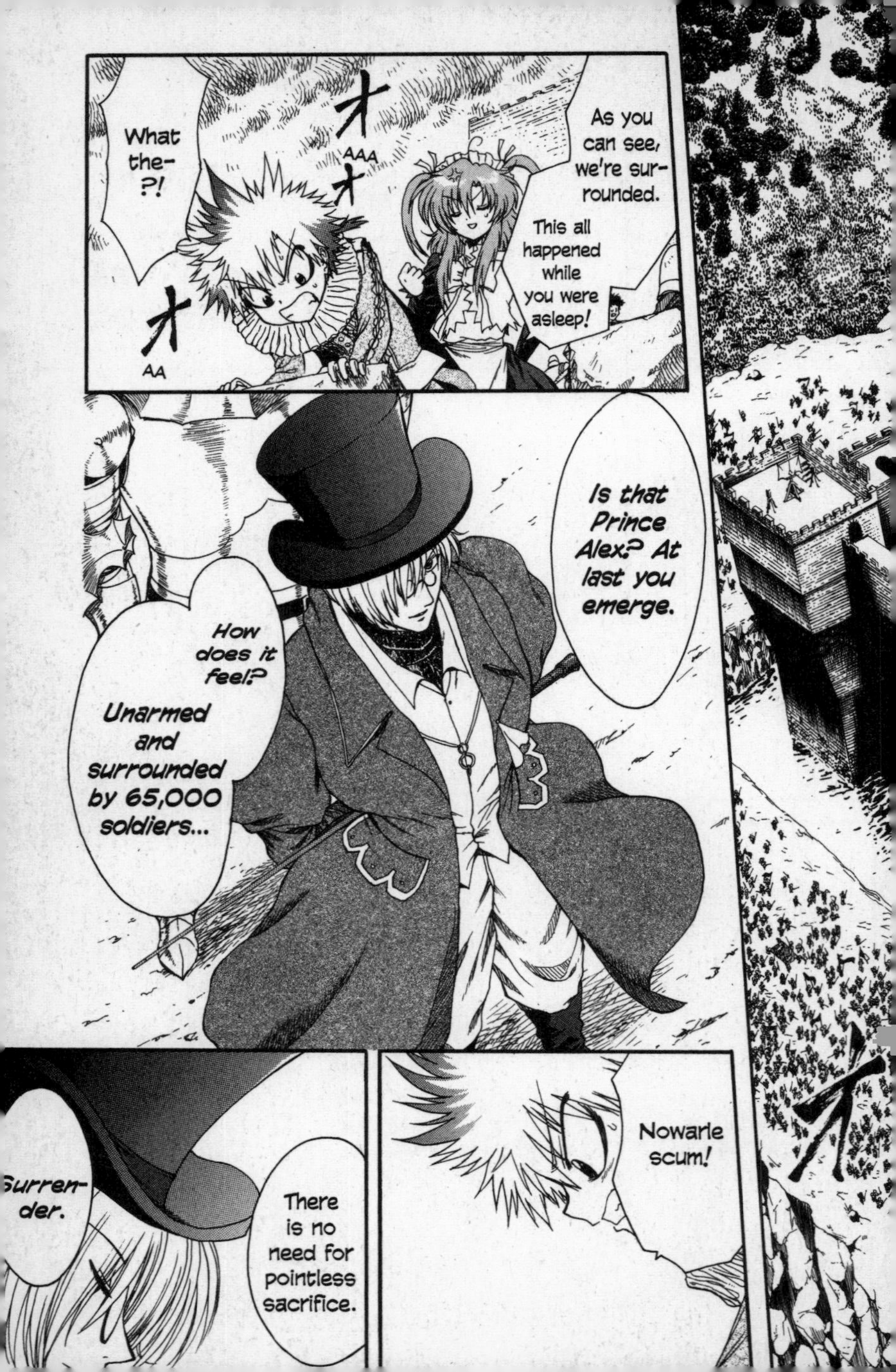
オ
As you can see, we're surrounded.
This all happened while you were asleep!
オ AAA
オ
What the-?!
オ AA
Is that Prince Alex? At last you emerge.
How does it feel?
Unarmed and surrounded by 65,000 soldiers...
Nowarle scum!
Surrender.
There is no need for pointless sacrifice.

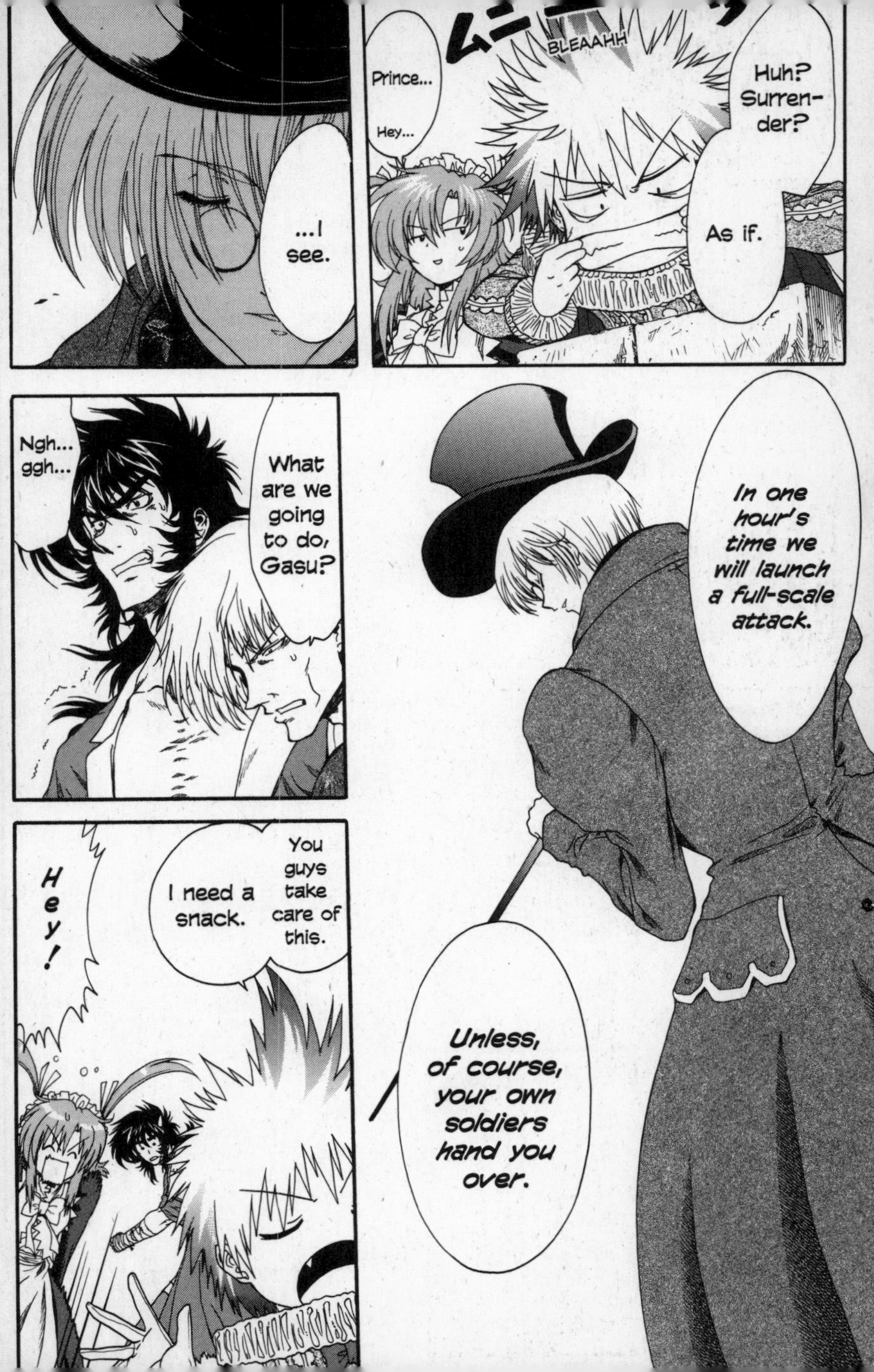
Huh? Surrender?
BLEAAHH
As if.
Prince...
Hey...
...I see.
In one hour's time we will launch a full-scale attack.
Unless, of course, your own soldiers hand you over.
What are we going to do, Gasu?
Ngh... ggh...
You guys take care of this.
I need a snack.
Hey!

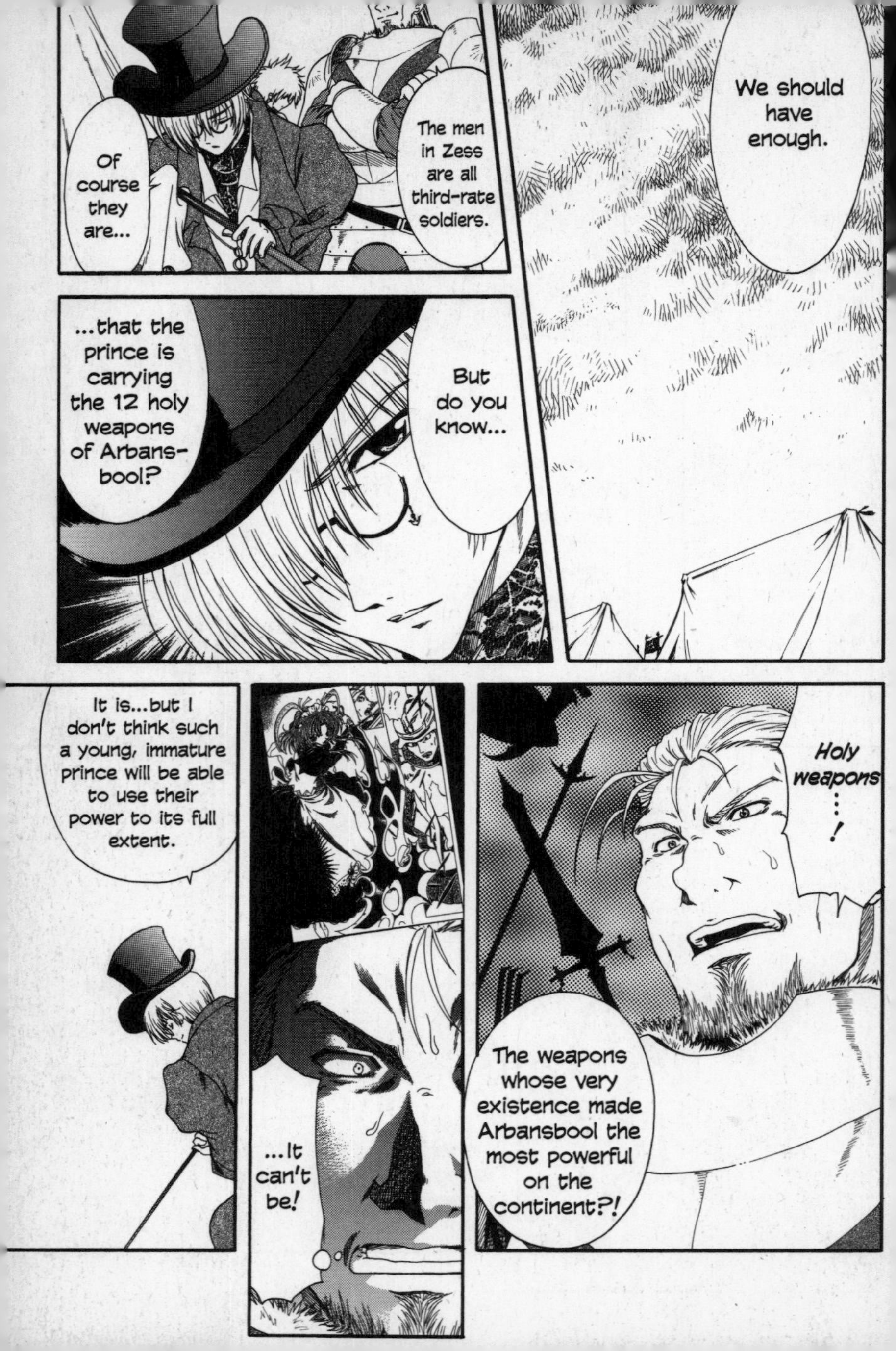
We should have enough.
The men in Zess are all third-rate soldiers.
Of course they are...
But do you know...
...that the prince is carrying the 12 holy weapons of Arbans-bool?
Holy weapons...!
The weapons whose very existence made Arbansbool the most powerful on the continent?!
...It can't be!
It is...but I don't think such a young, immature prince will be able to use their power to its full extent.

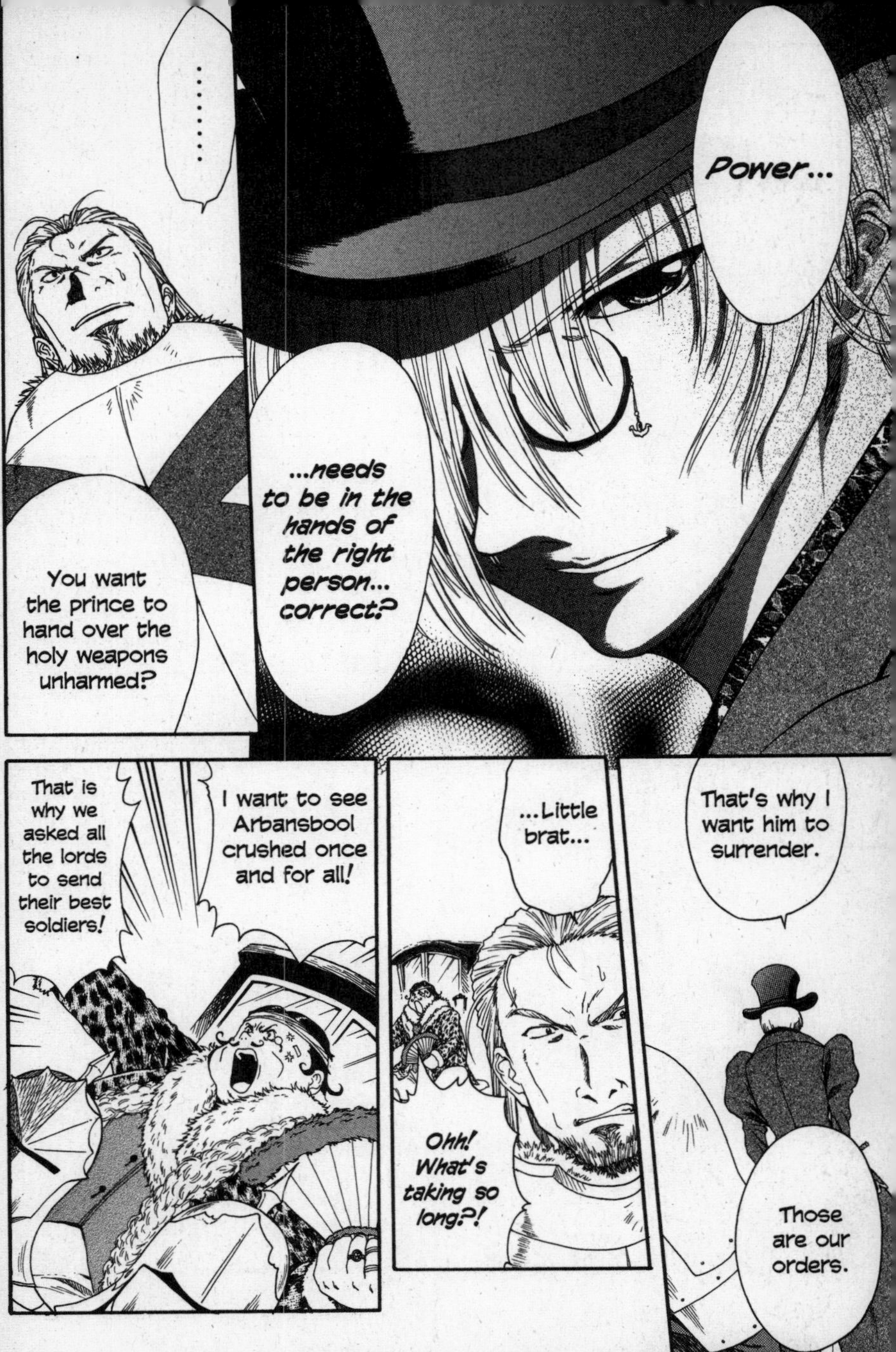
Power...
...needs to be in the hands of the right person... correct?
......
You want the prince to hand over the holy weapons unharmed?
That's why I want him to surrender.
Those are our orders.
...Little brat...
Ohh! What's taking so long?!
I want to see Arbansbool crushed once and for all!
That is why we asked all the lords to send their best soldiers!

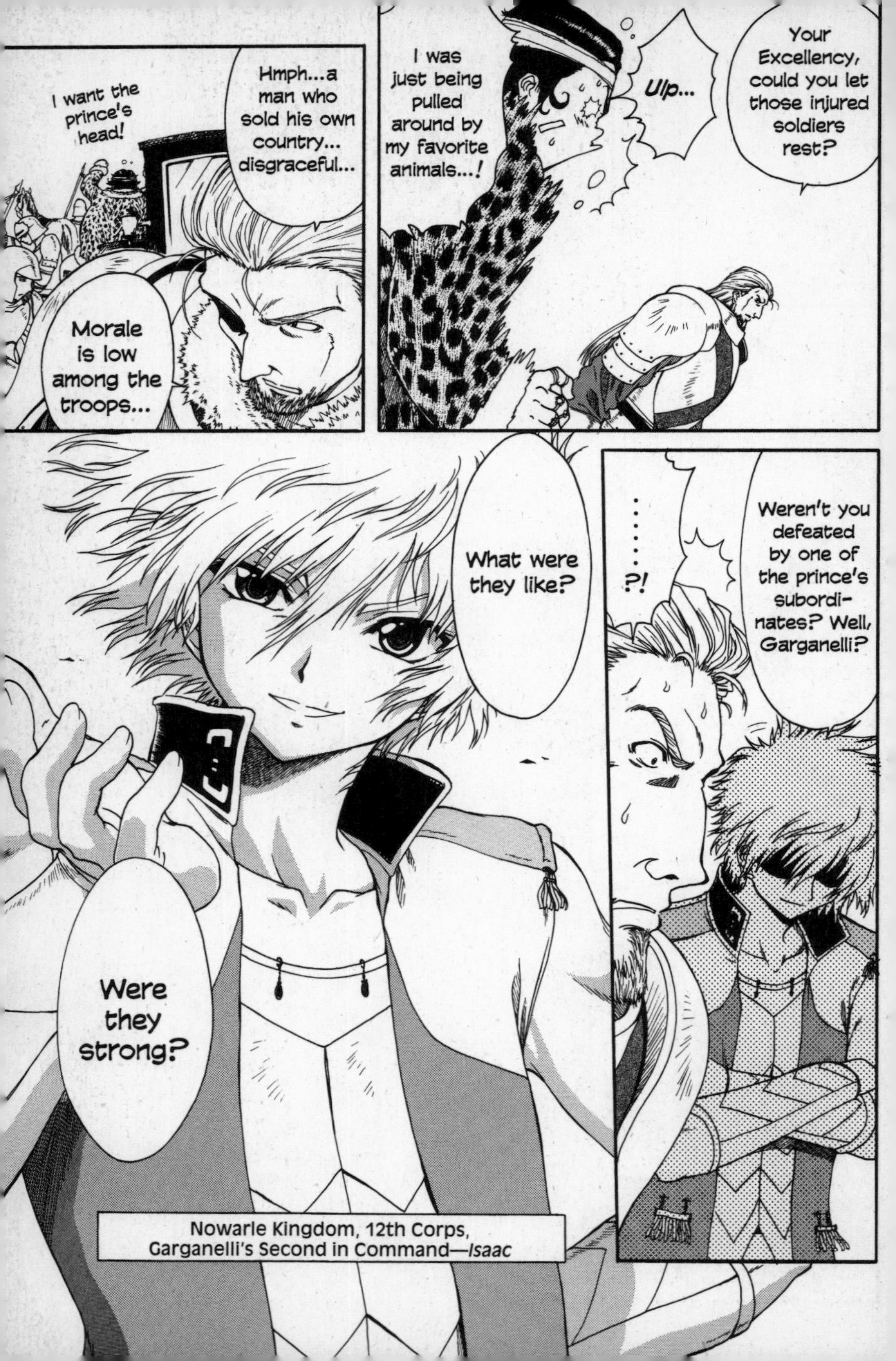

Your Excellency, could you let those injured soldiers rest?
Ulp...
I was just being pulled around by my favorite animals...!
Hmph...a man who sold his own country... disgraceful...
I want the prince's head!
Morale is low among the troops...
Weren't you defeated by one of the prince's subordinates? Well, Garganelli?
......?!
What were they like?
Were they strong?
Nowarle Kingdom, 12th Corps, Garganelli's Second in Command—*Isaac*

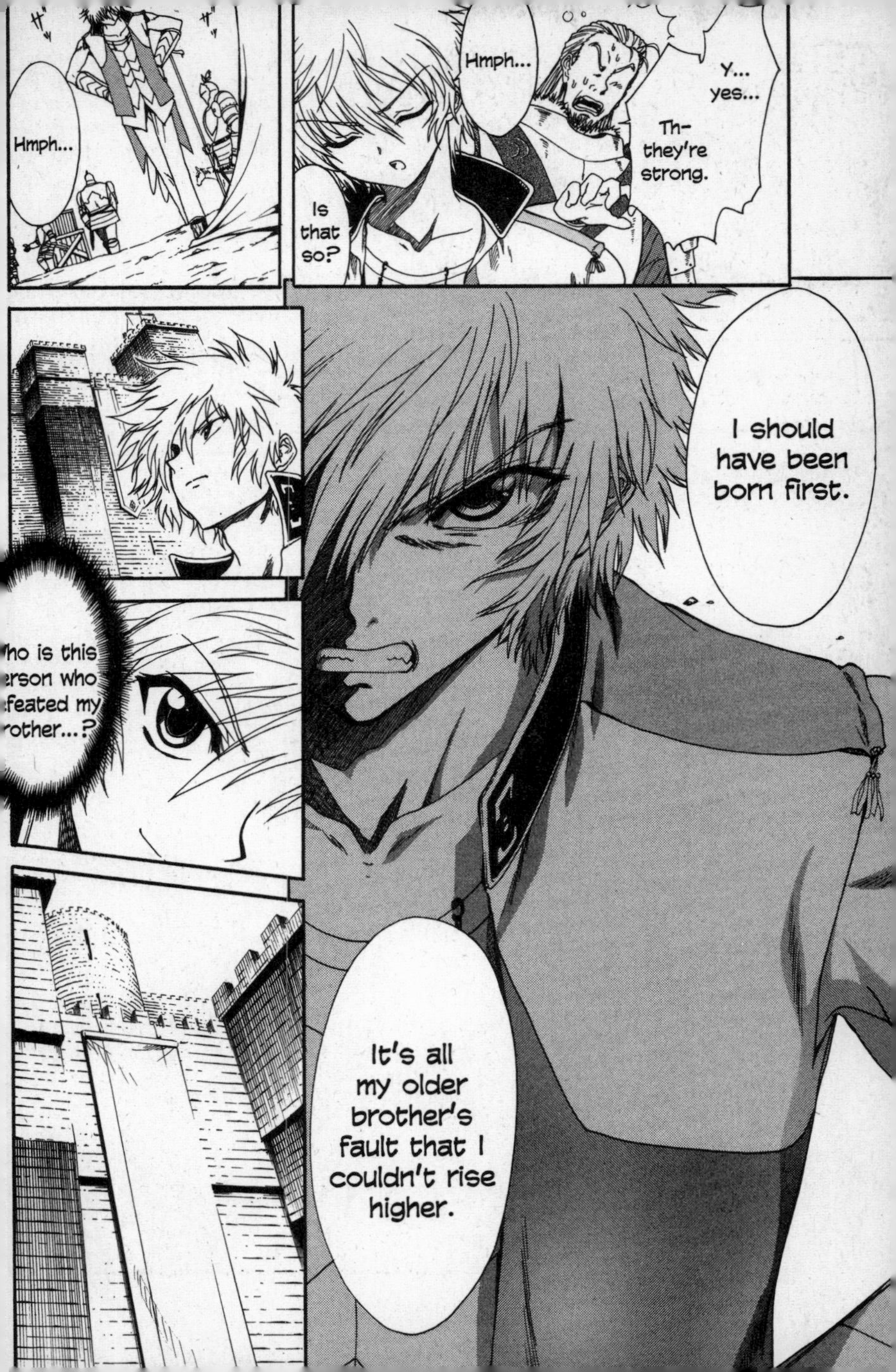
Y... yes...
Th- they're strong.
Hmph...
Is that so?
Hmph...
I should have been born first.
It's all my older brother's fault that I couldn't rise higher.
ho is this erson who efeated my rother...?

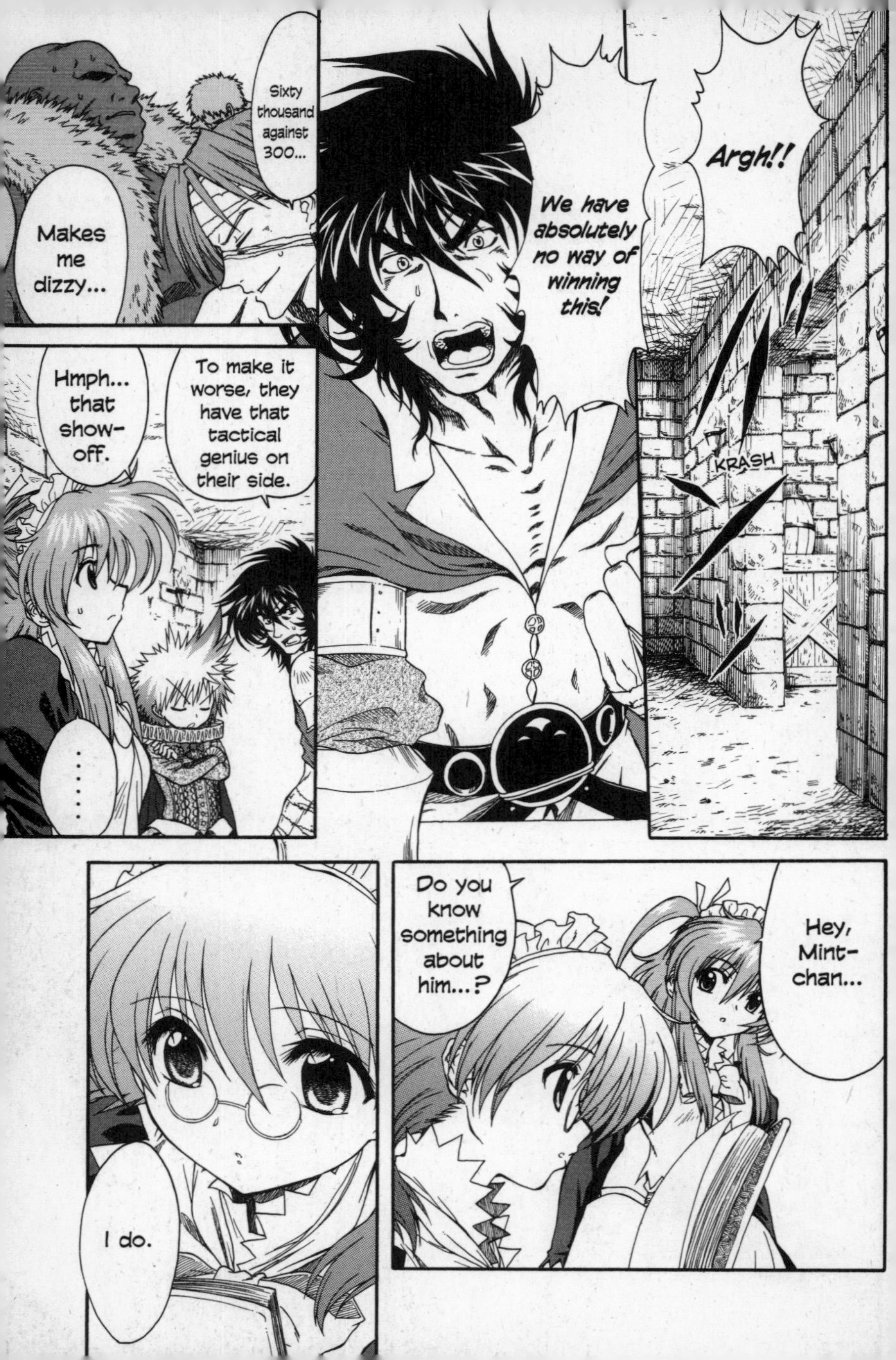

Argh!!
KRASH
We have absolutely no way of winning this!
Sixty thousand against 300...
Makes me dizzy...
To make it worse, they have that tactical genius on their side.
Hmph... that show-off.
......
Hey, Mint-chan...
Do you know something about him...?
I do.

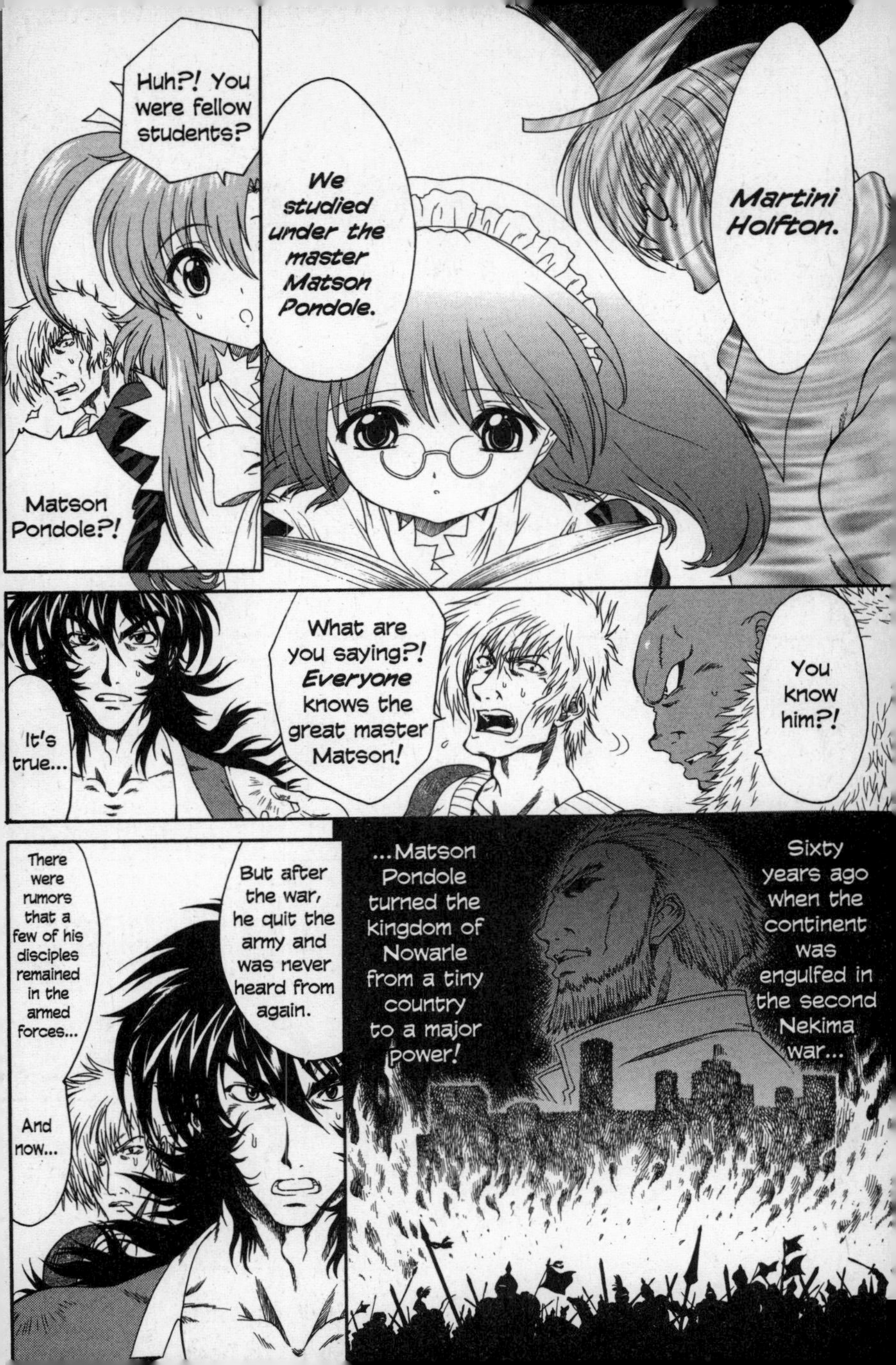
Martini Holfton.
We studied under the master Matson Pondole.
Huh?! You were fellow students?
Matson Pondole?!
You know him?!
What are you saying?! Everyone knows the great master Matson!
It's true...
Sixty years ago when the continent was engulfed in the second Nekima war...
...Matson Pondole turned the kingdom of Nowarle from a tiny country to a major power!
But after the war, he quit the army and was never heard from again.
There were rumors that a few of his disciples remained in the armed forces...
And now...

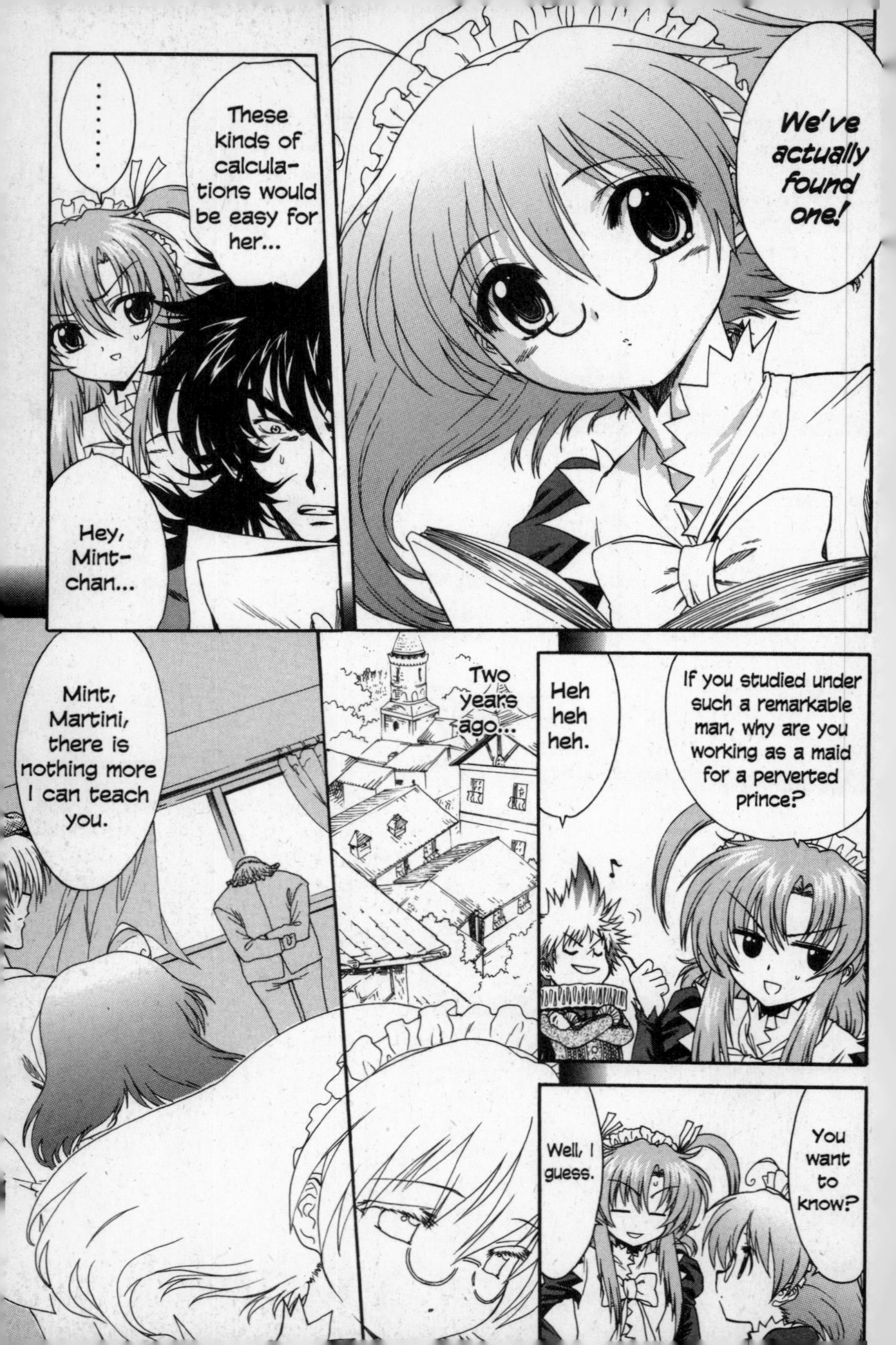
We've actually found one!
These kinds of calculations would be easy for her...
......
Hey, Mint-chan...
If you studied under such a remarkable man, why are you working as a maid for a perverted prince?
Heh heh heh.
You want to know?
Well, I guess.
Two years ago...
Mint, Martini, there is nothing more I can teach you.

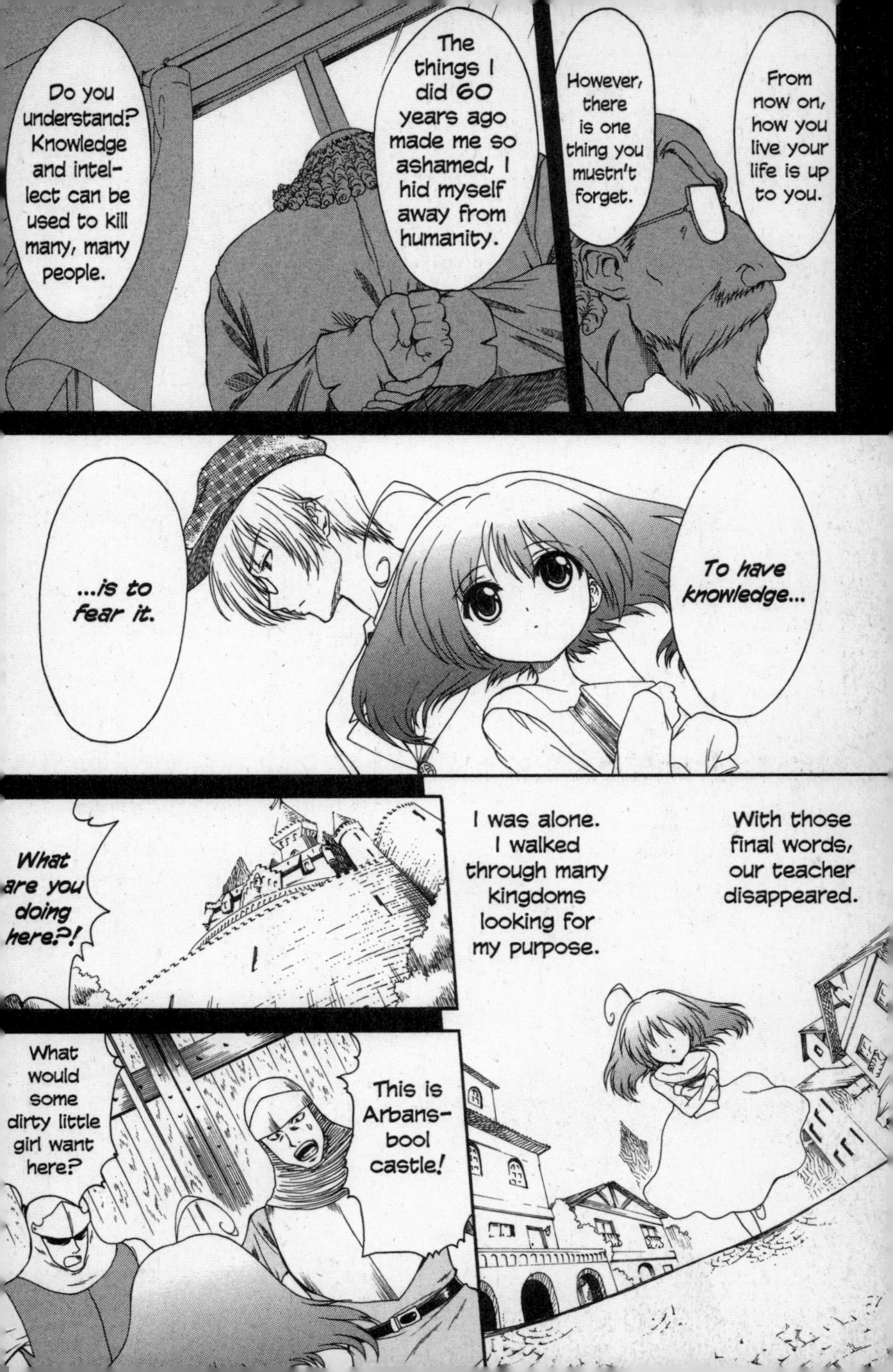

From now on, how you live your life is up to you.
However, there is one thing you mustn't forget.
The things I did 60 years ago made me so ashamed, I hid myself away from humanity.
Do you understand? Knowledge and intel-lect can be used to kill many, many people.
To have knowledge...
...is to fear it.
With those final words, our teacher disappeared.
I was alone. I walked through many kingdoms looking for my purpose.
What are you doing here?!
This is Arbans-bool castle!
What would some dirty little girl want here?

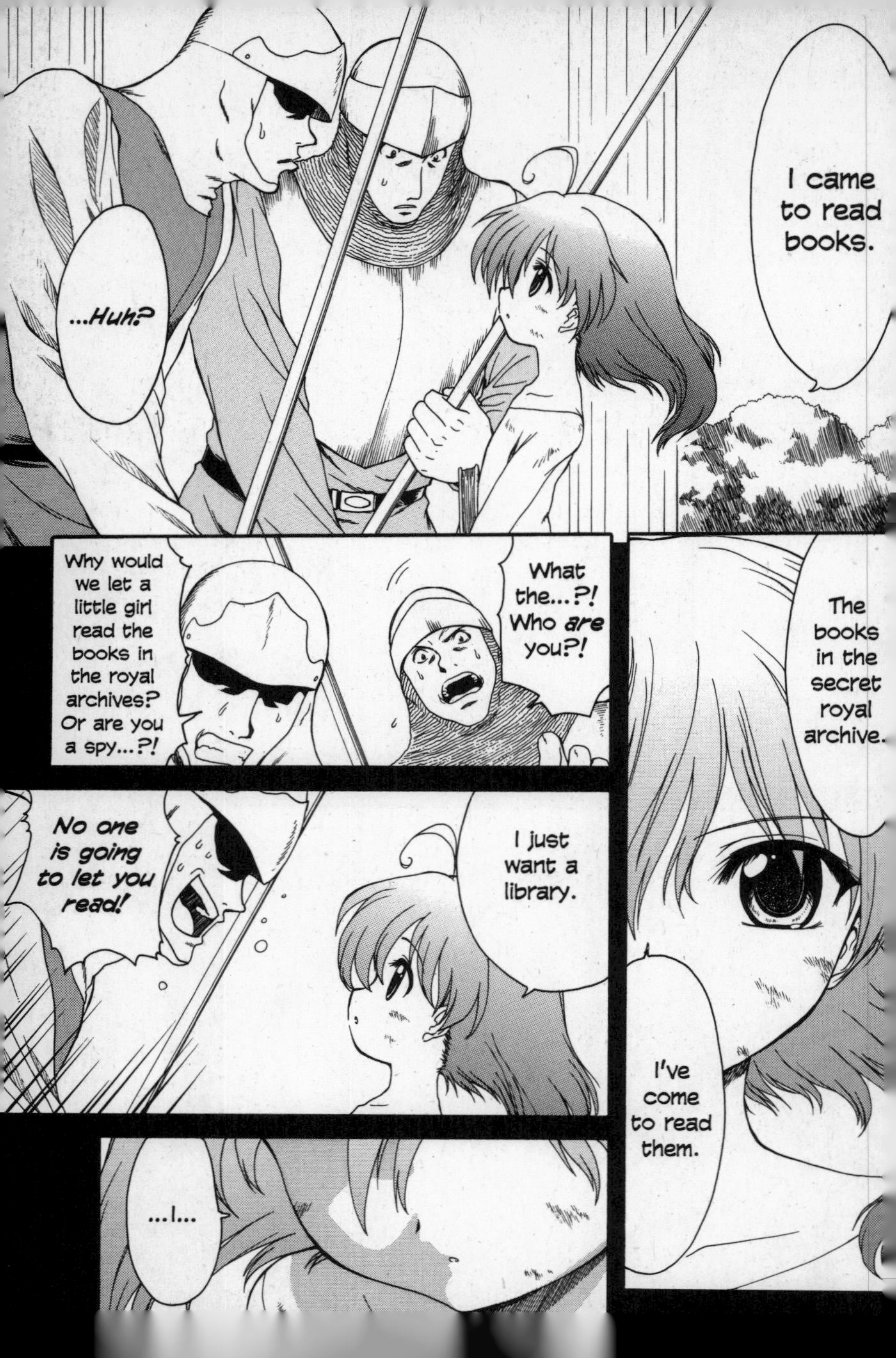
I came to read books.
...Huh?
The books in the secret royal archive.
I've come to read them.
What the...?! Who are you?!
Why would we let a little girl read the books in the royal archives? Or are you a spy...?!
I just want a library.
No one is going to let you read!
...I...

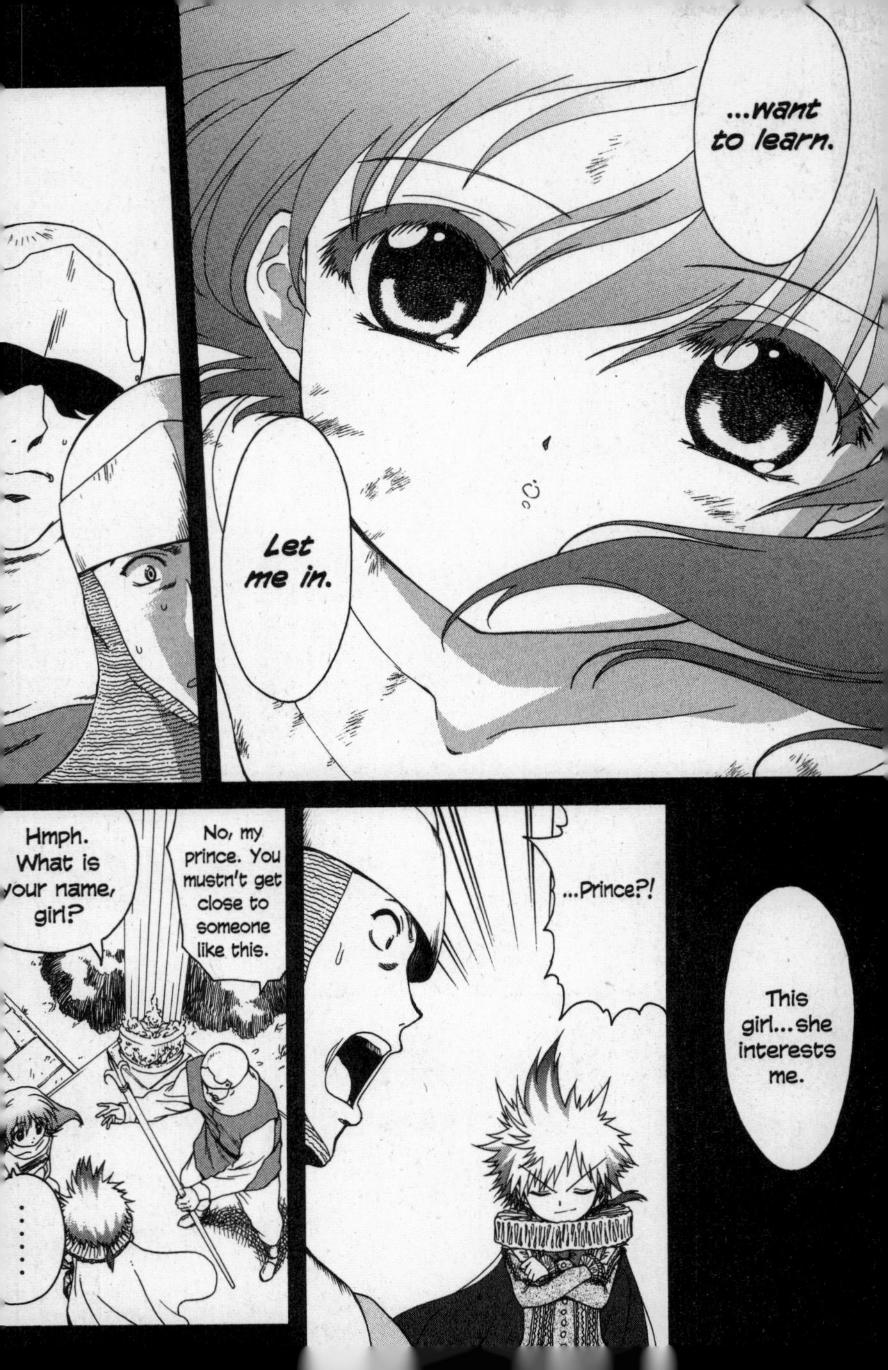
...want to learn.
Let me in.
This girl...she interests me.
...Prince?!
No, my prince. You mustn't get close to someone like this.
Hmph. What is your name, girl?
......

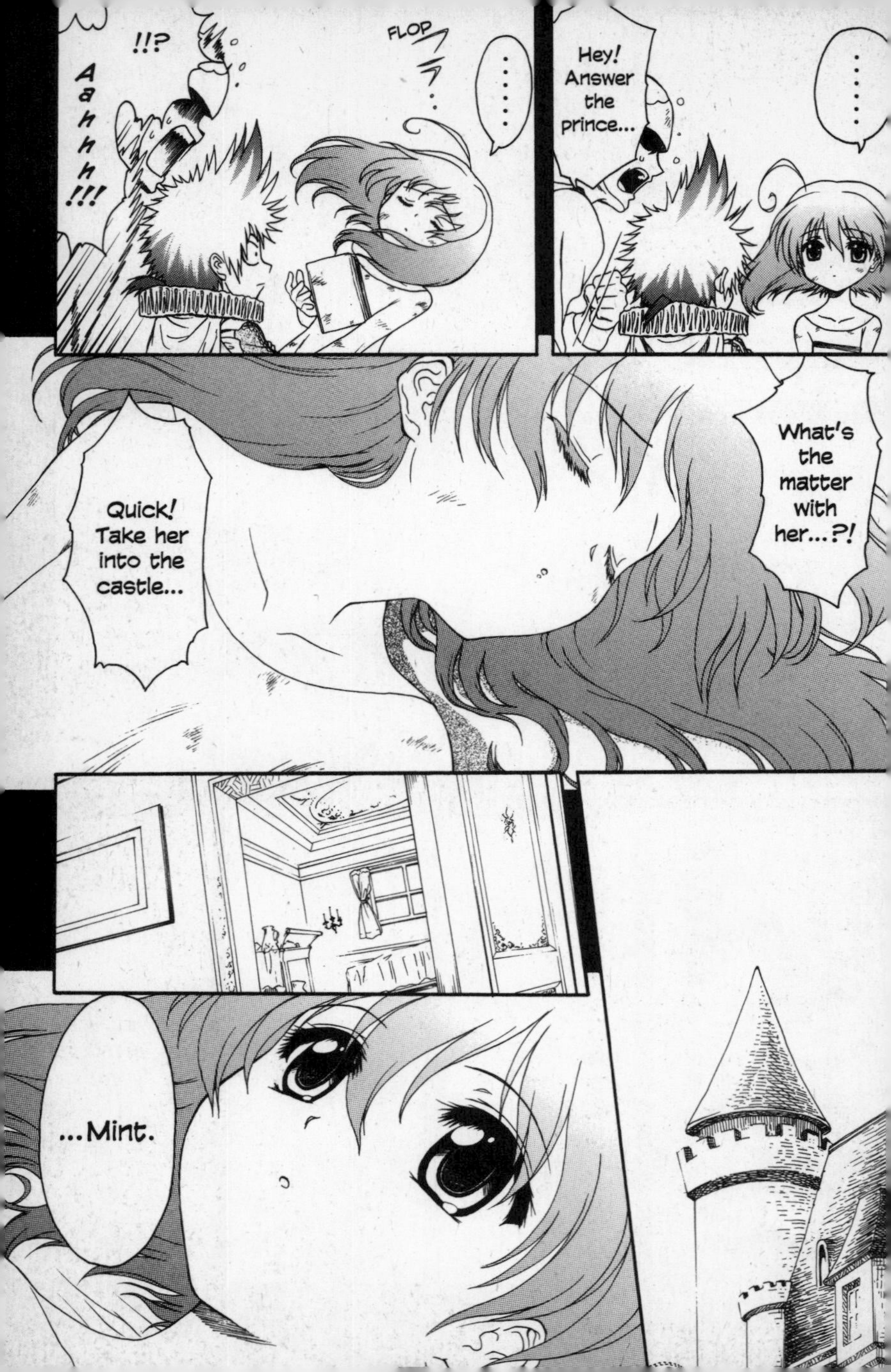
......
Hey! Answer the prince...
......
FLOP
!!?
Aahhhh!!!
What's the matter with her...?!
Quick! Take her into the castle...
...Mint.

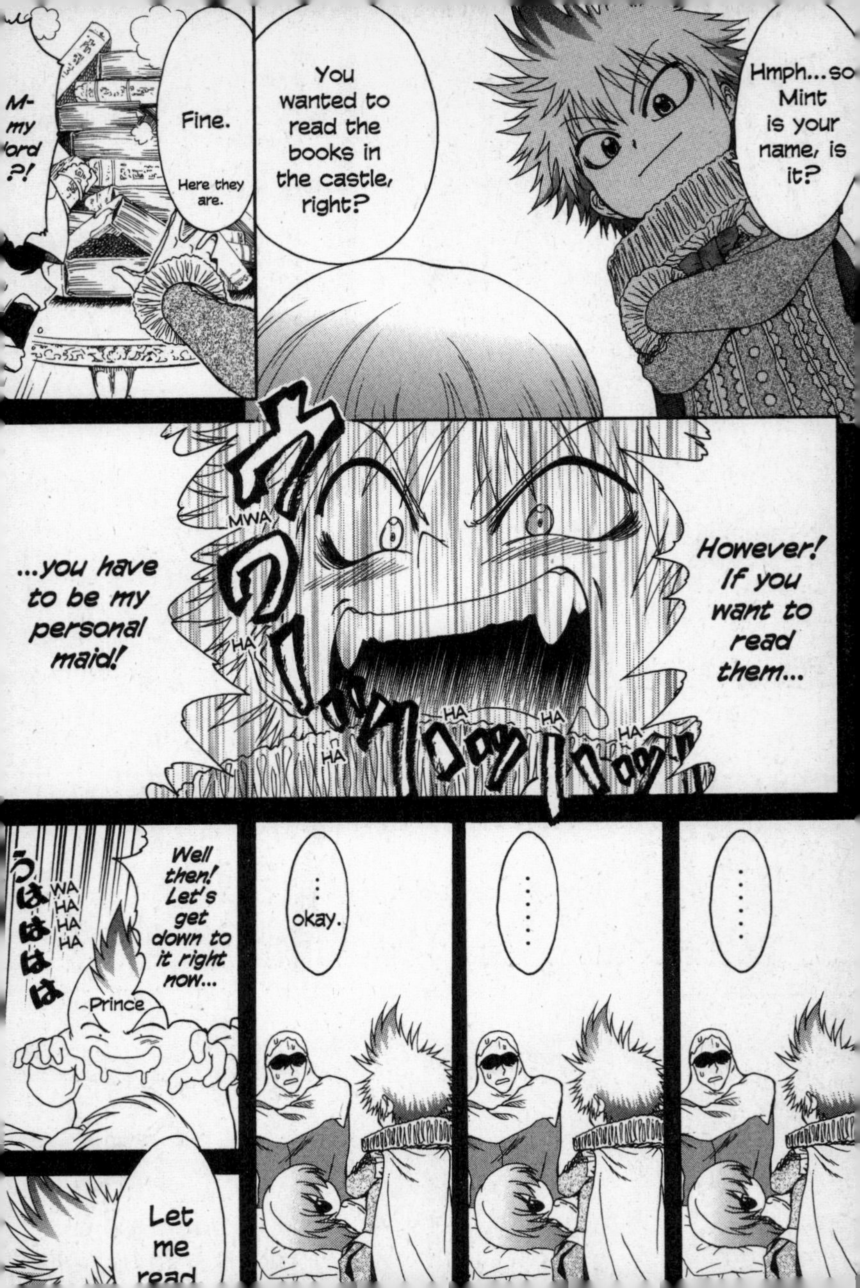
Hmph...so Mint is your name, is it?
You wanted to read the books in the castle, right?
Fine.
Here they are.
M-my ord?!
However! If you want to read them...
MWA HA HA HA HA HA
...you have to be my personal maid!
......
......
...okay.
うははは
WA HA HA HA
Well then! Let's get down to it right now...
Prince
Let me read

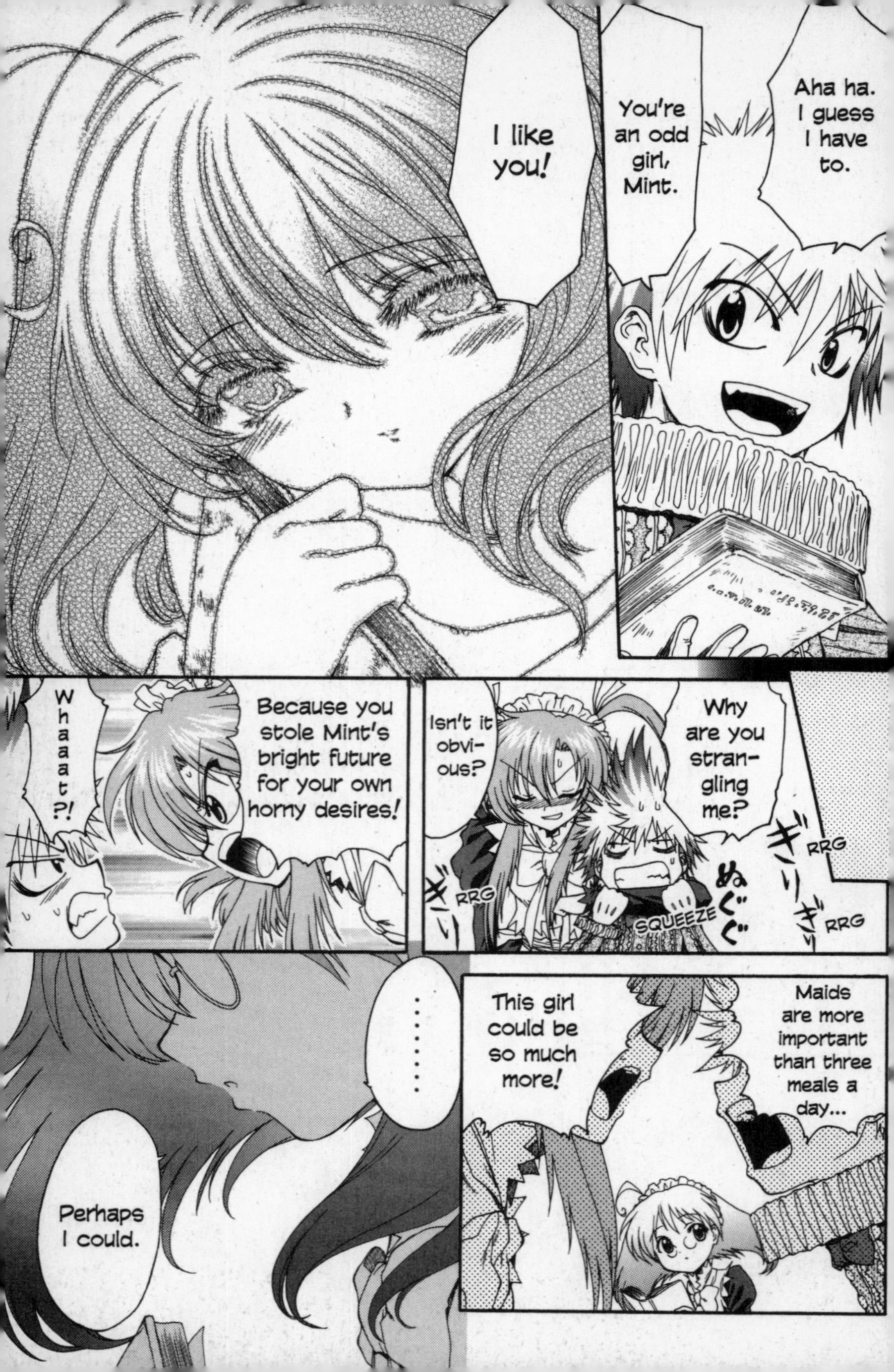

Aha ha. I guess I have to.
You're an odd girl, Mint.
I like you!
Why are you strangling me?
Isn't it obvious?
ギリ RRG
ぬぐぐ
SQUEEZE
ギリ RRG
ギリ RRG
Because you stole Mint's bright future for your own horny desires!
Whaaaat?!
Maids are more important than three meals a day...
This girl could be so much more!
......
Perhaps I could.

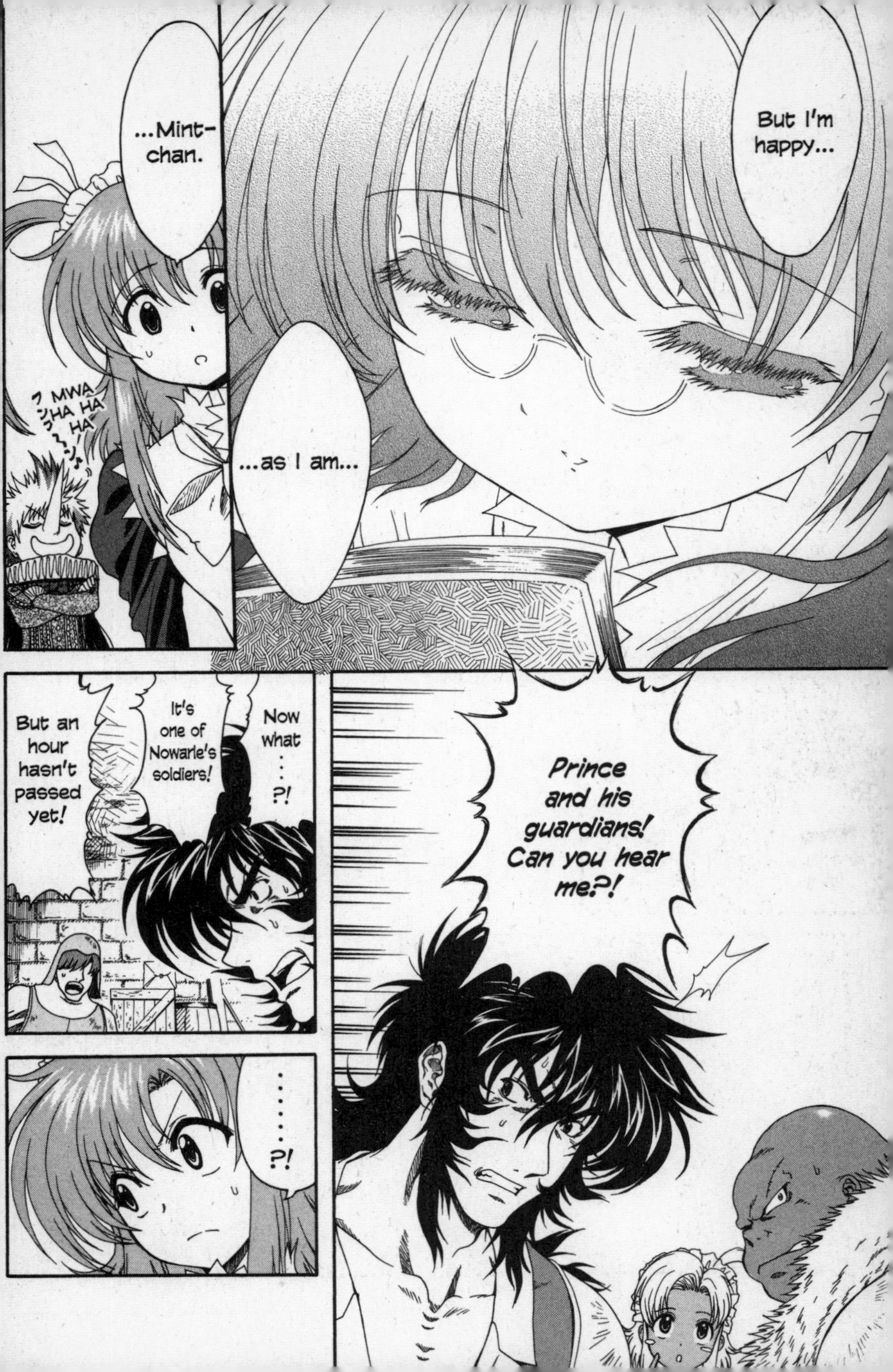
But I'm happy...
...as I am...
...Mint-chan.
MWA HA HA HA
Prince and his guardians! Can you hear me?!
Now what...?!
It's one of Nowarle's soldiers!
But an hour hasn't passed yet!
......?!

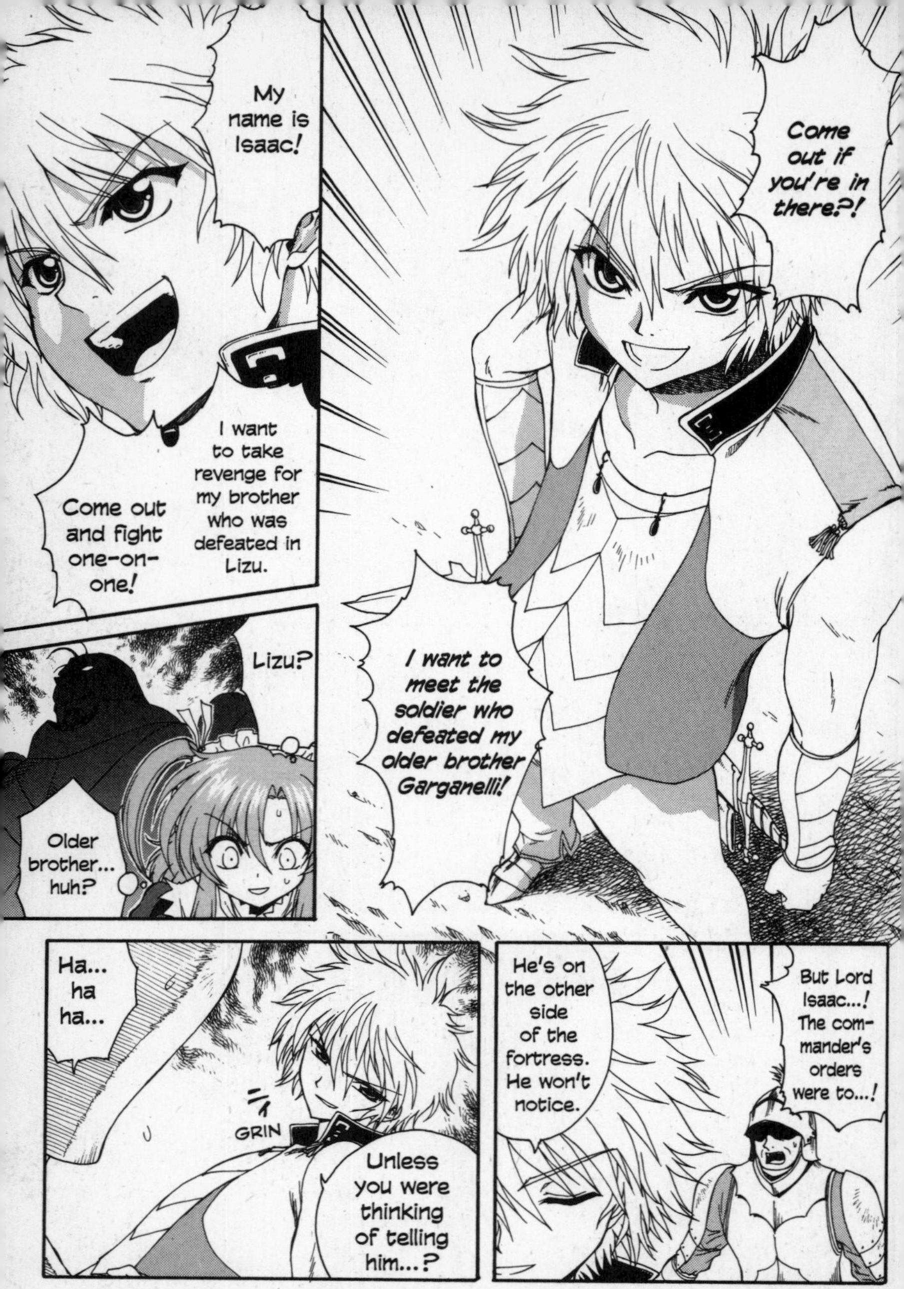

Come out if you're in there?!
I want to meet the soldier who defeated my older brother Garganelli!
My name is Isaac!
I want to take revenge for my brother who was defeated in Lizu.
Come out and fight one-on-one!
Lizu?
Older brother... huh?
But Lord Isaac...! The commander's orders were to...!
He's on the other side of the fortress. He won't notice.
Unless you were thinking of telling him...?
GRIN
Ha... ha ha...

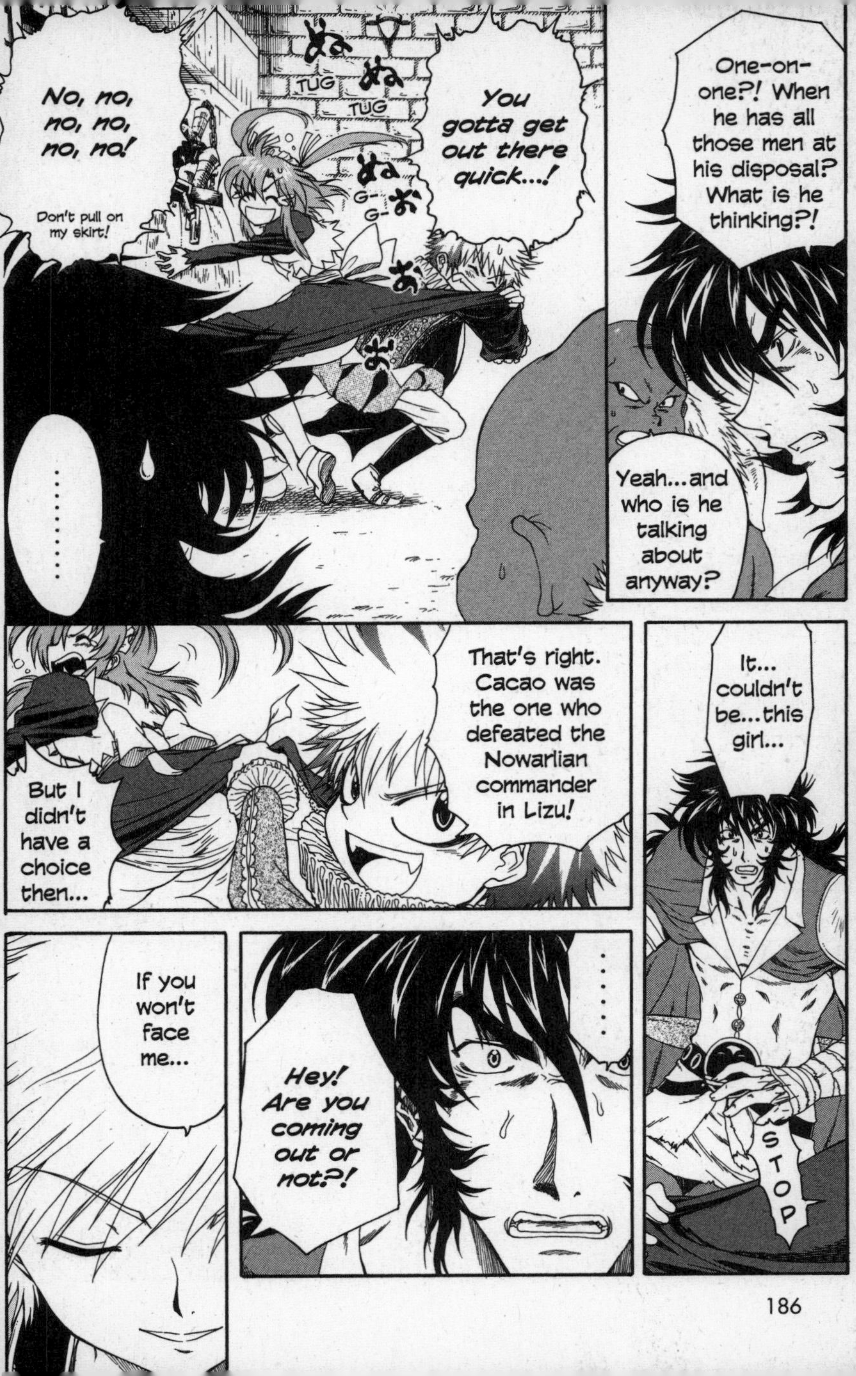
One-on-one?! When he has all those men at his disposal? What is he thinking?!
Yeah...and who is he talking about anyway?
You gotta get out there quick...!
TUG
TUG
ぬ ぬ
ぬ お
G- G-
お
お
No, no, no, no, no, no!
Don't pull on my skirt!
......
It... couldn't be...this girl...
STOP
That's right. Cacao was the one who defeated the Nowarlian commander in Lizu!
But I didn't have a choice then...
......
Hey! Are you coming out or not?!
If you won't face me...

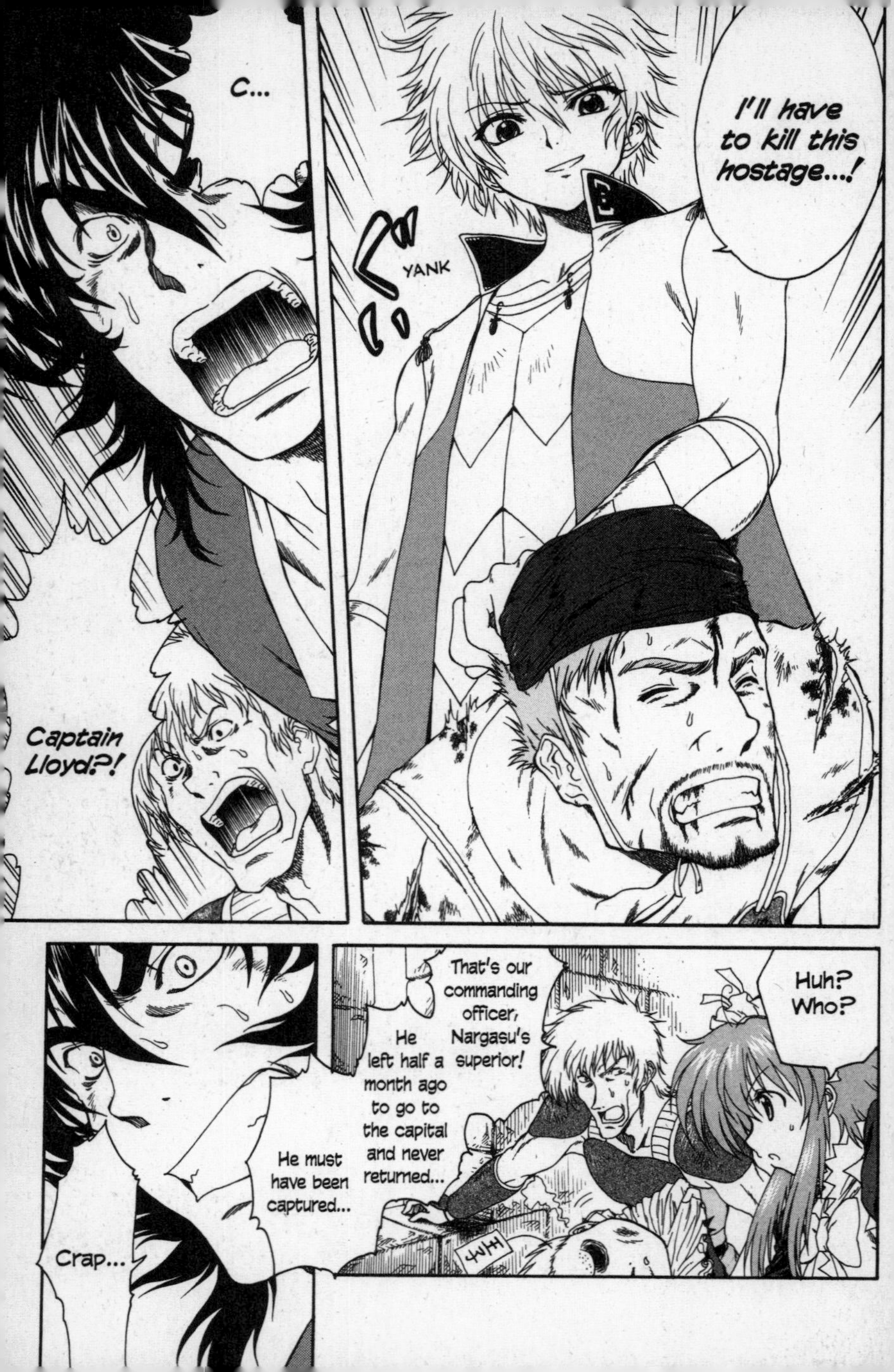
I'll have to kill this hostage...!
YANK
C...
Captain Lloyd?!
Huh? Who?
That's our commanding officer, Nargasu's superior!
He left half a month ago to go to the capital and never returned...
He must have been captured...
Crap...

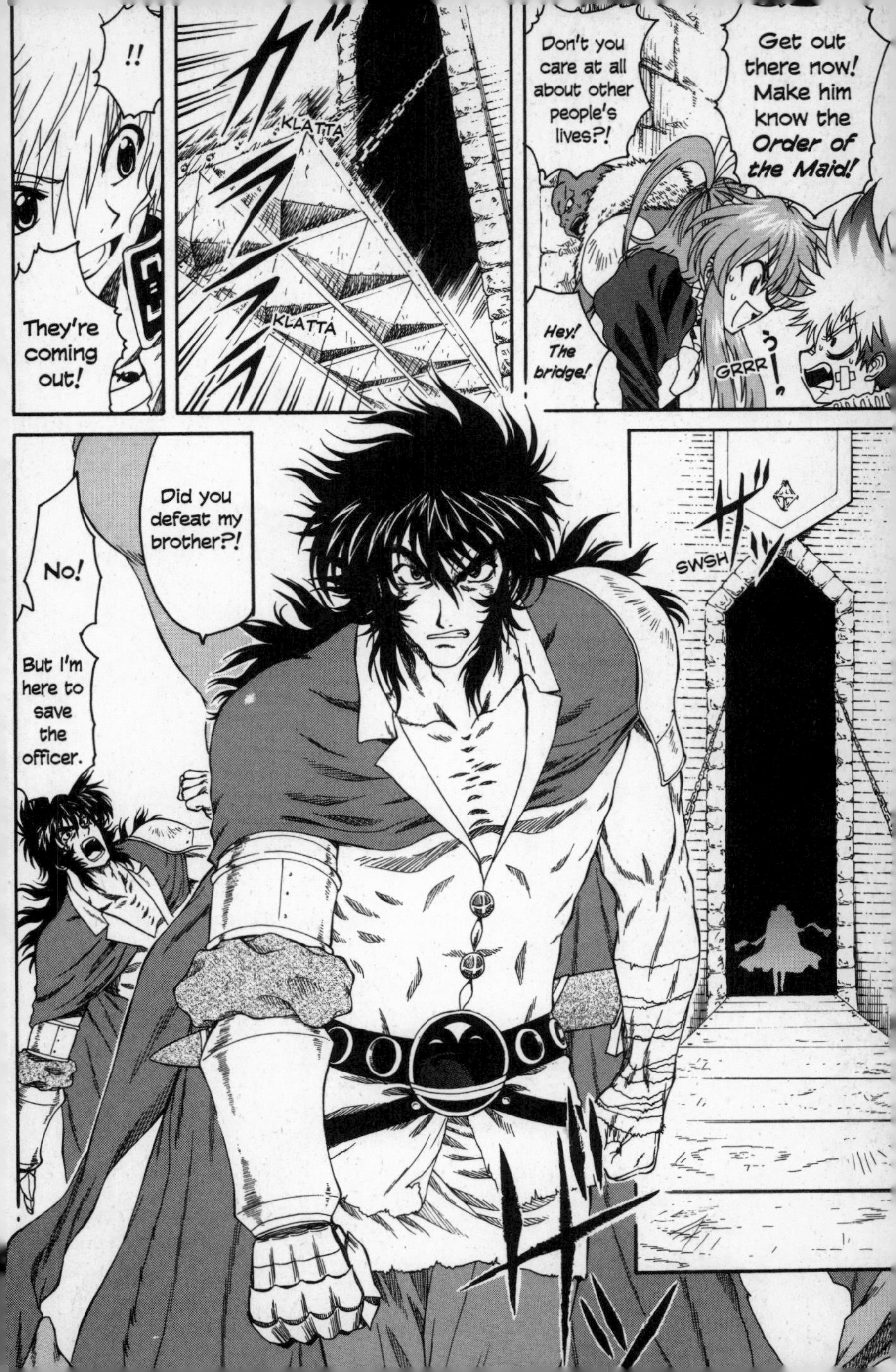

Get out there now! Make him know the Order of the Maid!
Don't you care at all about other people's lives?!
GRRR
Hey! The bridge!
KLATTA
KLATTA
!!
They're coming out!
SWSH
Did you defeat my brother?!
No!
But I'm here to save the officer.

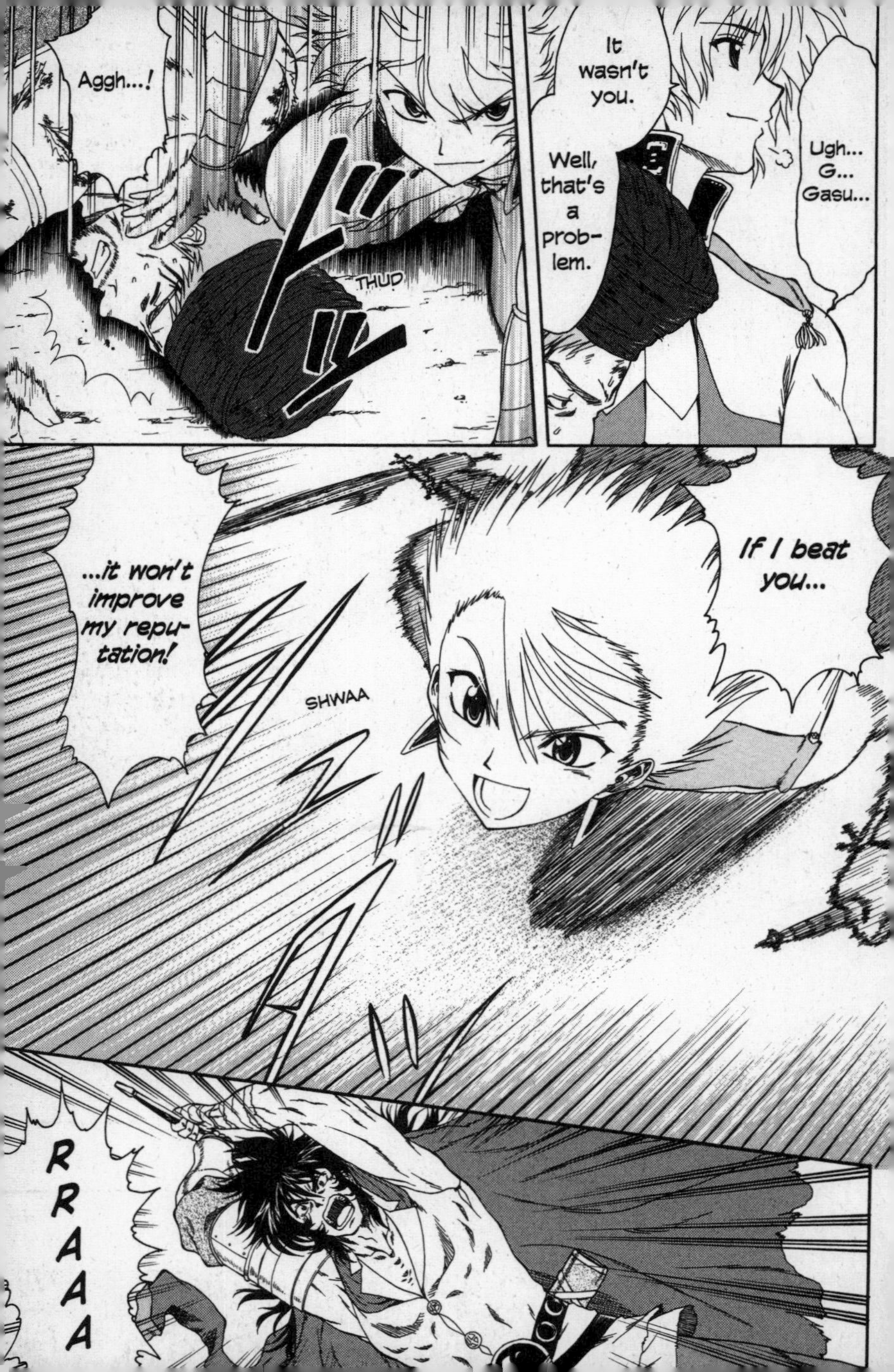
Ugh... G... Gasu...
It wasn't you.
Well, that's a problem.
Aggh...!
THUD
If I beat you...
SHWAA
...it won't improve my reputation!
RRAAA

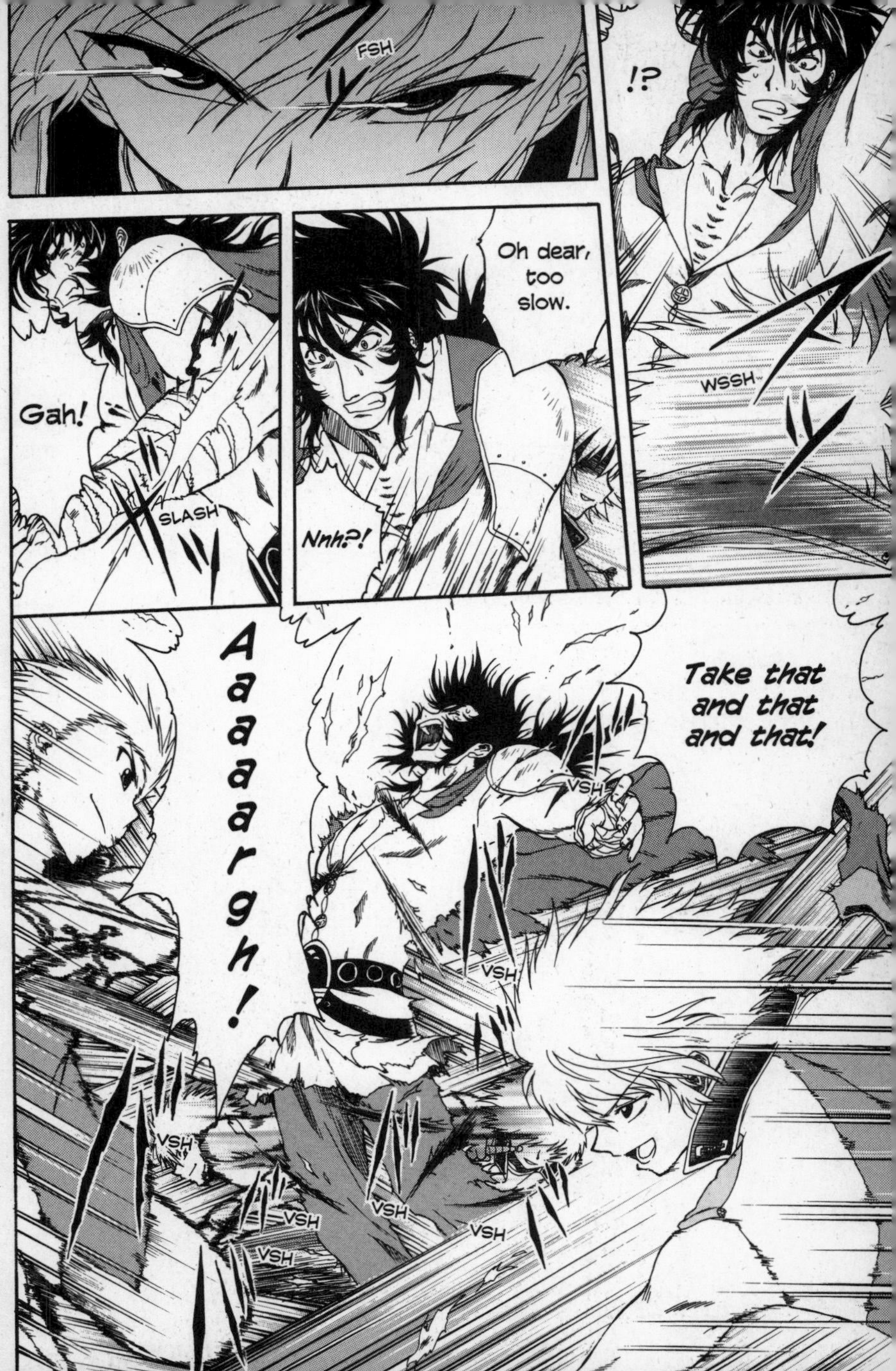
!?
WSSH
FSH
Oh dear, too slow.
Nnh?!
Gah!
SLASH
Take that and that and that!
VSH
Aaaaargh!
VSH
VSH
VSH
VSH
VSH
VSH

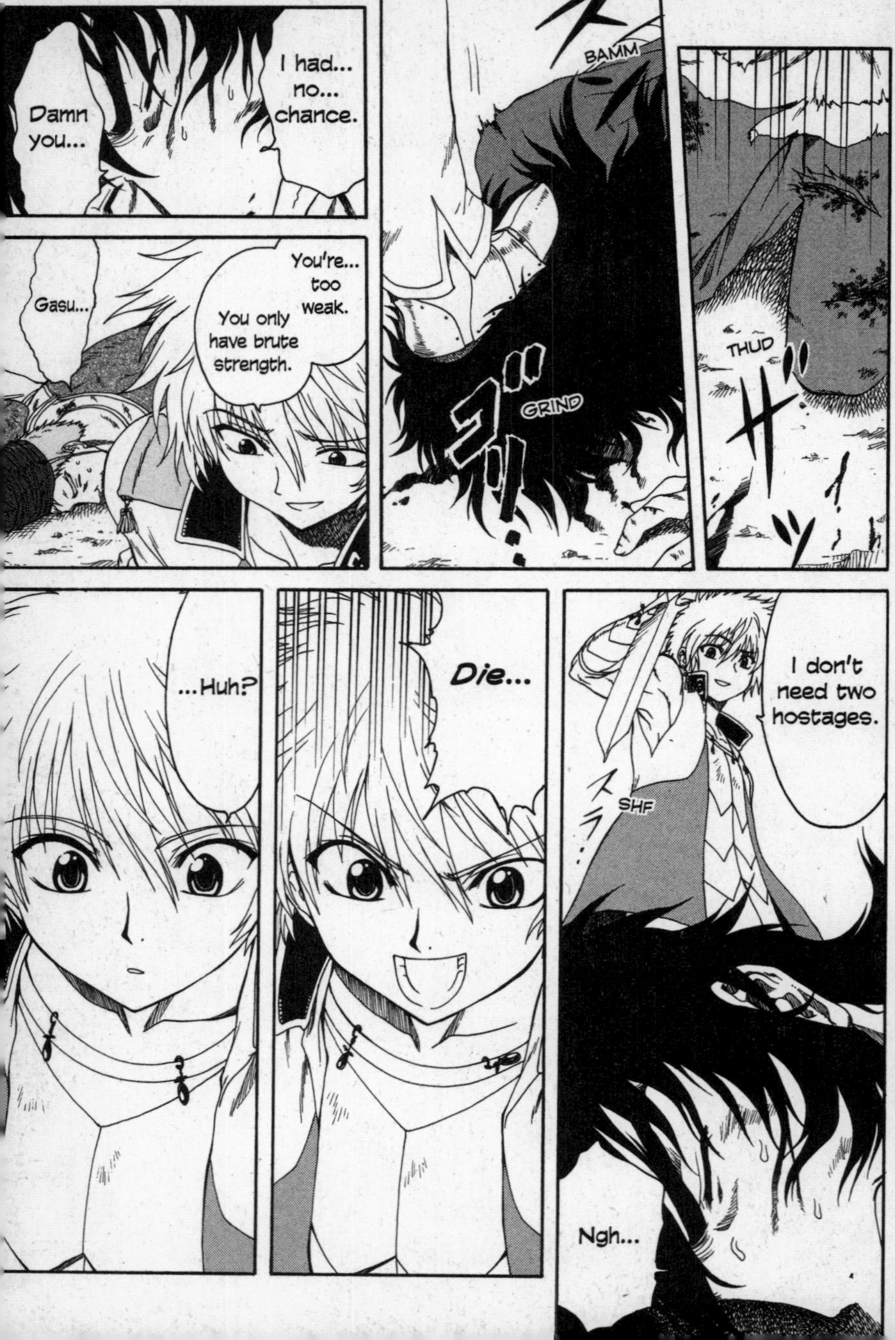
THUD
BAMM
GRIND
I had... no... chance.
Damn you...
You're... too weak.
You only have brute strength.
Gasu...
I don't need two hostages.
SHF
Ngh...
Die...
...Huh?

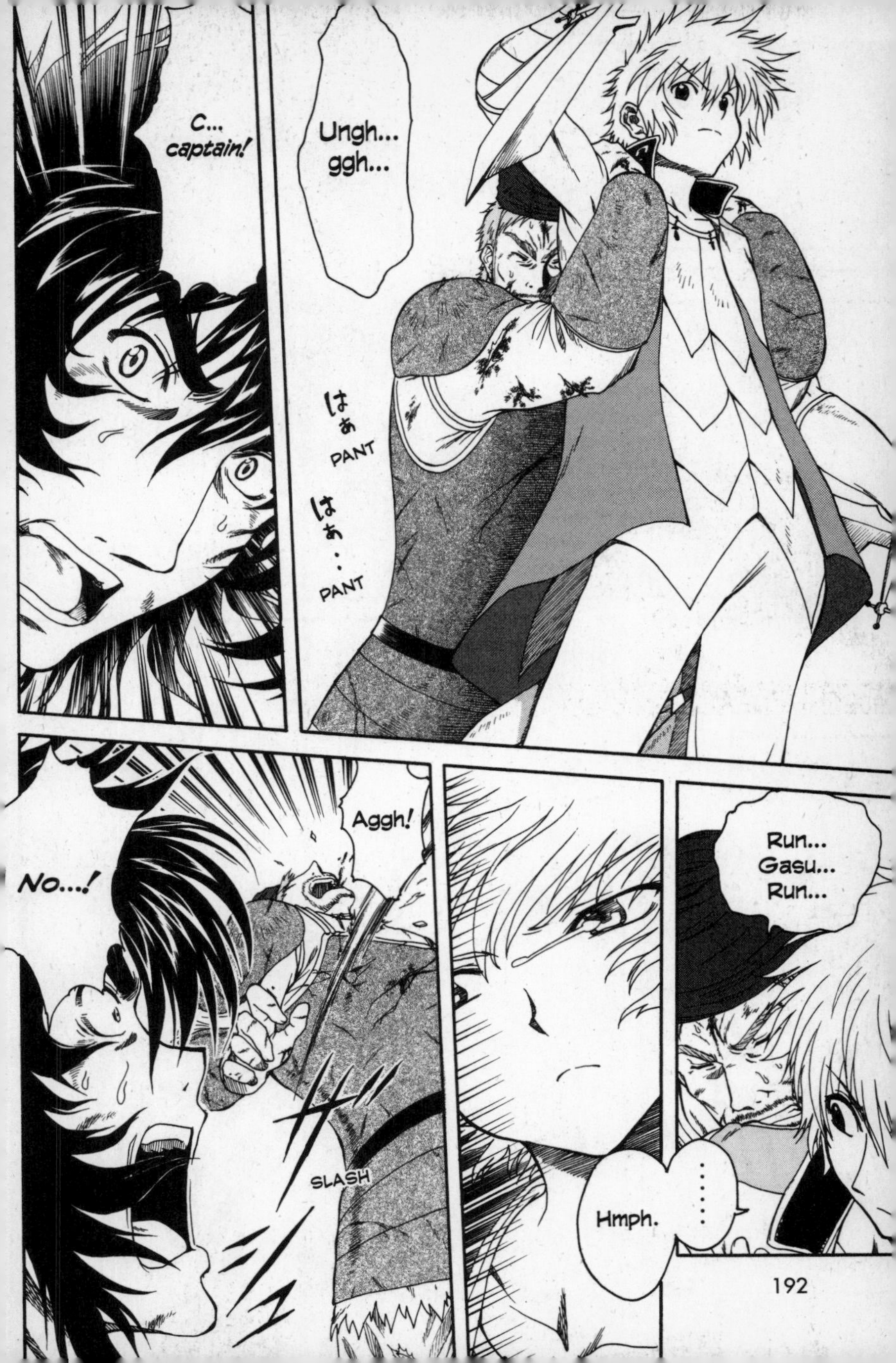
Ungh... ggh...
はぁ
PANT
はぁ・・
PANT
C... captain!
Run... Gasu... Run...
......
Hmph.
Aggh!
No...!
SLASH

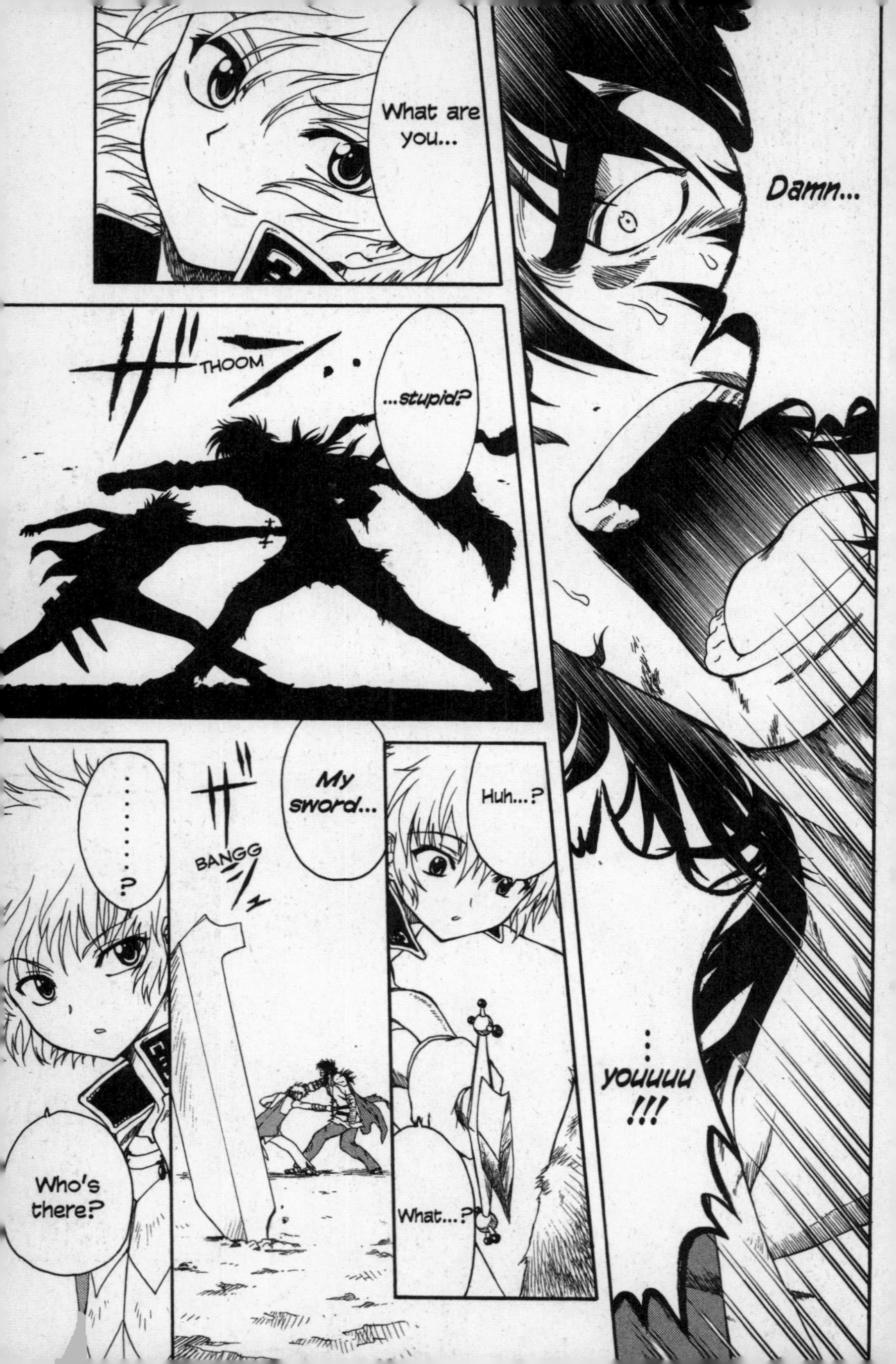

Damn...
...youuuu!!!
What are you...
...stupid?
THOOM
Huh...?
What...?
My sword...
BANGG
......?
Who's there?

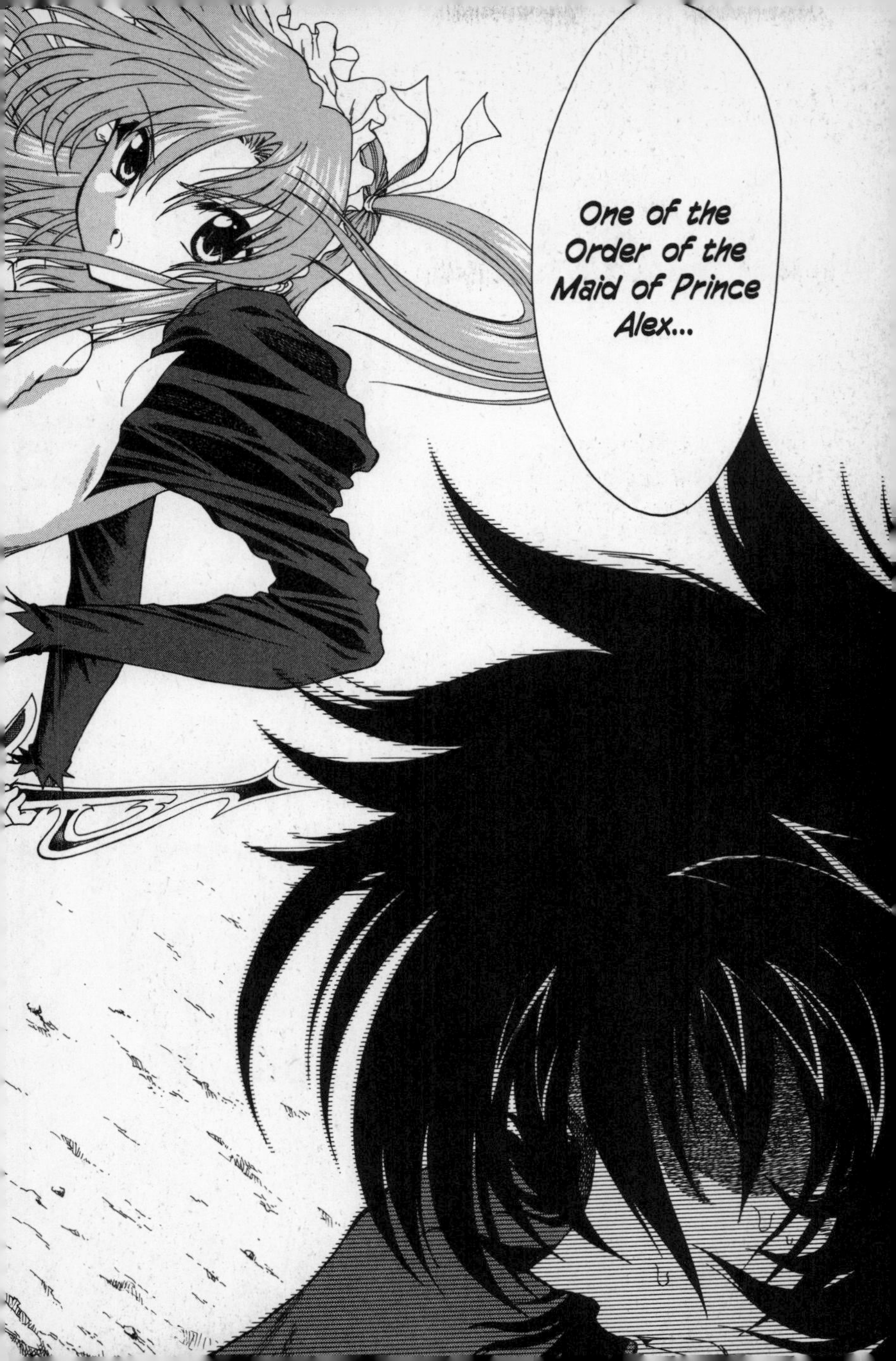
One of the Order of the Maid of Prince Alex...

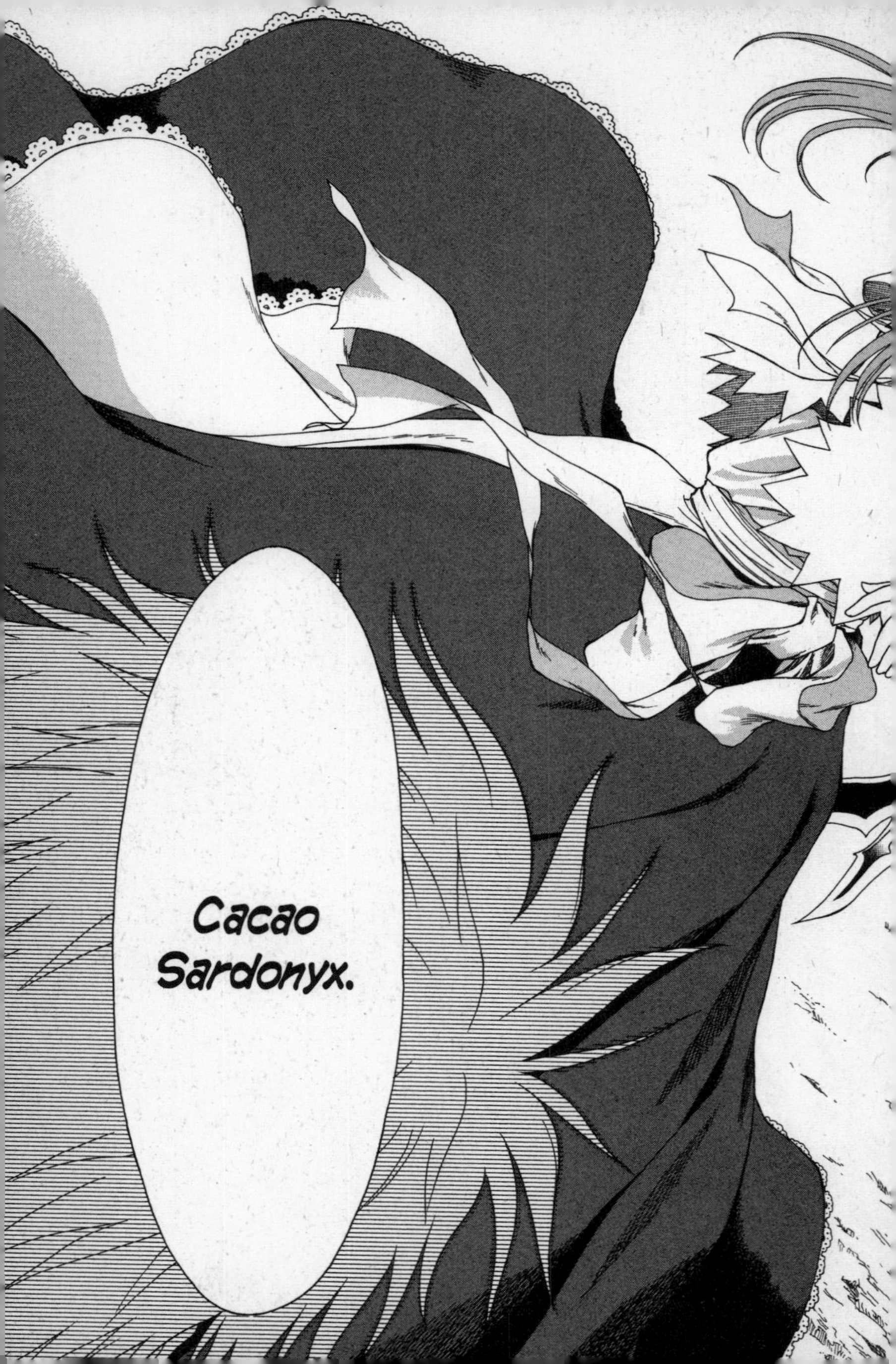
Cacao Sardonyx.

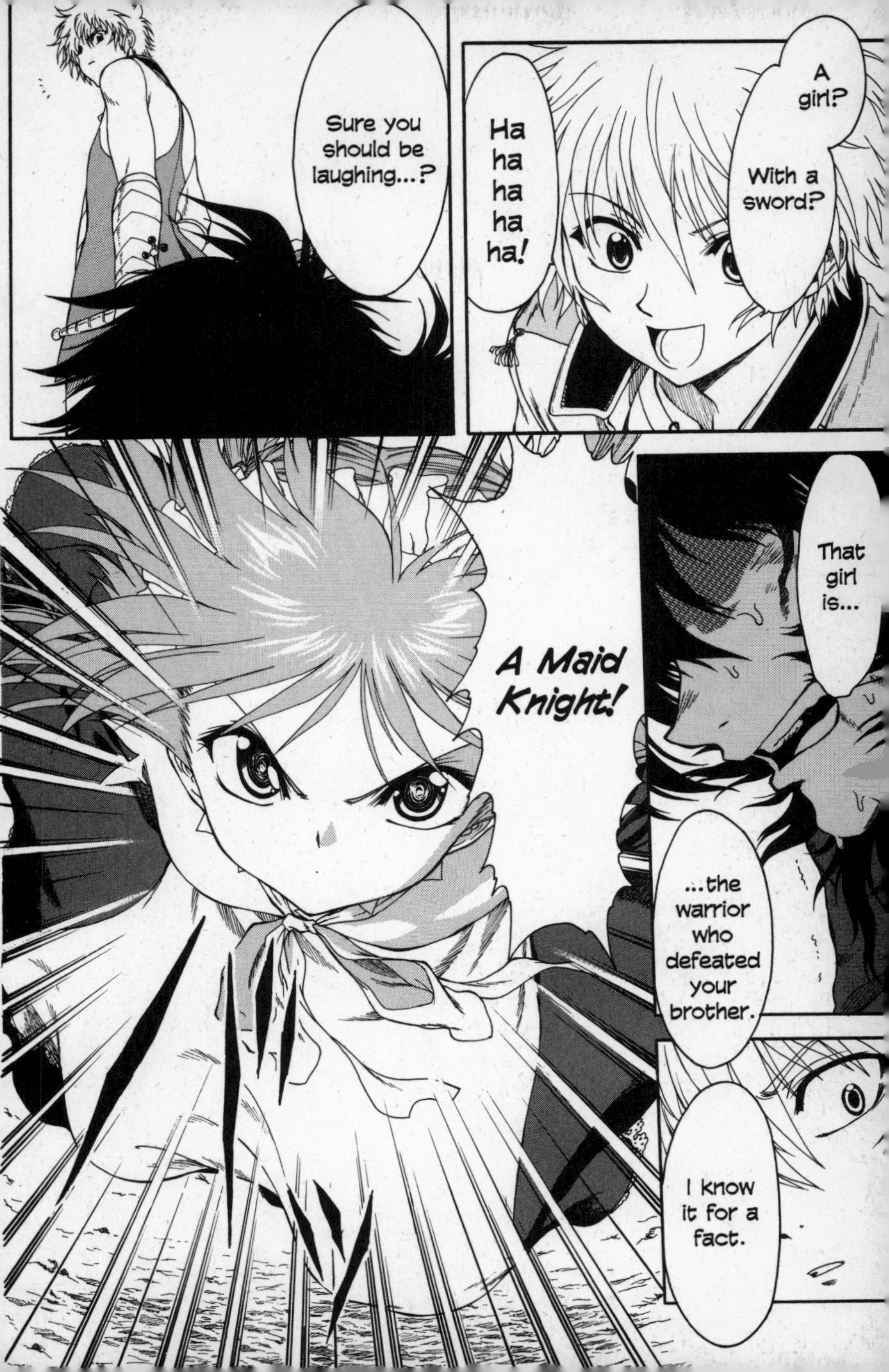
A girl?
With a sword?
Ha ha ha ha ha!
Sure you should be laughing...?
That girl is...
...the warrior who defeated your brother.
I know it for a fact.
A Maid Knight!

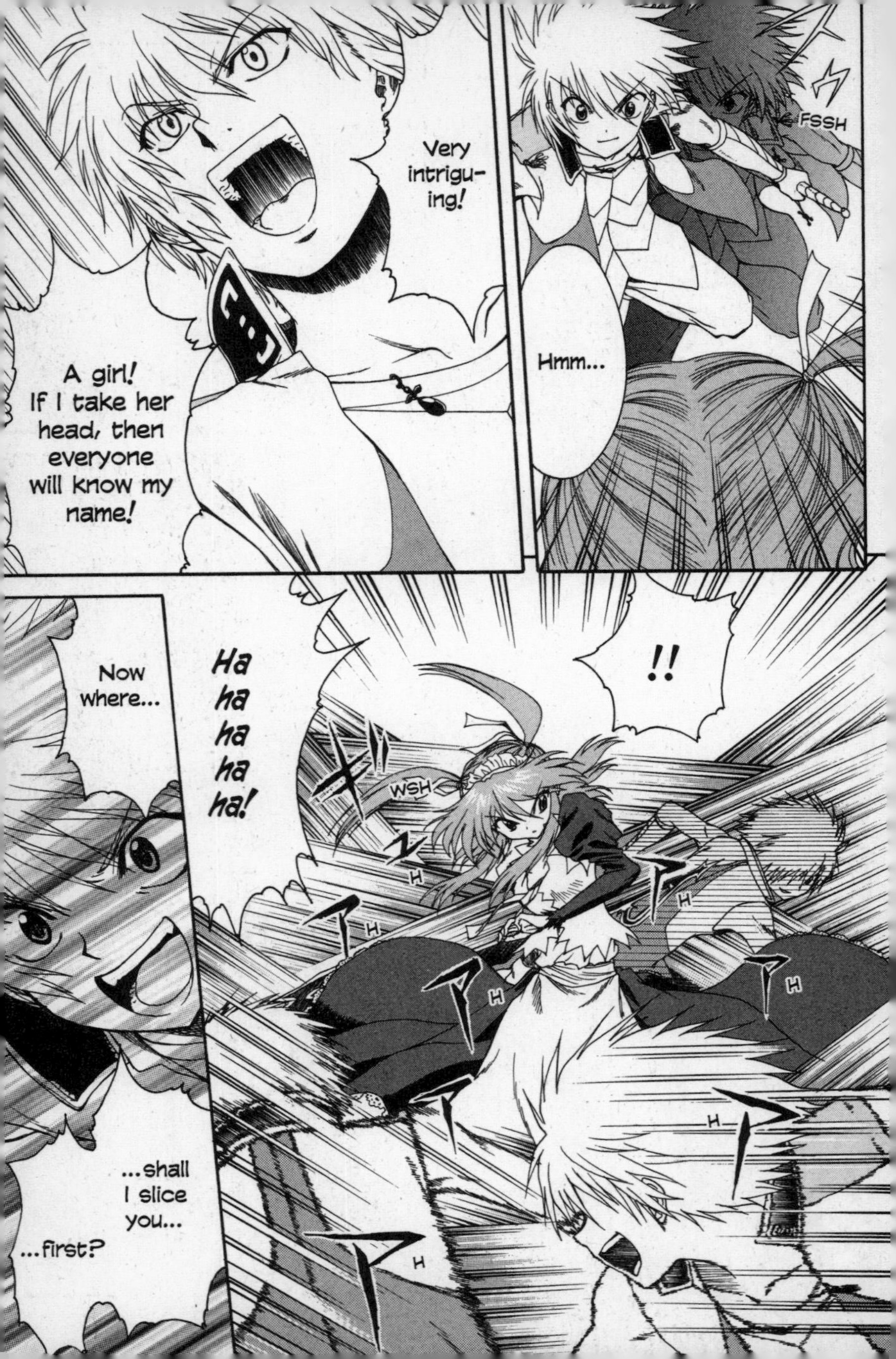
FSSH
Hmm...
Very intrigu-ing!
A girl! If I take her head, then everyone will know my name!
!!
Ha ha ha ha ha!
WSH
Now where...
...shall I slice you...
...first?

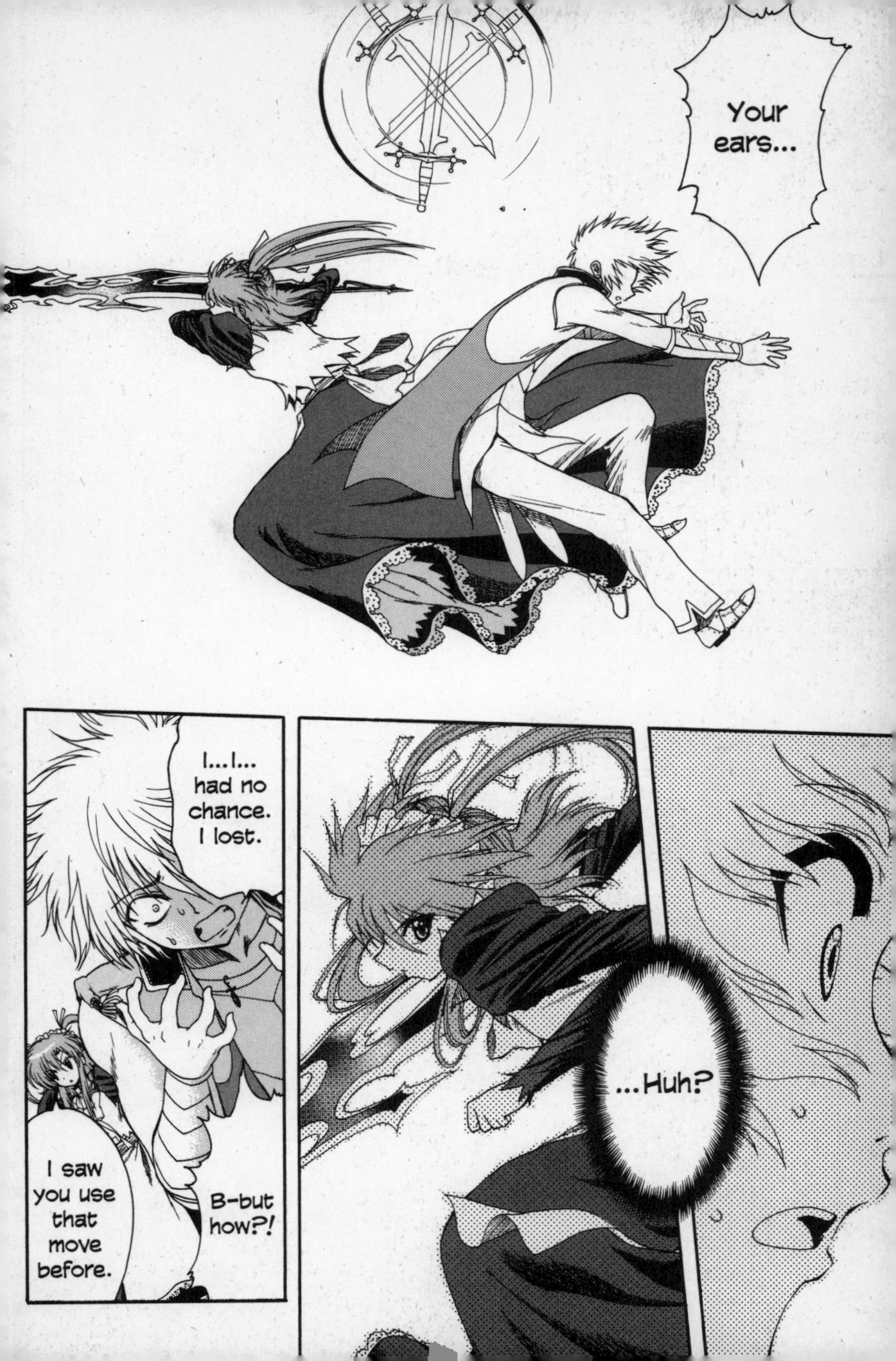
Your ears...
...Huh?
I...I... had no chance. I lost.
B-but how?!
I saw you use that move before.

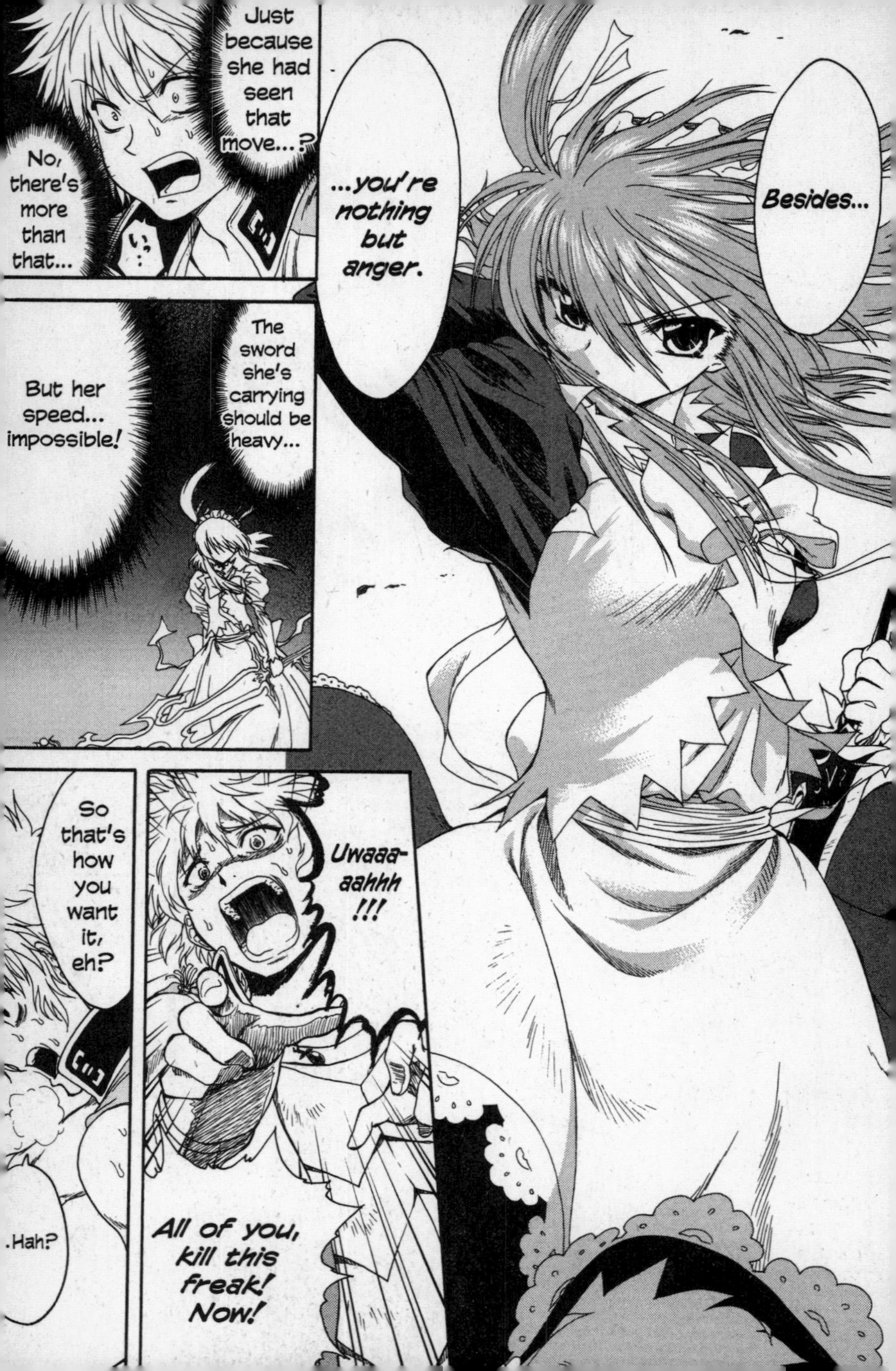

Besides...
...you're nothing but anger.
Just because she had seen that move...?
No, there's more than that...
The sword she's carrying should be heavy...
But her speed... impossible!
Uwaaa-aahhh!!!
All of you, kill this freak! Now!
So that's how you want it, eh?
.Hah?

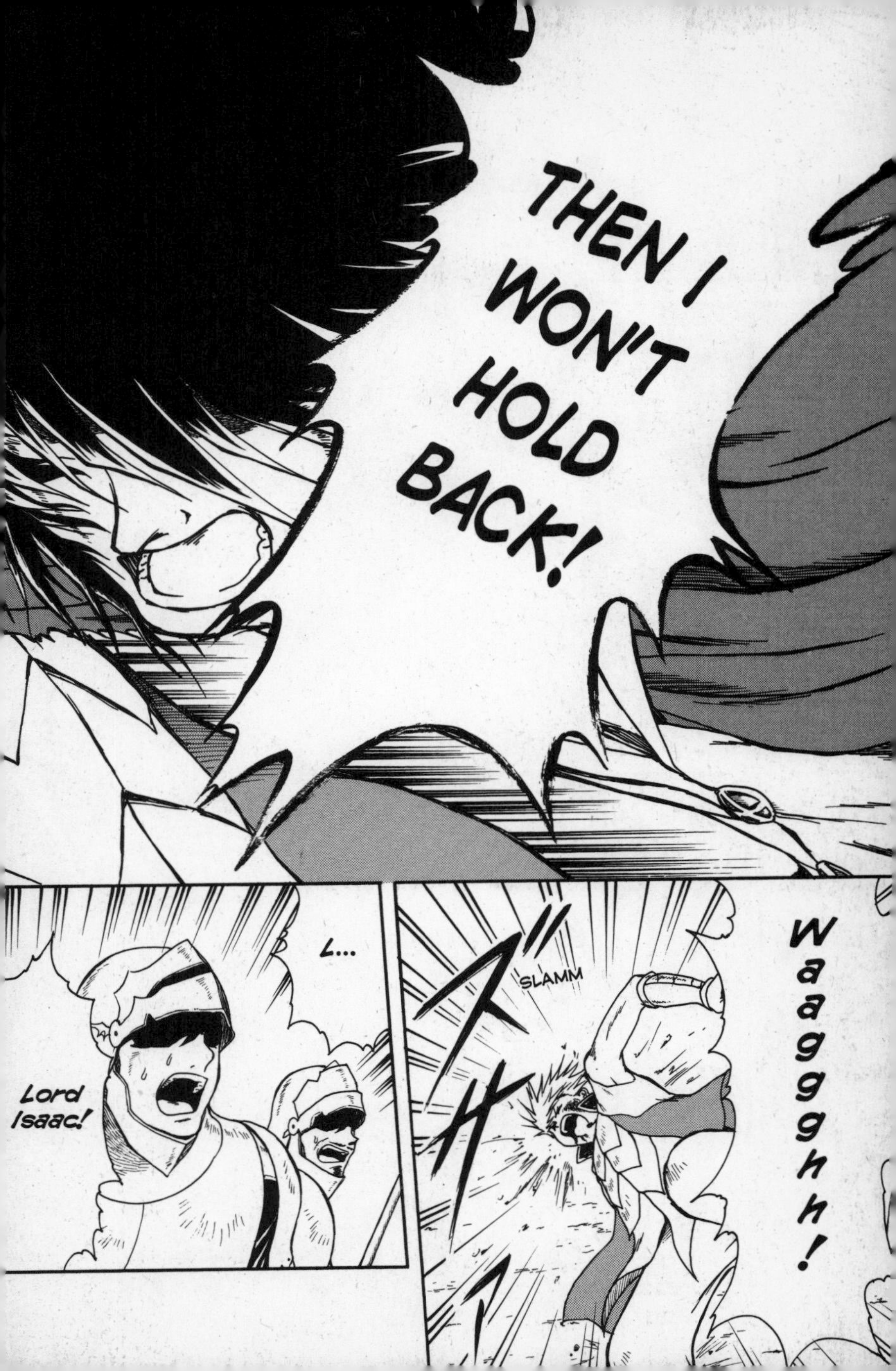
THEN I WON'T HOLD BACK!
Waaggghn!
SLAMM
L...
Lord Isaac!

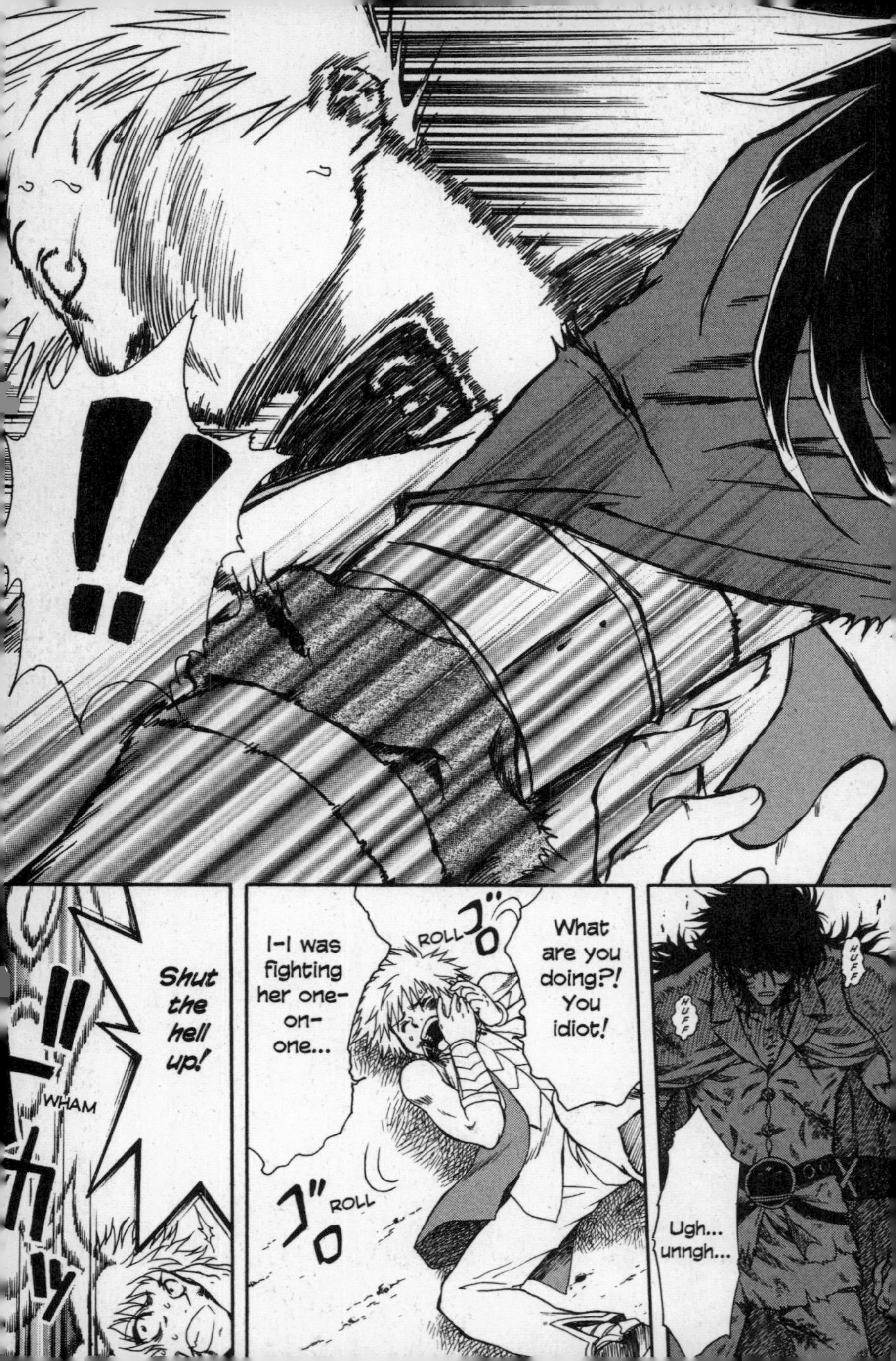
!!
HUFF
HUFF
Ugh... unngh...
What are you doing?! You idiot!
ROLL
I-I was fighting her one-on-one...
ROLL
Shut the hell up!
WHAM

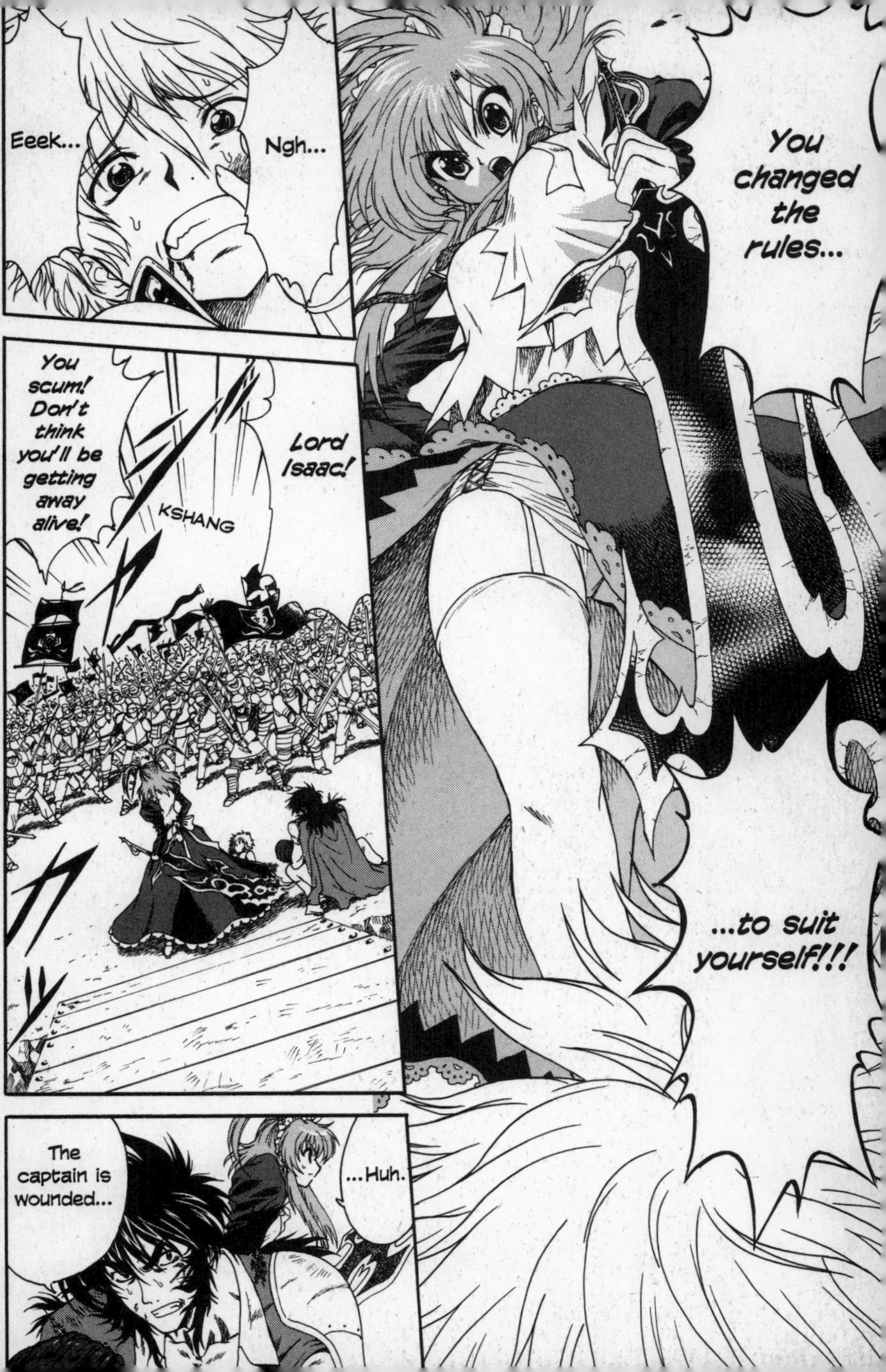
You changed the rules...
...to suit yourself!!!
Ngh...
Eeek...
Lord Isaac!
You scum! Don't think you'll be getting away alive!
KSHANG
...Huh.
The captain is wounded...

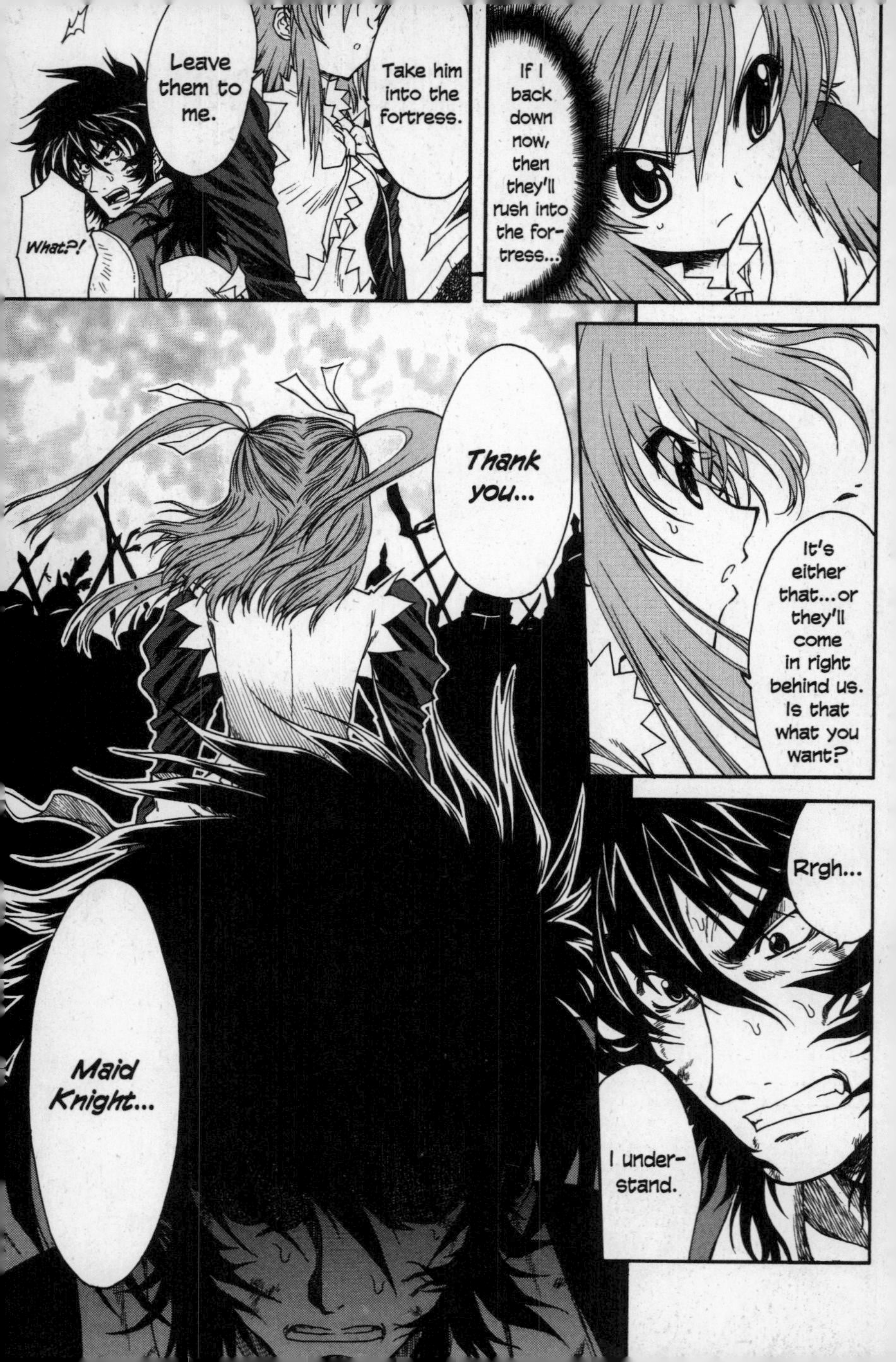
If I back down now, then they'll rush into the fortress...
Take him into the fortress.
Leave them to me.
What?!
It's either that...or they'll come in right behind us. Is that what you want?
Rrgh...
I understand.
Thank you...
Maid Knight...

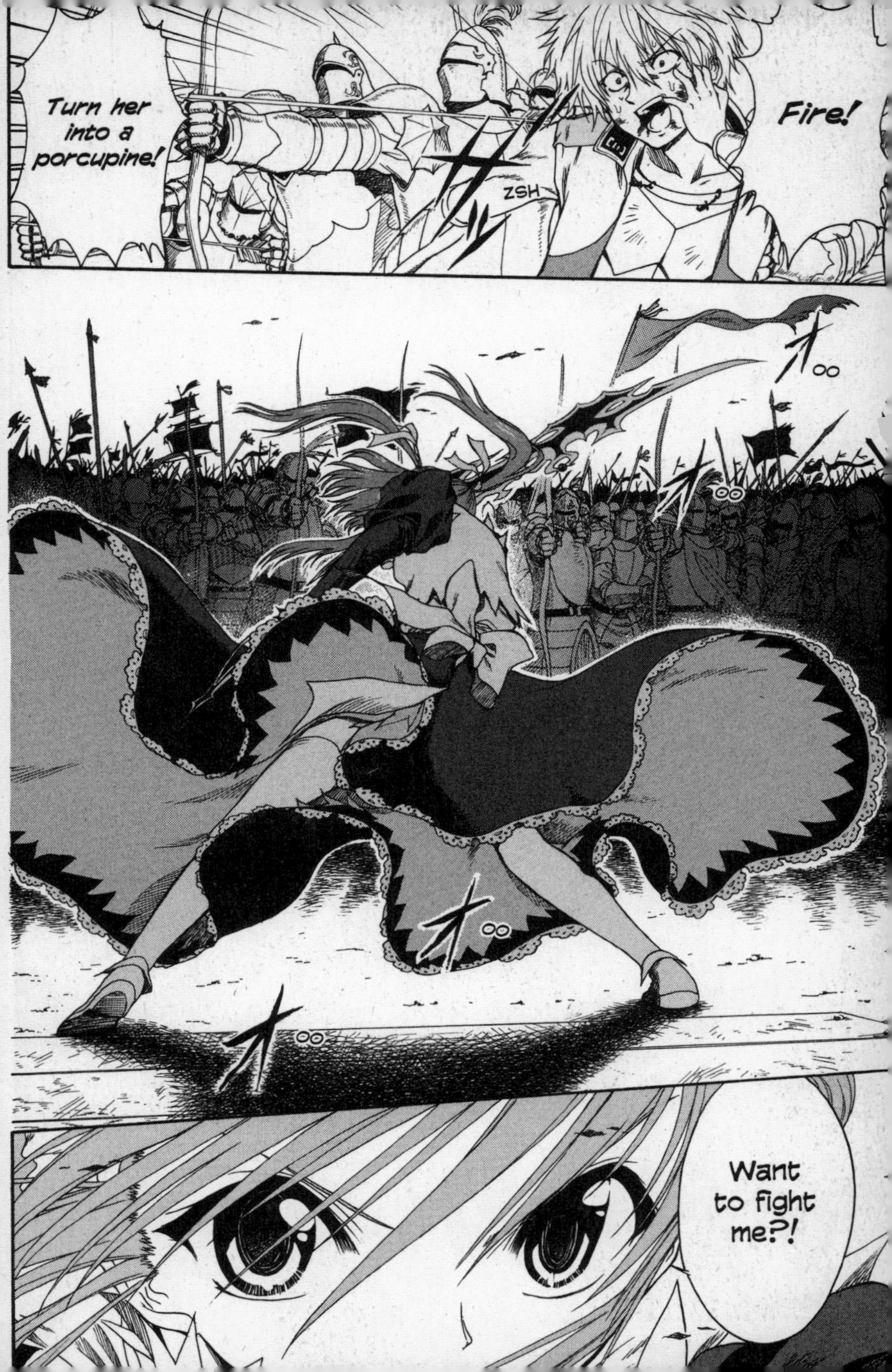
Fire!
Turn her into a porcupine!
ZSH
Want to fight me?!

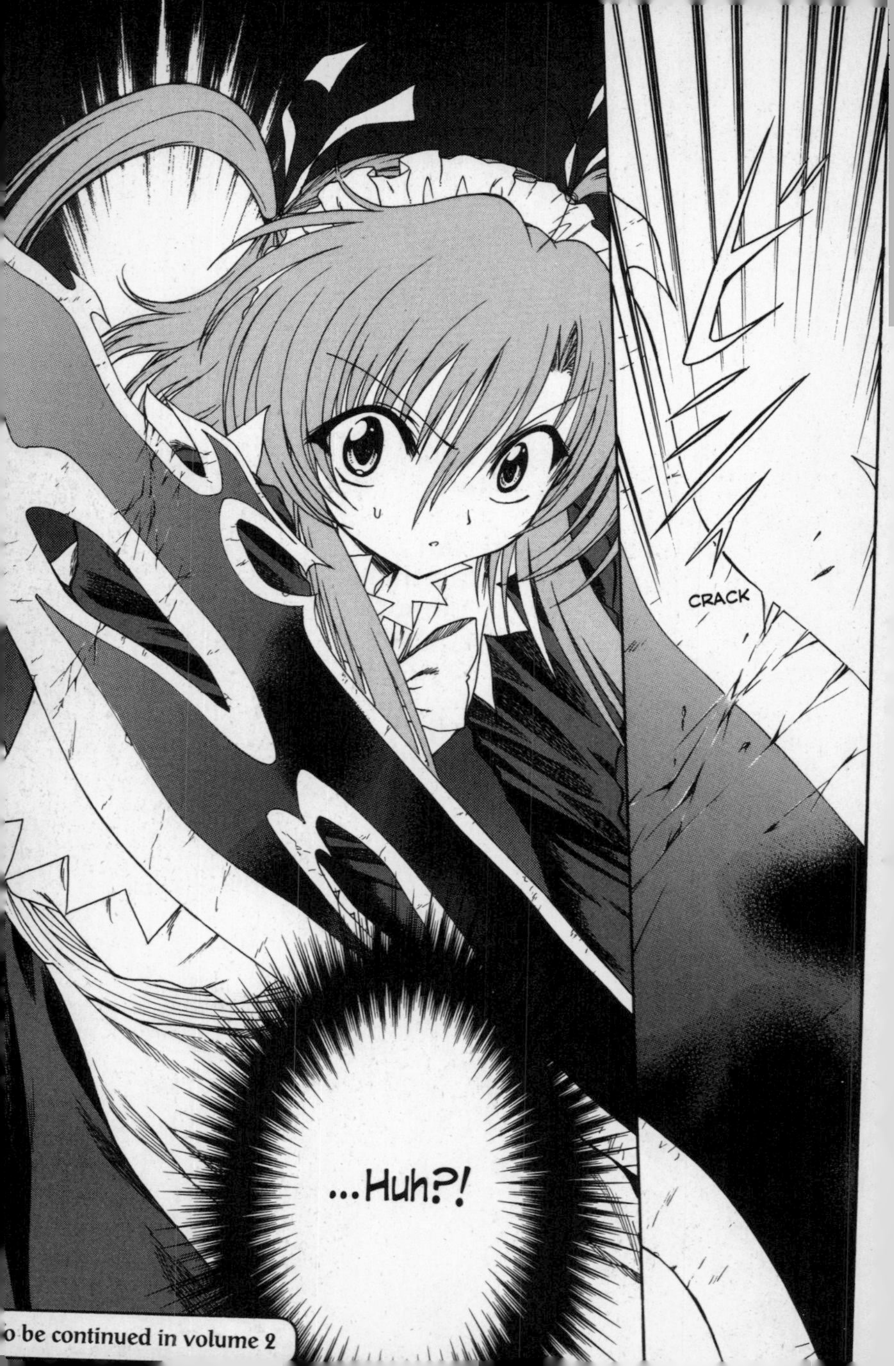
CRACK
...Huh?!
o be continued in volume 2

Story and Art
RAN

Assistants
Hiromi Kurashima
Sayaka Uemura
Hiromi Uchida
Miyuki Yagizawa

Design
Atsuji Kudo
(GxComplex)

And to all the people and
family members who supported this...
thank you!

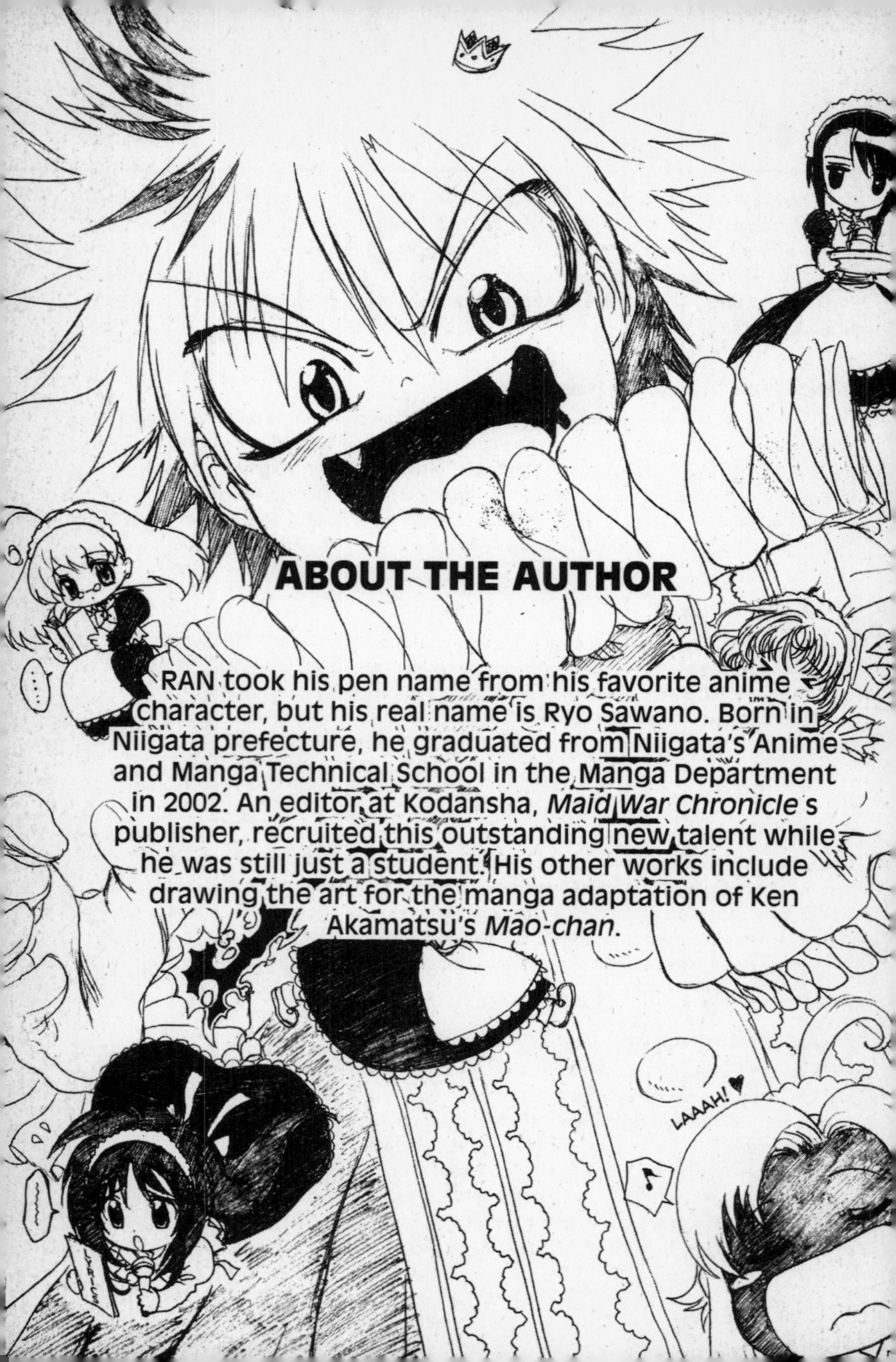
LAAAH! ♥
LYRICS

ABOUT THE AUTHOR

RAN took his pen name from his favorite anime character, but his real name is Ryo Sawano. Born in Niigata prefecture, he graduated from Niigata's Anime and Manga Technical School in the Manga Department in 2002. An editor at Kodansha, *Maid War Chronicle*'s publisher, recruited this outstanding new talent while he was still just a student. His other works include drawing the art for the manga adaptation of Ken Akamatsu's *Mao-chan*.

Translation Notes

Japanese is a tricky language for most Westerners, and translation is often more art than science. Although *Maid War Chronicle* is set in an imaginary pseudo-European setting, it still features some uniquely Japanese elements. For your edification and reading pleasure, here are notes on some of the places where we could have gone in a different direction, or where a Japanese (or European) cultural reference is used.

Maid War Chronicle (title)

The Japanese title of this manga uses the English loanword "maid" and the Japanese word *Senki*, meaning the record of a military campaign. It's usually translated as "war chronicle." It sounds a little formal in English, but it's a common element in anime and manga titles, such as *Makai Senki Disgaea* ("Demon World War Chronicle Disgaea"), *Shin Kidô Senki Gundam Wing* ("Mobile Suit Gundam Wing"), and *Lodoss Tô Senki* ("Record of Lodoss War").

Chivalric Orders

A chivalric order was a group of knights fighting for a cause. In modern fiction, they are often a romanticized imitation of military orders during the crusades. European monarchs created many different military orders during this period, some of which lasted for centuries. They became tied to the ideals of chivalry and also became reflected in Arthurian romances such as the Knights of the Round Table.

Court Maids

Court Maids were usually servants hired to perform domestic chores. Historically, they would not have been so close to the monarch's family and instead the monarch would be surrounded by "ladies in waiting"—women from good families who were chosen for their company. However, Prince Arbansbool clearly enjoys the power trip of having women dressed in cute costumes at his command.

Maid Phenomenon

Girls dressed in saucy French maid costumes are nothing new in manga, but in the last ten years they've gone from a minor fetish to a major part of Japanese *otaku* culture. Many manga and anime include a maid character or two, and even men dressed in maid outfits are not unknown, particularly in *yaoi* (male-on-male romance) manga. Cosplayers also enjoy the fun of dressing up in maid outfits. Many cities in Japan feature "maid cafés" where customers can enjoy being served by pretty girls in short skirts. Today, there are even maid cafés in America, such as temporary cafés at anime conventions, and the café/art gallery Royal/T in Culver City, California.

Prince Arbansbool, page 16

If you have maids, you need someone for the maids to work for, right? Prince Arbansbool falls into a long tradition of perverted manga characters obsessed with maids. On the one hand, as a spoiled little kid who abuses his maids, he's similar to the main character in the manga *He Is My Master*. On the other hand, with his unstoppable arrogance and his love of beautiful women in general, he's vaguely similar to the hero of the aptly titled fantasy manga *Bastard!!*. Will his sleaziness or his inexplicable charisma win out in the end?

Cacao, Vanilla, Liqueur, Bana, Cogna, and Mint, page 19

Pun names, particularly names based on food, are common in anime and manga. Well-known examples include *Dragon Ball*, with its characters named after vegetables, and *Saber Marionette*, with its characters named after fruits and berries. *Maid War Chronicle* follows in the footsteps of *Sorcerer Hunters* and *Sugar Sugar Rune* by naming its characters after sweets and sweet liquors (cocoa, vanilla, liqueur, banana, cognac, and mint).

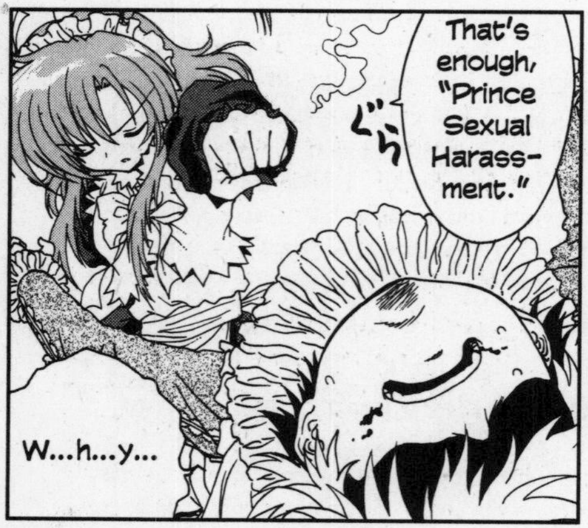
That's enough, "Prince Sexual Harass-ment."
W...h...y...

"Prince Sexual Harassment," page 42

In the original Japanese, Cacao refers to the prince as *sekuhara ôji*, literally "Prince Sexual Harassment." *Sekuhara* is a common Japanese abbreviation for the English loanword "sexual harassment," which became a well-known concept in Japan in the 1990s.

Cacao Sardonyx, page 56

Sardonyx is a form of the gemstone onyx, in which the quarz crystal is streaked with reddish-brown chalcedony. Like the character who bears its name, it's beautiful but tough.

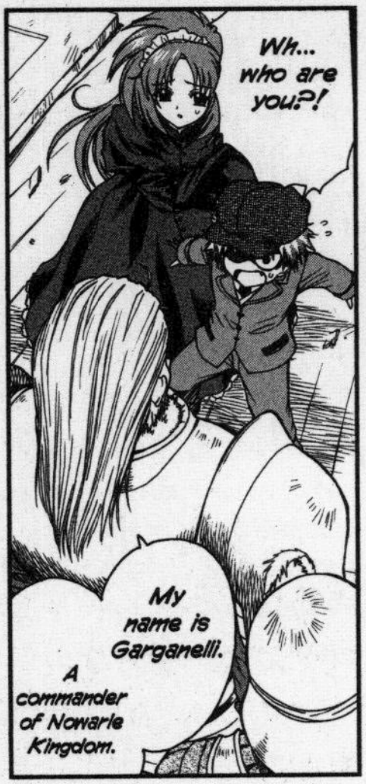
Wh... who are you?!
My name is Garganelli.
A commander of Nowarle Kingdom.

Garganelli, page 76

Garganelli's name is probably a reference to Garganelli pasta, a type of egg pasta shaped like a small cylinder which narrows to a point at the ends, similar to a quill pen.

Claymore, page 88

The claymore (written in Japanese as *daitsurugi*, "great sword") is an enormous sword used by the Highlanders of Scotland in the late Middle Ages. A classical claymore ran 55 inches (about four and a half feet) in length and had to be wielded with both hands, although from the eighteenth century onward the same term was applied to a different, one-handed sword with a basket hilt. Recently, the weapon has become famous through appearing in Japanese RPGs such as the *Final Fantasy* series (usually as the name for some type of ultimate weapon), as well as the manga *Claymore* by Norihiro Yagi.

"As punishment, you'll have to sleep in my bed for five nights!," page 99

In Japanese, the prince's threat "you'll have to sleep in my bed" means literally that—it doesn't imply anything sexual in the sense of "sleeping with" someone in English. However, given the prince's perverted sensibilities, it's possible he's not telling the whole truth.

Four-Panel Manga, pages 100 and 166

When *Maid War Chronicle* was originally printed in Japan in *Monthly Shônen Sirius* magazine, the four-panel manga (on pages 100 and 166) were part of a theme to write gag manga involving the number two. Thus the jokes about "ni" (Japanese for "two") and the numbers 12 and 200.

Preview of Volume 2

We're pleased to be able to present you a preview from volume 2. Please check our website (www.delreymanga.com) to see when this volume will be available in English. For now you'll have to make do with Japanese.

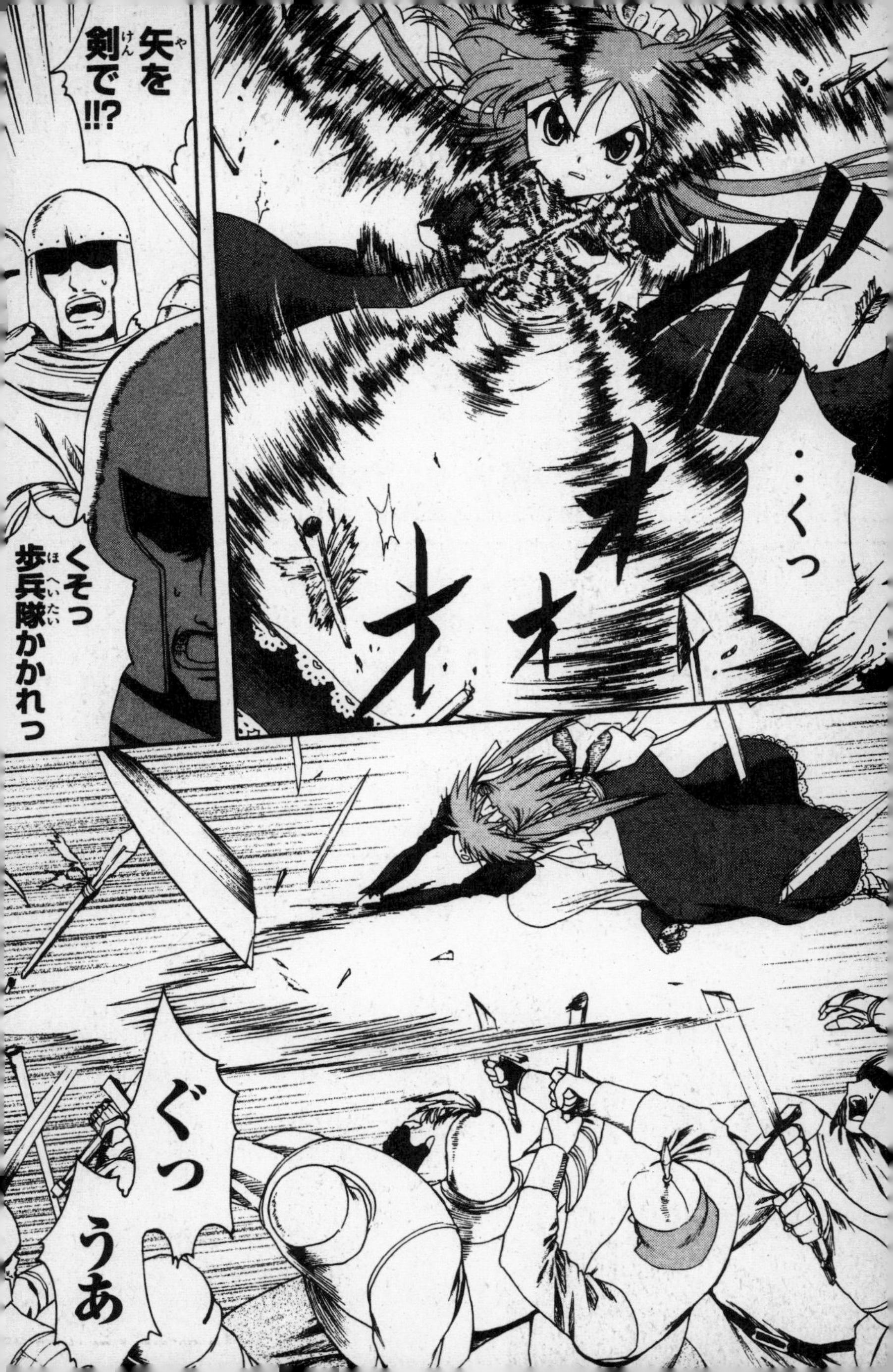
…くっ
オオオ
矢を剣で!!?
くそっ歩兵隊かかれっ
ぐっ
うあ

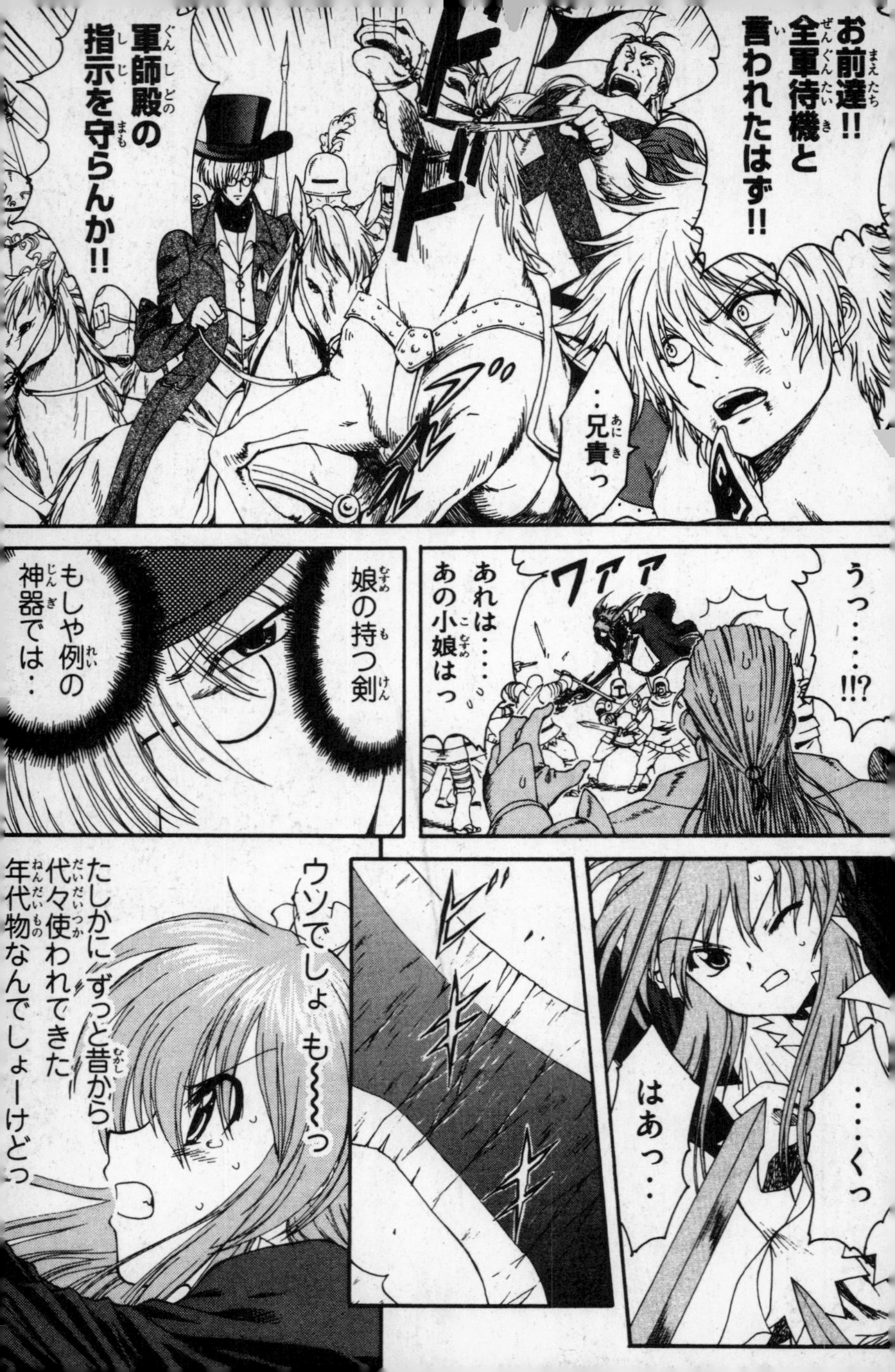
お前達!! 全軍待機と 言われたはず!!
軍師殿の 指示を守らんか!!
・・兄貴っ
うっ・・・・!!?
ワアア
あれは・・・・ あの小娘はっ
娘の持つ剣
もしや例の 神器では・・
・・・・くっ
はあっ・・・
ウソでしょも〜〜っ
たしかにずっと昔から 代々使われてきた 年代物なんでしょーけどっ

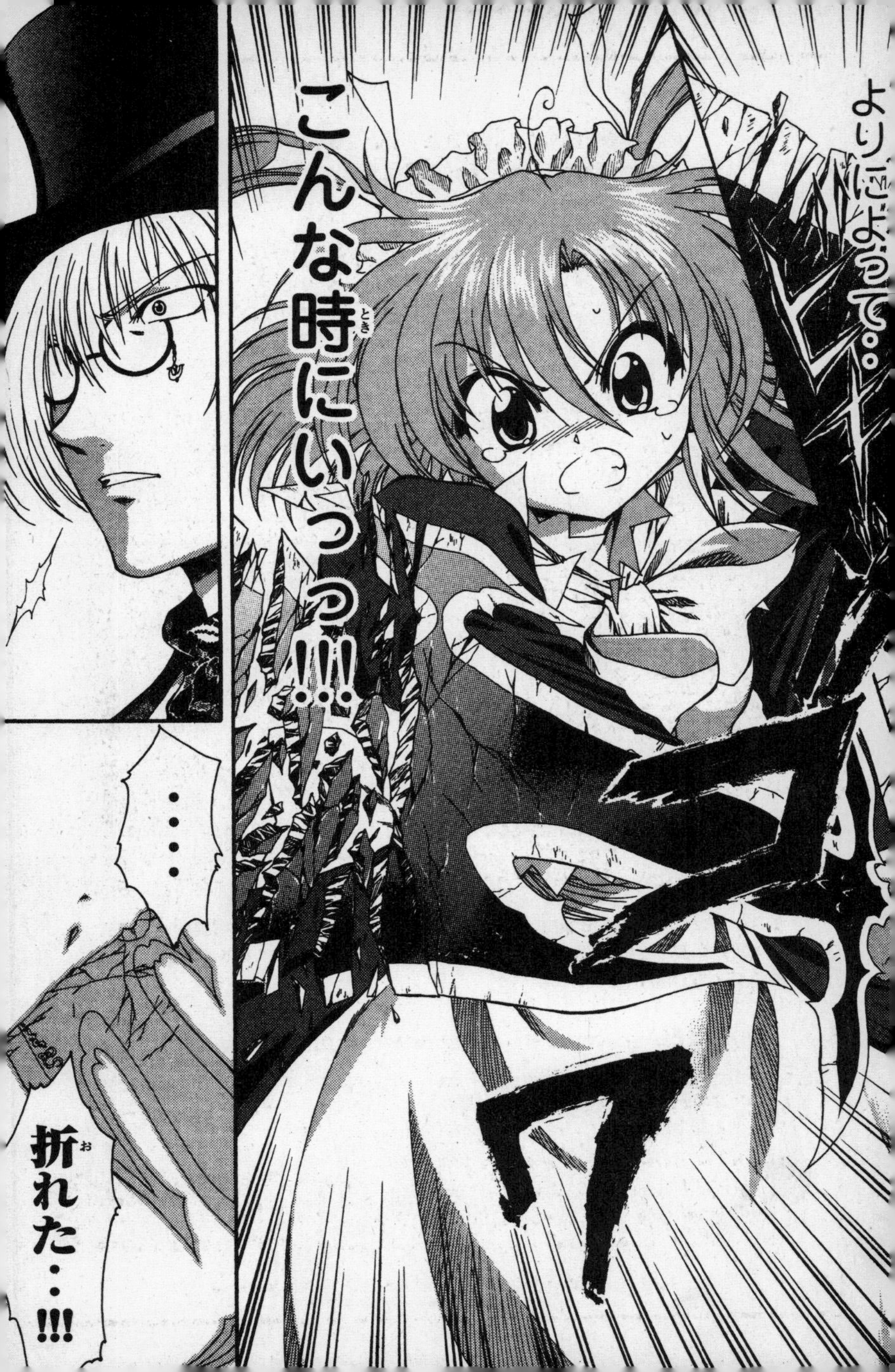
よりによって・・
こんな時にいっっ!!!!
・・・・
折れた・・!!!

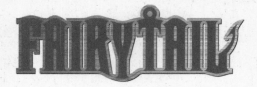
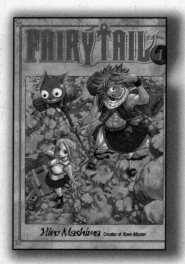
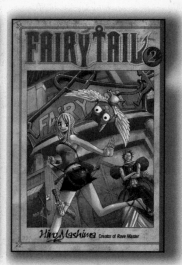
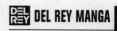

SHUGO CHARA!

PEACH-PIT

Creators of *Dears* and *Rozen Maiden*

Everybody at Seiyo Elementary thinks that stylish and super-cool Amu has it all. But nobody knows the *real* Amu, a shy girl who wishes she had the courage to truly be herself. Changing Amu's life is going to take more than wishes and dreams—it's going to take a little magic! One morning, Amu finds a surprise in her bed: three strange little eggs. Each egg contains a Guardian Character, an angel-like being who can give her the power to be someone new. With the help of her Guardian Characters, Amu is about to discover that her true self is even more amazing than she ever dreamed.

PEACH-PIT
CREATORS OF DEARS AND ROZEN MAIDEN
SHUGO CHARA!
1

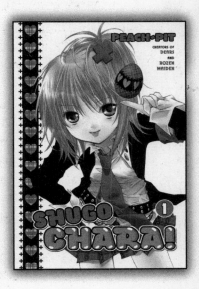

Special extras in each volume! Read them all!

VISIT WWW.DELREYMANGA.COM TO:

- Read sample pages
- View release date calendars for upcoming volumes
- Sign up for Del Rey's free manga e-newsletter
- Find out the latest about new Del Rey Manga series

RATING T AGES 13+

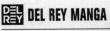

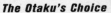

DEL REY MANGA デルレイ

The Otaku's Choice

TOMARE!

[STOP!]

You're going the wrong way!

Manga is a completely different type of reading experience.

To start at the *beginning*, go to the *end*!

That's right! Authentic manga is read the traditional Japanese way—from right to left. Exactly the *opposite* of how American books are read. It's easy to follow: Just go to the other end of the book, and read each page—and each panel—from right side to left side, starting at the top right. Now you're experiencing manga as it was meant to be!